THE FAMILY
Handyman®

Home Improvement

2013

THE FAMILY
Handyman.

Home Improvement
2013

by The Editors of *The Family Handyman* magazine

THE FAMILY HANDYMAN HOME IMPROVEMENT 2013
(See page 288 for complete staff listing.)
Editor in Chief: Ken Collier
Project Editor: Teresa Marrone
Contributing Designers: Joel Anderson, Bruce Bohnenstingl, Teresa Marrone
Contributing Copy Editors: Donna Bierbach, Peggy Parker
Indexing: Stephanie Reymann

Vice President, Group Publisher: Russell S. Ellis

The Reader's Digest Association, Inc.
President & Chief Executive Officer: Robert E. Guth

Warning: All do-it-yourself activities involve a degree of risk. Skills, materials, tools, and site conditions vary widely. Although the editors have made every effort to ensure accuracy, the reader remains responsible for the selection and use of tools, materials, and methods. Always obey local codes and laws, follow manufacturer's operating instructions, and observe safety precautions.

ISBN 978-1-60652-562-3   1-60652-562-3
118300027H
Address any comments about *The Family Handyman Home Improvement 2013* to:
Editor, Home Improvement 2013
2915 Commers Drive, Suite 700
Eagan, MN 55121

To order additional copies of *The Family Handyman Home Improvement 2013*, call 1-800-344-2560.

For more Reader's Digest products and information, visit our Web site at rd.com.
For more about *The Family Handyman* magazine, visit familyhandyman.com.

Printed in the United States of America.
 3 5 7 9 10 8 6 4 2

SAFETY FIRST–ALWAYS!

Tackling home improvement projects and repairs can be endlessly rewarding. But as most of us know, with the rewards come risks. DIYers use chain saws, climb ladders and tear into walls that can contain big and hazardous surprises.

The good news is, armed with the right knowledge, tools and procedures, homeowners can minimize risk. As you go about your projects and repairs, stay alert for these hazards:

Aluminum wiring

Aluminum wiring, installed in about 7 million homes between 1965 and 1973, requires special techniques and materials to make safe connections. This wiring is dull gray, not the dull orange characteristic of copper. Hire a licensed electrician certified to work with it. For more information go to cpsc.gov and search for "aluminum wiring."

Spontaneous combustion

Rags saturated with oil finishes like Danish oil and linseed oil, and oil-based paints and stains can spontaneously combust if left bunched up. Always dry them outdoors, spread out loosely. When the oil has thoroughly dried, you can safely throw them in the trash.

Vision and hearing protection

Safety glasses or goggles should be worn whenever you're working on DIY projects that involve chemicals, dust and anything that could shatter or chip off and hit your eye. Sounds louder than 80 decibels (dB) are considered potentially dangerous. Sound levels from a lawn mower can be 90 dB, and shop tools and chain saws can be 90 to 100 dB.

Lead paint

If your home was built before 1979, it may contain lead paint, which is a serious health hazard, especially for children six and under. Take precautions when you scrape or remove it. Contact your public health department for detailed safety information or call (800) 424-LEAD (5323) to receive an information pamphlet. Or visit epa.gov/lead.

Buried utilities

A few days before you dig in your yard, have your underground water, gas and electrical lines marked. Just call 811 or go to call811.com.

Smoke and carbon monoxide (CO) alarms

Almost two-thirds of home fire deaths from 2003 to 2006 resulted from fires in homes with missing or nonworking smoke alarms. Test your smoke alarms every month, replace batteries as necessary and replace units that are more than 10 years old. As you make your home more energy-efficient and airtight, existing ducts and chimneys can't always successfully vent combustion gases, including potentially deadly carbon monoxide (CO). Install a UL-listed CO detector, and test your CO and smoke alarms at the same time.

Five-gallon buckets and window covering cords

Since 1984, more than 275 children have drowned in 5-gallon buckets. Always store them upside down and store ones containing liquid with the covers securely snapped.

According to Parents for Window Blind Safety, just under 500 children have been seriously injured or killed in the United States in the past few decades after becoming entangled in looped window treatment cords. For more information, visit pfwbs.org or cpsc.gov.

Working up high

If you have to get up on your roof to do a repair or installation, always install roof brackets and wear a roof harness.

Asbestos

Texture sprayed on ceilings before 1978, adhesives and tiles for vinyl and asphalt floors before 1980, and vermiculite insulation (with gray granules) all may contain asbestos. Other building materials, made between 1940 and 1980, could also contain asbestos. If you suspect that materials you're removing or working around contain asbestos, contact your health department or visit epa.gov/asbestos for information.

For additional information about home safety, visit homesafetycouncil.org.
This site offers helpful information about dozens of home safety issues.

Contents

5 EXTERIOR REPAIRS & IMPROVEMENTS

6 OUTDOOR STRUCTURES, LANDSCAPING & GARDENING

7 VEHICLES & GARAGES

THE FAMILY
Handyman

More ways to get DIY jobs done right

The Family Handyman Magazine is North America's top DIY home improvement magazine, with new projects, repairs and tips in every issue. Subscribe and save at FamilyHandyman.com.

The Family Handyman for **iPad**® gives you each issue of the magazine, plus videos and bonus content. Get it on the App Store.

FamilyHandyman.com gives you instant access to thousands of projects, techniques and expert fixes. And it's all free!

We have **books** too! From storage projects to energy saving, get the tips and step-by-step advice you need at shopthefamilyhandyman.com.

Sign up for **FREE newsletters** at familyhandyman.com/freenewsletter. Get DIY tips, projects, expert repairs and more delivered to your inbox every week.

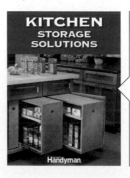

The Family Handyman eBooks cover a huge range of DIY topics, from tool tips and repairs to painting and flooring. Get them for your Nook, Kindle, iPad at familyhandyman.com/ebooks.

Whether you're an experienced DIYer or just getting started, we put know-how at your fingertips.

1 Interior Projects, Repairs & Remodeling

IN THIS CHAPTER

FIX A RATTLING DOOR

Some nights are just made for sleeping with the windows open. But if your interior doors are out of adjustment, they'll rattle with every breeze. The problem is always caused by a gap between the door stop and the door. Here are three simple fixes.

The simplest fix of the three is to bend the little tang on the strike plate toward the door (**photo, bottom left**). When the door latches, it pushes the door toward the stop just a bit and holds the latch a little tighter, sometimes enough to silence the door. It doesn't always work, but it's worth a shot. A pair of pliers always hacks up the finish on the plate, so use two adjustable wrenches instead.

The next easiest fix is to shim any gaps with self-adhesive "dots" (**bottom right**), which are usually used to soften cabinet door and drawer closes. You'll find them near the cabinet hardware at the store. The least obvious are the clear dots that blend in with the door finish.

The harder, but more elegant fix is to actually shift the door stop so it's tight against the door (**top photo**). If there's paint and/or caulk, score it first with a utility knife. Then use a block and smack the stop tight against the door. The existing nails will shift quite a bit but may hold the stop away from the jamb when they bend. If that happens, use the block again to smack the stop flat to the jamb to flatten the nails. Check the door operation to make sure it doesn't drag on the stop before you renail it. Here's the downside: With painted or stained trim, there may be a bit of retouching to do.

The most elegant fix: Shift the door stop. Close the door and hold a block of wood against the door stop. Smack the wood until the door stop moves enough to touch the door. Then secure the door stop with 1-1/4-in. finish nails.

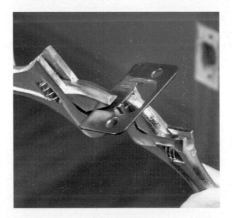

Or, bend the tang gently.
Tighten one adjustable wrench onto the curved "latch" side of the plate to hold it while you bend the tang. Then tighten the second wrench on the tang. Bend it toward the door and reinstall the strike to test the fit. Make several small bends rather than "overshooting" and having to bend it back and forth.

CORK DOT

DOOR STOP

Or, fill the gap with a "dot." Close the door and look for the largest gap between the door and the door stop. Fill the gap with a dot that matches the size of the gap. Just press the dot onto the door stop and cut off any overlap with a utility knife.

REMOVE VINYL FLOORING THE EASY WAY

There are several ways to remove vinyl flooring. The old-fashioned method is to use a handheld floor scraper; this usually takes the better part of a day, and your back and palms will probably be sore for a week. A better option is to use a rental oscillating floor scraper machine, also called a power floor scraper. The entire job can usually be done in less than an hour, and you won't even break a sweat. The machine rents for about $40 for four hours.

Start by scoring the vinyl (Photo 1). Next, adjust the angle on the floor scraper until it pulls up vinyl without gouging the subfloor. Then turn it on and let 'er rip (Photo 2).

1 **Score the vinyl flooring.** Measure out 10 in. from the wall and score the vinyl flooring with a utility knife. Then repeat scoring every 10 in. all the way across the room.

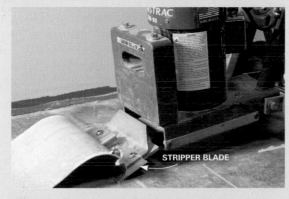

STRIPPER BLADE

2 **Guide the machine down each strip.** Steer the machine down the scored swath and let it do all the work. Let the stripped vinyl roll up in front of the scraper blade.

Use power to chip out floor tile

CERAMIC TILE BLADE

Ordinary floor scraper blades won't stand up to ceramic or porcelain tile. But some rental machines accept an optional tile chisel. If your rental store offers that feature, just remove the wide scraper blade, slide in the chisel attachment and secure it with the bolt and washer. Then fire it up and let the machine do the dirty work for you.

BEST LUBE FOR SQUEAKY BATHROOM DRAWERS

When using lubricants indoors, a bad smell is only one of the issues to consider, says Dr. Larry Beaver, a research expert at the company that makes Liquid Wrench products. "Some products can leave graphite stains, sticky residues that attract dust and dirt, and can even drip onto flooring or cabinet interiors."

For lubing drawer slides, door hinges, overhead fans and other sticking or squeaky things inside the house without causing stains or odor, Beaver recommends using a dry lubricant that contains PFTE (commonly known as Teflon). "It dries fast and leaves a durable, light-colored lubricating film right where you spray it."

Brands include Liquid Wrench Dry Lubricant, DuPont Teflon and Blaster Dry Lube (available at many home centers and hardware stores). Visit liquidwrench.com, blastercorporation.com and dupont.com for more information.

MEET AN EXPERT

Dr. Larry Beaver is the Vice President of Technology at Radiator Specialty Co. in Charlotte, NC. In this position, he oversees the product research and development, regulatory and environmental functions for all divisions of the manufacturing company, including GUNK and Liquid Wrench brands.

"Odor isn't the only factor. Some products leave stains and can even drip onto flooring."

—Dr. Larry Beaver

Web links: Get hinge-savvy

Replacing a cabinet or entertainment center hinge? Read up on all the styles and measuring techniques before you buy. hardwaresource.com/hinge-resource-center/resource-center/

HomeCare&Repair

REPAIR A CABINET-HINGE SCREW HOLE

Cabinets made from particleboard work great in utility and laundry rooms, and they're fairly inexpensive. But particleboard has a major weakness—it doesn't hold screw threads very well. So if you swing the door open too fast, the force can rip the hinge screw right out of the cabinet wall. Don't worry; the fix is easy and cheap. Here's how to patch things up. You'll need a bottle of wood glue, a 1/2-in. drill bit and a package of 1/2-in.-diameter hardwood plugs (about $2 at a home center).

Start by removing the hinge screws on the cabinet and flipping the hinge out of your way. If the accident pulled out a large chunk of the particleboard, glue it back into place and let the glue set up before proceeding with the rest of the repair. Drill out the stripped screw hole to accept the plug. Next, fill the hole with wood glue and install the plug (Photo 1). Then drill a pilot hole (Photo 2) and install the new screw—you're all set.

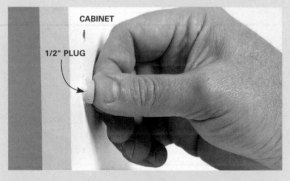

1 Pop in the plug. Smear some glue onto the plug and embed it in the hole. Tap the plug with a hammer to fully seat it. Then wipe up any glue ooze with a wet rag.

2 Drill a pilot hole. Mark the location for the new screw hole. Then drill a pilot hole with a bit that's smaller than the screw's diameter.

ADJUST BYPASS CLOSET DOORS

There's no reason to put up with sticking bypass closet doors, or doors that have uneven gaps against the jambs—especially since they're so easy to fix. Usually the mounting bracket screws have loosened up, making the door sag and rub against the carpet or floor.

To fix it, you'll have to work from inside the closet, so get a flashlight and screwdrivers. Start by pushing one door closed against the jamb. Hold it against the jamb while you adjust the brackets as shown. Do the same on the other door. If the screw holes are stripped, just move the bracket over a few inches and remount it.

1 Square the door. Push the door against the jamb and lock it in place with shims at both corners.

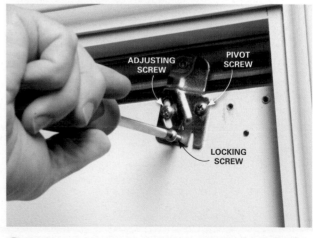

2 Tighten screws. Remount in new screw holes if necessary. Then test the door to make sure it rolls smoothly.

THE BEST FLOORING FOR A LAUNDRY ROOM

According to flooring expert Scott Lesnick, luxury vinyl tile, or LVT, is an excellent choice for wet areas such as laundry rooms and bathrooms. "LVT is more economical than ceramic tile and wood, it's easy to install and clean, it's moisture resistant, and very durable. And while you don't want any flooring product to soak in water, LVT can withstand a fair amount of moisture without damage." Vinyl flooring can also help absorb the noise of a washer and dryer.

The primary difference between LVT and the lower-priced vinyl composition tile (VCT) is that LVT is made with higher levels of solid vinyl, which makes it more durable over the long term. LVT also comes in a wide variety of patterns designed to look like natural wood, granite, tile and other materials.

Lesnick says the quality of vinyl flooring varies widely, and he warns against buying self-adhesive products. "Peel-and-stick vinyl is generally low-end and is not as durable as LVT. LVT can be installed direct glued or as a floating floor depending on the type. Make sure you know what you're buying and follow the manufacturer's guidelines."

MEET AN EXPERT

Scott Lesnick has been in the flooring business for 26 years. He works for Shaw Industries, the world's leading manufacturer of carpet, laminate, wood, luxury vinyl tile and pad.

"While you don't want any flooring product to soak in water, LVT can withstand a fair amount of moisture without damage."

—Scott Lesnick

FIX A SAGGING SELF-CLOSING DOOR

We get a lot of reader letters asking how to fix a door that closes by itself. Here are a couple of fixes that carpenters have been using for years that just might do the trick. These tips work only if a door slowly "creeps" closed. If it swings freely, the door or wall is out of plumb and will require more-draconian fixes, which we won't cover here.

Check the gap at the top of the door. If it's wider at the doorknob side, remove the center screw at the top hinge and replace it with a 3-in. screw (**Photo 1**). The screw will pull the jamb and door tighter to the framing and hopefully fix the problem.

If the door still creeps closed (but less so), go to the "Kleenex box" shimming technique (**Photo 2**). Put one shim behind the middle hinge and two shims behind the bottom hinge.

1 Draw in the top hinge. Draw the doorjamb toward the framing with a 3-in. screw. An impact driver works best, but if you don't have one, predrill first with a 1/8-in. drill bit.

2 Shim the hinges. Slip one shim behind the center hinge and replace the screws. Then place two shims behind the bottom hinge.

WALL REPAIR SIMPLIFIED

We know these products work— because we use them!

by **TFH Editors**

Ceiling stain solution

If you have a water-stained ceiling, a stain-blocking primer is mandatory to prevent the stain from bleeding through a fresh coat of paint. You could roll on primer, but there are two spray-can products you should consider first: Kilz Upshot and Zinsser Covers Up are both stain-blocking primers, and both have nozzles that shoot upward—perfect for ceiling work. Upshot is tinted to match aged, unpainted ceiling texture. Covers Up is a lighter shade of off-white. So if you're lucky, the primer will blend in and you won't have to paint the whole ceiling. You'll find one or the other (but probably not both) at home centers and paint stores for $5 to $6.

Cure for chronic cracks

Some cracks keep coming back no matter how well you repair them. For those pesky recurring cracks, we prescribe Good-Bye Cracks. It forms an elastic film that stretches and contracts along with the crack. It works best on hairline cracks, but it's worth a try on wider cracks too. Start by cleaning loose material out of the crack and fill it with joint compound. Then spray on two to three light coats of Good-Bye Cracks. The film isn't sandable, so a smooth, even coat is critical (practice on a scrap of cardboard first). When the film dries, prime and paint. You'll find Good-Bye Cracks (about $4) at some paint stores and home centers. Or search online for "Good-Bye Cracks."

"I first used this stuff three years ago, and the vast majority of those cracks never came back. Now it's my first choice for most repairs."

—Tom Dvorak

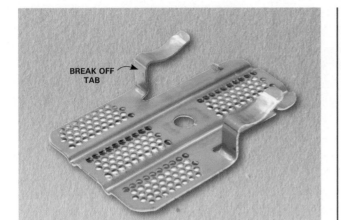

Fast patch backing

If you're installing a drywall patch, you gotta screw the patch to something. Usually, that means installing wood backing. But here's a quicker, easier way: Screw drywall repair clips to the surrounding drywall and screw in the patch. Then break off the tabs and you're ready for mud. Get a six-pack for about $4 at home centers.

—Bob Riley

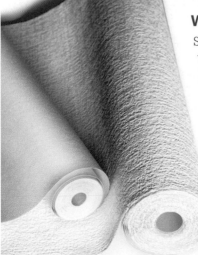

Mini texture gun

I've had some good results using texture from aerosol spray cans—and some disasters. The texture blasts out fast and heavy. One wrong move and you've got an over-textured mess.

This little hand-pump gun is much easier to control. It spits out just a little texture with each blast. So you can spray on a light texture, then add more until it looks right. Still, it's best to practice on some cardboard first. Also have a bucket and sponge handy in case you need to wipe away a misfire and start over. I got good results matching orange peel, splatter and knockdown textures, but lousy results with popcorn ceiling texture. The gun is available at some home centers for less than $20. Or search online for "Homax 4105." The kit comes with texture packets, but watered-down joint compound works fine too.

—Gary Wentz, Senior Editor

Chair rail

The walls in my parents' kitchen were banged up from decades of kids and grandkids impatient to get away from the table and slamming chairs into the wall. We talked about repairing the damage. But then I said, "Isn't that what chair rail is for?" So we just covered up the dings. Looks great.

—Donna Bierbach, Senior Copy Editor

Whole wall cover-up

Some walls are so bad that the best fix is to tear them out and install new drywall. Wall liner is the next-best fix. It's basically extra-thick, paintable wallpaper that acts as a big patch over the whole wall. Some versions are smooth; some have a textured or patterned surface. Fill cracks and holes with joint compound, prime the patches and then hang the liner just like wallpaper. A 55-sq.-ft. roll of wall liner costs about $17 at home centers, paint stores and online.

"My plaster walls had so many cracks that they looked like a road map. So I covered them with wall liner. Ten years later, they still look perfect."

—Gary Wentz, Senior Editor

Bigger cover plates

"Oversized" plates cover an extra 1/4 in. or so of wall on all four sides. And sometimes that's just enough to hide damage and save you the trouble of making a repair. Home centers carry oversized plates for common configurations like single and double switches and outlets.

Simplest crack solution

Step Saver Stress Crack Tape sounds like the perfect solution for cracks. Just stick it on and paint over it. So we gave it a try. The tape was still visible from across the room—even under two coats of paint. If you take a few minutes to skim over it with joint compound, the tape disappears completely. But will the tape stretch and stay stuck through seasonal crack movement? We'll get back to you on that...

Step Saver Stress Crack Tape is available at Sherwin-Williams, at Home Depot stores on the West Coast and online at stepsavers.com. The Stress Crack Tape Pack, containing 13 ft. of tape in various widths, costs about $6.

Instant patch

Every fix-it guy we know —DIYer or pro—loves self-stick metal patches. Just stick one over the hole and mud over it. Find them in sizes from 4 x 4 in. to 8 x 8 in. for about $5 at home centers.

Patch and protect

I dragged my feet for months after my wife asked me to fix a doorknob crater. Then one day I came home and saw that she had covered it with a stick-on bumper. Sometimes procrastination is the best strategy. Bumpers are sold at home centers for about $5.

—Travis Larson, Senior Editor

Texture in a jar

For small repairs on popcorn ceilings, dab on this stuff. Start with a light application, let it dry and add more if needed. With some careful brush work, you can perfectly match the surrounding texture. A quart costs about $6 to $13. If you don't find it at a home center, search online for "popcorn ceiling patch."

"Texturing with a brush is slow, fussy work. My 10 x 10-in. patch took two applications and a couple of hours altogether. But the patch is absolutely invisible."

—Gary Wentz, Senior Editor

HOW TO GET RID OF ANYTHING!

DIY jobs generate junk; here are some slick disposal tips

by **Jeff Gorton, Associate Editor**

Whether you're cleaning out your basement, replacing an old appliance or tackling a big remodeling job, getting rid of the old stuff is a pain. To help you out, we surveyed our staff and Field Editors for ideas and discovered tons of great tips and strategies for clearing out everything from cast iron bathtubs to old sidewalks.

"FREE" makes junk vanish

You know the old saying: "One man's trash is another man's treasure." The simplest way to get rid of stuff is to just put it on the curb with a "free" sign. When Gary Wentz, one of our editors, knocked down a stone retaining wall, he put a "free stone" sign on the curb. People were practically fighting over the rubble, and 12 tons of stone vanished in one afternoon. But don't be surprised if something reappears. Field Editor Cory Cochran put a freezer by the road with a sign that read "free—broke." It was gone the next day. Then a few days later, Cory found it back in his yard. Maybe he should have added "no returns" to the sign.

Dry out your old paint

If you have a bunch of almost-empty cans of latex paint, the best disposal method is to take them to the recycling center. But if that's not feasible, you can spread a sheet of painter's plastic in an out-of-the-way spot and dump a thin layer of paint on it to dry. When the liquid has evaporated, bundle it up and throw it in the trash.

Get money for metal

You can get money for almost any kind of scrap metal. You won't get much for steel (currently about 10¢ per pound), but that's better than paying to get rid of it. And other metals are worth a lot more: about $3 per lb. for copper and 80¢ per lb. for aluminum. You can even pull circuit boards out of electronic equipment and turn them in for bucks.

Turn waste wood into mulch

Here's an ingenious idea from Field Editor Tom Berg. After making sure the nails were removed, he ran 2,200 sq. ft. of siding through a wood chipper to make a mountain of great-smelling cedar mulch for his gardens. He saved a ton in trash container fees and had loads of free mulch to boot. You could do the same with pine or any other soft wood, but the mulch will decompose quicker than cedar.

READER PHOTO

BILL ZUEHLKE

Break up a cast iron tub

Some things are just so heavy to move in one piece that you shouldn't unless you absolutely have to. A cast iron bathtub is one of them. The trick is to break it up with a sledge. But be careful! Cast iron shrapnel is sharp and dangerous. Cover the tub with a blanket or drop cloth and be sure to wear long sleeves, safety glasses and hearing protection. Don't expect the tub to break easily on the first swing. You may have to hit the same spot repeatedly to get a crack started. It's hard work, but at least you won't break your back trying to lift the tub in one piece. This trick works for cast iron radiators and pipe too.

Give it away online

Even if you think no one would want the item, list it in the "free" category on a Web site. You'd be amazed at what people will take. Our Field Editors have gotten rid of all kinds of junk this way: half-rotten fence planks and worn-out appliances. Here's a list of Web sites where you can place listings to sell, give away or trade your stuff, plus find information about recycling and safe disposal.

> **craigslist.org**
> **earth911.com**
> **freecycle.org**
> **greenergadgets.org**
> **usell.com**

Tip Buy 3-mil heavy-duty contractor bags. They'll stand up to most tear-out debris without ripping.

Cut a water heater in half

It's a lot easier to move a water heater in two pieces—especially if it has 50 lbs. of sediment in the bottom—and it's surprisingly easy to cut one in half. You could use a recip saw, but a circular saw with a ferrous-metal cutting blade is faster. Be sure to wear goggles or a face shield, hearing protection and long sleeves. Many appliances can be cut; just be careful not to cut through refrigerant tubing or glass.

Cut it up fast with a ferrous-metal blade

Here's the blade we used to cut up the water heater (above). It's engineered to cut any mild steel, so when you're done cutting up your old water heater or refrigerator, you can cut angle iron, rebar, metal conduit or threaded rod, to name a few items. You'll find ferrous-metal cutting blades at home centers and hardware stores for about $40.

Buy a Bagster bag

If you have too much junk to fit in your trash can, but not enough to warrant renting a 10- or 20-yard trash container, then a Bagster bag is the answer. Buy the green poly bag at a home center or hardware store, fill it up and call the company for a pickup. The bag holds 3 cubic yards or up to 3,300 lbs. of debris. The Bagster bag costs $25 to $30. When you're done with it, you'll be charged a flat rate of $80 to $160 to have it picked up, depending on collection costs in your area. Find out more at thebagster.com.

He saved $400

For most of us, trash disposal is an unavoidable cost of remodeling. But Field Editor Tom Berg managed to complete an entire home addition without spending a penny on junk removal. He listed lumber, siding, windows and doors on freecycle.org and was surprised when people hauled them away for free. Even the scrap lumber got used as a bonfire for a church outing. He turned the cedar siding into mulch (see "Turn waste wood into mulch," p. 17) and threw the small amount of remaining stuff in the regular trash.

GETTY IMAGES/MARK TURNER

Recycle a sidewalk

Why spend a fortune hauling away old concrete when you can build a wall or path with it? Several of our Field Editors used old concrete from torn-out sidewalks and driveways to build paths, patios and walls. For walls, stack it like flat stones with the broken side facing out. For paths or patios, you can lay the broken pieces of concrete like flagstones and then plant a creeping ground cover or pour gravel between them.

BILL ZUEHLKE

Excess dirt is an opportunity

Digging a hole for a pond or fountain? You can save yourself time and money by turning the extra dirt into a landscaping feature. Here we piled the dirt along the back of the pond to create an earth berm. Covered with plants, the berm made a perfect backdrop for the pond.

Disassemble your old box spring

Field Editor Andrew Pitonyak stripped the fabric and padding from his box spring and left the metal springs on the curb for the local scrap collector to pick up. He saved the $20 cost of getting rid of the box spring and helped the environment by recycling the metal.

10 SIMPLE WAYS TO
ORGANIZE YOUR KITCHEN

Get the job done, get out and get on with life!

by **Gary Wentz, Senior Editor**

These projects are designed to give you efficiency, easy access and effortless organization. If you're like me, you'll appreciate the time savings. If you're not like me—if you actually enjoy your kitchen—you'll love the projects even more because cooking will be more convenient.

PERFECT PLACE FOR **LIDS**

You can mount a drawer for pot lids under your pot shelf—or under any other cabinet shelf. Before you remove the shelf, put some pencil marks on it to indicate the width of the cabinet opening at its narrowest point (usually at the hinges). Your

drawer front and slides can't extend beyond those marks (or you'll spend hours building a drawer that won't open). Then remove the shelf. If it's made from particleboard, I recommend that you replace it with 3/4-in. plywood and transfer the marks to the new shelf. If you can build a simple drawer box, the rest will be easy.

What it takes

Time: 1 to 4 hours, depending on the project
Cost: $10 to $50 if you have to buy all the materials. If you have some wood scraps lying around, most of these projects will cost less than $10.
Skill level: Beginner to intermediate
Tools: Drill, sander, table saw

Building notes

- All the wood projects shown here are finished with Minwax Wipe-On Poly (about $10 per pint at home centers).
- Unless otherwise noted, all the materials for these projects are available at home centers.
- If you want to cover plywood edges with iron-on edge band, find how-to help at familyhandyman.com (search for "edge banding").
- Several of these projects require joining 1/2-in.-thick wood parts. You can do that with a brad nailer, but if your aim is a smidgen off, you'll blow a nail out the side of the part. Trim-head screws are safer. Their thin shanks won't split thin wood (as long as you drill pilot holes), and their small heads are easy to hide with filler (or ignore).

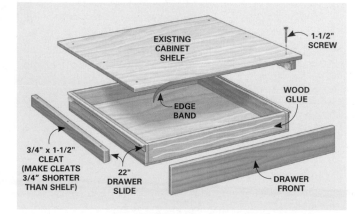

EXISTING CABINET SHELF

1-1/2" SCREW

WOOD GLUE

EDGE BAND

3/4" x 1-1/2" CLEAT (MAKE CLEATS 3/4" SHORTER THAN SHELF)

22" DRAWER SLIDE

DRAWER FRONT

DROP-DOWN
TABLET TRAY

This tray will keep your tablet computer off the counter-top. As it swings down, it also swings forward, so the tablet isn't hidden under the cabinet.

The mechanism is simple; just make and position the arms exactly as shown here and it will work smoothly. I cut the aluminum parts and rounded the corners with a grinder. When closed, the tray is held up by small cabinet door magnets. I clipped the plastic ears off the magnets and glued the magnets into place with epoxy. The liner in the tray is a foam placemat cut to fit. Don't worry, small magnets won't harm your tablet; it actually contains magnets.

FLIP-DOWN
PAPER TRAY

This tray is perfect for pens and paper. When closed, it's mostly hidden by the cabinet face frame. To install the tray, screw on the hinges first. Then open the cabinet door above and clamp the tray to the underside of the cabinet while you screw the hinges to the cabinet.

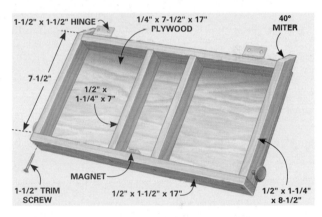

ADD A **SHELF**

Most cabinets come with only one or two shelves, leaving a lot of wasted space. So I added one (and sometimes two) shelves to most of my cabinets. All it takes is 3/4-in. plywood and a bag of shelf supports. The supports come in two diameters, so take an existing one to the store to make sure you get the right size.

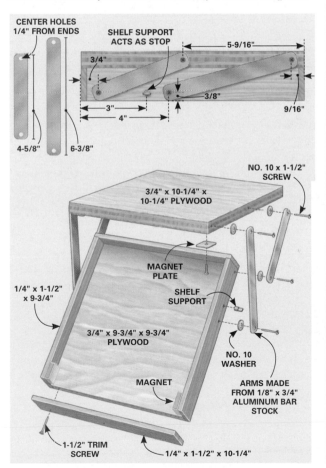

SHELF SUPPORT

DRAWER IN A DRAWER

Deep drawers often contain a jumbled pile of interlocking utensils. My solution is a sliding tray that creates two shallower spaces. Make it 1/8 in. narrower than the drawer box, about half the length and any depth you want (mine is 1-3/4 in. deep). When you position the holes for the adjustable shelf supports, don't rely on measurements and arithmetic. Instead,

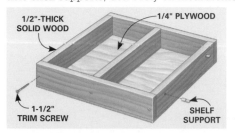

1/2"-THICK SOLID WOOD

1/4" PLYWOOD

1-1/2" TRIM SCREW

SHELF SUPPORT

position the tray inside the drawer box at least 1/8 in. lower than the cabinet opening and make a mark on the tray. My shelf supports fit tightly into the holes, but yours may require a little super glue.

ADD A DIVIDER FOR
UPRIGHT STORAGE

I don't know why the pan or tray you need is always the one at the bottom of the pile. But I do know the solution: Store large, flat stuff on edge rather than stacked up. That way, you can slide out whichever pan you need. Cut 3/4-in. plywood to match the depth of the cabinet, but make it at least an inch taller than the opening so you can fasten it to the face frame as shown. Drill shelf support holes that match the existing holes inside the cabinet. Finally, cut the old shelf to fit the new space.

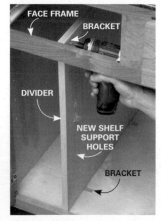

FACE FRAME

BRACKET

DIVIDER

NEW SHELF SUPPORT HOLES

BRACKET

Fasten the divider with brackets. Screw two brackets to the cabinet floor; one to the face frame and one to the back wall of the cabinet (not shown).

INSTANT
KNIFE RACK

You can size this knife rack to suit any cabinet door and any number of knives. To build it, you just need a table saw and wood scraps. Run the scraps across the saw on edge to cut kerfs. Adjust the blade height to suit the width of the knife blades. You have to remove the saw's blade guard for these cuts, so be extra careful. Also cut a thin strip to act as an end cap. Glue and clamp the kerfed scraps together and sand the knife rack until the joints are flush. To mount it, use two 1-1/4-in. screws and finish washers.

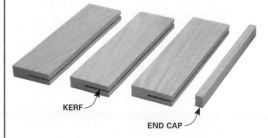

KERF

END CAP

ROLLOUT **STORAGE PANEL**

If you know how to mount a slab of plywood on drawer slides, you can take advantage of all the nifty shelves, hooks and holders sold at home centers. It's easy as long as you remember two critical things: First, make sure the drawer slides are parallel (**see photo below**). Second, make your cleats thick enough so that the slides will clear the cabinet door hinges. (I glued 1/2-in. plywood to 3/4-in. plywood to make my cleats.)

To install the panel in the cabinet, reassemble the slides. Hold the whole assembly against the cabinet wall and slide the panel out about 4 in. Drive screws through the cleats at the rear, then slide the panel out completely and drive screws at the front.

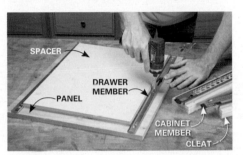

Mount the slides. They have to be absolutely parallel for smooth operation. So place a plywood spacer between the drawer members as you screw them to the panel. Screw the cabinet members to cleats.

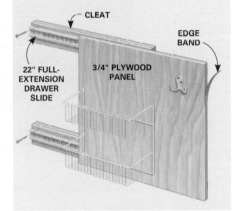

CONVENIENT CUTTING BOARD

The slickest way to store a cutting board for instant access is shown at right. But that only works for cutting boards less than 10-1/2 in. wide. For larger boards, mount a rack on a cabinet door. I used a sheet of 1/4-in.-thick acrylic plastic, but plywood would also work. You can cut acrylic with a table saw or circular saw as long as you cut slowly. Knock off the sharp edges with sandpaper. I also rounded the lower corners with a belt sander. For spacers, I used No. 14-8 crimp sleeves (in the electrical aisle at home centers). But any type of tube or even blocks of wood would work.

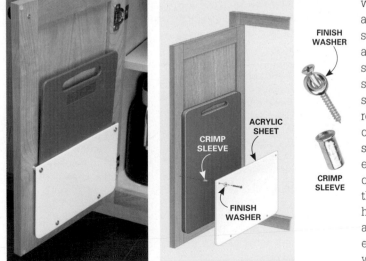

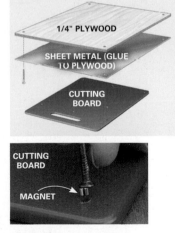

HIDDEN CUTTING BOARD

The secret to this project is "rare earth" magnets. The ones I used are just 5/32 in. in diameter and 1/8 in. tall. Browse online to find lots of shapes and sizes. Implant magnets at the corners of your cutting board; add more if needed.

Make the metal plate under the cabinet larger than the cutting board so the board will be easy to put away. Glue the sheet metal to plywood with spray adhesive. Drill holes near the corners and screw it to the cabinet underside.

Magnetize your cutting board. Drill holes sized for the magnets and drop in a dab of super glue. Insert magnets with a nail head. Slide the nail sideways to release the magnet.

BUILD YOUR OWN BAR

Tell your wife to think of it as an investment!

by **Gary Wentz, Senior Editor**

Every guy wants a place to hang out with friends. And the ultimate feature for any man cave is a bar. We talked with dozens of bar builders—DIYers and pros—and collected their best ideas for the perfect home bar.

Most of our bar builders just wanted a convenient spot to get together with the guys—a watering hole without crowds or noise, where you can flip on the game or music you want or switch it all off. But several also mentioned saving on entertainment. A night out on the town is expensive. But if your guests chip in for drinks and snacks, an evening in your home bar is dirt-cheap. So if your wife isn't too thrilled with your bar plan, present it as a smart investment strategy.

Anatomy of a bar

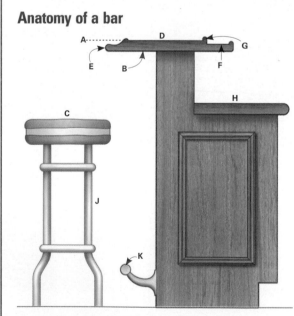

A. Standard **bar height** is 42 in. Bar stools will be easier to find if you stick with that height.

B. The **overhang** should be at least 8 in., but when it comes to knee room, more is better.

C. Most **bar stools** are 30 in. tall—perfect for standard bar height. But watch out: Some stools are several inches taller or shorter.

D. The **bar top** should be 16 to 20 in. wide, including the molding; more than that is a waste of space.

E. **Bar molding** serves three critical purposes:
1. It keeps spilled drinks from dribbling off the bar and onto your lap.
2. It provides a comfy armrest and lets you properly slouch over your beer.
3. Most important, it makes your home bar look more official.

F. The **drink rail** is where drinks get poured on a traditional bar. It's a nice feature, but not a necessity for a home bar.

G. A **drip lip**—simply a thin strip of protruding wood—keeps spills from running off the bar top.

H. A **lower counter** is the perfect place to slice lemons, set bottles or install a bar sink. But it adds complexity to the project and eats up a lot of space, so home bar builders often skip it.

J. The *minimum* **stool spacing** is 2 ft. of bar per seat. That will feel crowded to big guys, so go to 30 in. if you can.

K. The **foot rail** should be 7 to 9 in. off the floor. Metal railing (usually brass) is expensive ($200 for an 8-ft. run), so many home bars have a simple ledge instead.

Build in a drip tray

Beer drip trays catch spills, keep them off the finish and clean up easily. Just cut a recess out of the upper bar top layer to create a perfect pocket for the tray. The 6 x 12-in. stainless steel tray shown here (B005O1ASMA) costs $49 at amazon.com.

Advice on tap

At DIYer Roger Dunning's bar, beer flows from kegs kept cold by a fridge in the next room and propelled by CO_2 pressure. Aside from the fridge, the system came as a kit that cost about $300. After using (and loving) his system for a few years, Roger has this advice:

■ Buy small kegs. Depending on the type of beer, it stays fresh for just a month or two. After that, you have to shed a tear and send the left-over beer down the drain. For most home bars, 5-gallon kegs are big enough.

■ Every six weeks or so, you have to spend 20 minutes flushing the system with a cleaning solution. This is mandatory. If you're not willing to do it, stick with bottled beer.

■ Insulate the lines with pipe insulation and expanding foam. That keeps the beer cold and fully carbonated and prevents condensation from forming on the tubing and dripping inside walls.

■ Install one more tap than you think you'll need. You'll be glad you did.

"A tap system sounds complicated, but it's simple—mostly just running and connecting plastic tubing."

—Roger Dunning

Mock it up

Every bar builder we talked with told us that planning is tough. With so many dimensions and space considerations, using pencil and paper just doesn't provide a clear preview of the final results. So take an hour or two to build a model. Scavenge some cardboard or pick up some foam insulation at a home center (less than $10 for a 4 x 8-ft. sheet).

Granite top

Trim carpenter Dean Peacock wanted to top off his bar with something tougher than wood. He first thought about kitchen countertop materials like solid surfacing, granite and quartz. But those options are expensive and pro-installed—and Dean likes to do everything himself. Then he came across these Italian granite slabs at a tile store. Framed in oak, they made the perfect bar top. If you'd like to follow Dean's lead, contact a granite countertop fabricator. They often sell smaller leftover slabs at a bargain price.

"The friends who helped build my bar love to stop in for a glass of my excellent home brew." —Dean Peacock

Stone bar

DIYer Mike Kinross faced his basement bar with stone (manufactured stone instead of natural, but even Fred Flintstone couldn't tell the difference). Though it was his first stone project, Mike tells us it was easy—fussy and time-consuming, but not difficult. For installation tips, go to familyhandyman.com and search for "stone."

"It strokes my ego when friends say: 'You did this yourself? Amazing!'"

—Mike Kinross

Steel bar

Galvanized steel roofing has become a fashionable material indoors. But aside from style, DIYer John Solis found that steel has a ton of practical benefits.

- Inexpensive: John paid less than $1 per sq. ft.
- Fast and easy to install: no painting or finishing needed.
- Easy access: Need to run new beer lines to the taps? New speaker or TV wiring? Just unscrew the steel to open up stud cavities.
  - Durable and maintenance-free.

"If I had it to do over again, I might do a few things differently. But I would definitely use steel again." —John Solis

Bar molding tips

Most bar moldings fit over a bar top made from two layers of 3/4-in.-thick material (see **photo at bottom right**). The lower layer is usually plywood. The top layer can be plywood, solid wood, hardwood flooring, or even tile or stone. You won't find bar molding at home centers or lumberyards, but there are dozens of suppliers online. Costs range from $10 to $40 per linear ft., depending on wood species and width. It pays to shop around. Most suppliers carry lengths up to 8 ft., but a few offer 12-ft. lengths. Here are some tips for working with the stuff.

Some suppliers carry curved bar molding. But curves are costly; this radius corner was $150. Mitered corners are much cheaper!

Can your saw cut it?

Bar moldings range in width from 4-1/4 in. to almost 7 in. If you have a sliding miter saw, you can cut even the widest bar molding. But a standard 10-in. miter saw won't cut miters—and maybe not even crosscuts—on wide molding. Be sure to check your saw before ordering molding.

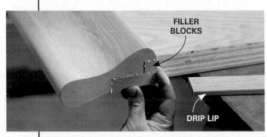

FILLER BLOCKS

DRIP LIP

Fill in dead ends

The butt end of bar molding leaves you with exposed rabbets. Some suppliers sell end caps ($20), which are easy to install but look awkward. So here's a better solution: Run the bar molding about 5/8 in. past the back edge of the bar top. Then fill the rabbets with blocks cut from wood with a similar grain pattern. Hold the blocks in place for about a minute. After the glue has completely dried, sand the end flush and add the drip lip. The lip shown here is simply a homemade strip of wood, 3/8 in. thick with rounded edges. The photo below shows it installed.

Prop it up for miters

The underside of most bar molding tilts downward when installed. So you can't just lay it on the saw bed when you make angled cuts. Instead, set the molding on blocks to hold it at the correct tilt. (You can lay the molding flat to make 90-degree cuts, however.) Tape the molding to limit tear-out where the saw teeth exit the wood.

Seal the end grain

With bar molding, you get a large area of exposed end grain. The end grain of wood sucks up more stain than the face grain and turns out a lot darker—almost black if you're using a dark stain. To prevent that, pretreat the end grain with sealer, which will partially fill the pores. A couple of ounces of polyurethane mixed with a couple of tablespoons of thinner (water or mineral spirits, depending on the type of polyurethane) works well. If you slop seal onto the face grain, sand it off.

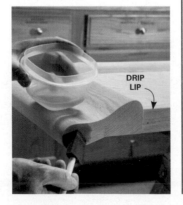

DRIP LIP

"Clamp" it with screws

Bar molding is almost impossible to clamp in place. So do some test fitting, fastening it with screws from below. Make sure all the joints are aligned and snug, then remove the screws, add glue and drive the screws back in.

HandyHints®

EASIER DOOR WORK

Before removing a door that will be reinstalled, snug a wooden wedge underneath it at the hinge side and duct tape the wedge to the floor. This makes reinstalling the door much easier because you'll get the height right on the first try.

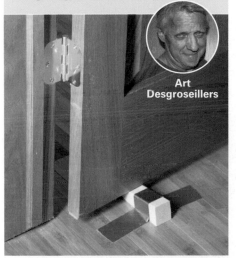

Art Desgroseillers

BEST COUNTERTOP SCRIBING TIP—EVER

Need to conform a new countertop to a wavy wall? Here's a great way to scribe it to create a perfect fit. Stick masking tape along the entire length of the countertop. Use a washer as a "pilot" wheel that'll spin as you run a marker through the washer hole to follow the wall contours. Cut and belt-sand to the line for a nearly seamless fit.

Jerry Matthews

CHRISTMAS LIGHT HANGER

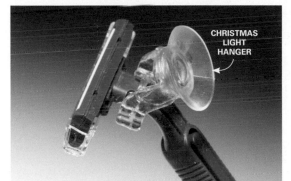

PACKING TAPE

RAZOR HOLDER FOR THE SHOWER

I found a great way to keep razors clean and dry in the shower: Use suction cup Christmas light hangers. They keep the razors high and dry, they're easy to remove for cleaning, and there's no need to drill holes in your beautiful tile job. You can find them at any home center or department store.

Bob Benedetti

SIMPLE SLAT REPAIR

Got a broken slat in your patio door vertical blinds? Here's a quick and easy way to fix it. Cover the broken area with two layers of packing tape. Use a hole punch to make a new hole for the clip. Clip the slat into place and move on to your next chore!

Clint Howe

HandyHints®

SPLASH-PROOF WALLS

With muddy dogs, hunters and teenagers coming and going, it's tough to keep the walls in our back entryway from getting dirty and needing to be repainted all the time. (I guess that's why it's called a "mudroom.") We solved the problem by "wallpapering" the walls with inexpensive vinyl flooring. Now all we have to do is wipe it down and it looks like new again.

—Dick and Diane Snyder

SOGGY
DOGGY

VINYL
FLOOR
TILES

SELF-SELECTING KEY

I have too many keys that look alike. So I drilled a second hole in my house key. That way, it hangs at an angle and stands out from the others. No more fumbling in the dark to find the right key!

—Gary Wentz,
Senior Editor

UTILITY SINK SPONGE HOLDER

Our wet sponges had always sat on the ledge of our utility sink. They never dried properly and became moldy and smelly and we had to toss a lot of them. But then we came up with the idea of screwing a sieve to the back of the sink to hold the sponges. They dry nicely, they're out of the way, and they last forever. We have a similar setup for our kitchen sink too.

—Julie Dieter

SIEVE

AMAZINGLY AFFORDABLE COUNTERTOPS

I don't know how IKEA does it, but you'd be hard-pressed to find high-quality wood countertops available for less unless you milled them yourself. Available in beech, oak and birch in various lengths, thicknesses and depths, these countertops are quality slabs of solid wood that you can cut, sand and finish as you like. The Numerär beech countertop shown (73-1/4 in. x 25-5/8 in. x 1-1/2 in.) costs $129. (You could use one for an awesome workbench top, too!) Find out more at ikea.com.

—Elisa Bernick,
Associate Editor

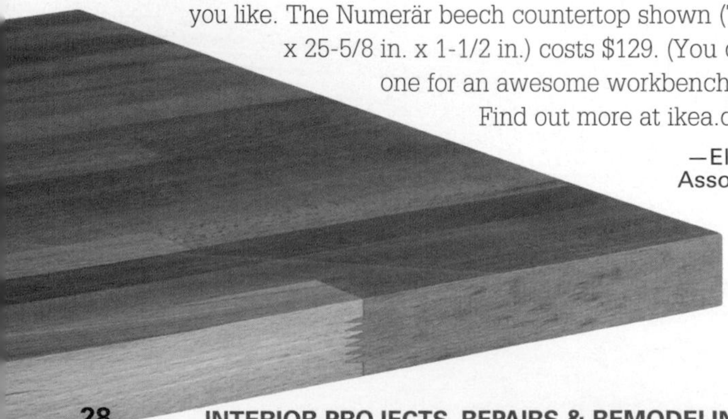

IKEA

NO-FADE CHALK LINES

I've been installing tile for 20 years. I always start a job by snapping a series of layout chalk lines on the area to be covered. Then I spray the lines with a clear coat of polyurethane. That way I can walk on the lines or sweep over them and they won't fade or disappear.

—Sissy Mcalpin

Holiday Handy Hints

EASY-CLIP TREE ORNAMENTS

The wire hooks that come with Christmas tree ornaments can be hard to use and can scratch the ornaments. Instead of wire hangers, we use plastic-coated paper clips to hang our ornaments. They're stronger and easy to use, and best of all, they won't scratch the ornaments, so you can leave them attached when you pack them away at the end of each season.

The Natales

PLASTIC-COATED PAPER CLIP

ORNAMENTS BY THE CUP

It's hard to store fragile ornaments without breaking them. That's why we came up with this solution: Use a plastic storage container and store each ornament in a separate plastic cup. By using cardboard to separate the layers, you can stack a lot of ornaments in one sturdy box without any tangling or breaking. We reuse the same cups and cardboard year after year.

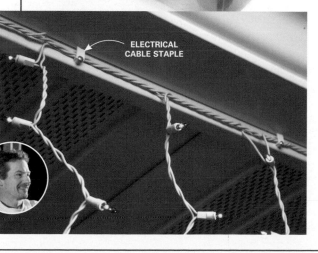

PLASTIC CUP

Bernie Wojek

BETTER HOLIDAY LIGHT CLIPS

I make inexpensive and long-lasting holiday light clips using a common staple for electrical cable wiring. I just snip the staple in half and fasten it to my fascia or trim with the remaining nail. It holds the wire securely, but it's still easy to slip the wire behind the clip. My clips have held up year after year no matter how cold it's gotten. If you have metal fascia, use stainless steel screws so they won't rust.

—Tom Dvorak

SNIPPED ELECTRICAL STAPLE

STAINLESS STEEL SCREW

ELECTRICAL CABLE STAPLE

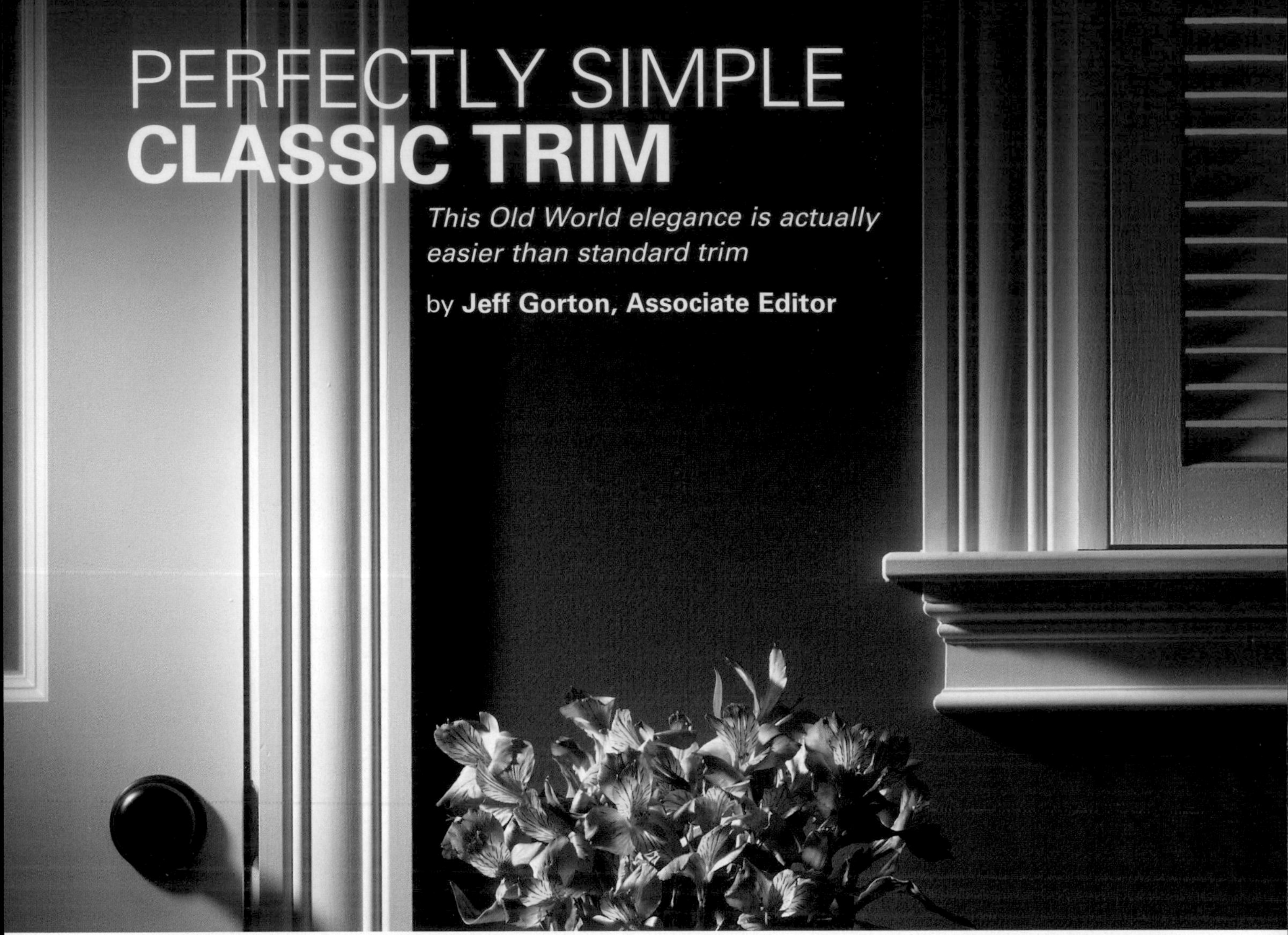

PERFECTLY SIMPLE
CLASSIC TRIM

This Old World elegance is actually easier than standard trim

by **Jeff Gorton, Associate Editor**

his traditional trim style may look like it requires old-school carpentry skills, but the truth is, it's easier to install than contemporary trim. Modern trim—four pieces of casing that "picture frame" a door or window—requires wide miter cuts, which look sloppy if they're not perfect. Traditional trim is more forgiving. While it also requires miter cuts, they're shorter and less visible. And the most prominent joints are assembled with simple square cuts.

If you're nervous about installing the mitered crown molding that tops off the trim, check out "Make Your Own Moldings" on p. 32 where we show you how to make a simple router-shaped version that doesn't require any miters. We'll walk you through the steps and give you some tips and pointers for cutting and installing the moldings to create this classic trim style.

Getting started

The first step is to prepare the jambs for trim. If you're replacing trim, pry it off and remove the nails from the jamb. Scrape or sand the face of the jamb to smooth out any paint or finish build-up. Finally, mark the reveal on the jambs to show where the edge of the trim goes (**Photo 1, inset**). A combination square set to 1/4 in. works great for marking the reveals. But you can also use a compass to scribe the marks, or simply measure and mark the reveals.

If possible, set up your miter saw in the room where you're installing the trim. Having the saw nearby will save you a ton of time. I like to rough-cut the casing and other moldings to length, allowing a few extra inches, and label them to make sure I have all the material I need and won't accidentally cut the wrong piece.

For tips on buying or making the moldings you'll need, see p. 32.

What it takes

Time: 90 minutes per window or door.

Skill level: Intermediate to advanced.

Cost: $35 per window and $40 per door for pine trim. Oak or maple trim would cost about twice as much.

Tools: A miter saw with at least a 40-tooth blade. A pneumatic trim nailer and compressor, and a table saw and router with a 1/4-in. roundover bit if you want to make a stool and fillet like the ones shown here.

MEET AN EXPERT

During his 20-plus years as a remodeling contractor, Associate Editor Jeff Gorton specialized in old-house renovations. He installed classic trim like this on hundreds of doors and windows.

Mark, don't measure

With the moldings and other parts cut to rough length, and the reveals marked on the jambs, the fastest and most accurate method for marking the trim for cutting is to simply hold the molding in place and mark it (**Photo 1**). It's foolproof. You don't have to measure, do math or remember any numbers.

Install the window casings, stool and apron

The order of trim installation for windows varies a little depending on whether you're working on old double-hung windows or newer-style windows. On older double-hung windows, the stool rests on the angled sill and butts into the lower sash (check out **Figure A** if you're not sure what a stool is). You have to notch the new stool to fit, and nail it to the windowsill before you install the side casings. But on newer windows like the one shown here, the stool isn't notched and doesn't rest on the sill, so it's a little trickier to nail. An easy way to attach this type of stool is

Figure A Window trim parts

Trim terminology can be confusing. Here's a labeled photo to show you the names of the parts we used.

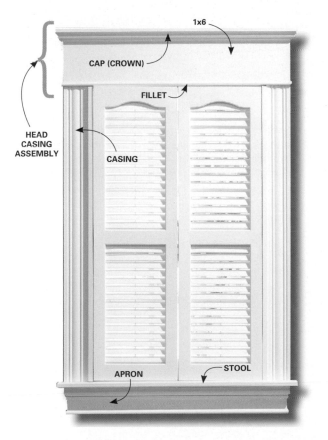

1x6
CAP (CROWN)
FILLET
HEAD CASING ASSEMBLY
CASING
APRON
STOOL

TOP REVEAL MARK
1/4"
BOTTOM REVEAL MARK
BOTTOM REVEAL MARK

1 **Mark the side casing.** Cut one end of the casing square. Line up the cut end with the pencil mark indicating the 1/4-in. reveal and mark the opposite end for cutting. Cut and install both side casings, keeping them aligned with the reveal marks.

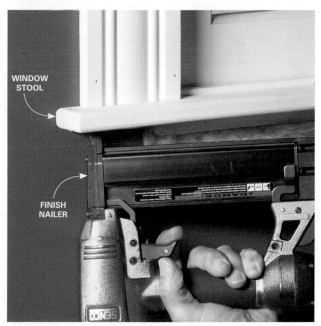

WINDOW STOOL
FINISH NAILER

2 **Install the stool.** Cut the stool so that it extends an inch past the casing on both ends. Then round the edges with a router or by sanding. Nail the stool to the side casings.

Traditional Molding

Tips for choosing, buying and making your own

Shopping for trim

We found the wide casing and base blocks at the home center, along with the fancy casing we used as an apron. We had to go to the local lumberyard for the 2-1/4-in. crown molding. If your local home center or lumberyard doesn't have what you want in stock, ask to see a molding book or chart that shows what styles are available to order. The Internet is also a good place to search for traditional moldings. Here are a few links to help you get started.

ferche.com

mouldingandmillwork.com

bosleymouldings.com

Make your own moldings

You don't have to buy moldings. With a little ingenuity and a few standard router bits, you can make your own. **Figure B** shows an example of a cap molding for a head casing that we made by stacking two pieces of 3/4-in. oak. Shaping the edges of wood strips with a router and stacking them to make bigger moldings is a great technique for making your own moldings.

You can make moldings with a hand-held router, but it's a lot easier and faster to mount your router in a router table. The Ryobi router table shown here (about $100) works well, but there are plenty of other options. For plans to make your own, go to familyhandyman.com and search for "router table."

The photo at right shows how to use featherboards for safer and more accurate routing. You can make your own featherboards, or buy plastic ones like these for about $10 to $20 each.

The ends of the boards shown in **Figure B** are routed. This method eliminates the need for mitered returns, but it does expose end grain and means you have to cut the parts to length before you shape them. To rout the end of boards, use a shop-made push block like the one shown at the top of the page. It serves two functions. First, it allows you to hold the board square to the fence. And second, the push block prevents splintering by providing a backer behind the board you're routing.

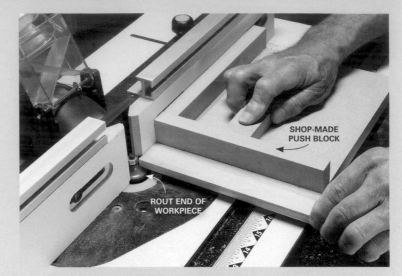

Build a simple push block to rout ends. Hold the board square to the fence and prevent tear-out with a shop-made push block like this.

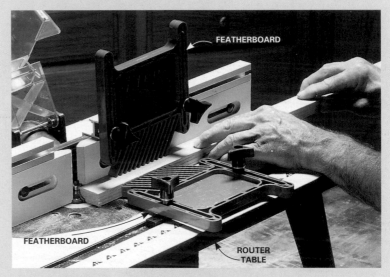

Hold the wood with featherboards. When you're making moldings with a router table, use featherboards to hold the wood tight to the fence and table. Set the featherboards to apply light pressure.

Figure B
Router-shaped cap molding

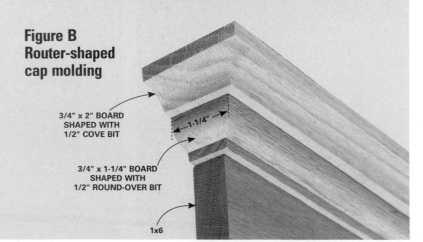

3/4" x 2" BOARD SHAPED WITH 1/2" COVE BIT

1-1/4"

3/4" x 1-1/4" BOARD SHAPED WITH 1/2" ROUND-OVER BIT

1x6

to install the side casings first, and then nail the stool to them (**Photo 2**).

The stool should protrude past the casings by about an inch (**Photo 2**). To find the length of the stool, make a mark 1 in. beyond the casing on both sides. Then hold the stool up and transfer the marks. After the stool material is cut to length, round the edges and ends. Or if you want a little fancier stool, rout the edges with a more decorative bit. You can even buy a special stool-shaping bit, but you may have to order it.

With the side casings and stool in place, the next step is to install the apron under the stool. Start by cutting a

45-degree miter on each end. Mark for the long point of the miters by resting the apron on the stool and making marks where the outside edges of the casings intersect the apron material. Snug the mitered apron against the bottom of the stool and nail it to the framing under the window. Then cut returns and glue them in (**Photos 3 and 4**).

Photo 3 shows how I used a sacrificial piece of wood behind the apron material. Any flat scrap of wood will work. This sacrificial backer board prevents the skinny piece of molding you're cutting off from getting caught by the blade and flung through the gap in the fence. Don't attach the sacrificial board to the saw. Just hold it in place

3 **Cut the mitered apron returns.** Set the miter saw to 45 degrees and cut a return from the apron molding. Use a sacrificial board to prevent the small cutoff from flying through the gap in the fence. Set the saw to the opposite angle to cut the other return from the opposite end of the molding.

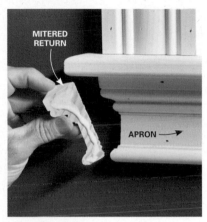

4 **Finish the apron.** Glue in the returns to complete the apron. Avoid nailing problems by letting the glue do the work. Just hold the return in place for 60 seconds while the glue grabs.

5 **Mark the crown molding for the end return.** Hold a piece of crown molding against the 1x6 you'll be using for the head casing and mark it for cutting.

6 **Build a crown-molding jig.** Build a simple jig to hold the crown molding at the correct angle while you cut it. Position the molding upside down and set the saw to 45 degrees. Avoid cutting all the way through the jig.

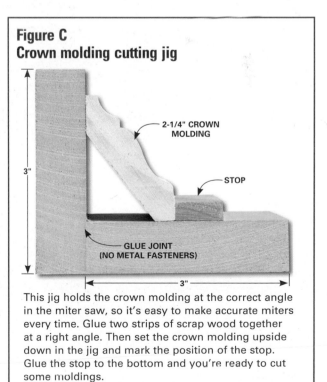

Figure C
Crown molding cutting jig

2-1/4" CROWN MOLDING — STOP — GLUE JOINT (NO METAL FASTENERS) — 3" — 3"

This jig holds the crown molding at the correct angle in the miter saw, so it's easy to make accurate miters every time. Glue two strips of scrap wood together at a right angle. Then set the crown molding upside down in the jig and mark the position of the stop. Glue the stop to the bottom and you're ready to cut some moldings.

along with the molding you're cutting. Then reposition it with each new cut so you're always making a fresh cut through the sacrificial board.

Build the head casing assembly

The final step for both the door and the window trim is building and installing the head casing assembly. It's made up of three parts: the fillet, a 1x6 and the cap molding. Traditionally this cap molding was solid, but since a solid molding this large is hard to come by, we substituted 2-1/4-in. crown molding. If you have a router and want to avoid using crown molding, check out **Figure B** on p. 32 for an attractive alternative.

Start by setting the 1x6 on top of the side casings and marking it at the outside edge of each casing. Cut the 1x6 to length. Then cut the fillet 3/4 in. longer than the 1x6. Round over the edges and ends of the fillet to make a bullnose shape using a router and 1/4-in. round-over bit. Nail the fillet to the bottom of the 1x6.

Finish the head casing by wrapping the front and sides of the 1x6 with crown molding. **Photos 5 – 8** show how. Make a jig (**Photo 6 and Figure C**) to hold the crown molding at the correct angle while you cut it. Remember to set the crown molding upside down in the jig. Mark and cut the short pieces of crown molding (**Photos 5 and 6**). Then cut a miter on one end of the long front piece and hold it in place on the 1x6 to mark the opposite end for the miter (**Photo 7**). Cut the second miter on the front piece.

Check the fit by holding the short mitered ends in place against the front crown molding. If the miters are tight and everything fits, complete the head casing by nailing the crown molding to the 1x6 (**Photo 8**). Complete the

window trim by nailing the head casing assembly to the framing above the window (**Photo 9**).

Finishing up

If you're installing painted moldings like ours, go to familyhandyman.com and enter "paint trim" in the search box for tips on how to finish your moldings with a flawless coat of paint. You can also find tips for staining and finishing wood by entering "stain trim" in the search box.

Doors are similar

Door trim starts with a base block at the bottom. Trimming a door is just like trimming a window, except you start out with base blocks at the floor, as shown above. The base blocks should be about 3/8 in. wider than the casings. Trim them if necessary. The height of the base blocks should be about 1 in. greater than the height of the baseboard you're planning to install.

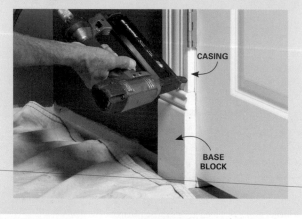

CASING

BASE BLOCK

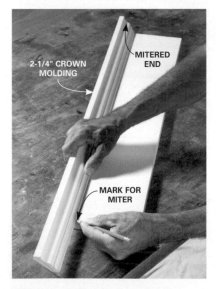

2-1/4" CROWN MOLDING

MITERED END

MARK FOR MITER

7 **Mark the front crown molding.** Cut a miter on one end of the front crown molding. Line up the cut with one end of the head casing and mark the opposite end for cutting. Set the molding in your jig and cut the opposite miter.

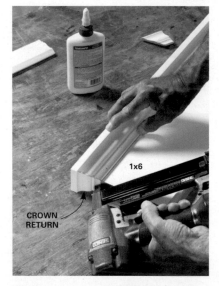

1x6

CROWN RETURN

8 **Attach the molding to the head casing.** Nail the crown molding to the 1x6. Then glue and nail in the end returns. Nail the fillet to the bottom of the 1x6 to complete the head casing assembly.

HEAD CASING ASSEMBLY

9 **Finish the window trim.** Set the head casing on the side casings, making sure the fillet overhangs evenly on both ends. Then nail it to the wall framing.

BETTER DRYWALL TOOLS

Here are three tips to ensure a more professional job

by **TFH Editors**

Best drywall tape for DIYers

Paper drywall tape is fine for skilled tapers. But for the rest of us, adhesive-backed mesh is a lot easier. You don't have to tool it into a bed of joint compound. Just stick it to the wall, then mud over it; no bubbles, ripples, wrinkles or slipping. That means you can concentrate on laying down a smooth, even coat of mud—which is hard enough for us non-pros.

The only weakness of mesh is...weakness. It's not as strong as paper and is more likely to allow cracks. To compensate, all the major manufacturers recommend stronger joint compound for the first coat. That means mixing powdered "setting-type" compound with water—a messy, time-consuming pain in the neck.

I know lots of guys who routinely ignore this advice and use standard premixed joint compound with mesh (and get away with it). But I prefer this low-risk recipe: mesh and a thin coat of lightweight setting compound for the first coat, standard compound for the following coats. I've done miles of joints this way. Zero cracks.

One last tip for rookie tapers: On inside corners, use tape that's made especially for corners. It's stiff and provides a guide for your knife, so you get straight corners every time.

—Gary Wentz, Senior Editor

Paper tape creates strong joints, but embedding it in joint compound takes some practice.

Corner tape is stiff and keeps your knife on a straight path along inside corners.

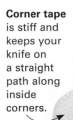

Mesh tape is bonehead simple. Just stick it to the wall and trowel on the mud.

Banish rusty mud

For a small job or two, an ordinary steel knife is fine. But after a few uses, rust sets in. That means rust in your joint compound and—possibly—rust stains that bleed through your paint job. A stainless steel knife costs three times as much (about $15) but will last forever. If you already have a rusty steel blade, remove the rust before you sling any mud.

—Elisa Bernick, Associate Editor

Better mud mixing

When I use my power drill to mix mortar or drywall mud, the drill jerks around in circles in the bucket instead of doing a good mixing job. To control the shaft of the mixer better without injuring my hands, I slip a short piece of 1/2-in. PVC pipe around the shaft of the mixing paddle. Mixing up mud just got a whole lot easier.

1/2" PVC PIPE

Damian Cordel

BATHROOM BUMP-OUT

Discover the magic of six square feet!

by **Gary Wentz, Senior Editor**

Building a "bump-out" is a big project that adds only a few square feet to a room. But in some rooms—especially bathrooms—an extra 6 or 7 sq. ft. allows for a complete transformation. With this wee addition, you can actually turn a half bath into a full bath, install a luxury two-sink vanity or even install a spa. The bump-out shown here allowed Charlie Avoles to expand a bathroom and replace a small tub with an oversized, easy-access shower.

A bump-out is a home addition. And though a lot smaller than most, it raises many of the same planning issues. This article covers the main issues Charlie had to wrestle with; they're the same things you'll have to consider if you're interested in a bump-out of your own.

If, after working through all these considerations, you decide a bump-out is worth the effort, get a building permit. That might seem like a pain in the neck. But think of it this way: An expert will check your plans in advance to make sure your bump-out will be built right. Then, during construction, another pro will make a house call to inspect your work. Not bad for $50 to $100 (not including plumbing and electrical permit fees).

"A bump-out doesn't add a lot of square footage, but think of it this way: This bathroom grew by more than 25 percent!"

—Charlie Avoles

Before you cut a hole in your house...

In most cases, you'll need to build a "shoring wall" (a temporary stud wall) inside the house, a couple of feet from the exterior wall. The shoring wall will support the ceiling and walls above while you cut a hole in the wall and install the header.

PHOTO BY CHARLIE AVOLES

How far can a bump-out bump out?

Floor joists can typically cantilever up to four times their depth. So if your existing joists are 2x8s (7-1/4 in. deep), the new joists can extend 29 in. outside (7-1/4 x 4 = 29). Check with your building inspector. A bump-out set on footings is limited only by setback requirements and other local codes.

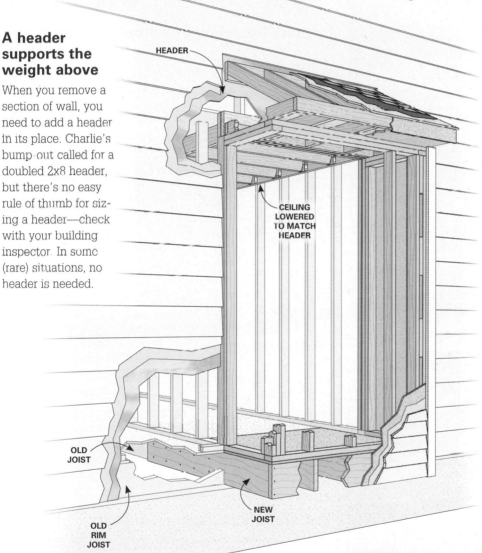

Consider a lower ceiling

Sometimes, a header extending down from the ceiling creates an attractive break in a room. In this case, the header would have been an eyesore centered above the shower. Charlie's solution was to lower the whole ceiling. That created a flat, uninterrupted ceiling. Plus, a small room feels bigger with a lower ceiling.

Roof lines

A lean-to roof like the one on Charlie's bump-out is the easiest type to build, and Charlie was able to connect to the existing roofline, for a neater appearance. On many homes, the solution is even simpler: Run the new exterior walls right up to the existing roof soffit and you won't need any roof at all. You'll have to limit the depth of the bump-out to the depth of the roof overhang, of course.

A header supports the weight above

When you remove a section of wall, you need to add a header in its place. Charlie's bump-out called for a doubled 2x8 header, but there's no easy rule of thumb for sizing a header—check with your building inspector. In some (rare) situations, no header is needed.

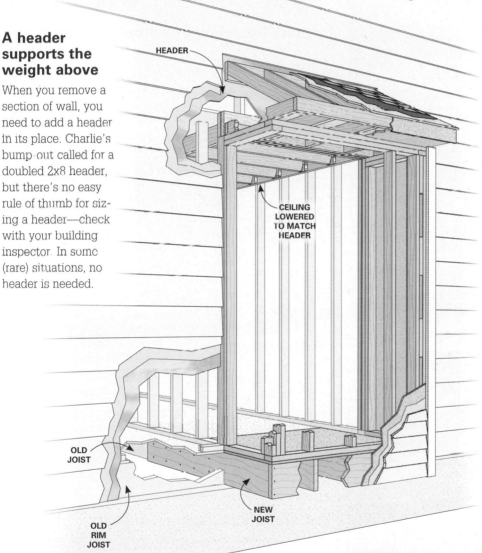

HEADER

CEILING LOWERED TO MATCH HEADER

OLD JOIST

OLD RIM JOIST

NEW JOIST

Two ways to support the floor

Charlie's bump-out rests on joists that protrude from the house and have no support under them—kind of like a balcony. These "cantilevered" joists are nailed onto the sides of the old joists (called "sistering") inside the basement. This approach works only if existing joists run the right direction, of course. You can also set a bump-out on footings, just like you'd build a deck. Charlie chose the cantilevered method to avoid digging holes to frost depth (42 in. in southern Minnesota) and pouring concrete footings. Footings are much less work in warmer climates.

New joists must reach far inside

In most cases, cantilevered joists must extend 2 ft. inside the foundation for every 1 ft. outside, so joists that cantilever 2 ft. must reach 4 ft. inside. That may mean moving plumbing, electrical or heating lines that run between existing joists. (So figure out what you're getting into before you start!) One more thing: You're going to have to cut out the rim joist to access the joists for sistering in the new ones.

MEET A PRO

Charlie Avoles is one of the licensed master plumbers who checks and double-checks every bit of plumbing info that appears in *The Family Handyman*. When he's not nitpicking magazine articles, Charlie is co-owner of St. Paul Pipeworks in St. Paul, Minnesota, and sometimes wears a general contractor hat, as he did for the bump-out shown here.

SUSPENDED CEILING DO'S AND DON'TS

These tips will help you hang a perfect ceiling

by **Mark Petersen, Contributing Editor**

Wade Sides (pictured at left) has been hanging suspended ceilings for more than 30 years. He started out working with his dad while still in high school. Wade has hung ceilings just about everywhere, from residential laundry rooms to casinos and megamalls. With these tips, $75 worth of tools and a little elbow grease, you'll save about 40 percent of the total cost of professional installation.

Lay it out on paper

Even the pros use graph paper to lay out the ceiling grid for each room. It helps not only with your materials list but also with getting equal-size panels at each side of the room. Include items like light fixtures and heat registers. The room should be bisected at the center by either a main tee or a centered row of tiles. Wade's tip on ordering materials: order by even numbers. If a room is 9 x 11 ft., order enough for a 10 x 12-ft. room.

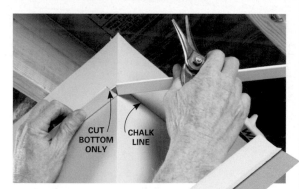

Nail up the wall angle

Pick a height so the ceiling tile will clear the lowest ceiling obstruction, like plumbing lines or ductwork. Snap a chalk line marking the top of the wall angle. Nail the wall angle at every stud with 1-1/4-in. drywall nails. Try to avoid nailing on or near the corner beads—it's a sure way to cause nail pops and cracks. Instead, run the wall angle long, snip the bottom and then bend it around the corner. Finish it with a "slip-on" outside corner.

Make rivet holes with a grid punch

Drilling your rivet holes works fine, but it's slow going. If you've got more than one suspended ceiling project in your future, a grid punch will save you a bunch of time. You can buy one at amazon.com for less than $30.

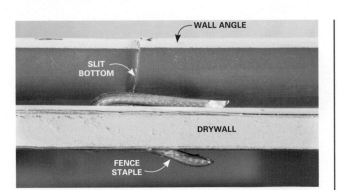

Use fence staples to hold the angle tight

Wade uses fence staples to secure the wall angle between the studs, especially where there's a gap between the wall and the angle. If there's a severe bow in the wall, you may have to cut the lower part of the channel so it will flex and follow the contour.

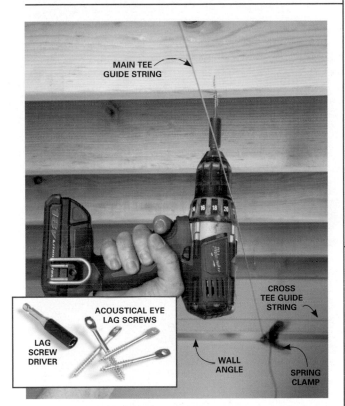

Run guide strings and drive in the hanging screws

Use strings as a guide to position the hanging screws (lag screws) and to keep the main tees straight while hanging. Offset the strings 1/2 in. so they line up with the sides of the tees rather than with the center. Wade wraps the end of the strings around a nail and uses a spring clamp to secure them to the wall angles. Sight along the string to position and drive in the hanging screws—they don't have to be perfectly centered. These acoustical eye lag screws require a special driver, which can be purchased for $4 at the home center where you get your other ceiling materials and tools.

Use your finger as a depth gauge

Follow the scribe to cut halfway through the face of the panel first, and then finish it by cutting through the side. Use your finger as a depth gauge. Gloves will prevent the oil in your hands from making smudge marks on the panels—and, of course, protect your hands.

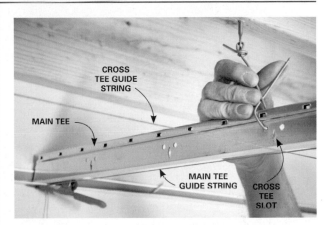

Line up the cross tee slots

Once you've figured out the size of the border row, measure back from the cross tee slots, and cut your main tees to size. Don't assume the wall is straight. Instead, run a string and use that as a guide to make sure all the cross tee slots line up.

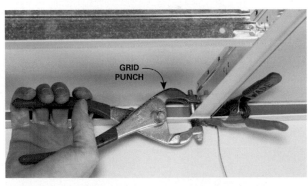

Pop-in rivets hold the grid square

Once you've hung a couple of main tees and locked in 8 to 12 ft. of cross tees, it's time to square up the grid. Check the diagonal measurements of at least a couple of the openings. When everything is square, rivet the main tees and cross tees to the wall angle. "This is where most people get into trouble," says Wade. If things are out of whack in the beginning, the problem will telegraph out across the room. Before you're done, you may end up trimming full panels instead of just plopping them into place.

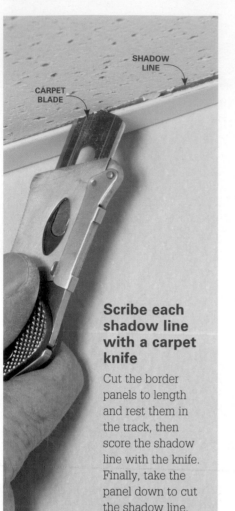

SHADOW LINE

CARPET BLADE

Scribe each shadow line with a carpet knife

Cut the border panels to length and rest them in the track, then score the shadow line with the knife. Finally, take the panel down to cut the shadow line.

DRYWALL CIRCLE GAUGE

KEYHOLE SAW

Mark your holes with a drywall circle gauge

Scribe holes with a drywall circle gauge, and then make the cuts with a drywall saw. With just these two tools, you can cut a wide variety of hole sizes.

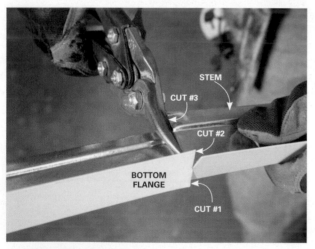

STEM

CUT #3

CUT #2

BOTTOM FLANGE

CUT #1

Cut the flanges first

The cleanest way to cut the main tees to length is to cut the bottom flange first from both directions. Then cut the stem last. That'll give you a clean, flat cut. Wade's cutting tool of choice is a pair of high-quality, yellow-handled (straight-cut) aviator snips.

Repair panels with flat latex caulk

Wade insists that only rookies damage ceiling panels. But when a panel does get damaged at his job site, he uses white caulk (or "apprentice putty" as he calls it) to patch it up. Make sure you use a flat latex caulk—shiny silicone will stand out worse than the hole. If the damaged area is bigger than a pencil eraser, you may want to set that panel aside to use as a partial in another location.

INSTALLING CABINETS

Do the job right with these easy step-by-step instructions

by **Mark Petersen, Contributing Editor**

Kitchen cabinets aren't cheap, and while you shouldn't be afraid to install them, you don't want to screw them up, either. We asked Jerome Worm, an experienced installer, to show you what it takes to install basic box cabinets successfully. His tips can save you time and help you avoid costly mistakes on your next installation.

MEET AN EXPERT

Jerome Worm has installed cabinets in hundreds of kitchens. These days, he can hang them in his sleep. Here are some of his best tips.

Mark up the wall first

Every good cabinet installation starts with a good layout. Jerome calls it "blueprinting" the wall. Here's how to do it: Measure from the highest point in the floor (see "Raise the Cabinets for Flooring," p. 44), and draw a level line marking the top of the base cabinets. Measure up 19-1/2 in. from that line and draw another line for the bottom of the upper cabinets. Label the location of the cabinets and appliances on the wall. Draw a vertical line to line up the edge of the first cabinet to be installed. Finally, mark the stud locations.

Remove the doors and drawers

Removing shelves, doors and drawers makes installation easier and prevents damage. Mark the location of the doors on painter's tape, and make a pencil mark at the top of the hinges so you have a good starting point when you reinstall them. Remember that many upper cabinets have no designated top or bottom. They can be hung either direction depending on which way you want the doors to swing. So decide that before you mark the hinges.

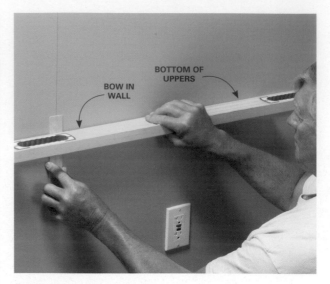

Shim extreme bows

Most of the time you can shim the cabinets as you go, but if there's an extreme bow in the wall (more than 3/8 in.), shim it out before you hang the cabinet. If you don't, you may accidentally pull the back off the cabinet while fastening it into place. Hold a level across the wall, and slide a shim up from the bottom (go in from the top when you're doing the top side) until it's snug. Then pin or tape it into place.

Start with the upper cabinets

It's easier to hang the uppers when you're not leaning way over the base cabinets. Rest the uppers on a ledger board—it'll ensure a nice, straight alignment and eliminate the frustration of holding the cabinets in place while screwing them to the wall.

Clamp, drill and fasten

When connecting two cabinets to each other, line up the face frames and clamp them together. Both cabinets should be fastened to the wall at this point, but you may have to loosen one cabinet or the other to get the frames to line up perfectly. Jerome prefers hand-screw clamps because they don't flex, and less flex means a tighter grip. Predrill a 1/8-in. hole before screwing them together with a 2-1/2-in. screw. Choose the less noticeable cabinet of the two for drilling and placing the screw head.

Use a block of wood for scribing

Find the largest distance between the outside of the cabinet and the wall. Take that measurement and make a pencil mark on your filler strip (measure over right to left in this case). Clamp the filler onto the cabinet flush with the inside of the vertical rail. Measure over from the wall to your pencil mark, and make a scribing block that size. Use your block to trace a pencil line down the filler strip. Masking tape on the filler strip helps the pencil line show up better and protects the finish from the saw table.

FILLER STRIP

SCRIBING BLOCK

Mark the stud locations on upper cabinets

Jerome prefers to predrill the screw holes from the inside of the cabinet so the drill bit doesn't "blow out" the wood on the inside where it can be seen. Do this by marking the stud locations on the inside of the cabinet and drilling pilot holes. Start by finding the distance from the wall or adjacent cabinet to the center of the next stud. For 1/2-in.-thick cabinet walls, subtract 7/8 in. from that measurement, and measure over that distance from the inside of the cabinet. Make a pencil mark on both the top and the bottom nailing strip. The outside of the cabinet walls are not flush with the rest of the cabinet; that 7/8 in. represents the thickness of the cabinet wall and the distance the walls are recessed.

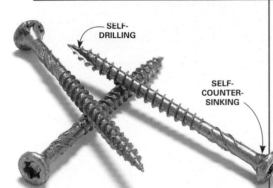

SELF-DRILLING

SELF-COUNTER-SINKING

Use good screws

Jerome prefers GRK's R4 self-countersinking screw, which he calls "the Cadillac of screws." You'll pay accordingly, but why scrimp on screws when you're spending thousands of dollars on cabinets? Whatever you do, don't use drywall screws—they'll just snap off and you'll end up with an extra hole. Learn more about the R4 screws at grkfasteners.com.

Fasten the back, then shim

Line up the base cabinets with the level line on the wall. Fasten the back of the cabinets to that line. Once the backs of the cabinets are level, use shims to level the sides. Take your time on this step—nobody likes to have eggs roll off a slanted countertop.

2x2

FLOORING BLOCK

Use 2x2s to secure cabinets to the floor

Cabinets that make up islands and peninsulas need to be secured to the floor. Join the island cabinets and set them in place. Trace an outline of the cabinets on the floor. Screw 2x2s to the floor 1/2 in. on the inside of the line to account for the thickness of the cabinets. Anchor the island cabinets to the 2x2s with screws. If needed, place flooring blocks under the 2x2s (see below left).

Raise the cabinets for flooring

If the kitchen flooring is going to be hardwood or tile, and you're installing it after the cabinets, you'll have to raise the cabinets off the floor or the dishwasher won't fit under the countertop. Use blocks to represent the finished floor height, and add those distances to the guide line for the base cabinet tops. Hold the blocks back a bit from the front so the flooring can tuck underneath.

FLOORING BLOCK

GAP FOR FLOORING

Cut oversize holes

Cutting exact size holes for water lines and drainpipes might impress your wife or customer, but such precision is likely to result in unnecessary headaches for you. Cutting larger holes makes it easier to slide the cabinet into place and provides wiggle room for minor adjustments. No one's going to notice the oversize holes once the cabinet is filled with dish soaps, scrubbers and recycling bins.

GreatGoofs®

Window blind bungle

I consider myself an advanced DIYer. I have tiled, laid flooring, built custom furniture, etc. So when my wife needed blinds hung in the guest room, I knew it would be an easy task. After spending about 15 minutes installing the brackets, I hung the new blinds and pulled them all the way up. I noticed there was a lot of extra string, so I neatly trimmed it and called in my wife to show her my quick handiwork.

She immediately pointed out that thanks to my clever trimming, the blinds couldn't be lowered more than a few inches. I hung my head, went to the hardware store and bought a roll of string. Needless to say, my "easy" project turned into a four-hour nightmare because I had to totally restring the new blinds. Lesson learned. Cut the extra string when the blinds are lowered.

Matthew Guilfoy

Belly gaffes

In an attempt to be neat while taking down the backsplash in my kitchen, I covered the counters, stove and sink with newspaper. I was leaning over the stove to get at the backsplash behind it, and my belly (not me!) turned on a burner. The newspaper started burning while I was trying to figure out what that clicking noise was. I saved the house but learned a lesson: Keep combustibles away from sources of fire and always know where the faucet is, especially if it's covered up!

—Keith Hetrick

The new fandango

My wife picked out an expensive new ceiling fan. While I was installing it, I noticed a red tag with some printing on it, but I was eager to proceed, so I figured I'd read it after the fan was up and running.

I followed the directions and included the extra bracing for the fan. When I was done installing it, I proudly called in my wife to admire it. As I flicked on the switch to take our new fan for its maiden spin, the fan immediately unscrewed itself from the threaded support pipe and came whirling down in what looked like slow motion and crashed to the floor. The fan was a complete wreck, there were ugly scratches in our brand new hardwood floor, and you can guess what my wife had to say!

When I finally got around to reading the red tag, here's what it said: "After the pipe is screwed in, use the locking screw provided to lock the pipe onto the main support."

—Stephen Finegan

Painting & Staining

SPATTER-PROOF WINDOW TREATMENTS

We were painting our bedroom and didn't want to spatter paint all over our white window treatments. Taking them down and putting them back up again would have taken us longer than the actual painting. Instead, we wrapped the window treatments in plastic bags and painted around them. No drips, spray or spatter, and we just threw the plastic away when we were done.

—Frank Miske III

PLASTIC BAG

CUSTOM-COLOR STAIN MARKERS

You don't have to settle for a stain touch-up marker that's close enough. Get an exact match by loading this Perfect Match Stain Marker ($5) with the same stain you used on the project. The pen loads like a syringe. Remove the felt tip, stick the end of the pen into the stain, and pull the plunger back to suck stain into the pen. Remember to stir the stain first. Replace the felt tip and you've got a custom-color stain touch-up marker. Go to perfectmatchstainmarker.com to find a retailer in your area, or search online.

Fill the stain marker with stain to match your project. Replace the felt tip and you've got a custom-color touch-up marker.

BETTER PAINT STIRRER

Instead of using a paint stick to stir your paint, use an old kitchen whisk. It mixes the paint better and it's a lot faster.

—Bradin Wyffels

WHAT'S THE BEST PAINT FOR A STUCCO PATCH?

According to Steve Revnew at Sherwin-Williams, dealing with patched stucco requires a two-step process. "Since the patch is new stucco, before you paint, prime the patch with a masonry primer designed with specific resistance to high pH and efflorescence." Revnew says these primers typically have elastomeric properties that provide for expansion and contraction throughout the life of the stucco. "If you don't do this, you risk paint failure."

Revnew suggests painting with a high-quality 100 percent acrylic latex. "These products allow moisture to escape and give great color and gloss retention." To find the right primer and paint for your stucco project, read the can label or ask at the paint store. High-quality options include Sherwin-Williams' Loxon line and SuperPaint, Behr's Elastomeric Masonry, Stucco & Brick Paint and UGL's DRYLOK masonry waterproofer.

MEET AN EXPERT

Steven Revnew is Vice President for Product Innovation at Sherwin-Williams. A chemist by training, Revnew practiced his profession in the Sherwin-Williams research and development labs before venturing into the world of marketing and sales.

TAPING BUMPY WALLS

Getting painter's tape to stick well to a semi-smooth wall is a challenge, but I found a great method. Use a tennis ball to smooth the tape! The ball lets you apply more pressure over a larger area than fingers alone. I find that an older tennis ball has more give and works better than a brand new one.

Greg Carroll

READER PHOTO

SLICK CORNER PAINTING TIP

Here's a neat trick I learned from my father-in-law for painting corners where two different colors meet on adjoining walls. Instead of taping right at the corner, cheat the tape a quarter inch away from the corner and run it down the wall's nice flat surface. It's much easier to get the tape to look straight and you don't fight the corner. This works especially well when you're butting darker and lighter colors together.

Shaun Kalis

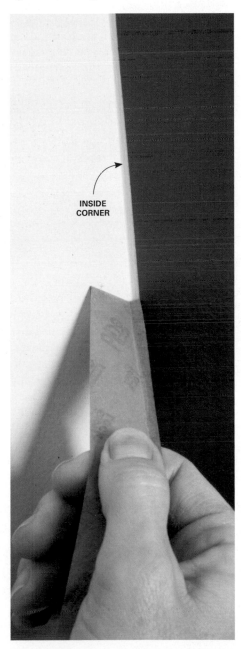

INSIDE CORNER

Painting&Staining
FASTER, BETTER PAINTING

Secrets from a painting pro for a speedy, great-looking paint job

by **Jeff Gorton, Associate Editor**

MEET A PRO

Jay Gorton got his first painting lessons more than 30 years ago when he worked for his father-in-law painting houses in the Minneapolis area. Since then he's perfected his trade and grown a business from a one-man operation to a team of more than 30 painters at times. Most of his work is in high-end new construction where he specializes in enamel finishes, faux-finished walls, and antiqued and distressed woodwork.

Prep varnished wood carefully

Every surface should be cleaned before it's painted, but painting over clear finishes like varnish or polyurethane requires extra care to ensure that the new paint bonds well. Thorough sanding is one way to prepare the surface. But a liquid sander/deglosser is easier and faster. Jay uses Klean-Strip Easy Liquid Sander Deglosser (about $7 per quart), but other types are available.

Read and follow the instructions on the container. Some types of "liquid sandpaper" require you to paint over them before they dry. Others, like the one Jay is using, should dry first. Follow the sander/deglosser with a coat of bonding primer. Ask for it at the paint department. Most major paint manufacturers sell it. Valspar Bonding Primer (about $21 per gallon at Lowe's) is one example.

Caulk every crack

Rather than trying to decide which cracks are large enough to require caulk, just caulk everything. It's actually faster because you don't have to waste time deciding what to caulk and because you're not constantly starting and stopping. Caulk every intersection between moldings and between moldings and walls or ceilings. You'll be amazed at how much better the final paint job looks when there are no dark cracks showing.

Patch with glazing putty

If you've done much auto body repair, you're probably familiar with glazing putty. On cars, glazing putty is used to fill small scratches and imperfections before painting because it spreads easily, dries quickly and is easy to sand. These same properties also make glazing putty ideal for filling shallow damage in trim. A 4.5-oz. tube of 3M Bondo Glazing and Spot putty costs about $3. You'll find glazing putty in auto parts stores, hardware stores and some well-stocked paint stores.

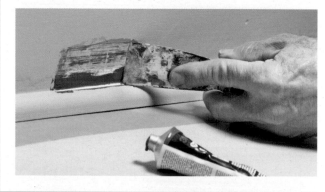

Look for a shed-resistant, woven roller

If you're picky about how your walls look when you're done rolling on the paint, then you'll want a way to avoid leaving a trail of roller fuzzies behind. Look for rollers that are labeled "shed resistant woven." They cost a little more than some covers, but the smooth, lint-free finish is worth it.

Paint twice as fast with this extra-wide roller

An 18-in.-wide roller setup like this may not be for everybody. Painters use them for the obvious reason that they can paint twice as fast as they can with a standard 9-in. roller.

If you have a lot of large, unbroken walls and ceilings, the investment in a large paint pail (about $30), 18-in. roller cage ($15 and up) and 18-in. cover (about $10) makes sense for you, too. You'll definitely save a bunch of time. Plus, because the roller is supported on both edges instead of just one, it's easier to apply consistent pressure and avoid roller marks left by paint buildup at the edge of the roller.

You'll find 18-in. roller equipment at most home centers and paint stores.

Replace your roller tray with a pail

If you're like most homeowners, you have a paint tray that you use to roll walls. And if you've done much painting, you've probably stepped in or spilled the tray at least once. Plus, as you know, trays are awkward to move around, especially when they're fully loaded with paint. A paint pail solves these problems and more. Pails hold more paint than trays, and you'll find them easy to move around and tough to step in! As an added bonus, if you use the plastic lining tip we show here, you can practically eliminate cleanup. You'll find standard-sized paint pails at home centers and paint stores for $15 to $20.

1 Line the pail to simplify cleanup. Use thin painter's plastic to line the pail. Cut a piece of plastic and drape it into the pail. Add your paint and then run a band of masking tape around the perimeter to hold the plastic in place.

2 Drain the leftover paint back into the can. When you're done painting, just bundle up the plastic and pull it out. If there's leftover paint, hold the plastic over your paint can and slit the bottom with a utility knife to drain the paint back into your paint can.

A quicker way to mask windows

Unless you're a really good painter, it's quicker to mask window glass than to try to neatly cut in with a brush, especially if you use the masking method we show here. The three photos at right show the technique. If you're going to spray-paint the window trim, cover the glass entirely by attaching a piece of paper under the first strip of masking tape. Precut the paper so it's about 1-1/2 in. narrower and shorter than the glass size.

1 Tape both sides of the glass, letting the ends run wild. Push the tape tightly into the corners with a flexible putty knife.

2 Slice off the excess with a utility knife.

3 Finish by taping the top and bottom.

Painting&Staining

Use a mini roller and screen

A mini roller is great for all kinds of painting tasks. Fit it with a woven sleeve to match the nap on your large roller and use it to touch up, and to paint areas where your big roller won't fit.

Buy a small screen and just drop it in your gallon paint can so it'll be handy when you need it. If you use a plastic screen like the one shown, you can push it down into the can and still get the paint can cover on. Then when you need to do a little touch-up, just take off the lid and start rolling.

Put a foam cover on your mini roller for painting doors and woodwork. You'll find a large selection of mini rollers at hardware stores, paint stores and home centers.

Drop-cloth substitute

Drop cloths can be a hassle. They slip on hard floors, get bunched up under ladders and are difficult to fit tight to baseboards. Eliminate the hassle and save time by using rosin paper instead. For about $12, you can buy a 160-ft.-long roll of 3-ft.-wide heavy masking paper. Roll it out, leaving about a 1/2-in. space along the wall for the tape. Then cover the edges with tape to keep it in place. You'll find rolls of masking or rosin paper at home centers and paint stores.

Don't start in corners

It's natural to load your brush with paint and stick it into the corner to start painting. But you'll end up with too much paint in the corner, where it's difficult to spread out. Instead, start laying on the paint about 4 to 6 in. from inside corners, and then spread the paint back into the corner with the brush. You'll get a nice, smooth paint job without excess paint buildup at inside corners.

Speedy, accurate masking

The key to perfect masking is to keep the tape straight and tight to the wall. Here's a tip to simplify the job. Stick about 6 in. of tape to the molding. Then, with the tape roll held tight against the wall, unroll about 6 more inches of tape. Rotate the roll down until this section of tape is stuck and repeat the process. The trick is to keep the roll of tape against the wall. It takes a little practice to master this technique, so don't give up. Once you learn to tape this way, your speed and accuracy will increase dramatically.

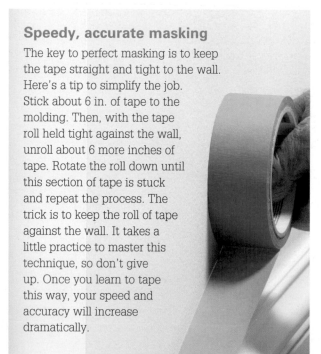

THE BEST PAINTBRUSH FOR CUTTING IN WITH LATEX PAINT

Professional painter—and ballroom dancer extraordinaire—Bill Nunn says the clear choice is a high-quality synthetic "sash" paintbrush. (That's the type with the angled bristles.)

"They can be found in nylon, a nylon and polyester blend, and Chinex. Nylon is a soft and fine filament and feathers paint well. In combination with polyester, it has a firmer feel and can help you spread a heavier paint. The firmness is usually marked on the paper wrapper, to which I always return a brush at day's end to preserve the shape. Chinex is a trade name for a synthetic bristle designed to help you with cleanup. It sheds paint well, especially the newer acrylics, but also applies oil paint well."

MEET AN EXPERT

For more than 30 years, Bill Nunn, owner of William Nunn Painting, has specialized in interior and exterior painting, wallcoverings and wood finishing.

THE BEST SOLVENT FOR OIL-BASED PAINT, STAIN AND VARNISH

Mineral spirits or paint thinner...which is better? For cleaning brushes, paint thinner is best since it's half the cost of mineral spirits and basically works the same. Other than the price, the differences between the two solvents are subtle:

- Both are petroleum products.
- Both can be used to thin oil-based paints and varnishes and to clean paintbrushes.
- Paint thinner is mineral spirits, but in a less refined form. It contains other types of solvents, which makes it a lot smellier and more volatile.
- Mineral spirits is not as stinky. Because it's more refined, it's slightly more effective in smaller quantities than paint thinner.

No matter which solvent you choose, use it in a well-ventilated space and observe proper safety precautions.

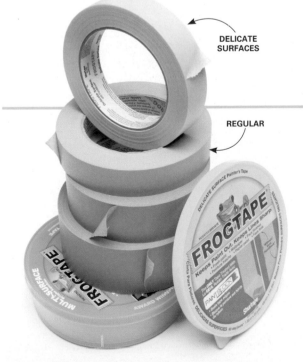

DELICATE SURFACES

REGULAR

NO-BLEED TAPE

We've used dozens of rolls of FrogTape over the last two years and have been impressed with it every single time. We've decided to give it one of our innovation awards. It not only works as advertised but also is the first genuine innovation in the painter's tape biz in years.

FrogTape has all but eliminated "bleeding," the problem of paint seeping behind the tape you've applied to protect your woodwork or to create accents. The company's big idea was to embed a chemical in the adhesive along the tape edges to turn the water in latex paints into gel. That effectively seals the edges of the tape. Buy FrogTape at home centers for a wee bit more than ordinary painter's tape. Brilliant!

Painting&Staining

CAULK IN ANY COLOR

Your kitchen wall is Colonial Green. Your new granite countertop is Arctic Blue. Which color caulk are you going to use to seal the backsplash: white, almond or brown? Don't like those options?

Pick up Sashco's eXact color kit and mix 1 oz. of leftover wall paint into the eXact color tube, shake it up and you've got yourself a tube of Colonial Green caulk. The directions on the packaging are very simple, and Sashco has a great video on its Web site (sashco.com/hi/exactcolor.html).

We tried it with orange paint. It came out a little light at first but matched great once it cured. There will be an air bubble or two, which could cause a splatter, so you might want to tape off each side of the bead and plan on tooling it. You can get a kit at some hardware stores or buy one at amazon.com for about $13

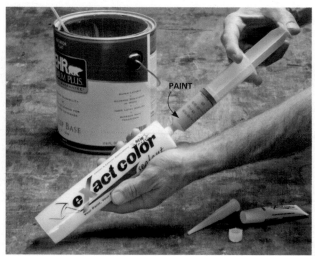

PAINT

EDITORS' CHOICE: PAINT BUCKET

One of our pro painting consultants turned us on to this paint bucket, and we think it's perfect for DIYers, too. We like it because it holds more paint than a tray so you don't have to refill as often. And unlike a tray, it's easy to move around without spilling. If you use our tip on p. 49, it's also super easy to keep clean. You'll find the Wooster 4-gallon paint bucket (about $20) at some paint stores and online.

EDITORS' CHOICE: MINI HAND MASKER

We've tried all kinds of masking tape dispensers. But for a simple, affordable way to speed up your masking, it's hard to beat this little applicator from Scotch. After you get a few inches of tape stuck down, hold the dispenser against the surface you're masking and slide it along the wall. Wheels press the tape to the surface, and a built-in cutter slices it off at the end of the run. We applied a straight, accurate line of masking tape along the moldings in this room in record time.

The 3M Scotch-Blue Painter's Tape Applicator is available for about $10 at home centers and hardware stores. It's refillable and comes with Scotch Edge-Lock tape, a special type of masking tape that prevents paint from creeping underneath.

SLIDE THE TAPE APPLICATOR ALONG THE WALL FOR A PERFECT MASKING JOB IN NO TIME

2 Electrical & High-Tech

IN THIS CHAPTER

HomeCare&Repair

TIPS, FIXES & GEAR FOR A TROUBLE-FREE HOME

REPAIR CHARRED WIRING

So you're finally getting around to replacing the ceiling light fixture when you discover that the wiring insulation has turned to charcoal and cracked off. The usual reason insulation gets ruined is that the bulbs in the fixture exceeded the fixture's wattage rating. That extra heat literally baked the insulation. Usually the insulation outside of the ceiling box is OK. But you'll have to repair

the damaged insulation inside the box. No, you can't just wrap the bare wires with electrical tape. That's not an acceptable long-term fix. Here's the right way to fix the problem.

Since the wiring in a ceiling fixture is usually 14-gauge, you can fix it with insulation stripped from a 12-gauge wire. Pick up a short length of 12-2 nonmetallic cable and a package of heat shrinkable

tubing. Strip insulation off the 12-gauge wires (**Photo 1**). Next, slide the new insulation onto the old wires (**Photo 2**). Then secure the new insulation with heat shrinkable tubing (**Photo 3**). When you're done, you can connect the new fixture without worrying about the old wires shorting out. Just be sure to follow the wattage maximum of the fixture when you select bulbs.

1 **Get new insulation.** Peel off the outer jacket of 12-2 nonmetallic cable. Then strip off about 8 in. of insulation from the black and white wires.

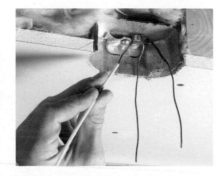

2 **Reinsulate the old wires.** Remove as much old insulation as possible. Then straighten out the old bare wire. Slide on new insulation (white goes on the neutral, black on the "hot"). Hold the insulation in place and slide on a short piece of heat shrinkable tubing.

HEAT SHRINKABLE TUBING

3 **Shrink the tubing.** Wave the flame from a lighter under the heat shrinkable tubing. Keep the flame moving so the heat does all the work and the tubing doesn't burn.

WIRELESS BOOM BOX

Creating a home-wide audio network in decades past would have involved a ton of expensive wiring to set up wall-mounted control panels in each room. Only those with deep pockets ever bothered. Achieving this goal today is much easier and less expensive—and wireless.

One way to start is with iHome's iW1, a handsomely understated mini speaker system that interacts with Apple iOS devices via a Wi-Fi–enabled, easy-to-use wireless technology called AirPlay.

Using another kind of phone or tablet, such as an Android device? Logitech's Wireless Boombox (not shown) is for you. It's cheaper than the iW1, connects over Bluetooth, and sounds great. You can use it with iOS devices too, but it has fewer features than iHome's unit.

The iW1 is $300 at ihomeaudio.com. The Wireless Boombox is $150 at bestbuy.com.

Web links: Energy upgrade rebates

Want to find out what energy upgrade rebates are available in your area? Click on your state and view all of them at dsireusa.org.

54 ELECTRICAL & HIGH-TECH

CFL BULBS IN OUTDOOR FIXTURE WON'T TURN OFF

I installed outdoor-rated CFL bulbs in my outdoor motion sensor fixture. They always turn on, but sometimes they don't turn off unless I flip the indoor switch. The fixture worked fine with incandescent bulbs. What gives?

Older motion sensor fixtures were designed for incandescent bulbs. The electronic ballasts in some CFLs interfere with the solid-state circuitry in the motion sensor.

First visit the sensor manufacturer's Web site and look for compatible CFL bulbs. If you can't find any, either buy a CFL-compatible fixture or go back to incandescent bulbs.

WHAT'S THE BEST ELECTRICAL TAPE?

"A lot of electricians, including me, swear by Scotch 33+," says Master Electrician Al Hildenbrand. "It's an amazing tape. The glue is stable and non-gumming or running, so it doesn't leave a residue on your hands or the material if removed. But more importantly, the plastic has a 'stretch' and 'return memory.' When the tape is pulled off the roll, it stretches slightly, and over the next five to ten minutes, attempts to return to its original length. This 'memory' helps to put a slight compression on a smoothly wrapped splice to hold it in place. And the 'stretch' allows an irregular surface to be wrapped over the high spots, where the stretch is greatest, and the 'memory' generally allows the tape on either side to snug down onto the smaller diameters. The result is a smoother, tighter and more uniform insulating of what is being covered."

> *"There are cheaper tapes, but they seriously lack the quality of Scotch 33+."*

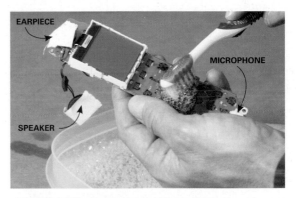

Scotch Super 33+ Vinyl Electrical Tape

MEET AN EXPERT

Al Hildenbrand is a licensed Minnesota Class "A" Master Electrician with a bachelor of science degree in electrical engineering. He's the owner of Al's Electric Works in Minneapolis, MN.

FIX A GUNKED-UP PORTABLE PHONE

Nobody knows who spilled the soda on the portable phone. But now the buttons are all gummed up and you can't use it. You may have to pitch the phone and buy a new one. But here's a last-ditch cleaning method that may save it from the recycling center.

Remove the batteries and any screws inside the battery compartment. Check for other screws holding the case together and remove them, too. Then use a butter knife to pry open the case.

Remove the entire circuit board and the silicone push buttons. Cover the speaker, microphone, earpiece and any mechanical switches with duct tape to keep them dry. Then clean all the parts with water/dishwashing detergent solution and a soft toothbrush (**Photo 1**).

Once you get the crud off, rinse the parts with lukewarm tap water. Blow off the excess water with compressed air (**Photo 2**). Remove the tape and store the circuit board and push buttons in a bag of rice for a few days. Then reassemble and try making a call. If it works, you just saved yourself some bucks. If not, you're just out a little time.

1 Scrub off the crud. Dip the toothbrush into the cleaning solution and gently scrub the soda residue from the push buttons and the circuit board.

2 Dry off the parts. Shoot compressed air into the earphone jacks, mechanical switches and all over the circuit board to remove excess water.

PROTECT THE WHOLE HOUSE FROM **POWER SURGES**

Appliances and other devices need protection—not just your computer!

by **Rick Muscoplat, Contributing Editor**

You might have plug-in surge protectors on some of your electronics, but you probably don't have them for appliances with electronic circuit boards. Those electronics are sitting ducks for power surges generated by lightning strikes (even if the strike is miles from your home). Most newer appliances, cable boxes, exercise machines and that new Bose Wave are all at risk. And it's not just lightning. Damaging power surges on the grid are common even when there isn't lightning around. It doesn't take much of a power surge to wipe out delicate electronics. It often costs as much to replace a circuit board as it does to buy a new device.

That's why everyone should have a whole-house surge protector. Those who live in rural areas are particularly vulnerable, especially if you live near the end of the power line. There's nowhere else for the surge to go but into your house.

A full-featured whole-house surge protection device (SPD) can protect all your electronics, appliances, telephone, Internet and cable TV equipment (the Square D No. SDSB1175C is one type; about $250 at homedepot.com). Electricians charge about $175 to install it. But if you're comfortable working inside the main panel, you can do the job yourself and save the installation fee. The job takes about an hour. I'll show you how to do it.

First buy the right SPD

There's a lot of manufacturer hype surrounding surge protectors. Ignore all the mumbo jumbo and head right for the specifications. SPDs are rated in kiloamps (1kA equals 1,000 amps). The really inexpensive SPDs start at about 10kA. They can handle one really large surge and then they're toast—so they're a bad long-term investment.

Instead, look for an SPD with a minimum rating of 50kA. It'll last longer than a 10kA device.

If you've got telephone, DSL, cable or satellite service, get an SPD that protects those lines as well. Finally, make sure the device you choose complies with the most recent UL No. 1449 rating. Not all the equipment on the market

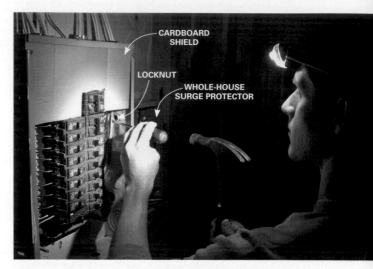

CARDBOARD SHIELD
LOCKNUT
WHOLE-HOUSE SURGE PROTECTOR

1 **Secure the offset nipple to the main panel.** Remove a knockout on the main panel and insert the offset nipple. Spin on the dimpled locknut with the locking "ears" facing the wall of the panel. Then tighten it with a flat-blade screwdriver and hammer.

meets the newer standard. Once you decide on an SPD, you'll also need a double-pole 15-amp breaker, one 1/2-in. rigid offset nipple and two 1/2-in. locknuts.

Can you install it yourself?

You'll need two blank spaces, one on top of the other, in your main panel to hook up the SPD. Or, you can connect it to an existing two-pole 240V breaker—but only if that breaker is rated for two wires. To find out, call the breaker manufacturer's tech support line. If you don't have two blank spots in your main panel or the existing breakers aren't rated for two wires, you'll have to hire an electrician to install a subpanel. Or consider buying an SPD that installs right in the meter box (see "Is a Meter Socket SPD the Answer?" on p. 57).

First, the warnings

Even with the main breaker (service disconnect) off, there are still live wires inside the panel. If you touch them, you could die. So before you loosen a single screw on the main panel cover, go to familyhandyman.com and search for "how to connect a new circuit." Read the entire article and pay particular attention to the diagram showing the dangerous areas. If you have any reservations about working inside the main panel, call a licensed electrician.

> **WARNING: Electrocution hazard!** Even with the service disconnect turned off, there are still live wires inside the main panel. If you don't know which ones remain live, don't attempt this project. Call a licensed electrician.

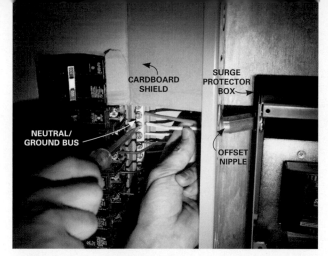

CARDBOARD SHIELD

SURGE PROTECTOR BOX

NEUTRAL/ GROUND BUS

OFFSET NIPPLE

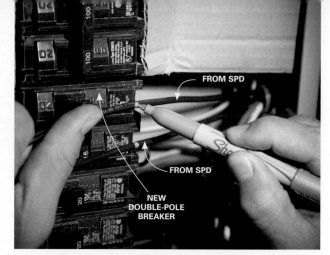

FROM SPD

FROM SPD

NEW DOUBLE-POLE BREAKER

2 **Connect the neutral and ground to the bus.** Strip off 3/4 in. of insulation from the neutral (white) and ground (green) wires and secure them to separate screws on the neutral bus.

3 **Cut the black wires to length and install.** Mark the two black wires from the SPD (a silver permanent marker works well). Then cut them to length and strip the insulation. Insert the bare wire into the breaker screws and tighten.

Start the installation

Remove all rings and jewelry before unscrewing the main panel cover. Then flip the service disconnect to "off." Cut a cardboard protector and place it inside the panel to prevent contact with live wires. Remove the two circuit breakers directly below the service disconnect and relocate them and the wires running into them elsewhere in the panel. Position the SPD next to the main panel so the wires enter it as close as possible to the two vacant spots. Connect the offset nipple to the SPD and then to the main panel (**Photo 1**). Secure the SPD to the wall with screws.

Next, thread the wires from the SPD into the main panel. Route the neutral (white) and ground (green) wires to the nearest screw terminals on the neutral bus (**Photo 2**). Make the bends as gradual as possible. Keep all the wires (white, green and black) as short as possible. Then snap in the new breaker and connect the two black wires from the SPD (**Photo 3**).

To install telephone and cable surge protections, find the service "demarcation boxes" on the outside of your house. Run lengths of telephone and coaxial cable to the new SPD and connect them (**Photo 4**).

As with all electrical projects, local electrical regulations always trump our advice. Always pull a permit and have your work inspected.

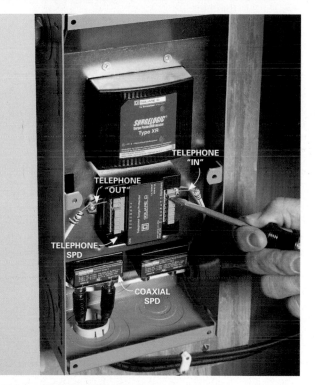

SURGELOGIC Surge Protection Module Type XR

TELEPHONE "IN"

TELEPHONE "OUT"

TELEPHONE SPD

COAXIAL SPD

4 **Connect the telephone wires to the SPD.** Run the telephone wires from the demarcation device to the "in" connectors on the telephone SPD. Connect the house phone lines to the "out" terminals. Follow the same procedure for the cable TV lines.

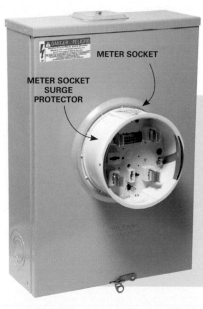

METER SOCKET

METER SOCKET SURGE PROTECTOR

DANGER PELIGRO

Is a meter socket SPD the answer?

If your electrical panel is full or you're not up to doing your own installation, a meter socket SPD may be the perfect alternative. It snaps into the meter socket. Start by checking with your local power utility to see if it will allow a meter socket SPD. If so, find out how much it charges for installation—you can't install it yourself. Shown is the Leviton No. 50240-MSA, which is $210 at amazon.com.

8 COMMON ELECTRICAL
CODE VIOLATIONS

Be careful to avoid these common mistakes

by **Mark Petersen, Contributing Editor**

We sat down with a state chief electrical inspector as well as a seasoned field inspector to find out which electrical codes DIYers and pros mess up most often.

Many of the problems stem from the newest additions to the National Electrical Code (NEC). For example, DIYers often install GFCIs where AFCIs are required, and vice versa.

However, we also found that other common mistakes, like inadequate clearances for service panels, violate codes that have been on the books for years.

We hope the info here helps clear up the confusion that could lead to a failed electrical inspection.

1. CHOOSING THE **WRONG CIRCUIT BREAKERS**

The big picture

To help you understand which protection goes where, consider what each type of breaker was designed to do.

- **Circuit breakers** protect wiring and equipment like furnaces, air conditioners, dryers and stoves.
- **GFCIs** protect people in areas where they are likely to be using small appliances and where water is present.
- **AFCIs** prevent fires in all living areas where appliance cords are prone to be pinched or crimped, or chewed by pets.

Standard circuit breakers

Standard circuit breakers are better at protecting wiring and equipment than preventing fires and protecting people. That's why they have largely been replaced by GFCIs and AFCIs. There are only a few places left where standard circuit breakers can be used, typically for larger appliances such as furnaces, A/C condensers, dryers and stoves.

Ground fault circuit interrupter

GFCI breakers and outlets have been around for a while, and most people know they're required in bathrooms, kitchens and outdoors, but our experts are still finding violations, especially in these areas: garages, crawl spaces, storage/work areas in unfinished basements, wet bars (within 6 ft. of a sink), and sump pumps. And don't forget that GFCIs need to be readily accessible in order to be reset. This means they shouldn't be installed on the ceiling or buried under a hydro massage tub without an access panel.

Arc fault circuit interrupter

AFCIs are the newest type. They used to be required only on bedroom circuits, but the NEC now requires AFCI protection in all living areas. AFCIs were designed with fire protection in mind. They're equipped with sophisticated electronics that can detect an arcing condition (like in a frayed lamp cord), which may not be detected by a standard circuit breaker until after a fire has started. AFCI protection is not just required for new construction; it's now also required where branch-circuit wiring is modified, replaced or extended into existing homes.

Common violations

- No GFCI protection in wet bars.
- GFCI installed on inaccessible spots such as ceilings.
- No AFCI protection on basement finish or remodeling projects.

2. FORGETTING THE **TAMPER-RESISTANT** RECEPTACLES

Tamper-resistant receptacles are designed to stop a kid from inserting an object such as a paper clip. They're required for all locations, indoors and out. Tamper-resistant receptacles are a great invention, so use them—it's code.

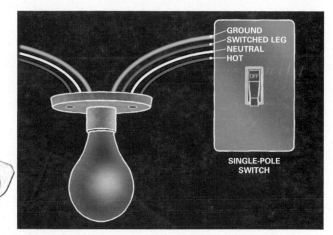

GROUND
SWITCHED LEG
NEUTRAL
HOT

OFF

SINGLE-POLE
SWITCH

TAMPER
RESISTANT

Common violation

Replacing an existing receptacle with a conventional one. When an existing receptacle is replaced, the NEC requires the installation of a tamper-resistant receptacle.

3. WIRING SWITCHES **WITHOUT A NEUTRAL**

All switch locations now need a neutral wire. This code was mainly implemented to accommodate potential future uses. Electronic switches require a small amount of constant electricity and therefore need a neutral wire run to them. There are exceptions to this code, but if the walls are currently open anyway, don't make the next guy fish in a wire. Do it right and make sure there's a neutral wire in the box.

Common violation

One common occurrence of a missing neutral wire is a dead-end single-pole switch loop. One way to solve this problem is to run a three-wire cable with ground to the last switch on the run.

4. USING A **GROUND ROD ELECTRODE** WHEN A BETTER SYSTEM IS AVAILABLE

For a long time, metal underground water piping was considered the best grounding electrode available, but virtually all underground water piping today is plastic. And it turns out that rebar in concrete footings or the foundation for a house is actually a more effective grounding system than the ground rods we've been using for decades. So if there's rebar in the new footings, that rebar needs to be used as the primary grounding electrode. This new provision in the NEC requires a lot of coordination between the trades and project managers. Electricians usually show up long after the concrete guys have moved on, but good communication is much easier work than busting up concrete.

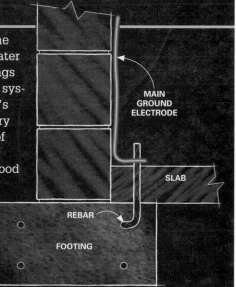

MAIN
GROUND
ELECTRODE

SLAB

REBAR

FOOTING

The bottom line

If a new home has footings with at least 20 ft. of 1/2-in. rebar, the rebar embedded in those footings needs to be used as the primary grounding electrode.

5. INSTALLING A **FLAT WEATHER-RESISTANT COVER** ON AN OUTDOOR RECEPTACLE

DOES NOT MEET CODE

Flat covers provide protection only when a receptacle isn't in use, but it's not uncommon for extension cords to be plugged in for extended periods of time—for holiday lights, for example. In-use or "bubble covers" provide protection at all times. The NEC defines a "wet location" as an area that is subject to saturation with water or other liquids, and unprotected locations exposed to the weather. The NEC has another definition for "damp locations" that is more subjective, but if you think the receptacle is going to get wet, use an in-use cover. And don't forget the weather-resistant receptacle. The NEC requires that all 15- and 20-amp receptacles be rated as weather-resistant and tamper-resistant when installed in *both* wet and damp locations.

IN-USE BUBBLE COVER

Common violation

Often it's assumed that an exterior outlet that's sheltered by a roof overhang can be covered with one of the older, flap-style outlet covers. But that decision is up to the inspector, so it's better to play it safe and install a bubble cover.

6. **CROWDING** A SERVICE PANEL

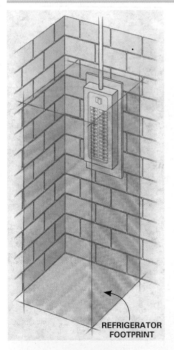

REFRIGERATOR FOOTPRINT

A service panel requires a working clearance that's 30 in. wide, 3 ft. deep and 6 ft. 8 in. high. Here's a good rule of thumb: If you can't park a refrigerator in front of the panel, you don't have enough working space. These clearances are designed to protect the person working on the panel. It's difficult to work safely when your arms are pinned to your sides. Also, the panel needs to be readily accessible, meaning the area should not be used as storage space or require a ladder for access.

Common violations

- Panels in closets, crawl spaces and bathrooms.
- Panels encroached upon by laundry tubs, sump basket, ducting and pipes.

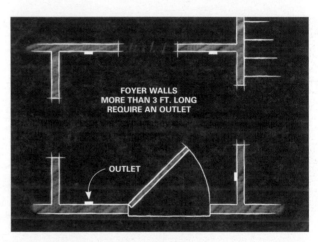

FOYER WALLS MORE THAN 3 FT. LONG REQUIRE AN OUTLET

OUTLET

7. **NOT ENOUGH RECEPTACLES** IN THE FOYER

The purpose of this code is to reduce the use of extension cords. From any point along a wall line, a receptacle outlet needs to be within reach of a 6-ft. appliance cord, and that 6 ft. cannot be measured across a passageway. The bottom line is that extension cords start fires and create tripping hazards—the fewer of them, the better.

Common violation

Failure to install receptacles in walls that are 3 ft. long or longer.

8. INSUFFICIENT BONDING

Grounding is not bonding. Plumbing, phone lines, coaxial cable and gas piping systems need to be not only *grounded* but also *bonded* to one another. Bonding equalizes the voltage potential between conductive systems. This greatly reduces the risk of a person becoming the path for current flow between two conductive systems in case one of the systems becomes energized. Also, in a lightning strike, equalized voltage potential minimizes the risk of a very high current jumping (arcing) between two systems and causing a fire.

Common violations
- Replacing an old fuse box and assuming the system is bonded.
- Unbonded satellite and cable installations.

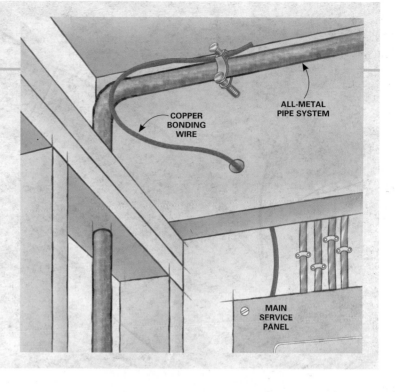

COPPER BONDING WIRE

ALL-METAL PIPE SYSTEM

MAIN SERVICE PANEL

GreatGoofs

A bit of a mistake

When my wife and I moved into our first apartment, I decided to run cable from the living room to our bedroom TV. So I bought a long drill bit and started drilling through the bedroom wall. After a few moments, I went into the living room, expecting to see the bit coming through the wall. Nope, not yet. So I went back into the bedroom and drilled a little farther until I felt the bit push through the wall. Aha! I threaded the coaxial cable through the hole and then went out into the living room to hook it up. But there was no sign of the cable. What was going on? Only then did I notice that the living room wasn't as deep as the bedroom. I looked at the front door and thought Uh-oh. I slowly opened the front door, looked to my left and there was the cable coming out of the nice stucco wall of the apartment complex.

—Charlie Porzio

HandyHints®

EXTERNAL BATTERY PACK

UPS

TO MODEM

TO PORTABLE PHONE

TO ROUTER

MAINTAIN DIGITAL SERVICES DURING A POWER FAILURE

A long power outage can ruin more than just the food in your fridge. It can stop all your communication with the outside world. No power means no computer or wireless Internet and limited cable or Vonage-style phone service.

To stay up and running, you need a voltage-regulated uninterruptible power supply (UPS). It converts internal battery power to clean, steady 110 volts AC to run your wireless modem/router, VoIP adapter and portable phone base station. In a typical home setup, those devices use a maximum of 50 watts (less when the units are idling). So an 865-watt unit (like the APC BR1500G; $193 from amazon.com) will run your digital communications for a minimum of 2.6 hours. Turn off the UPS when you're not using your modem to extend the run-time. But if you typically experience long power outages and want to double the run-time, add an external battery pack (APC BR24BPG; $160 from amazon.com). Yeah, it's a lot of money. But this setup can provide a working wireless signal and phone service for a few days—without the need for a generator.

Stay connected with backup power. Hook up your wireless modem, VoIP telephone adapter and portable phone base station to a voltage-regulated battery backup system.

CAN YOU ADD MORE CIRCUIT BREAKERS TO A FULL BOX?

I need to add more circuits to my main panel. I bought a few tandem breakers (in the correct brand for my box), but they don't fit. What gives?

Not all slots in a panel will accept tandem breakers, and each panel will accept only a certain number. To find out where the tandem slots are located and how many you can install, first see if the information is on the label inside the main electrical panel. If it's not, you'll have to call the manufacturer's help line and supply the model number. That's the only way to get the answer.

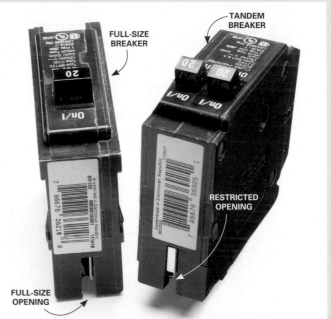

FULL-SIZE BREAKER

TANDEM BREAKER

RESTRICTED OPENING

FULL-SIZE OPENING

SMARTPHONE SMARTS

Maribeth Boyle

I always keep my cell phone in my back pocket, and keeping it clean when I'm painting or working in the garden is hard.

My phone was getting pretty grimy, but I didn't want to buy an expensive phone cover, so I came up with this easy (and cheap!) solution: Stick it in a zipper-top plastic bag. You can still work all the buttons right through the plastic while keeping the phone itself clean and dry.

DISH SOAP WIRE LUBRICANT

Tom Dvorak

Whenever I pull wire through a long run of metal or PVC conduit, I first squirt some liquid dish soap into the conduit at the feed point of the pull. Then, as I feed the wire and my helper pulls, I continue to add a squirt of soap every 10 ft. or so. The soap acts as a lubricant, and the wire glides through with minimal resistance. You can buy special wire lubricant, but dish soap is much cheaper and as close as the kitchen. Plus, this is probably the only remodeling job that leaves my hands cleaner than when I started!

A BETTER WAY TO FISH WIRE

Trying to run a fish tape through an insulated stud bay is a nightmare. The fish tape curls up and snags the insulation, making it impossible to reach the hole you've cut out for your new junction box. I now use a 10-ft. stick of 1/2-in. PEX as my fish "tape."

The PEX is rigid enough that I can slide it between the insulation and the drywall. Once the PEX reaches the hole, I tape my Romex to it and pull the PEX back to the starting point of the operation. This also works great when you're fishing wire above a ceiling and below a batt of insulation between joist bays (to install a ceiling fan or light fixture, for example).

—Tom Dvorak

CABLE MANAGEMENT 101

I've seen lots of products for tidying up the mess of cables behind my TV, but these spiral wrapping bands (No. 7028; 30mm x 1.5 meters; $3 at monoprice.com) are dirt cheap and drop-dead simple to use. The bands are available in black and gray and come in different sizes. Just clamp and pull to encase the cables in a nice, tidy bundle.

—Rick Muscoplat, Contributing Editor

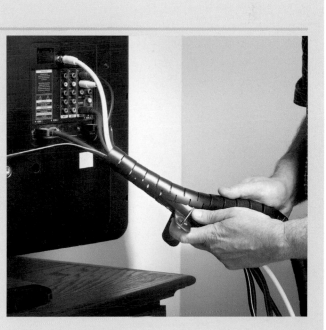

Security&Safety

CUT-PROOF PADLOCK

Most padlocks are no match for some creep with a $15 bolt cutter. That's why Master Lock developed its Pro Series padlocks. These locks have a steel shroud that protects the hasp from the jaws of any bolt cutter. Makes sense, eh? Buy one at amazon.com for $29.

LB FITTING

HANDSOME SLIDING DOOR SECURITY

Like a lot of folks, we needed something to secure our sliding patio door. But I wanted it to be a little more stylish than a 2x4 or an ugly metal bar. So I picked up an oak handrail, then stained and sealed it. I finished it with an attractive drawer pull. It works great, it's easy to handle and it gets tons of compliments from everyone who sees it.

—Ryan Velthuis

HANDRAIL

HIDE A HOUSE KEY IN PLAIN SIGHT

Jake Blohm

Burglars can easily find a house key hidden under a mat or over the door molding, but they'll never think to look inside plastic conduit. Just glue 1/2-in. plastic conduit to a 1/2-in. LB fitting. Drive the conduit into the ground next to the house so it looks like the conduit enters there. You can leave out the bottom screw or just glue a screw in place to completely fool the crooks. Leave the top screw a little loose so the cover will swivel open easily. Pop the key inside and no one's the wiser (except you—and all the thieves reading this tip!).

WHAT'S THE BEST WAY TO CHOOSE A DEAD BOLT?

Look for the "ANSI Grade" on the label. Don't even consider a Grade 3, despite the tempting price tag (about $10). A Grade 2 dead bolt (about $25) is adequate, but spend an extra 10 bucks and buy a Grade 1. Aside from higher security, you'll get a better-built lock that will give you years of trouble-free service.

LOCKS THAT WORK WITH VEHICLE KEYS

File this in the "why didn't I think of it before" department. Strattec, a large manufacturer of automotive lock cylinders, has just developed several styles of locks that work with your vehicle key. Order the locks to match your vehicle brand. Then insert your key into the Bolt Lock and turn the cylinder. Bolt Lock is self-learning, so you don't need a locksmith.

Choose a regular padlock ($28), cable lock ($45) or receiver lock ($39). View a demo and buy the locks from boltlock.com.

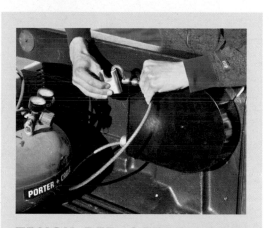

CABLE LOCK

RECEIVER LOCK

PADLOCK

NEW-STYLE LOCK AND SHACKLE LAUGH AT BOLT CUTTERS

These days even the dumbest crooks carry bolt cutters. In less than five seconds, they're into your shed and carting off your expensive tools.

Thwart the bums (or at least make them break a sweat) with a high-security hasp and hidden shackle lock. Attach the hasp to your doors with carriage bolts. Then slap on a bump-proof, case-hardened lock. It completely covers the hasp, protecting it from bolt cutters. And crooks can't pry the lock off because it's surrounded by a ring of high-strength steel. Both the lock (Master No. 6270NKA-402K190; $27) and the hasp (Master No. 770; $19) are available at amazon.com.

HASP

LOCK

TRUCK BED CABLE LOCK

No cable lock can protect against thieves who carry bolt cutters. But this truck bed cable lock can sure slow them down. The Toylok base unit includes a 3/8-in.-thick, 18-in.-long retractable cable and mounts in a stake pocket with a mounting bracket (Toylok TL1020, $85, and stake pocket mounting bracket TL006; $22, at etrailer.com). Or buy other mounting brackets to mount the lock to your trailer hitch, RV bumper or toolbox.

Security&Safety

LOCK, UNLOCK YOUR DOOR FROM ANYWHERE

Schlage is all but synonymous with home automation and home security. One of its signature products is the LiNK Wireless Keypad Deadbolt, a sturdy door lock that connects to the Internet so you can control it from anywhere. Lock and unlock the dead bolt from your computer or phone on a moment's notice, or program it to unlock at preset times.

You don't need a Wi-Fi network; just plug the dead bolt's companion Schlage Bridge into your broadband router and you're set. Monitor activity at your front door at any time, and receive alerts via texts or e-mail. Since the dead bolt has a keypad, you can assign up to 19 four-digit codes to household members or the furnace repair guy. The dead bolt is $200 to $250 from vendors such as amazon.com, and you'll have to pay a subscription fee. Find out more at schlage.com.

SCH_AGE

WIRELESS SECURITY LIGHT

Need a motion detector spotlight outside but don't want the hassle of fishing and running wiring? The Mr. Beams MB360 Wireless LED Spotlight is the simplest answer available. You can hang it any-where you want with two screws. What could be easier? Because it uses an LED bulb, three ordinary D-cell batteries will power it for two full years. Or 2,400 thirty-second activations, whichever comes first. Find one at amazon.com for about $20. Mr. Beams has other cool lighting stuff too. Check it out at mrbeams.com.

EMERGENCY LABELS

I label all the important switches and valves around the house with shipping labels. These include the main water shutoffs and the well electric switch. Then I take photos of all the shutoffs with the tags attached and put them in a "House Reference" binder. If there's a leak when I'm not home, everyone will know what to do to prevent a disaster. I did the same thing at our cabin.

Terry R. Boylan

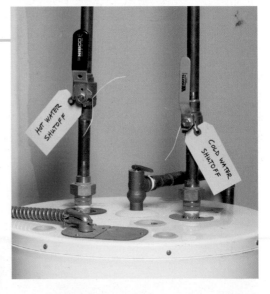

3 Plumbing, Heating & Appliances

IN THIS CHAPTER

GAS FIREPLACE ADVICE

It's smart to leave your pilot light running year-round on your gas fireplace. If you turn it off during the summer, spiders can plug up the pilot orifice and you'll have trouble relighting it next fall. Every year fireplace service companies get a slew of complaints from customers who can't relight the pilot in the fall. Sure, the customer saved $1.50 in gas over the course of the summer. But that pales in comparison with a $125 service call to clean out the gas valve and pilot assembly. So leave it on!

WHICH IS BETTER— BLACK OR WHITE PLASTIC PIPE?

When it comes to longevity, there isn't any reason to choose one over the other. If you install them right, either black or white plastic pipe will remain in service a lot longer than you will.

So how do you choose? First, check with your building inspector. A few local building codes allow only PVC (white) or only ABS (black). That doesn't make sense, but it doesn't matter; comply or else.

If code allows both PVC and ABS, make a pass through the plumbing aisle at your favorite home center. Even if the store carries both PVC and ABS, you'll probably find that it stocks a much wider selection of fittings for one of the types. A big selection makes your plumbing life easier.

If code and selection turn out to be non-factors, go with ABS, which is a little easier to work with. Unlike PVC, which requires purple primer and cement, ABS is joined with cement only. ABS is also easier to cut and a bit more flexible.

If, for any reason, you need to join one to the other during a remodeling project, don't just cement the two together. Instead, use a rubber transition coupling with stainless steel clamps.

KEEP A TOILET SEAT TIGHT

Many people change out the plastic toilet seat bolts to steel in an attempt to keep the toilet seat tight. That does help, but the fix may last only a month or two.

Here's a more permanent fix. Buy a toilet seat tightening kit (about $3) from a home center or amazon.com. Remove the toilet seat nuts and insert one of the rubber bushings (**Photo 1**). Then install a set of toilet seat stabilizers (**Photo 2**), such as Safe-T-Bumpers ($5 at amazon.com). That'll eliminate loosening caused by side-to-side movement.

TOILET SEAT BOLT

BUSHING

TOILET SEAT NUT

TIGHTENING TOOL

BUSHING

1 **Slide on a rubber bushing.** Install the rubber bushing with the tapered side facing up toward the toilet seat. Then use the tightening tool from the kit to snug up the nut.

STABILIZER

2 **Locate and install the stabilizers.** Loop the rubber band around the toilet seat and center the stabilizers so they touch the inside rim of the bowl. Drill a starter hole and secure the stabilizers with screws from the kit.

AVOID FLOODING DISASTERS

Flooding from washing machines happens far more often than you think. In fact, washing machine floods hold a prominent place in the "Top 10" list of homeowner's insurance claims.

Even if you've already switched out your rubber hoses for "no-burst" braided hoses (you did that, right?), you're still at risk. The machine's water valve, drain hose and pump can fail and cause major damage. This is especially important if your washing machine is located on an upper floor, in a finished room or in a condo, where major flood damage can cost tens of thousands of dollars.

A washing machine valve shutoff kit (one choice is FloodStop No. FS3/4H-90; about $148 from amazon.com) puts all that concern to rest. When the floor-mounted sensor detects puddling, it instantly shuts off the water valve. The unit installs in less than 30 minutes with just slip-joint pliers (no soldering required). Here's how.

Turn off the water to the washing machine and remove the fill hoses from the valves. Install the new motorized valves (**Photo 1**). Then mount the controller close to the nearest electrical receptacle and connect the wires (**Photo 2**). Locate the flood sensor below the washing machine

1 **Install the valves.** Screw the new motorized valves onto the manual shutoff valves. Then attach the washing machine hoses. Tighten until snug with slip-joint pliers.

(Photo 3). For additional protection, buy a few more sensors and daisy-chain them onto the first sensor. Then wet them and adjust the sensitivity at the controller.

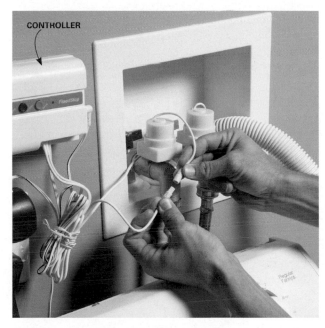

CONTROLLER

2 **Connect the valves.** Plug the valve connectors into the wiring harness from the controller. It doesn't matter which wire goes to which connector plug.

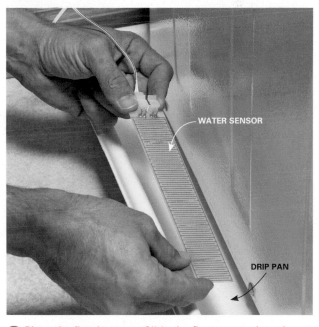

WATER SENSOR

DRIP PAN

3 **Place the flood sensor.** Slide the floor sensor into the washing machine drain pan (if you have one) or lay it on the floor below the washing machine.

A FIX FOR A SPINNING DRAIN

If you're trying to remove an old kitchen sink, you may be frustrated because the entire drain turns every time you smack the spanner nut.

To make this operation easier, you have three options: Buy a P.O. plug wrench that'll fit in the drain cross and hold the drain (Wolverine No. PST148, $9 from amazon.com). Or, jam pliers handles into the cross and hold it while you turn the nut (this works best with two people). Or just cut the large spanner nut with a rotary tool and cutoff wheel. The last option is the easiest and fastest.

HomeCare&Repair

WHAT'S THE BEST TYPE OF COPPER PIPE TO USE FOR INSIDE WATER LINES?

You may be surprised to find two types of copper pipe on the home center shelf: Type M and Type L. The difference is the wall thickness of the pipe and how much bursting pressure it can handle. The exterior dimensions are identical, so you use the same copper fittings. You also use the same tools, materials and techniques to cut and sweat them. Most plumbers use the cheaper, thinner-walled Type M pipe for normal "in the wall" household plumbing projects, but check with your local plumbing inspector for regional requirements.

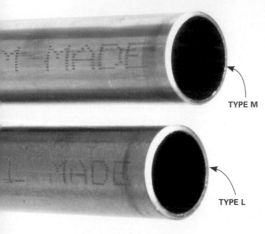

TYPE M

TYPE L

However, if you have corrosive or "aggressive" water (have yours tested if you're not sure), which can be hard on copper pipe, you may want to use the beefier Type L pipe, which is often used underground, in hot water heating systems and for commercial plumbing. Some plumbers avoid copper in those cases and use CPVC. But according to veteran plumber Charlie Avoles, the best alternative to copper is PEX (flexible plastic pipe). "We're seeing that many properties of PEX are actually tougher than copper, and PEX doesn't appear to get fragile with age and exposure to ultraviolet light like CPVC does."

MEET AN EXPERT

Charlie Avoles is co-owner of St. Paul PipeWorks Plumbing and Remodeling. The company was a 2010 Angie's List Super Service Award Winner.

JOINING THREADED PLUMBING FITTINGS

Wrapping Teflon tape around pipe threads to create a seal is standard procedure for DIYers. But it's not foolproof. Burrs inside the female fitting can catch the tape and roll it around. The leak will only show up after you've finished the job and turned on the water. At that point, you'll have a mess on your hands, cutting and refitting pipes.

Here's a tip from master plumber Les Zell. Go ahead and wrap Teflon tape around the male threads just like always. Then add pipe thread sealant as shown. The sealant will fill any gaps caused by tape failures. It's cheap insurance against a leak. Les says he's never had a leak since he started adding this second step.

Add a dab of pipe dope. Grab a brush full of pipe thread sealant and wipe it right on top of the Teflon tape. Then assemble the fittings.

SKIP THE WAX RING

Plumbers and handymen have been using beeswax toilet rings ever since toilets were invented. Now there's something completely different—a soft plastic toilet ring called the Sani Seal (about $12). Just set the toilet down and the soft ring squishes for a perfect seal. It can even be reused if you ever need to pull the toilet. No wax to clean off either. If you have a recessed flange, you can stack them up just like you can with wax rings. Find out more and place an order at sanisealgasket.com.

► Web links: Find a dryer belt diagram

Replacing the belt on your dryer but don't remember how to reroute it? Find dryer belt diagrams here:
forum.appliancepartspros.com/dryer-repair/25860-dryer-belt-diagrams.html

FIX A CLOGGED CONDENSATE DRAIN

If water is puddling near the furnace with the A/C running, you have a clogged condensate drain tube. Condensation from air conditioning coils contains bacteria that can form slime and clog the condensate pan drain tube. You can prevent slime and eliminate drain tube clogs in two easy steps. First, remove the drain tube and fitting from your A/C condensate pan. Toss them. Next, buy a package of slime preventing tablets (one choice is AC-Safe Air Conditioner Pan Tablets; about $3 at homedepot.com). Follow the package dosing directions and insert the tablets right in the drain pan (**Photo 1**).

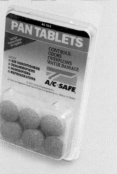

Next, buy a 3/4-in. MIPT barb fitting, a small coil of 3/4-in. I.D. vinyl tubing, and several tubing straps. Then install the larger tubing (**Photo 2**). The pan tablets will reduce slime formation, and the larger-diameter tubing will enable faster condensate flow. That usually eliminates clogging for good.

1 **Treat the pan with tablets.** Shove the tablets into the drain pan opening and push them in farther using a dowel or long screwdriver. Add new tablets monthly during air-conditioning season, or less often if you rarely use your A/C.

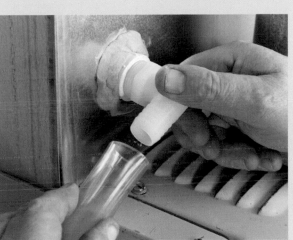

2 **Install new tubing.** Screw the new fitting into the drain pan and slide on the tubing. Route it to the floor drain and secure it with tubing straps.

TIP FOR CAULKING THE TOILET TO THE FLOOR

Toilets should be caulked to the floor to prevent side-to-side movement that can break the wax seal (and to prevent splashes or overflows from puddling under the toilet and rotting the floor). DIYers often set the toilet and then apply a tiny bead of caulk along the outside edge. That doesn't always provide a good enough bond to the floor, and it leaves a prominent caulk line. There's an easier way to secure the toilet and provide a cleaner caulk line. Just follow this tip from master plumber Les Zell.

First set the toilet in place (without the wax ring) and square it up to the wall. Then make an outline of the toilet on the floor with masking tape. Remove the toilet and turn it on its side. Measure the depth and width of the gluing edge of the bowl. Next, move your caulk gun to the inset depth you just measured and apply caulk directly to the floor, maintaining the inset depth as you follow the tape (**photo right**). Install the wax ring and lower the toilet onto the flange. Stand on the toilet to compress the wax ring and ensure good contact with the caulk. Then use paper towels to clean up any caulk that oozed out.

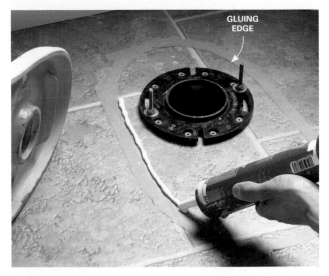

Caulk the floor. Cut the caulk tube tip square and drag the caulk gun toward you as you lay in a thick bead of caulk along the inside edge of the tape.

HomeCare&Repair

FIX YOUR CENTRAL A/C

You can't cool off in front of the open fridge forever. It's time to decide: You can either wait four days for the service guy to show up or try fixing your central air conditioner yourself. Read on to learn which A/C failures can be handled by a DIYer and how to safely replace the three parts that cause the majority of all outdoor condenser unit failures. You'll need a standard multimeter, an insulated needle-nose pliers and ordinary hand tools.

First, be sure you've checked the A/C and furnace circuit breakers in the main electrical panel, as well as any cartridge fuses in the outside disconnect. Replace all three parts at once (about $150 total; see "Buy the Right Parts," p. 73). Of course, that might mean you'll replace some good parts. But if the fixes work, your A/C will be up and running much sooner and you'll save about $150. Or you can replace the parts one at a time and test the unit after each one.

If these fixes don't work, at least you've covered the most common failures, and your service guy can concentrate on finding the more elusive problem. Plus, with the new parts, you'll likely add years of breakdown-free air conditioning.

Make sure the problem isn't the furnace

Set your thermostat to A/C mode and lower the temperature setting. If the furnace fan kicks in, the problem isn't in the furnace. If the fan doesn't run, try resetting the furnace circuit breaker. If the fan still won't start, call a pro—the fixes shown here won't work.

Next, check the outside condensing unit. The compressor (which sounds like a refrigerator) and fan should be running. If not, follow the troubleshooting and repair procedures shown here.

CAUTION: Turn off the A/C and furnace breakers in the main electrical panel before pulling the outdoor disconnect or removing the condensing unit's access panel. Then use a voltage sniffer on the wires coming into the contactor to make sure the power is really off.

Clean or replace the contactor relay

The contactor relay switches power to the condenser fan and the compressor. It rarely fails. But it often gets jammed with beetles, bugs and spiders that perished checking things out. Remove the condenser unit's access cover and locate the contactor relay—it'll have at least six wires attached to it. Try cleaning the critters out with compressed air (Photo 1). If that works, fine. But if you can't remove all the fried bug parts, replace the contactor with a new unit (about $30). Don't think you can file the contacts to clean them. That fix won't last.

Replace the capacitor(s)

The "start" and "run" capacitors store electrical energy to jump-start the compressor and fan motor. You may have a combination start/run capacitor or two individual ones. Both styles have a very high failure rate, and when they go, the compressor or fan won't start. They're cheap (about $30), so replace them.

First discharge any remaining electrical charge from the capacitor(s) before you work on them. Fabricate a shorting resistor pack by twisting four 5.6k-ohm, 1/2-watt resistors in series (part No. 271-1125; $1.25 at RadioShack). Then discharge the capacitor (Photo 2).

Next, move each wire lead from the old capacitor to the new capacitor (Photo 3).

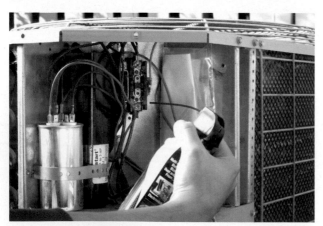

1 **Blow out the contactor.** Blow compressed air into all sides of the contactor relay to clean out dead insects. If you're not able to remove all the debris, you'll have to replace the contactor. Then try starting the unit.

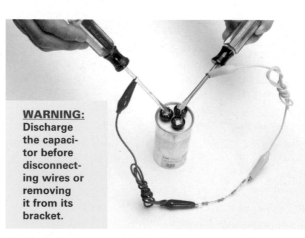

WARNING: Discharge the capacitor before disconnecting wires or removing it from its bracket.

2 **Discharge the old capacitor.** Attach a jumper lead to each end of the resistor pack. Clip the other ends to insulated screwdrivers. Then touch the screwdrivers to the capacitor terminals.

CONSULTANT: JAMES HAUGEN, PRIORITY HEATING & COOLING, WOODBURY, MN

RICK MUSCOPLAT

3 Swap capacitor wires to the new unit. Wiggle each wire off the old capacitor, noting the terminal markings. Place the wire on the matching terminal on the new capacitor. Then secure the new capacitor in the mounting bracket.

Replace the fan motor

Remove the fasteners that hold the fan guard in place or remove the entire cover assembly from the condenser unit. Lift out the fan assembly and mark the bottom of the blade so you replace it in the right direction. Then loosen the blade-retaining nut and pull it off the motor shaft. Disconnect the fan motor electrical connector. Then swap in the new fan motor (**Photo 4**). Reconnect the fan guard or condenser cover.

Check out the operation

Reinstall the access cover and the outside disconnect block. Raise the temperature on the thermostat. Then flip the A/C and furnace breakers to "On." Wait 15 minutes for the thermostat and furnace electronics to reset. Then lower the temperature setting. The condensing unit should

4 Install the new fan motor. Align the fan motor studs with the holes in the fan guard or condenser cover. Then spin on the acorn nuts and tighten. Install the fan blade and the electrical connector. Tuck the new fan wires into the old conduit.

start up. If it doesn't, your system may need more time to reset. Wait one hour and try it again. If it still doesn't work, schedule a service call. Be sure to specify exactly what you did. That'll keep the repair person from replacing brand new parts, and you'll be able to have your work checked by an expert.

Buy the right parts

Buy replacement parts from your local appliance parts store or A/C dealer. You'll need the make, model and serial numbers from the nameplate on your outdoor condensing unit—not the furnace nameplate. Or, if you're willing to pay for overnight delivery, you can buy discount parts online (source1parts.com is one site).

PLUM—WONDERFUL PLUMBING SHORTCUT

I'm a professional engineer who designs plumbing systems. I have a shortcut to pass along that may save you some time when you're venting a sink. Most municipalities (but not all, so check) allow engineered air admittance valves (AAVs). You can use an AAV instead of running a vent up through the roof or connecting to an existing vent pipe. A HUGE time and labor saver.

The only downside is that an AAV needs to be located in free air space, meaning you can't completely enclose it in a wall or joist space. But you can buy a recessed box with a grille that makes it look like a heating vent. You can find AAVs at some home centers and online retailers, including oatey.com and studor.net.

—Steven J. Gala

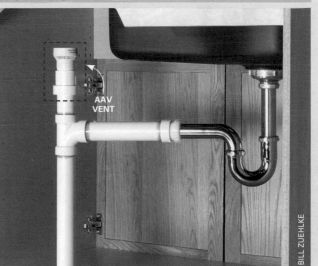

AAV VENT

BILL ZUEHLKE

An AAV lets air in but doesn't release sewer gases.

HomeCare&Repair

REMOVE A STUCK CLEANOUT PLUG

Snaking a clog in a drain line isn't exactly neurosurgery. Just remove the cleanout plug and ram the snake down the line. But what if you can't remove the plug?

"I see rusted-in cleanout plugs a lot in older homes with galvanized pipe," says master plumber Les Zell. He recommends investing no more than 30 minutes trying to free one. After that, go to Plan B: Cut out a whole section of pipe and replace it with new plastic piping rather than beat yourself up and possibly break fittings.

"It's much cheaper for my customers if I just hack out the old stuff rather than struggle with rusted connections for two hours," Les says.

MEET AN EXPERT

Les Zell has been a master plumber for 25 years and runs his own plumbing business in the Minneapolis/St. Paul area.

First try finesse & force...

Start by applying gentle heat to the fitting to soften the old pipe dope (Photo 1). If that doesn't work, wait for the pipe to cool, apply rust penetrant, and then apply double hammer blows around the fitting (Photo 2). The vibrations from the shocks break up the corrosion and allow the rust penetrant to do its work. If the plug unscrews, go ahead and snake the line. But don't reuse the metal plug. Buy a plastic plug and coat the threads with Teflon paste before installing. Then snug it up with a slip joint pliers (not the pipe wrench).

CLOGGED DRAIN LINE

CLEANOUT PLUG

BIG, HONKIN' PIPE WRENCH

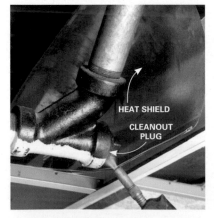

HEAT SHIELD

CLEANOUT PLUG

1 **Heat the fitting.** Clean away any cobwebs, and shield surrounding wood with a metal baking pan. Grab a fire extinguisher and apply just enough heat to warm the fitting. Don't get it cherry red.

2 **Apply rust penetrant and vibration.** Soak the plug with rust penetrant. Then smack opposite sides of the tee or wye fitting at the same time using two hammers. Rotate the double blows around the entire fitting. Then try using a pipe wrench again.

3 **Apply muscle and leverage.** Slip one pipe wrench onto the fitting and the second one on the plug. Then give it all you've got. If the plug breaks loose, you're home free.

If that doesn't work, get out the saw...

If the fitting won't budge, saw off the old section (Photo 4) and replace it with new parts. Once it's free, use the old fitting as a cutting guide to glue up a replacement wye, stub pipes and a new cleanout adapter (Photo 5). Don't mess around with steel replacement parts. Go right to black ABS or white PVC plastic fittings and pipes and join them with rubber mission couplings. Slide both couplers onto the old pipe. Hold the new pipe in place, slide the vertical coupler into place and snug it up. Then connect the horizontal coupler. Tighten both to the proper torque.

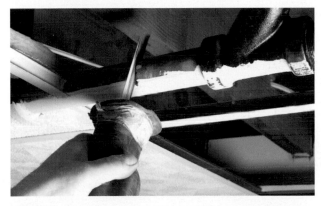

4 Cut out the old section. Use a recip saw and a metal-cutting blade to cut out the fittings and the pipe leading to and from the cleanout wye or tee.

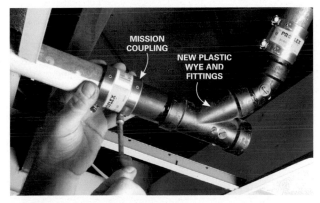

MISSION COUPLING

NEW PLASTIC WYE AND FITTINGS

5 Replace the fitting. Slide the mission couplings onto the old pipe and slip in the new plastic fitting and repair couplings. Tighten the worm-drive clamps. Then wrap Teflon tape around the new plug and screw it into the adapter.

Tip
When cutting pipe, saw through the horizontal pipe, but leave about 1/4 in. of the pipe uncut. Then saw off the vertical pipe. The horizontal "tab" prevents the vertical pipe from wiggling while you saw. Then finish the cut on the horizontal pipe.

HYBRID WATER HEATERS

The ads for hybrid electric water heaters claim energy savings of almost 50 percent. How can a heat pump with a mechanical compressor be more efficient than electric heating coils that are supposedly 100 percent efficient?

Simple. It's more energy efficient to move existing heat produced by natural gas or propane from the surrounding area into the water inside the tank than to create heat. If you have an electric water heater, it would be wise to check out the savings from a hybrid.

The GE GeoSpring Hybrid Water Heater is one choice. It uses the same electrical supply as your existing heater and requires only minor height changes to existing plumbing. And, prices on hybrid water heaters have dropped lately, making them an even better investment. Go to dsireusa.org to check for rebates and tax incentives in your area.

CHOOSING A QUIET BATH FAN

Bath fan noise is measured in "sones," and most fans carry a rating right on the packaging. Home centers stock a range of fans; from cheap and noisy (5 sones, $10) to quiet and pricey (1 sone or less, starting at about $120). But what does all that mean? Well, you probably watch TV at about 4 sones and have a normal conversation at 2 to 3 sones and a whispered conversation at .5 to 1 sone. If you choose a fan rated at 1 sone or less, put it on a timer switch. You won't have the noise to remind you to shut it off.

Sound		Sones
Jet	✈	256
Truck	🚌	64
Traffic	🚗	5–8
TV or Radio		3–4
Quiet home		2
Rustling trees		0.5

ALLERGY FURNACE FILTER PROS & CONS

My kids have allergies, so I buy those ultra-pleated furnace filters. My neighbor told me they damaged his furnace, so he doesn't use them anymore. Should I be worried?

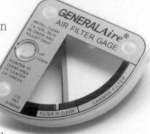

Pleated air filters work great for reducing allergens in your home. But when homeowners leave them in too long, they clog. The reduced airflow causes overheating and burner shutdown. If that happens too many times, the "limit switch" fails and then the furnace won't fire up at all. The service call and new part can easily cost you $175.

No filter manufacturer can predict how long its filters will last because none of them know the dust conditions in your home. So you have to check it often. The rule of thumb is, "If it looks dirty, it is dirty." If you want a smarter way to determine when it needs replacing, install an air filter gauge (General G-99 Air Filter Gauge Kit; $16 at amazon.com). It measures airflow between the filter and the furnace via a small hose.

EXTEND THE LIFE OF YOUR WELL PUMP

If you have a well and you do a lot of watering, here's a tip to add life to your pump. Run as many sprinklers as you can while still maintaining reasonable water pressure. In other words, do all your watering at once.

Here's why. When you run a single sprinkler, the pump cycles on and off every few seconds. That repeated starting and stopping overheats the pump and shortens its life. However, if you run two, three or four hoses at the same time, the pump runs more or less continuously.

Besides being easier on the pump, continuous running saves on your electric bill. For a given volume of water, it takes much more electricity to start up a pump every few minutes than to have it run continuously.

GET READY NOW FOR GAS EMERGENCIES

Don't ask how I know this, but trust me, sometimes projects involving gas lines don't go as planned. When a gas project goes bad, that's not the time to be searching for the right tool to shut the gas off at the meter. And just for the record, screaming at your son to "go find a big pliers!" doesn't work well either. A much wiser strategy is to buy an emergency gas meter wrench shutoff tool and secure it to the meter as shown. Pick one up at a home center for about $12.

—Rick Muscoplat, Contributing Editor

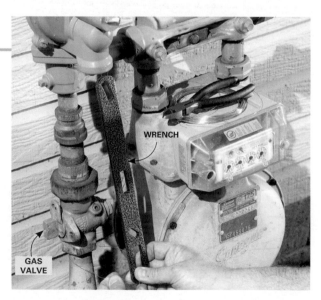

Secure the wrench with wire. Hang the wrench from the gas meter supply pipe with a piece of stainless steel wire. Then secure the bottom portion. Twist the wire just a few times so it'll release quickly in an emergency.

LES TALKS
PLASTIC PIPES

A master plumber gives straight advice about pipes

by **Mark Petersen, Contributing Editor**

We asked Les Zell, our resident master plumber, to tell us some of his tips on working with plastic plumbing. Not surprisingly, with 25 years in the biz, he had plenty to share. Here are a few of his best.

Les is an ABS guy

"I pretty much only use ABS black pipe and rarely use the white PVC stuff. It's all about the glue. Gluing ABS is a one-step process, which makes it faster to work with than PVC. Purple PVC primer is messy, emits noxious fumes, and it's just ugly."

ABS cement lasts longer in the can and dries clear, making it more forgiving if you get a drip or two on the floor. ABS cement also dries faster, which reduces the risk of connections pushing apart before they set up. Les believes the labor saved by using ABS more than makes up for the extra money spent on pipe and fittings. ABS is also lighter and more flexible. He says that makes it easier to flex for bending it into tight spaces.

"It's not only me. None of my plumber buddies use PVC either." The only downside—retailers don't always carry ABS.

Les on plumbing wisdom

Les believes that new plumbers will learn 75 percent of what they need to know during the first year on the job, but that it takes 20 years to learn the next 24 percent, and the rest is unknowable.

Use dull blades for bigger or tighter cuts

When Les cuts larger pipe or has trouble getting the tubing cutter (p. 79) into tight spaces, he uses a recip saw fitted with an older, dull wood blade. "A new wood blade with aggressive teeth tends to grab on to the pipe

DULL BLADE

and rattle the whole works, and a metal blade melts the plastic rather than cuts it."

You can reuse a landlocked fitting

SOCKET SAVER

If you have to replace some piping but it's tough to replace the fitting, it's possible to ream out the old fitting and reuse it. This happens a lot. Let's say there's a tee coming out of the back of a cabinet with a broken pipe leading to it. Or the fitting is so buried up in the floor joists that you can't get at it. Les just cuts off the pipe near the knuckle, then uses a Socket Saver to ream out the pipe to expose the inside of the fitting. Then he can cement a new pipe into the old fitting and reuse it. "It's a lot simpler than ripping out cabinets or drywall or concrete to replace the fitting." Find Socket Savers for $18 to $35 at plumbest.com or amazon.com.

Don't glue yourself into a corner

In many assemblies, there are pipes that move and pipes that don't. If you start gluing fittings together willy-nilly, you may end up in a situation where you're unable to attach the last fitting because one or both of the pipes don't move enough to slide the fitting on.

"The last fitting to be glued should be the one on a pipe that has a little wiggle room." That's usually where a vertical run meets a horizontal one so you can snug on an elbow or a tee from two directions.

MOVABLE PIPE

Avoid callbacks—use straps

Changes in temperature can cause changes in the length of plastic pipes. When you hang pipe from plastic J-hooks, you'll hear a tick when the pipe slips past the J-hook. Les says he gets tons of service calls from panicky customers believing these ticks to be water drips from a leaky pipe. "But they can never find the leak!" He generally uses plastic straps and never gets false alarm calls on his plumbing.

PLASTIC STRAP

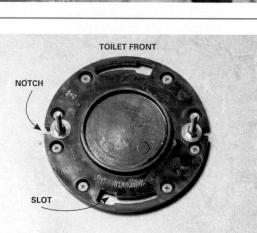

TOILET FRONT

NOTCH

SLOT

Skip those closet flange slots

Les has serviced dozens of toilets with broken closet flanges. Toilets are top-heavy, which stresses the closet bolts that hold a toilet to the closet flange. The plastic on the sides of the adjustable slots that receive the bolts is thin and prone to cracking. Les always turns the flange 90 degrees and anchors the toilet using the notches instead. He makes sure the notches are parallel to the wall behind the toilet. "One more thing: Don't use flanges with metal collars—metal rusts."

2" SUPPORT PIPE

PLASTIC J-HOOK

1-1/2" WASTE LINE

Support hot drain lines

Drain lines that routinely drain extremely hot water need continuous support. "Lines under sinks that are connected to dishwashers are the most common culprit." Those pipes will sag between ordinary supports.

Here's another Les trick: "Slide a larger pipe over the drain line before attaching any fittings, and then attach the supports to that."

Seal the ends!

Most ABS pipes have either a cellular or a foam core that air will actually pass right through. "If you don't believe it, wrap your lips around the pipe wall and blow through it." If you don't seal pipe ends with cement, air will escape into the porous center core and find its way out of the plumbing system and you'll fail a pressure test every time. "Can you even imagine that disaster? You'd have to replumb everything!"

FOAM CORE

Les loves tubing cutters

For pipes up to 2 in., Les prefers a tubing cutter (a giant version of the type used for copper tubing). "It makes a perfectly straight cut with no burrs or shavings to clean up. But best of all, it doesn't take up much room in the tool bucket." You can get them for about $25 at home centers.

Deburr for leak-free connections

Leftover burrs on the end of a pipe will create channels in the cement when you push the fitting onto the pipe—and then stay there like little canals. That's when you'll get leaks or flunk a pressure test. Les always scrapes away burrs with a utility knife before joining the pipes.

Learn Les's elbow rule

For pipes under 3 in., there are three basic types of 90-degree elbows: vent, short sweep and long sweep. Vent elbows are easily identified by their drastic bend and can only be used on a vent run that carries air, not water.

Les has a good system to remember when to use the other two types of elbows. "If water is speeding up as it turns the corner (usually going from horizontal to vertical), use a short sweep. If water is slowing down (usually from vertical to horizontal), use a long sweep."

LONG SWEEP

SHORT SWEEP

VENT ONLY

PLUMBING A
BASEMENT BATH

Installing the drain system is a big job; the DIY savings are even bigger

by **Gary Wentz, Senior Editor**

Adding a basement bathroom is a big, complicated project. But that doesn't mean you can't do it. Thousands of DIYers successfully tackle the job every year, and so can you.

This article will focus on the most difficult part of the project: installing the "DWV" system (drain, waste and vent). The DWV system requires some hard labor—breaking up concrete—and enough know-how to construct it so waste will be carried away without problems. You supply the labor; this article will supply the know-how.

MAIN STACK

TOILET DRAIN

WALL

SHOWER DRAIN

SINK DRAIN

MAIN DRAIN

FUTURE DRAIN LINES

Figure A
Plumbing a basement bath

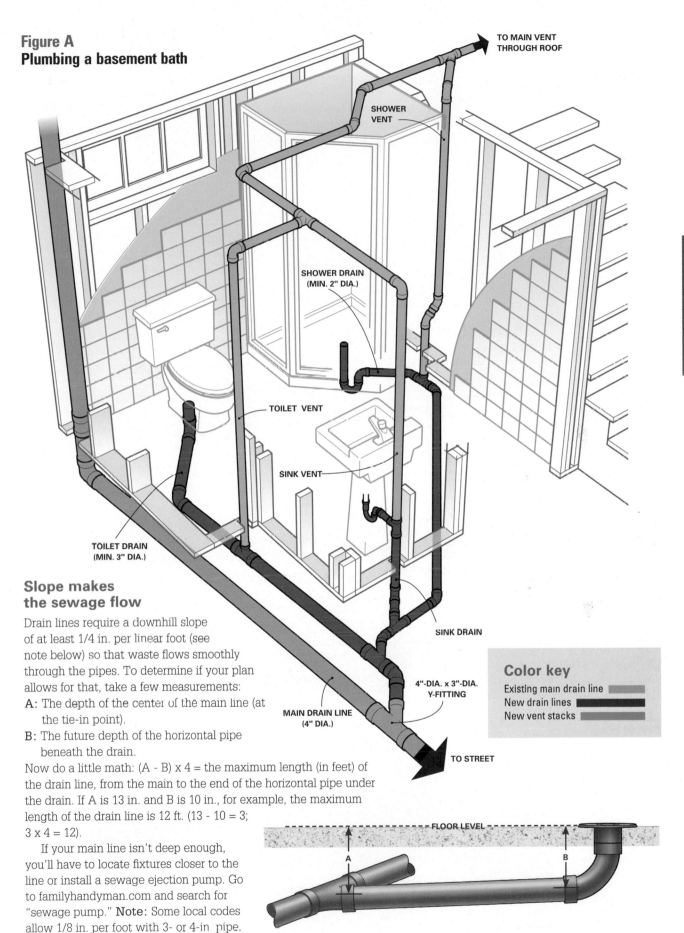

TO MAIN VENT
THROUGH ROOF

SHOWER
VENT

SHOWER DRAIN
(MIN. 2" DIA.)

TOILET VENT

SINK VENT

TOILET DRAIN
(MIN. 3" DIA.)

SINK DRAIN

4"-DIA. x 3"-DIA.
Y-FITTING

MAIN DRAIN LINE
(4" DIA.)

TO STREET

FLOOR LEVEL

A

B

Slope makes the sewage flow

Drain lines require a downhill slope of at least 1/4 in. per linear foot (see note below) so that waste flows smoothly through the pipes. To determine if your plan allows for that, take a few measurements:

A: The depth of the center of the main line (at the tie-in point).

B: The future depth of the horizontal pipe beneath the drain.

Now do a little math: (A - B) x 4 = the maximum length (in feet) of the drain line, from the main to the end of the horizontal pipe under the drain. If A is 13 in. and B is 10 in., for example, the maximum length of the drain line is 12 ft. (13 - 10 = 3; 3 x 4 = 12).

If your main line isn't deep enough, you'll have to locate fixtures closer to the line or install a sewage ejection pump. Go to familyhandyman.com and search for "sewage pump." **Note:** Some local codes allow 1/8 in. per foot with 3- or 4-in. pipe.

Color key
Existing main drain line
New drain lines
New vent stacks

The materials for the DWV system shown here cost about $250. Plumbers' labor rates vary a lot by region, but most licensed pros would charge $1,200 to $2,000 for a job similar to the one shown here.

Find the main drain line

You'll have to connect new drain lines to an existing line under the basement. So before you can do any real planning, you have to find that line. First, locate the "main stack," the large (3 or 4 in. diameter) vertical pipe that runs into the basement floor (see photo, p. 80). From there, the pipe runs under the floor and out to the city sewage system under the street. But it may run at an angle rather than straight out to the street.

Look for a cleanout plug along the street-facing wall of the basement. If you find one, that's most likely the spot where the line exits your home. And usually, the line runs straight from the main stack to the cleanout. If you have a private septic system, your main line will run toward the location of the drain field.

If you're unsure where the line is, you have a couple of options. You can punch through the floor where you think it is (Photo 1). You might end up enlarging that hole or breaking a second exploratory hole, but that's not as bad as it sounds; all it will cost you is some wasted time and a couple of extra bags of concrete mix when you patch the floor. Your second option is to get a plumber to help. In most areas, a brief house call will cost you $75 to $150. Some plumbers have access to high-tech equipment that locates lines precisely, but expect to pay $200 for that service.

What it takes

Time: 20 hours
The locations of the existing drain line and vent and the layout of your bathroom will determine how much concrete you'll have to break up and how much pipe you'll have to run. Expect to spend at least three full days on this project.

Cost: $250
Even if your situation is a lot different from ours, your materials cost will be similar. You'll need a similar number of fittings and—since plastic pipe is inexpensive—longer runs means only small cost increases.

Skill level: Intermediate
Careful planning and attention to detail, rather than hands-on skills, are critical for this project. If you're willing to do your homework and carefully plan the job, you can do a pro-grade job.

---

1 Locate the main drain. Break through the concrete to verify that the main line is where you think it is and that it's deep enough to allow adequate downhill slope in the new drain lines.

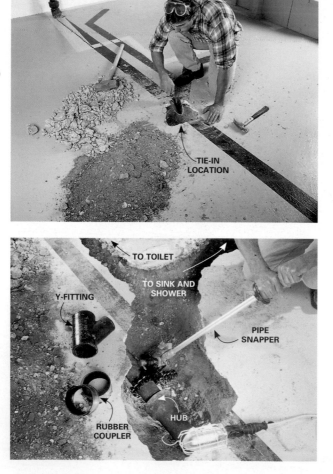

TIE-IN LOCATION

2 Break out a section of drain. After completing the trenches for the new lines, cut into the main line so you can install a Y-fitting. Our tie-in point was near an existing hub, so we cut out the hub. Make sure no one runs water (or flushes!) while the line is open.

TO TOILET

TO SINK AND SHOWER

Y-FITTING

PIPE SNAPPER

RUBBER COUPLER

HUB

Rent a snapper

A cast iron pipe snapper works by tightening a cutting chain until the pipe cracks. Rent one for about $20. Old cast iron pipe can crush rather than crack. If that happens, you'll have to abandon the snapper and cut the slow way: with a reciprocating saw. If you have plastic pipe, cutting into the main is quick and easy with a reciprocating saw.

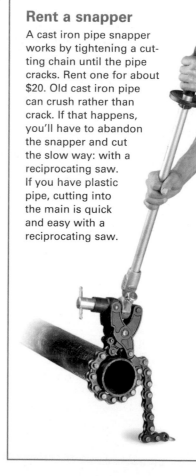

Plan the system

Once you've located the line, you'll have to make sure it's deep enough to allow downward slope in the new drain lines that will run from your future bathroom (for more on that, see "Slope Makes the Sewage Flow," p. 81). Then grab a pencil and mark out the whole bathroom on the basement floor: walls, toilet, sink, shower and finally the drain lines.

Consider it all a preplan at this point. Chances are, you'll have to make some changes as the plan develops. You may want to mock up sections of the system and lay them out on the basement floor using sections of pipe and an assortment of fittings. When the whole system is planned, mark it out on the floor. For photo clarity, we marked out bold lines on the floor. But simple spray paint is fine for drain lines.

Trench the floor

A plain old sledgehammer will bust up a basement floor. Breaking through at the tie-in point (see **Photo 1**) may take a few dozen whacks. But once you have a starter hole, the job gets easier because the concrete has space to crack and break off. Within a few minutes, you'll learn to aim your blows and bust out a neat trench line. Pick out the larger chunks of concrete as you go. Ideally, most of your trench will be just wide enough for your spade. When digging, toss the dirt on a pile separate from the larger chunks of concrete. You don't want big chunks in the soil you'll use for backfill later.

Build the drain system

Begin the drain system by cutting into the main line (**Photo 2**) and splicing in a Y-fitting (**Photo 3**). We used a no-hub cast iron Y-fitting to tie into our cast iron main. But you can use a plastic Y-fitting instead if you glue short sections of pipe into the Y-fitting to accommodate the rubber couplers. Use that same method to tie into a plastic main.

For your DWV system, you can use ABS plastic (as we did; **Photo 4**) or PVC. Both are easy to cut and join. The hard part of any underground pipe work is building branches that end up exactly where you want them while maintaining a constant slope of at least 1/4 in. per running foot.

Here are tips to help you get it right:

■ Buy twice as many fittings as you think you'll need and a few types that you don't think you'll need. Return the leftovers when the job is done.

■ If you don't have a torpedo level, buy one (see **Photo 7**). It's the handiest tool for checking the slope of pipes.

■ When a section of pipe is complete, pack dirt under and around it to keep it from shifting as you build other sections.

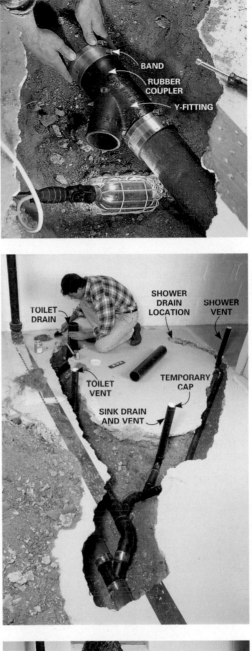

3 **Tie into the drain.** Slip rubber couplers onto the main line, insert the Y-fitting, slide the couplers over the joints and tighten the bands. Then plug the inlet and grant your family the freedom to flush again.

BAND
RUBBER COUPLER
Y-FITTING

4 **Build the drain system.** The location of the drains and vents is critical—check and double-check your work before you glue joints together. Determine where the exact location of the shower drain will be after the walls are framed. Cap open pipes to keep sewer gas out of your home. Don't bury the lines until the building inspector has approved your work.

SHOWER DRAIN LOCATION
SHOWER VENT
TOILET DRAIN
TOILET VENT
TEMPORARY CAP
SINK DRAIN AND VENT

5 **Patch the floor.** Backfill the trench with soil and screed 3 in. of concrete over it. Pack the soil firmly so it won't settle later. Smooth the concrete with a steel trowel.

6 Build the vent system. After framing the bathroom walls, assemble the vent lines. We ran our vent lines below the floor joists and later framed a lower ceiling to hide the pipes.

TOILET VENT

SINK VENT

7 Connect to an existing vent. Glue short sections of plastic pipe into a T- or Y-fitting, cut out a section of the existing vent pipe and make connections with rubber couplers.

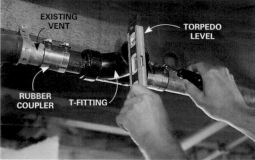

EXISTING VENT

TORPEDO LEVEL

RUBBER COUPLER   T-FITTING

8 Position the shower drain. Set the shower pan in place and measure from the walls to determine the exact location of the drain. Assemble the drain and trap without glue. Then set the pan in place again to check your work before you finally glue up the fittings.

SHOWER PAN

SHOWER DRAIN

■ Know the "rough-in" of your toilet (the distance from the wall to the center of the drain, most likely 12 in.). Don't forget to account for the thickness of framing and drywall.

■ Backfill the trenches with care (**Photo 5**). You want to pack the soil tightly to prevent settling later, but be sure not to move the pipes as you tamp the soil.

Build the vent system

The vent system is a lot simpler than the drain system. We ran vent lines under the floor joists (**Photo 6**) and framed in a lower ceiling later. If you want to preserve ceiling height by running pipes through the joists, you'll have to bore some large holes, which can weaken the joists. To avoid that, go to familyhandyman.com and search for "drill joists."

In most basements, you can tie your new vent system into the line that vents the laundry sink. Our plumbing inspector allowed us to connect our new 2-in. vent line to an existing 1-1/2-in. vent. Before cutting a section out of the old steel vent, we installed extra metal strapping to support the pipe during and after cutting.

What size drainpipe should I use?

The toilet requires 3-in. or larger. Use 2-in. for the others; pipes smaller than 2 in. aren't allowed beneath a concrete slab.

When should I use a T-fitting?

Use a T-fitting in drain lines to connect a horizontal pipe to vertical pipes. It can also be used to tie vent lines into horizontal drains or to join vent lines.

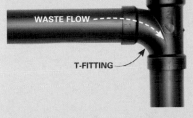

WASTE FLOW

T-FITTING

When should I use a Y?

In the drain system, use a Y-fitting to connect horizontal pipes (Photo 3, p. 83). Along with a 45-degree "street" fitting, you can use a Y-fitting to run vertical drainpipes into horizontal pipes as shown. A Y-fitting can also be used in vent systems.

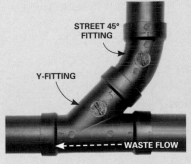

STREET 45° FITTING

Y-FITTING

WASTE FLOW

What's a street fitting?

Standard fittings have hubs that fit over pipes. A street fitting has a "streeted" end that fits **into** a hub, so you can connect it directly to another fitting without using a section of pipe. That saves labor and space.

HUB

STREETED END

Why does the home center carry three types of L-fittings?

WASTE FLOW

STANDARD L-FITTING

■ A standard L-fitting is used for horizontal-to-vertical flow in drain systems.

■ A "sweep" or "long-turn" L-fitting is OK for almost any situation and is required in two situations: horizontal-to-horizontal turns and vertical-to-horizontal turns (as shown). But it can be used in any situation where space allows.

LONG-TURN L-FITTING

VENT L-FITTING

■ A vent L-fitting can be used anywhere in the vent system, but only in the vent system—never where waste flows. The other two types of L-fittings are OK for venting, too.

What's the vent for?

A plumbing vent is kind of like the air intake on a gas can; it lets in air. Without venting, a slug of sewage racing through a waste line creates air pressure and vacuum in the pipe. That means noisy, gurgling drains. Even worse, vacuum can suck all the water out of traps, allowing sewer gas to flow freely into your home. Yuck.

Vent-to-trap distance— there's a limit

Every drain needs a trap (see note below), and every trap needs a vent. The maximum distance between the trap and vent depends on the diameter of the pipe. Memorize this table for midterm exams:

Pipe size	Max. horizontal distance to vent
1-1/4"	30"
1-1/2"	42"
2"	5'
3"	6'
4"	10'

Note: A toilet has a built-in trap, so it doesn't need one in the drain line. It still needs a vent, though.

Can vents run horizontally?

Yes, but horizontal vent lines must be at least 6 in. above the "spill line," which is the level where water would overflow the rim of a sink, tub or toilet.

What size vent pipes do I need?

A typical bathroom like the one we show (sink, toilet, shower or tub) requires a 2-in. vent. You could run smaller pipes to the sink or shower, but it's usually easier to use one size for the whole system.

Plumbing codes vary by locality. The rules we give in this article generally follow the strictest codes. Your local rules may be more lenient about issues like vent sizing, the choice of fittings, etc.

HandyHints®

BETTER CAULK TOOLING

Who hasn't used their finger and a little bit of spit to get that line of caulk around the tub or sink just perfect? Try this instead: Mix a small cup of water with a few drops of dish soap. Then all you have to do is dip your finger in the cup and wipe the seam. A perfect caulk line—spit free!

—Andrew Betzner

5-GALLON BUCKET PVC PIPE CUTTER

Here's a nifty way to cut PVC pipe on the fly. Just make a couple of notches in the top of a 5-gallon bucket. Set the pipe in the notches and you've got a stable spot for sawing. As a bonus, you can load up the bucket and carry your tools along, too!

—Jim Penick

RADIATOR HOSE

HOSE CLAMP

NO-RUST TOILET SCREWS

It doesn't take long for the hinge screws on a toilet seat to rust, and then you have rust dust all over the toilet rim every time the seat slams. To prevent this, all you need to do is dab a little clear nail polish onto the screw heads. If the screws are already rusted, fill the holes with caulk. (Don't worry—you'll never have to get at the screws, because you'll be replacing the whole seat and lid assembly someday.)

—Mike Scholey

SUMP PUMP NOISE REDUCTION

Our basement sump pump runs pretty often in the spring, and we can hear the vibration all over the house. To dampen the sound, I replaced a section of the plastic pipe with a radiator hose secured with hose clamps. To ensure I got the right hose size, I took a section of pipe to the auto parts store. It works great!

Dave MacDougal

> **Web links: Need parts for a sick ceiling fan?**
>
> eceilingfans.com carries ceiling fan parts for all major brands. Whether you need a switch, flywheel, new blades or glass globes, you'll find it here.

COOL FAUCET—REMOVAL WRENCH

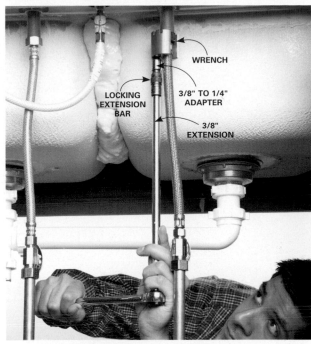

WRENCH

LOCKING EXTENSION BAR

3/8" TO 1/4" ADAPTER

3/8" EXTENSION

Remove faucet nuts from below. Slide the open end of the wrench over the supply tube and push it up to the faucet nuts. Then turn the ratchet and it will self-center on the nut. Remove and reattach the ratchet handle as you rotate the nut.

Replacing a faucet is easy once you get the retaining nuts off. But that's easier said than done. If you're like most DIY plumbers, you probably use a cheap basin wrench. That means you have to crawl on your back all the way into the sink base. Then you have to arch your back, reach all the way up to the sink deck (while holding a flashlight in your mouth) and hook the jaw onto the faucet nuts.

Forget that. Just buy a Basin Buddy wrench (about $25) and snap it onto a long, 3/8-in. extension from your socket set. (One online source is simplyplumbing.com.) Then twist the ratchet handle as shown to loosen the nuts. You'll save your back and do the job in a fraction of the time.

WRENCH

3/8" TO 1/4" ADAPTER

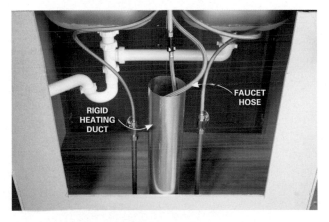

RIGID HEATING DUCT

FAUCET HOSE

PULLOUT FAUCET FIX

I can't be the only one whose pullout faucet hose gets wrapped around things under the sink. One time, it wrapped around a water valve and shut off the water to the dishwasher. After an embarassing (and expensive) service call, I came up with a solution to the problem. I bought a 2-ft. piece of 4-in. rigid heating duct. I propped the duct up under the sink and pushed the faucet hose down into the duct. Now the hose slides freely without getting wrapped around anything. If the duct won't stay upright, screw it to a block of wood that's screwed to the bottom of the cabinet.

Michael Grimes

ICE CUBE CATCHER

Our ice dispenser sometimes sends cubes flying. I turned a magnetic vent deflector upside down to use as a catch basin. You can find these at any home center for a few dollars.
If the magnets won't stick, use hot glue. You can easily remove the deflector without damaging the finish on your fridge.

Wm. W. McCandlish

VENT DEFLECTOR

PLUMBING, HEATING & APPLIANCES

WORKING WITH
ROUND DUCT PIPE

These tips from a pro will help you avoid frustration—and get a better job

by **Mark Petersen, Associate Editor**

Whether you're adding new heat runs in a basement or changing the layout of an existing HVAC system, you'll probably be working with round metal duct pipe. We invited Bob Schmahl to give us a few pointers. Bob's been a tin bender for more than 40 years. He insists he still doesn't know everything about ductwork, but we weren't convinced. These tips should help make your next job run that much smoother.

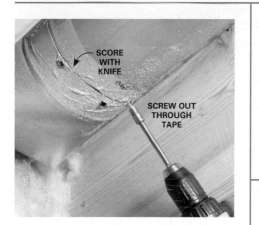

Install dampers at the registers

Adding heat runs in a basement may change the airflow in the rooms above. Each register should have its own damper that can be accessed for adjustment. If those dampers can't be accessed from below, you'll want to install them close enough to the register so that you can reach them through the register opening. Bob likes 4 x 10-in. boots (not shown)—you can easily fit your hand in them to adjust dampers, and there are more grate cover options for that size.

DAMPER

Bob's not a fan of flexible duct

There's no question that flexible duct is easier to install than metal pipe, but consider this: Flexible duct can degrade over time. It collects dust and is almost impossible to clean. Flexible duct needs to be larger than pipes to allow the same amount of airflow. The most common problem Bob has seen: "People get careless and turn corners too sharp, which creates kinks that severely restrict airflow."

SCORE WITH KNIFE

SCREW OUT THROUGH TAPE

Don't peel off old tape

If you have to disassemble existing fittings, there's no need to peel off the old foil tape first. Instead, just score the tape at the seam with a utility knife and remove the screws right through the tape. When it comes time to retape, just clean off the dust and apply new tape right over the old.

HOLD EDGES CLOSE

Assemble the pipe like a zipper

When assembling pipe, start at one end and work the seam together like a zipper. Use one hand to keep the two edges close and the other to apply downward pressure. Use your leg, a workbench or the ground to support the back side of the pipe. If you make a mistake and have to dismantle a pipe, slam it down flat on the ground, seam side up. It should pop right apart.

PUSH DOWN

START AT END

ANGLE DRILL

A hole cutter works great in tight spots

Aviator snips work fine to cut holes in a trunk line, but only if there's enough space. If you're dealing with close quarters and you own a right-angle drill or attachment, you may want to invest in a sheet metal hole cutter. Otherwise you might have to take down the trunk line. You can buy them online for about $65. Malco is one manufacturer.

Caulk the take-offs

Caulk (don't tape) the connection between the trunk line and a take-off (elbow) before you connect pipes to it. That way, you'll be able to turn the take-off out of the way to caulk above it. Regular silicone is fine.

Overlap butt joints with draw band connectors

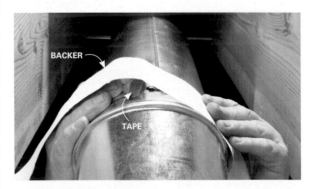

When you're installing a pipe between two fixed parts, it's impossible to slip in the piece using the crimped ends and still get the required 1-1/2-in. overlaps at both ends. Overlap one side as you normally would and create a butt joint on the other. Use a draw band connector to complete the butt joint. If your supplier doesn't carry them, make your own by cutting a piece of pipe to overlap the ends, and then screw and tape the band into place. If you're working with 6-in. pipe, you'll need to use 7-in. pipe for the bands.

BACKER

TAPE

Leave backing on the tape

If the ducts are going to be concealed, all seams need to be taped or caulked. Here's Bob's trick for taping a seam on a pipe that's installed close to the subfloor: Cut a piece to length. Peel off part of the backing. Slide the backing up and over the pipe. Finally, pull down on the backing, which will pull the tape along with it. Inspectors will want to know you've used an approved tape, so buy the stuff with writing on it, or keep the roll on-site until inspection.

Make two marks for cutting

When cutting pipe, Bob likes to mark the size he needs on each side of the open seam with a marker. Flat metal is easier to cut than curved, so he uses his knee to support and flatten the pipe while he opens it up. Then you just sight on the far mark while you make the cut. It'll be straight and perfect every time. Bob prefers snips made by Malco, which cost less than $35 at Amazon. Unless you enjoy trips to the ER, wear gloves when cutting pipe—the stuff is razor sharp.

MARK

MARK

Move one ring at a time

Figuring out the right combination of turns to get an elbow to point in the right direction can be perplexing. Bob recommends moving one "gore" (elbow ring) at a time, starting with the connected side. And don't make 90-degree turns if you don't have to. A 90-degree elbow creates the same resistance as adding 5 ft. of pipe.

3 SCREWS

SUPPORT BRACKET

Use support brackets and three screws

Each pipe needs support. You can use just about any support you want, but adjustable steel support brackets are quick and easy. And don't forget to screw the pipe to the joist hanger so the pipes won't rattle when someone stomps across the floor above. Every connection needs three screws. They don't have to be evenly spaced. Use 1-in. galvanized zip screws designed for sheet metal.

COMSTOCK

TIME FOR A NEW FURNACE?

Before you sit down with an HVAC contractor, read up on what our pros and Field Editors think you need to know

by **Elisa Bernick, Associate Editor**

New furnaces are more complex than ever with lots of new features, higher efficiencies and higher costs. Knowing what to ask an HVAC contractor is key to buying the right furnace for your home and getting a quality installation.

We asked experienced TFH Field Editors—HVAC pros who do this for a living as well as fellow DIYers who have recently bought a furnace—for their top tips, warnings, lessons learned and best advice about buying a new forced-air furnace.

Top tips from an HVAC pro

■ **Don't go with the lowest bidder.** "Service calls are twice as likely to be related to poor installation as to defective equipment. The guy with the lowest bid often makes the biggest mistakes."

■ **Contractor markup makes a difference.** "The heating contractor actually pays about $300 to $500 more for a 95 percent furnace than he does for a 90 percent furnace. So, if that added cost is passed through with little markup, you might be able to cost-justify it. If the contractor marks up the price a whole bunch, then you have no chance of making a payback in your lifetime."

■ **Have a pro install a new thermostat.** "Furnaces and thermostats, just like cars, have gotten increasingly computerized, and they can require some pretty serious know-how to get them to work right."

■ **High vs. very high efficiencies.** "Higher efficiency means higher complexity, and I like to keep the machinery as simple as possible. The more complex it is, the more expensive it is, and the more it will cost to fix when it breaks. Generally, your very best value is to get a 92 percent efficiency furnace with one of the new ECM fan motors."

■ **Get a proposal, not a bid.** "Go with someone who provides a detailed written proposal that outlines exactly what

he will and won't do. He should list the manufacturer and model number of the proposed equipment as well as the cost of any plumbing, venting changes or electrical work required."

■ **Buy a reputable brand.** "Stick with the major brands or one of their subsidiaries. If you don't recognize the brand, don't trust what the contractor says about it. Do your own checking online before you buy."

■ **You may need a smaller furnace.** "Older furnaces were usually oversized so that the house was always warm enough. But new higher efficiency furnaces can have a lower Btu rating and still put out the same amount of heat. For example, a new 94 percent efficient furnace that is rated at 80,000 Btu puts out as much heat as an old 75 percent efficient 100,000 Btu furnace."

MEET AN EXPERT

Dave Jones is a 35-year licensed professional engineer and a TFH Field Editor. He is the Engineering & Design Manager at Temperature Systems Inc. in Madison, WI, and has been involved in the design and construction of hundreds of HVAC projects across the United States, ranging from lake cabins to large research facilities.

Assess your entire HVAC system

When you're shopping for a furnace, get your ducts checked at the same time. There's no sense in getting a new furnace if you'll let the hot/cold out through leaks or poor insulation in your ductwork.

—Thomas Czerwinski

New law may affect your choice

Beginning in May 2013, a new U.S. Department of Energy rule requires newly installed residential gas furnaces in 30 northern states to be rated at least 90 percent AFUE (annual fuel utilization efficiency). That means your new furnace will vent directly through the wall instead of up your chimney or stack. Check with a local HVAC professional for more information or visit appliance-standards.org/product/furnaces.

MID- OR HIGH-EFFICIENCY FURNACE?

Mid-efficiency

Cost: $1,500 to $2,500 installed (no A/C). AFUE: 80 to 89 percent.
Savings: 15 to 20 percent of current heating costs (when replacing a 65 percent efficient unit).
Venting: Into a masonry or metal chimney (existing chimney might require upgrading).

High-efficiency

Cost: $3,000 to $5,000 installed (no A/C). AFUE: 90 to 97 percent.
Savings: 25 to 30 percent of current heating costs (when replacing a 65 percent efficient unit).
Venting: Directly through a wall to the outside through plastic PVC pipe. Known as "condensing units" because they recover extra heat from combustion gases by extracting water from them.

Highest efficiencies make sense when...

- You live in a cold climate (may be required by law—see p. 92).
- You will be staying in your house for 10 years or more.
- Local energy costs are high.
- You're replacing an inefficient heating system.
- The contractor markup is low (see "Top Tips from an HVAC Pro" on p. 92).
- You can take advantage of local, state and utility rebates and incentives. Federal tax credits on high-efficiency furnaces are no longer available as of this writing, but state, local and utility rebates may still be available in many areas. Visit dsireusa.org for more information.
- The payback calculation is reasonable. To run a payback calculation online, visit yourmoneypage.com/energy/furnace1.php.

SINGLE-STAGE OR TWO-STAGE FURNACE?

Single-Stage

A traditional single-stage furnace runs the burner at full blast and shuts off until heat is called for. It costs $500 less than a two-stage furnace, but the trade-off is lower energy efficiency, hot and cold spots, and inconsistent temperatures.

Two-stage

A two-stage furnace has a high and a low burner setting. It normally runs on low unless full blast is needed. It costs $500 more than a single-stage unit, but it delivers consistent heat, which means fewer drafts and temperature swings, and is quiet and energy efficient.

TWO-SPEED OR A VARIABLE-SPEED BLOWER?

Standard two-speed

A standard two-speed blower (aka "multi" speed) with a pSC MOTOR has one blower speed for heating and one for cooling. It's $600 cheaper than a variable-speed blower and is less complex, which means lower future repair costs. But it's noisier than a variable-speed blower and uses more electricity.

Variable-speed

A variable-speed blower uses an ECM motor, which runs on DC power and continually adjusts its speed to your home's needs. It uses a fraction of the electricity of most standard motors and is quiet and comfortable. It costs $600 more than a standard blower and is a more complex system, which potentially means more expensive repairs.

■ Use an experienced pro

Stick with reputable furnace contractors who have been in business for a long time. Chances are they're still in business because they do quality work, and they'll still be around if you have problems down the line.

Bruce Fox

■ Incentives can slash the price

My gas company gave me a $100 rebate, the manufacturer gave me a $500 rebate and the city gave me a five-year interest-free loan to make the upgrade. I ended up saving a bundle.

Thomas Czerwinski

■ Know the true cost of the furnace

I got quotes from $2,800 (furnace and ductwork) to $12,000. Do your own research on the Internet and find out how much you can purchase the unit for online so you can separate the unit from the labor.

David Youngblood

■ Highest efficiencies have higher repair bills

I'm an HVAC repairman. Most furnace installers prefer that you buy the most efficient furnace and claim it will save you money. What they don't tell you is that the parts to repair it are about three times as expensive and in the long run you're not saving anything. You can buy a furnace rated at 95 percent and still stay away from the high repair bills of a 97 or 98 percent.

—Lee Schmidt

■ Don't assume the contractor knows everything

Most contractors I've talked to don't recommend variable-speed blowers because they don't really understand them. I dug into manufacturers' documentation and a few contractors' message boards on the Internet and read until I understood them. I guess that's what DIY is all about.

Tom Berg

■ Consider buying through a home center

We got quotes from a few local contractors but went with a home center instead. The home center hired a reputable local company but backed the work, and even gave us a small discount for opening a credit card and charging the work on it.

Steve Markman

■ Put details in writing

Confirm that your contractor will remove your old furnace without additional charges.

Jeff Montgomery

GreatGoofs®

What goes up...

To show my nephews how I practiced catching as a child, I was throwing a tennis ball up on my roof, letting it bounce a few times and catching it. After a few throws and catches, I heaved one up and the three of us stood looking at the roof for the rebound. Nothing. We looked on the other side of the house, in the bushes and all around. No luck. Oh well, I figured it would eventually show up.

Later that day, I noticed the laundry sink in the basement wasn't draining. Hmmm...plugged trap? Then we realized *none* of the drains was draining. We called a plumber, who snaked a camera down the cleanout and found the tennis ball stuck in the sewer drain! Seems my throw to the roof was a perfect shot down the vent pipe. The $500 service call was bad enough. But now I'm constantly getting my chops busted by family members holding tennis balls and asking if I want to play catch.

—Joe LaRosa

The sound of ... quality

Our garbage disposer had been making loud grinding noises for over a year. When it finally gave up the ghost, I bought a top-of-the-line InSinkErator. After installing it, I plugged it in, ran the water and turned it on. Nothing. I thought I might have done something wrong, so I took it out, rewired it and tried again. Still nothing. I went down to the basement to see if I had blown a fuse. Everything was fine. While I was sitting there scratching my head, my wife came into the kitchen and dumped her ice cubes into the sink and turned on the disposer. I could hear the cubes being ground up. The disposer was working fine. It was just so quiet that I couldn't tell it was running.

—David Soper

Exploding toilet trick

Our toilet wouldn't stop running because the float wouldn't turn the water completely off. I'd fixed the same problem in our old toilet by bending the float arm down a little to increase the pressure on the shutoff valve in the tank. But since our new toilet had a plastic arm, I decided to apply a little heat to soften it so I could bend it.

First I sprayed silicone lube on everything in the tank to help things slide better. Then I leaned over the tank with my lighter, clicked it and...WHOOOOMPP! The aerosol silicone spray I had just shot into the tank exploded. Luckily, I escaped with only singed hair and eyelashes. But now my wife can't stop telling people about our exploding toilet.

—Ron Woodward

Feeling a little blue

My husband, Dan, is a businessman, but he loves the construction process and was the general contractor on our first and second homes. Our second home was built 15 years after the first, and certain things had changed a bit in the interim. Dan ordered a new bathtub for one of the bathrooms, but when it arrived he saw that it was blue instead of the white one we ordered, so he sent it back. We waited another two weeks for the white tub to arrive and when it did, unbelievably it was blue, too. Dan was furious! He was about to send that one back when he (luckily) realized that the "blue" was just plastic wrap over the white tub underneath.

—Ann Delicato

Cleaning

CLEAN VENT HOOD GREASE FILTER

I've run my vent hood grease filter through my dishwasher but had disappointing results. And I've tried "grease cutting" household cleaners. I finally got great results when I used water-based degreaser from the auto parts store. I filled the sink with hot water and degreaser, dropped in the filter and let the degreaser do all the work. The filter came out sparkling clean in just a few minutes. Then I rinsed it off.

—Rick Muscoplat, Contributing Editor

CLEANING DULL-LOOKING FIBERGLASS DOOR

If your fiberglass entry door looks weathered and dull but the stain is still dark, clean the door and lightly sand the surface with 220-grit sandpaper. Then dust off the door and recoat it with a few coats of a marine spar varnish (one choice is McCloskey Man O'War Spar Marine Varnish; $19 at amazon.com). Apply with a roller to achieve the smoothest coat. If the stain has faded, restain and then varnish.

RUST BUSTER

I've written before about how much I love using Acid Magic for removing rust from sinks, toilets and showers. Well, I obviously have lots of iron in my well water—the latest evidence is that all our ground-level windows had a reddish tint from the sprinklers. I had no idea how to remove it until I thought of Acid Magic again. I brushed it on with a paintbrush and the rust instantly dissolved and ran down the glass.

If you have other mineral deposits in your water, I'm certain it'd take care of them, too. You can buy it by the gallon for about $15 at online sources and some hardware stores.

—Travis Larson, Senior Editor

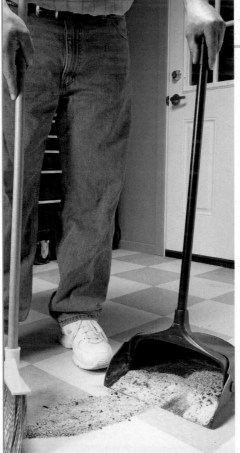

LAZY MAN'S DUSTPAN

I'll admit it—I'm not a fan of bending over. That's why I own four lobby dustpans: one for my house, one for my garage and two for my shop. I discovered lobby pans when I worked for my brother's cleaning company as a kid. The one regular dustpan I've bought in my life was for my first apartment. When I finally moved out, I left it there for the next tenant, got myself a lobby pan and never looked back. Get one at a home center for under $20. If you want a higher-quality model, check out a janitorial supply company.

—Mark Petersen, Contributing Editor

DE-STINK YOUR FRIDGE

When your power goes out and the food in your fridge and freezer goes bad, you've got a really stinky mess on your hands. Obviously the first step is to remove the food and wipe everything down with a disinfecting cleaning spray. But our appliance expert, Costas Stavrou, gave us the rest of the story.

Turns out the most common mistake DIYers make is not cleaning all the nooks and crannies inside the freezer. The biggest culprits? The shelf supports in your freezer. Costas says to remove them and clean behind them with detergent and disinfectant to get rid of any blood or crud. If they're permanently attached, soak them with cleaning spray. Next, forget about those expensive charcoal odor removers or coffee (which is even more expensive). Just use newspaper and charcoal briquettes. Finally (and this is the most important part), replace the old newspaper and charcoal with fresh stuff **every day for about a week** or until the smell is gone. Don't think a single treatment is enough. It isn't.

Absorb the odor with newspaper and charcoal. Smash about 12 charcoal briquettes from your grill and spread the chunks on two trays. One goes in the fridge, the other in the freezer. Then crunch up newspaper and fill the shelves with it. Close the doors and walk away. Repeat every day for a week.

SHOPPING BAGS

WINDOW WASHING SMARTS

When you're up on a ladder washing windows, it can be a hassle to keep all your equipment within easy reach. I loop my belt through the handles of two old plastic shopping bags so they hang at my sides. I put window spray and a roll of paper towels in one bag and my used paper towels in the other. I look a little goofy (or a lot), but it sure beats going up and down the ladder to retrieve a dropped roll of paper towels.

William Elias

GREASE-DESTROYING HAND WIPES

I always try to wear nitrile gloves when working on dirty projects. But sometimes I don't have any, and I just have to reach in and "get 'er done."

That's where Grime Boss Hand Wipes come in handy. One side is embedded with grease-dissolving cleansers and grit to really scrub the grease off. The flip side is smooth and contains a disinfectant plus vitamin E and aloe to soften up those ham hocks of yours.

Throw a 10- or 30-count dispenser pack into your trunk or toolbox and you're covered. The packs cost $2 and $6 at amazon.com, target.com and auto parts stores.

—Rick Muscoplat, Contributing Editor

Cleaning

THE BEST CLEANER FOR UNGLAZED PORCELAIN TILE

First, make sure you know whether you have glazed or unglazed porcelain tile. "Glazed porcelain typically has a complex design or veining pattern that only happens with a baked-on glaze finish," says tile cleaning expert Troy Roberts. "Unglazed porcelain tiles will all look basically the same with monotonous designs and no shade variations among the tiles." If you're not sure, Roberts suggests letting water sit on the tiles for five minutes and then wiping it off. If the tiles darken, they're most likely unglazed.

Clean glazed porcelain the same way you clean ceramic tile. Cleaning unglazed porcelain tiles is trickier. There are no industry standards governing porcelain tile quality, so you can't be completely sure what you're dealing with. For that reason, Roberts says it's critical to test a cleaning product on out-of-the-way tiles before using it "to make sure your scrub pads don't scratch the tiles and the cleaners won't damage or discolor them."

Roberts recommends starting with a soft, non-abrasive scrub pad and a good-quality alkaline cleaner like StoneTech's KlenzAll to emulsify and dissolve dirt, grease and grime. "If you still see smudges, swipe marks or a hazy appearance, it's probably a grout haze leftover from the tile installation." In that case, he suggests using an acidic cleaner, such as StoneTech's Restore, which will safely remove grout haze from tiles that are not sensitive to acid. "Again, test it first on an out-of-the-way tile to make sure the acid cleaner doesn't etch the tile." For more information, visit tilecleaning.org.

MEET AN EXPERT
Troy Roberts has been in the tile cleaning and restoration business for 20 years. He is the president of NATCO, the North American Tile Cleaning Organization.

"Test first on an out-of-the-way tile to make sure the acid cleaner doesn't etch the tile."
—Troy Roberts

KlenzAll, an alkaline cleaner, tackles grease and grime. Restore, an acidic cleaner, removes grout haze. Both are available at tile shops and online.

SUDS BUCKET

AUTOMOTIVE "CAR WASH" SOAP

RINSE BUCKET

TOP TWO CAR-WASHING TIPS

If you wash your car yourself rather than taking it to the car wash, be sure to do it right. Here are the top two car-washing tips to get your vehicle clean and protect its finish.

■ Always use automotive "car wash" soap on your car's finish—never dishwashing detergent, household spray cleaners or glass cleaner. Those chemicals can pull essential oils out of your vehicle's paint and shorten its life.

■ Use two wash buckets—one for soapy water and one for rinse. Dip your wash mitt in the soapy water and wash a section of your car. Then swish the mitt in rinse water to clean off the crud before you redip it in the sudsy water. Change the rinse water often.

4 Woodworking & Workshop Projects & Tips

REMOVE A STUCK PHILLIPS HEAD SCREW

1 **Fill the screw head.** Squirt a dollop of valve grinding compound into the head of the screw. Then jam in the screwdriver and turn.

No matter how simple the repair, it seems like there's always one stuck screw. You try to muscle your way out of the jam, but all that does is cam out the screw head slots. It doesn't have to be that way. Here are a few tricks to coax out a stubborn Phillips screw.

At the first sign of trouble, spray the screw with rust penetrant (Liquid Wrench and PB Blaster are two really good brands). Let the penetrant work for at least 15 minutes. Then spray it again and tap the screw head dead-on several times with a hammer. Then try the screwdriver again.

Next, apply valve grinding compound (**Photo 1**). The compound (about $4 at any auto parts store) contains a fine grit that helps the screwdriver bite into the head.

If the screw still won't budge and the surrounding surfaces can tolerate some heat, aim a lighter flame directly onto the screw head. Then douse it with cold water before trying it again.

Still stuck? Invest in an impact screwdriver (**Photo 2**). Pick one up for about $20 at a home center or an auto parts store.

If you've stripped out the head, cut a new slot with a straight-groove rotary tool (**Photo 3**). Then crank it out with a flat-blade screwdriver.

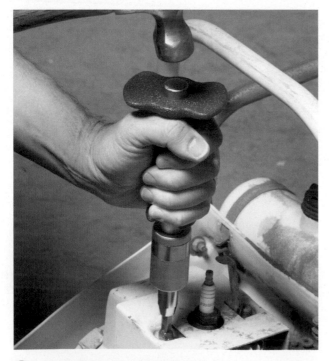

2 **Hammer the impact driver.** Hold the body of the impact driver to prevent it from turning. Then hit the end with a serious blow.

Stripped out? Cut into the head. Slice a deep groove into the screw head with a cutting wheel and rotary tool. Make it wide enough to accommodate your largest flat-blade screwdriver.

BEST WOOD GLUE FOR OUTDOOR FURNITURE

According to adhesives expert Bob Behnke, the best all-around outdoor wood glue is a PVA-type glue with at least a Type II ANSI-HPVA rating (such as Gorilla Wood Glue or Titebond II). "A Type II ANSI rating on the label means it's a water-resistant product that can get wet and stay wet for a sustained period, such as a soaking rain, but it will dry out without losing strength."

ANSI ratings signify different levels of water resistance for ply-wood adhesive. A Type I rating means the bond is waterproof and won't weaken when submerged and exposed to high temperatures. A Type II rating means the bond is water resistant, which is fine for most outdoor projects. Behnke says that with so many glue choices, finding the right glue for a project can be confusing. "Always consider two things: the substrate you're holding together and what the glue needs to do after it's dry."

For example, if you're making a wooden cutting board that's going to go through a dishwasher, you'll need a glue that can not only handle getting wet but can also stand up to the high heat of a dishwasher. In this case, Behnke says, you need a glue with a Type I ANSI rating (such as Titebond III or original Gorilla Glue). Another consideration is open time (how long you have before the adhesive sets up). Wood glues have distinct differences in open and assembly times, so choose an adhesive based on the project and your working style. If you're confused about which adhesive to use for your project, Behnke suggests you check the technical data sheets or call the manufacturer's hotline and ask an expert.

MEET AN EXPERT

Bob Behnke, Senior Technical Specialist at Franklin International, maker of Titebond glues and other products, is a chemist with 30 years of experience in adhesives, sealants and coatings.

"You can have the greatest glue in the world, but if you use it in the wrong situation, it will be the worst glue in the world."

—Bob Behnke

MAKE YOUR OWN TACK CLOTHS

Store-bought tack cloths aren't expensive (about $2 each). But if you need a lot of them for a big project or you've run out and need them right now, here's a quick way to make your own.

Start with a section of cheesecloth or an old white T-shirt. Cut it into 12-in. squares. Wearing gloves, dip the cloth into a bowl of mineral spirits. Wring it out. Then lay it out on an old baking pan and dribble on some varnish. Knead the cloth to spread the varnish. Store the homemade tack cloths in a sealed container to prevent spontaneous combustion.

CHOOSING NAIL HOLE PUTTY FOR FINISHED TRIM

Oil-based putties (in the little jars) are the best choice for prestained and prefinished trim. These come in a wide range of colors, and you can even knead different shades together to get just the right color where the grain is lighter or darker.

After you've applied the putty, make sure you apply a coat of polyurethane to protect it. Oil-based putty stays soft, so it's not a good choice on floors or to fill large holes or gaps. And don't use oil-based putty on bare wood. The oils soak into the wood around the nail holes, and stain and finish will absorb differently and look blotchy.

SUPER BENCH

- Simple enough to build on a Saturday
- Easy enough for a beginner
- Strong enough to hold a V-8
- Tough enough to last a lifetime

This project is both a workbench and a storage unit

by **Mark Petersen, Contributing Editor**

What it takes

Time: One day. If you plan to varnish it, add another day.

Cost: $100. That doesn't include the finish or the drawer pulls.

Skill Level: Beginner. But even a heavy-duty DIYer will love this bench.

Tools: Circular saw and drill.

Does your current workbench consist of two sawhorses and an old door slab? Well, my friend, it's time to upgrade. There are hundreds of workbench plans out there, but not many of them call for plywood. Plywood makes a flat, stable work surface, and it doesn't need to be clamped, glued or planed. And it can easily be replaced if it gets too beaten up after years of abuse.

If the idea of building drawers makes you break into a cold sweat, then build your workbench with two shelf sections and forget about the drawers. But if your mantra is, "The more storage the better," then get yourself an additional half sheet each of 3/4-in. and 1/4-in. plywood, and build another two drawer sections to take the place of the lower shelf.

Cut the workbench components

It's always nice to cut as many parts as possible before starting the assembly. That way, you can set aside the dust mask, safety glasses and hearing protection for longer periods of time, and the air isn't continually filled with sawdust. Cut

1 **Cut plywood parts perfectly straight.** Cut the shelf top first and use the factory-cut edge as a guide for your other cuts. Measure the distance between the saw blade and the edge of the saw baseplate, and align the shelf top that same distance away from your cutting line.

2 **Frame the drawer compartment.** Drill 1/8-in. pilot holes through the frame back and into the plywood drawer dividers. If you skip this step, you're guaranteed to split the plywood.

everything except the lengths of the drawer components. In case things get a little out of whack during assembly, you'll be able to measure and fit the drawers to the actual openings.

Mark the cutting lines for your big sheets with a chalk line. Use a framing square to mark the lines for the smaller components, but don't forget that the blade will remove about 1/8 in. on every pass, so either add that space when you're marking, or mark and cut one at a time.

Start with the shelf top (C). Cut the whole length of the plywood. You'll have to freehand this one, but don't worry if your cut isn't perfect. The cut edge will be down low and backed up against the wall. Use the factory edge of the shelf top as a guide to cut the three other larger pieces (A, B, D; **Photo 1**). Think you might have trouble lugging around full sheets of plywood? Some home centers will cut them for you if you ask.

After cutting the big parts to length, you'll have some medium-size chunks of plywood you can use as a guide to cut the smaller components, or you can clamp down your framing square as a guide. Next, cut the 2x4 legs (L). You can get two legs out of each 8-ft. 2x4 with about a 2-ft. piece left over. Set aside the remaining four 2-ft. pieces for use later. Cut the 2x4s that make up the shelf and drawer compartment frames (M – Q), starting with the long boards first.

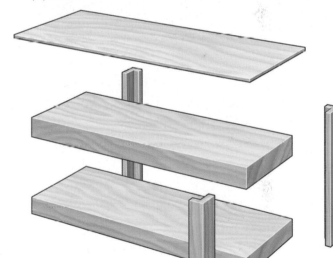

Assemble the shelf section

Use the benchtop (D) as a temporary workbench (if you don't have a door slab). Join the 2x4 frame with one 3-in. screw in the middle of each corner. This will reduce the chances that screws will collide when you attach the legs. Secure the plywood shelf to the frame using 1-5/8-in. screws about 12 in. apart. Use

4 legs, 2 boxes and a top

That's all there is to it. The legs are just 2x4s screwed together. The shelf and work surface could be constructed as simple boxes or made with drawer components. It's a perfect project for a beginner but a great bench for even the most advanced DIYer.

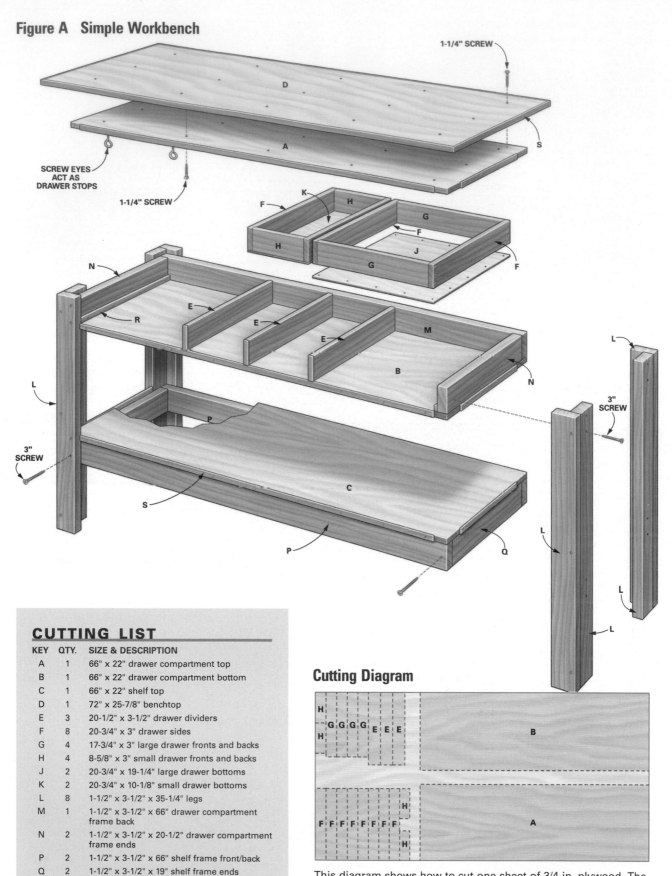

Figure A   Simple Workbench

1-1/4" SCREW

D

S

A

SCREW EYES
ACT AS
DRAWER STOPS

1-1/4" SCREW

F

K

H

G

F

H

J

G

F

N

R

E

E

E

M

B

N

L

L

3"
SCREW

P

S

C

L

3"
SCREW

P

Q

L

L

CUTTING LIST

KEY	QTY.	SIZE & DESCRIPTION
A	1	66" x 22" drawer compartment top
B	1	66" x 22" drawer compartment bottom
C	1	66" x 22" shelf top
D	1	72" x 25-7/8" benchtop
E	3	20-1/2" x 3-1/2" drawer dividers
F	8	20-3/4" x 3" drawer sides
G	4	17-3/4" x 3" large drawer fronts and backs
H	4	8-5/8" x 3" small drawer fronts and backs
J	2	20-3/4" x 19-1/4" large drawer bottoms
K	2	20-3/4" x 10-1/8" small drawer bottoms
L	8	1-1/2" x 3-1/2" x 35-1/4" legs
M	1	1-1/2" x 3-1/2" x 66" drawer compartment frame back
N	2	1-1/2" x 3-1/2" x 20-1/2" drawer compartment frame ends
P	2	1-1/2" x 3-1/2" x 66" shelf frame front/back
Q	2	1-1/2" x 3-1/2" x 19" shelf frame ends
R	2	3/4" x 1/4" x 8' screen mold drawer guides
S		Screen mold/plywood edging cut to fit

Cutting Diagram

H

G G G   E E E

B

H

H

F F F F F F F F

H

A

This diagram shows how to cut one sheet of 3/4-in. plywood. The second 3/4-in. sheet is much simpler: just cut lengthwise to yield parts C and D. Cut the drawer bottoms (J and K) from a 4 x 4-ft. sheet of 1/4-in. plywood.

glue on every joint except the top sheet of plywood—you may want to replace it someday.

Assemble the drawer compartment section

Assemble the three 2x4s that make up the drawer compartment frame (M, N) with one 3-in. screw at both corners. Mark lines for the location of the drawer dividers (E). Driving screws into the end grain of plywood can cause it to split. You can avoid this by predrilling holes with a 1/8-in. drill bit. Attach the plywood drawer dividers to the frame using two 3-in. screws in each one (Photo 2).

Lay the drawer compartment bottom (B) on top of the frame, and mark lines on the front of the plywood to line up the front of the drawer dividers. Then mark lines across the top of the plywood for the location of the screws. Clamp the box down with the drawer dividers aligned, then predrill holes for the dividers (Photo 3). You can often eliminate small warps and bows in the plywood by starting at one end and working your way down the line. Screw the plywood down with 1-5/8-in. screws. Space the screws about 12 in. apart the long way and 8 in. the short.

Before you repeat the process to attach the top of the drawer compartment, install screen mold on each end of the drawer compartment with 3d 1-1/4-in. brad nails. This will help the outside drawers slide in straight once the legs are installed.

Attach the legs and shelf

Preassemble the legs with three 3-in. screws in each leg. Flip the drawer box

3 **Add the top and bottom to the drawer compartment.** Install the bottom first. Mark the locations of the dividers, and clamp everything in place before predrilling and fastening. Install the top the same way, but don't forget to add the drawer guides (R) first.

LINE FOR SCREWS

DRAWER ALIGNMENT LINES

4 **Screw on the legs.** Square up one side of the leg and fasten it with one screw, then square up the other side of the leg and fasten with two screws. Double-check the first side before driving in the final screw.

PREASSEMBLED LEG

5 **Install the shelf.** Set the shelf on spacers to hold it in perfect position. Then screw through the legs just as you did with the drawer compartment.

SHELF

TEMPORARY SPACER

MATERIALS LIST

ITEM	QTY.
4' x 8' x 3/4" BC plywood	2
4' x 4' x 1/4" plywood	1
2x4 x 8'	8
1/4" x 3/4" x 8' pine screen mold	5
1-1/4" self-drilling exterior-grade screws	1 lb.
1-5/8" self-drilling exterior-grade screws	1 lb.
3" self-drilling exterior-grade screws	1 lb.
3d 1-1/4" brad nails	1 lb.
Chest handle	4
No. 10 screw eyes	8
Bottle of exterior-grade wood glue	1 qt.
Minwax PolyShade stain/polyurethane	1 qt.
Water-based polyurethane	1 qt.

6 **Cover the plywood ends with screen mold.** Nail on the screen mold with 1-1/4-in. brads. Start with the long sections, and then use the scraps on the shorter ones.

SCREEN MOLD

7 **Build simple drawers.** Glue and clamp the front, back and sides together first. Then nail on the bottom. Finally, nail the sides to the front and back.

upside down. Position the legs so the seams are facing the ends of the workbench. Secure the legs with two 3-in. screws on each side of each leg. Use a framing square as a guide (**Photo 4**). Next, cut the four 2x4s you have left over from the legs to 16 in., and use them as temporary spacers for the shelf. Secure the shelf to the legs with two 3-in. screws on each side (**Photo 5**).

Install the top

Before you screw down the benchtop, predrill holes for the screw eyes that will act as drawer stops. Drill two 3/32-in. holes for each drawer opening, 2 in. in from the sides and 1-1/2 in. from the front (see **Figure A**, p. 104). Align the benchtop flush with the back legs and even on each side. Secure it with a row of 1-1/4-in. screws down the front, back and middle, spaced about every 16 in. Again, you'll have more luck getting a flatter surface by starting at one end and working your way down the line.

Attach the screen mold

Attach the screen mold to the end grain of the plywood. Don't worry about the back side if your bench is going to sit against a wall. Nail on the screen mold pieces with 1-1/4-in. brads (**Photo 6**).

Build the drawers

Double-check the sizes of your drawer openings, and cut each drawer bottom width 1/4 in. smaller than its opening. Cut the sides of the drawers (F) so they will be exposed at the front. This won't look as nice, but it will make the drawer front stronger and keep it from pulling off after you

fill the drawer with heavy tools and hardware.

Glue and clamp the drawer sides together, but before you nail them, attach the bottom with 1-1/4-in. brads. Remove one clamp and set the drawer on edge with the other clamp hanging off the side of the workbench. Nail each corner together with three 1-1/4-in. brads. Remove the other clamp, and nail the remaining two corners together. Work fast so the glue doesn't set up before you get it all put together. Repeat the process for the other three drawers (**Photo 7**).

Finish

It's hard to stain plywood without getting a blotchy look, so after sanding down the rough and sharp edges, we finished our workbench with Minwax PolyShade, a combination stain and polyurethane. It can be brushed on like regular polyurethane but adds a little color in the process. We did one coat on the whole bench and then added a couple more coats of regular polyurethane to the work surfaces. Apply an extra coat or two to the bottom of the legs so they won't wick up moisture from your garage floor.

Attach the drawer pulls. We chose chest handles instead of standard drawer pulls because of their low profile. They won't get in the way when you're clamping projects down to the front edge of the workbench.

Install the screw eyes/drawer stops after you insert the drawers. You may need a small screwdriver for leverage on the last few turns. All that's left is to show off your handiwork to your wife or neighbor, and get started using your new workbench on your next project.

Storage cabinet

TV stand

Entry bench

CHEAPSKATE FURNITURE

The secret is to start with kitchen cabinets!

by **Gary Wentz, Senior Editor**

How cheap? Materials for the TV stand cost $160, the storage cabinet $175, the entry bench $100!

As a world-class penny pincher, I've found that stock cabinets are the key to low-cost, good-quality furniture. I get handsome, sturdy, real-wood furniture for the cost of assemble-it-yourself pieces sold at discount stores. And the advantages go way beyond saving money. Cabinets make furniture building incredibly quick and easy by eliminating the difficult, fussy process of building and hanging doors.

In the following pages, I'll show you how to build three weekend furniture projects. Along the way, you'll see different methods of covering the sides and tops of cabinets and adding legs, feet or a base. You can mix and match these various approaches to build your own furniture with the look and function you want.

Finding cabinets

Used cabinets from remodeling jobs are my first choice for furniture projects (they're free!). I also like damaged cabinets from the local salvage store (cheap!). The trouble with these tightwad options is that the cabinets are already finished, and finishing raw wood to match the factory finish is tough. To get around this, I've painted the furniture or stained the new wood surrounding the cabinets a contrasting color for a two-tone look.

When neither paint nor a two-tone look is suitable, I buy unfinished stock cabinets like the ones shown in this article. Home centers usually carry one style only and one wood species only (typically oak). For the projects shown here, I used 12-in.-deep "upper" cabinets ranging in cost from $30 to $60 each. The cabinets you find may not be exactly like mine, so you may have to alter the measurements given in my plans.

TV STAND

With technology changing so fast, it didn't seem smart to sink a lot of money into a TV stand. But inexpensive stands didn't have the features I wanted: enclosed storage and lots of shelves for electronic components. This stand gives me those things, plus it's rock solid. Some inexpensive stands are rated to support 75 lbs. or less. This thing would hold a V-8 engine block. It's sized for a 42-in. TV, but you could easily make it bigger by spacing the cabinets farther apart or choosing wider cabinets. It's taller than most stands, which may be good or bad, depending on your situation. The materials cost me about $160.

Build up the cabinets

A TV stand based on the standard 12-in. depth of upper cabinets would have a top and shelves that are too shallow for some TV bases and electronic components. To add depth to the stand, extend the backs of the cabinets using plywood frames. I extended the cabinets by 3 in.

Assemble the extension frames using nails or screws and a little glue. Note that one side of the frame (G) is 1/4 in. narrower than the other (H). That creates a recess for the 1/4-in. plywood back (S). Next, skin the cabinet sides with 1/4-in. plywood (**Photo 1**). After spreading glue, I tacked the plywood in place with a couple of brad nails and then weighted it down with paint cans. Also glue the fillers (E) into the recesses at the top and bottom of the cabinets. Fillers give you a solid core to drive screws through when you screw the cabinets to the base and top—without them, screws might pop right through the flimsy 1/2-in. particleboard of the cabinets.

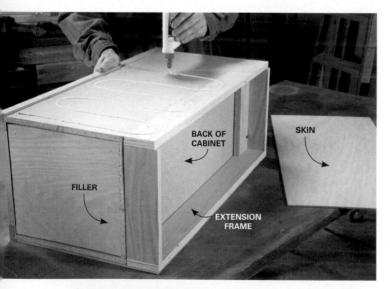

1 **Extend the depth and cover the sides.** "Skin" the sides with plywood after you screw extension frames to the cabinets. The frames give the TV stand extra shelf depth for electronic components and create a cavity for wires behind the cabinets. Also glue fillers into the recesses at the top and bottom of the cabinets.

2 **Build the base.** Rout a decorative cove after the base is assembled. That gives you perfect corners without fussy miter cuts. To avoid splintering at the corner, clamp on a breakout block.

MATERIALS LIST

ITEM	QTY.
12" x 12" x 30" cabinet	2
3/4" x 4' x 8' oak plywood	1
1/4" x 4' x 4' oak plywood	1
1x4 x 8' oak boards	2
3/4" oak cove molding	8'

1-1/4" and 2" screws, wood glue,
Minwax Ebony stain, Minwax
Wipe-On Poly

CUTTING LIST

KEY	QTY.	SIZE & DESCRIPTION
A	2	12" x 12" x 30" cabinets
B	1	3/4" x 16" x 41-1/2" top
C	2	3/4" x 5" x 41" top front & back
D	2	3/4" x 5" x 5-3/4" top sides
E	4	3/4" x 10-3/8" x 10-3/8" fillers
F	8	3/4" x 3" x 10-1/16" frame rungs
G	2	3/4" x 2-3/4" x 30" frame inner sides
H	2	3/4" x 3" x 30" frame outer sides
J	2	1/4" x 14-1/4" x 30" outside panels
K	1	3/4" x 15" x 40" base top
L	1	1/4" x 15-1/2" x 41" base subtop
M	2	3/4" x 3-1/4" x 41" base front & back
N	3	3/4" x 3-1/4" x 14" base rungs
P	2	3/4" x 3-1/2" x 15-1/2" base facing*
Q	1	3/4" x 3-1/2" x 42-1/2" base facing*
R	2	1/4" x 14" x 30" inside panels
S	1	1/4" x 18-1/2" x 29-7/8" back panel
T	2	3/4" x 1-1/2" x 17" back cleats*
U	4	3/4" x 13-1/2" x 16-7/8" shelves

*Base facing, cleats and all bandings
are solid wood cut from 1x4 boards.
Bandings are 3/4" x 1". All other parts are
plywood.

Figure A
TV stand

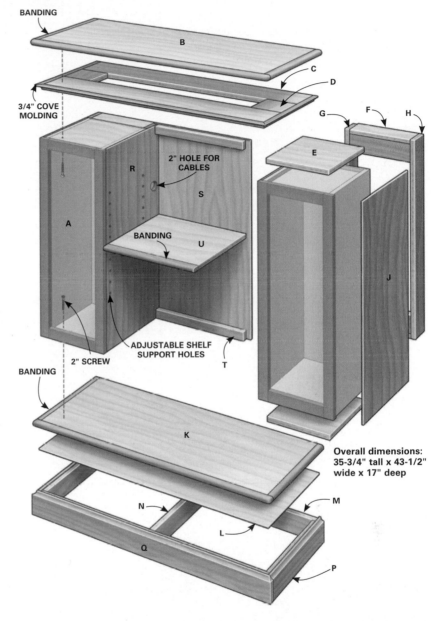

Overall dimensions:
35-3/4" tall x 43-1/2"
wide x 17" deep

The base and top

The base starts with a plywood frame constructed much like the extension frames: nails or screws, plus glue. Top off the frame by gluing on 1/4-in. plywood (L). Now you're ready to wrap the frame with solid wood facing using one of my favorite woodworking shortcuts: Instead of routing the facing, then fussing with mitered corners, glue on the facing before you rout and just form simple 90-degree butt joints at corners. Sand the corners flush and then rout the facing (Photo 2). You'll get tight, perfect corners—fast.

I used a 1/2-in.-radius cove bit and cut to a depth of 1/2 in. That's too deep

Cheap trick

Routed finger pulls

A recess cut with a 1/2-in. cove bit lets you open doors with your fingertips. No hardware needed. Sometimes—like with this TV stand—that's a sleek design choice. And sometimes, it's a big money saver: I recently cut finger pulls in a whole set of laundry room doors and drawers. Compared with the cost of knobs (even inexpensive ones), that saved almost $100.

for a single router pass, so I made three passes, removing and replacing the breakout block after each pass.

To make the base top, use the same wrap-and-rout procedure. Round the top and bottom of the banding (see **Figure A**, p. 109) with a 3/8-in. round-over bit. Again, use a breakout block to prevent splintering. Repeat this entire process to build the top of the stand, which is simply a larger version of the base top. To complete the top, add scraps of plywood and cove molding on the underside (**Photo 3**).

Assembly and finishing

Assemble the entire stand to make sure all the parts fit together correctly. Use screws only—no glue! This TV stand is heavy, and screws will allow quick disassembly for moving.

Screw the cabinets first to the base, driving screws from inside the cabinet boxes (see **Figure A**). Then set the top in place and fasten it the same way before adding the back panel (S).

Measure between the cabinets and subtract 1/8 in. to determine the width of the shelves. To make the shelves, glue banding to a long piece of plywood and rout it with a round-over bit, just as you did to make the top. Then cut the plywood into sections. The shelves rest on adjustable supports. I drilled 2-in. holes into the extension frames for cables to exit behind the stand. Those holes also provide a nook to stuff excess wires into.

Disassemble the stand for finishing. I used two heavy coats of Minwax Ebony stain followed by two coats of Minwax Wipe-On Poly. Later, with the stand assembled and in place, I drove a single screw through the top cleat (T) into a wall stud—insurance against tipping forward.

3 Make the top. Edge the plywood top with solid wood and round the edges with a router. Glue scraps of plywood to the underside of the top and add cove molding.

COVE MOLDING

SOLID WOOD EDGING

STORAGE CABINET

This is my favorite cabinet furniture project because it's so versatile. Use it to store books, small appliances, games and more. Assembly is amazingly fast and easy when you use a brad nailer and glue. My materials cost was about $175.

First, screw the face frames of the two cabinets together. Drill pilot holes and drive screws through the lower face frame into the upper. Then lay them on one side and hold a straightedge across the fronts of the face frames to be sure they form a straight, flat surface. I had to slip a strip of cardboard between the two cabinet boxes to get the face frames aligned.

Next, add spacer strips that match the thickness of the protruding edge of the face frames. For my cabinets, I cut strips just a hair thicker than 1/4 in. from a 2x4. Cutting thin strips on a table saw can be tricky, even dangerous. For tips, go to familyhandyman.com and search for "ripping safely."

Fasten the strips with plenty of glue and a few brad nails. Then add the side panel (**Photo 1**). Make sure the front edge of the panel is perfectly flush with the face frames, and remember that the panel overhangs the lower cabinet by 1 in. Follow the same steps on the other side.

Lay the unit on its back and check that the doors are centered on the cabinets and in line with each other before you add legs and rails. The doors on my cabinets were a mess—I had to slip paper spacers behind one of the hinges and completely reinstall another.

Now you're ready to glue and nail on the legs and rails (**Photo 2**). Glue front leg parts (L, M and N) together, then add them to the cabinet. The top rail (T) is too thin to nail to the face frame, so just nail it to the center stile (S) and clamp it in place until the glue sets. Then remove the doors, finish-sand the whole cabinet and add the top, which is just two layers of plywood edge-banded and glued together (**Photo 3**).

Cheap trick

EDGE BAND

Edge banding

Every cheapskate should learn how to use iron-on edge band. It's the easiest way to cover plywood edges, and it makes inexpensive plywood look like solid wood. The top on this chest, for example, used less than $20 worth of plywood. Solid wood would cost more than twice as much. To see how easy it is, go to familyhandyman.com and search for "edge banding."

MATERIALS LIST

ITEM	QTY.
12" x 15" x 30" cabinet	1
12" x 30" x 30" cabinet	1
3/4" x 4' x 8' oak plywood	1
1x6 oak	30'

Edge band, knobs, wood glue, 2" screws, Minwax Early American stain, Minwax Wipe-On Poly

CUTTING LIST

KEY	PCS.	SIZE & DESCRIPTION
A	1	12" x 30" x 15" cabinet
B	1	12" x 30" x 30" cabinet
C	1	3/4" x 13-3/4" x 35" top*
D	1	3/4" x 13-1/8" x 33-3/4" subtop*
E	2	3/4" x 3" x 28-1/4" fillers*
F	4	1-1/2" x 45" spacers (thickness varies)
G	2	3/4" x 12" x 46" side panels*
H	4	3/4" x 1-1/2" x 9-1/4" side rails
J	2	3/4" x 1-3/4" x 49" back legs
K	2	3/4" x 1-3/4" x 3" back leg blocks
L	2	3/4" x 1" x 3" front leg blocks
M	2	3/4" x 1" x 49" front leg sides
N	2	3/4" x 1-3/4" x 49" front legs
P	1	3/4" x 1-1/2" x 30" rail backer*
Q	1	3/4" x 1-1/2" x 29-1/2" bottom rail
R	1	3/4" x 5/8" x 29 1/2" middle rail
S	1	3/4" x 7/8" x 14-3/8" stile
T	1	3/4" x 1/4" x 29-1/2" top rail

*Plywood parts

Figure B Storage cabinet

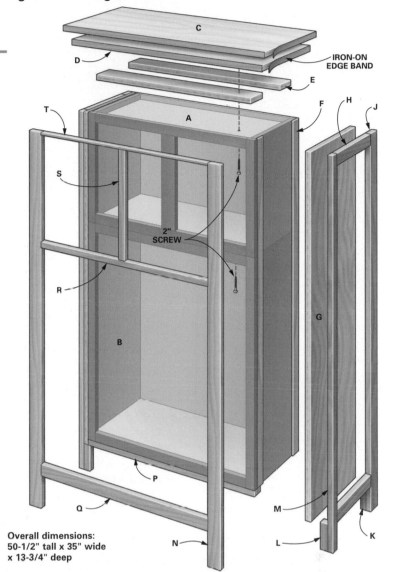

IRON-ON EDGE BAND

2" SCREW

Overall dimensions:
50-1/2" tall x 35" wide
x 13-3/4" deep

SIDE PANEL

SPACER

UPPER CABINET

LOWER CABINET

RAIL

FRONT LEG

BACK LEG

TOP

FILLER

1 **Cover the sides.** Screw two cabinets together and glue spacer strips to the sides. Then glue on the side panels. Tack the panel into place, positioning nails where they'll be hidden by the legs or rails later.

2 **Add the legs and rails.** Attach one of the front legs, then dry-fit the rails and the other leg. When they all fit right, glue and tack them in place. Follow the same dry-fit routine for the side rails and the back legs.

3 **Top it off.** Glue the two layers of the top together. To attach the top, drive screws from inside the cabinet, through the fillers and into the top.

ENTRY **BENCH**

This just might be the easiest piece of furniture I've ever built. And the handiest, too: Besides the storage space, it's the perfect perch for slipping on your shoes. The building materials cost about $90. The upholstery supplies cost $10 to $40.

I covered the sides of the cabinet the same way I skinned the sides of the TV stand cabinets (see **Photo 1**, p. 108), but used primed beadboard paneling instead of 1/4-in. plywood. The next step is to build a base (parts E, G and H) and wrap it with trim.

Your local home center may not carry the same chair rail molding I used, but it will have a similar profile. Glue fillers into the recess at the top and bottom of the cabinet. (Actually, most stock cabinets don't really have a "top" or "bottom"—just pick one.) Then screw the base to the spacers and add the bun feet (**Photo 3**).

I used 3/4-in. particleboard for the seat, though plywood or MDF would work just as well. For a better-looking upholstery job, round all the corners and edges of the seat like I did. A router and 1/4-in. round-over bit work best, but a sander will work too.

Cut the foam to size so it overhangs all four sides of the seat by about 1 in. and glue it to the seat. Spray adhesive is the standard glue for this job, but I just dribbled a few lines of wood glue onto the seat— that saved me $5—and then set the seat onto the foam.

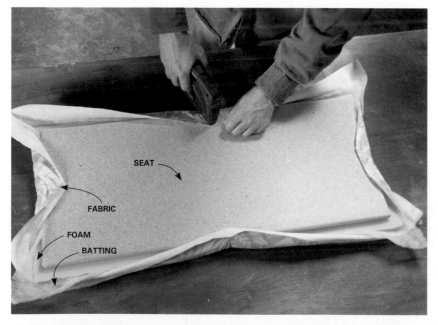

1 Upholster the seat. Lay out the fabric, batting and foam. Stretch and staple the fabric to the seat, starting at the middle of each side and working toward the corners.

Labels on image: SEAT, FABRIC, FOAM, BATTING

Cheap trick

DIY bun feet

There are lots of online sources for bun feet, but I wasn't going to spend $30 or more when I could make my own for free. I gathered up some 3/4-in.-thick wood scraps, glued two layers together and cut out circles with a hole saw. After sanding the rough edges, I screwed each foot to a scrap of wood to hold it securely and rounded both sides with a round-over bit. A 3/4-in. round-over bit will cost you just as much as factory-made bun feet would. But spending on tools is always the right thing to do, even for a cheapskate.

Labels on image: 3/4" SCRAPS GLUED TOGETHER, 4" HOLE SAW, 3/4" ROUND-OVER BIT, 1/4" DOWEL SCREW

MATERIALS LIST

ITEM	QTY.
12" x 15" x 30" cabinet	1
3/4" x 4' x 4' plywood	1
Chair rail molding	6'
3/16" beaded paneling sheet	1
Fabric, batting, 1" foam	2' x 3'
Scrap wood for bun feet, wood glue, cabinet knobs, 2" screws, dowel screws	

CUTTING LIST

KEY	QTY.	SIZE & DESCRIPTION
A	1	12" x 30" x 15" cabinet
B	1	3/4" x 13-1/2" x 31" seat
C	4	3/4" x 3" x 28-1/4" fillers
D	2	3/16" x 11-1/4" x 15" side panel
E	1	3/4" x 12-3/4" x 30" base
F	3	1-5/8" chair rail molding (cut to fit)
G	2	3/4" x 3-1/2" x 9-1/4" base side
H	1	3/4" x 3-1/2" x 30" base front

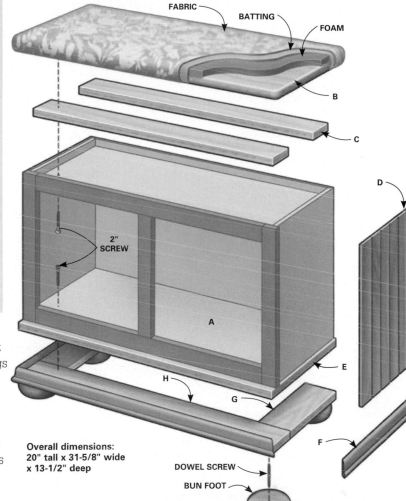

Figure C Entry bench

Overall dimensions:
20" tall x 31-5/8" wide x 13-1/2" deep

Cut the batting so it overhangs the seat by about 3 in. and the fabric so it overhangs by 4 in. Then stretch and staple the fabric (**Photo 1**). There are a few ways to deal with seat corners. **Photo 2** shows the method I find easiest. Don't worry about mistakes—the nice thing about upholstery work is that you can always pry out staples and fix mistakes. To fasten the seat to the cabinet, drive screws through the cabinet and fillers and into the seat.

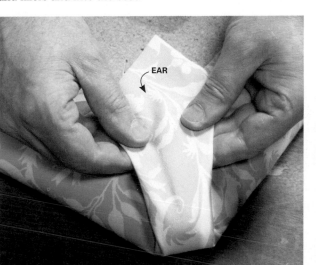

2 **Staple the corners last.** Fold the fabric inward to create an "ear." Then pull the ear back, staple it and cut off the excess fabric.

3 **Add the bun feet.** Drive dowel screws halfway into the bun feet. Drill pilot holes in the bench base 2-1/4 in. from the edges and then screw in the bun feet.

22 WAYS TO
WORK SMARTER

Here are some of our favorite tips and tools to help you get the job done easier, better and faster

by **TFH Editors**

Wire soldering made easier

"I do some minor soldering for hobbies, and I always have problems holding the wires together to solder them, even when I'm using alligator clips to hold things in place. What I've found works best is a simple washer. I clamp the wires on each side of the washer with alligator clips. The hole in the washer gives me nearly 360-degree access to the solder joint."

—Joseph Johnson

Low-wage helper

Hanging upper cabinets is a tough task for one person. Having a lifting buddy to help is usually a good idea but costs extra.

Little Hands HD is perfect for the guy who mostly works alone. The 6 x 6-in. base keeps the cabinets stable, and each lift can handle 150 lbs. The lever action can be raised a tiny fraction of an inch at a time, but sneak up on your target height because lowering the lifts isn't quite as easy.

Little Hands HD has a range of 16.5 in. to 22.8 in., so the lower cabinets need to be installed first. With this guy on site, if you can lift it, you can hang it completely solo. You can buy one for about $30 at online retailers (search "Little Hands HD").

—Mark Petersen, Contributing Editor

Choosing router bits

If your router takes both 1/4- and 1/2-in. shank sizes, go with the beefier 1/2-in. bit. It's not much more expensive, and because it's a thicker, stronger bit (more than four times the mass of a 1/4-in. bit), it will be less prone to breaking, wobbling or vibrating. A more solid bit means a cleaner cut. And the additional mass will also do a better job of dissipating heat and lessen the chance of burning a profile.

If you have a 1/4-in. router that doesn't come with an optional 1/2-in. collet (the part that receives the bit), you may be tempted to buy an adapter so it can take a bigger bit. Don't. It doesn't have the same power and torque to run 1/2-in. bits. Save your 1/4-in. router for light stuff such as profiling edges and laminate work. Buy a router designed to accept 1/2-in. bits for heavier work.

—Elisa Bernick, Associate Editor

1/4" SHANK

1/2" SHANK

Toolbox and shop vacuum in one—brilliant!

Back when I was installing replacement windows, we would drag a big, old, clumsy construction vacuum from window to window, fighting cords and losing attachments along the way. We kept our other tools and supplies in a 5-gallon bucket because it was easier to carry than most toolboxes.

Shop-Vac's Tool Mate combination toolbox and wet/dry vac would have made life a lot easier. Being able to grab all your tools and the vac in one hand is huge—less trips means more money. Any tradesmen who do small, dedicated jobs in finished homes could use one. The Tool Mate is available from various online retailers for about $100 (search "Shop-Vac Tool Mate").

—Mark Petersen, Contributing Editor

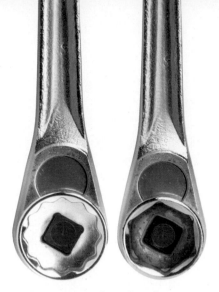

Shed some light on the subject

Seems like ads for headlamps always target spelunkers, campers and rock climbers. But I bet that for every one of those guys, there are about 1,000 of us DIYers and tradesmen who need them too.

If you're looking at headlamps, don't get one of those dim, battery-eating lightbulb ones. Look for one that sports an LED bulb, preferably with a dimmer switch because the batteries will last for dozens of hours if you're judicious with the dimmer. Try one and you'll be strapping it on every time you go into the attic, crawl space, under the car—anywhere that light is an issue.

Think about it. No more propping up flashlights, no broken trouble lightbulbs, no shadows—none of those hassles. Wherever you look, there's good light right where you need it. You'll find headlamps at any camping or sporting goods store, or search online for "LED headlamp."

—Travis Larson, Senior Editor

This Surefire Saint Minimus dimming headlamp costs $139 at amazon.com.

This Coast TT7497CP LED dimming headlamp costs $46 at amazon.com.

Socket wrench selection: 6- or 12-point?

Twelve-point sockets work great for most household repairs and projects. But for vehicle, mower or motorcycle repairs, I always use six-point sockets. They have thicker walls and apply force to the flat shoulder of the hex bolt/nut instead of the corners. So I can apply more torque without rounding off shoulder corners.

The number of points refers to the number of angles cut into the socket. Most modern fasteners have a hexagonal shape (six sides). But 12-point sockets do offer some advantages for the average homeowner. The biggest plus of a 12-point socket is that it gives you twice the number of starting positions. So you only need to rotate the socket a maximum of 30 degrees before it slips onto the fastener (as opposed to 60 degrees for a six-point socket). That's an important feature when you're working in tight spaces or hard-to-see locations—like inside an appliance.

It's not a bad idea to have 12-point tools around. But if I had to choose only one type, I'd go with the six-pointers.

—Rick Muscoplat, Contributing Editor

Simplified miter measuring

I've installed casing on a hundred windows but never figured out a good way to measure the overall length of the trim board once the first angle was cut. The problem is, there's no way to hook onto the short side of the angle, and that's usually where you have to measure from.

Somebody smarter than I finally figured it out and invented a tool called Miter Aid. After cutting the left angle, you just clamp the Miter Aid onto the cut edge. It has a slot for your tape measure that lines up perfectly with the short side of the angle—simple but ingenious. Buy one at amazon.com for $15.

—Mark Petersen, Contributing Editor

MOVE **HEAVY STUFF** THE SMART WAY

Need to move a shed? Or maybe wrestle a refrigerator down a flight of stairs? Brute strength may have served you well back in high school. But growing older means using your mind more than your muscles when it comes to moving heavy or awkward things. Otherwise, you risk wrecking your back, your house and the item you're moving.

We asked veteran movers and our Field Editors for their top moving tips. Their brains can make your next move faster and easier, even if you don't have the brawn of a high school he-man.

Rolling right along

I moved a 10 x 10-ft. shed by myself recently. I put 2x4s down and used 10-ft. sections of PVC pipe to roll the shed into position.

—Karl Schroeder

Lift plants the smart way

PotLifter plant straps let you tote up to 200 lbs. without straining. The straps are available for about $23 at online retailers such as amazon.com.

—Elisa Bernick, Associate Editor

Remove your door stop molding

Sometimes, an extra 1/2 in. is all it takes to get through a doorway. If removing the door doesn't open up enough space, pry off the door stop molding. That will give you another 3/4 in.

Take apart what you can

When you're lugging a sofa through a doorway, remember: You can always make it a few inches smaller by removing the feet. The same principle applies to any piece of furniture you need to make sleeker or lighter: Take off any and all knobs, drawers, shelves, racks and legs.

—Elisa Bernick, Associate Editor

SOFA FEET

Use chains, not your back

I love my chain hoist ($60 at harborfreight.com). It lets me load just about anything into my pickup without breaking a sweat. Here's how: I beefed up one of my garage roof trusses by screwing and gluing 3/4-in. plywood to both sides. Then I hung my chain hoist from the truss. Now I can lift any load a few feet off the floor, back my pickup in under it and lower the load into the bed.

—Gary Wentz, Senior Editor

Carry mirrors and glass with suction cups

Available in single and double versions, FastCap Handle on Demand suction cups can be attached to any nonporous surface. They're not for unfinished wood surfaces. A single pad can support 100 lbs. and the double pad twice that. They cost $8 and $11, respectively, at fastcap.com, amazon.com and other online retailers.

—Elisa Bernick, Associate Editor

Move it on ice

We were setting granite stair treads, and moving them around was tough. We poured bagged ice on the ground, set the treads on top and moved them easily into place. When the ice melted, those treads were there forever.

—Jim Haglund

Slippery pads really work

You can buy furniture slides in many shapes and sizes at home centers and online retailers. Use hard plastic sliders for carpeting, and soft, carpeted sliders for hard flooring.

—Elisa Bernick, Associate Editor

Ramp it up (and down)

Use lumber, scaffold planks and blocks to create ramps to maneuver items.

To load my wheeled generator into the back of my SUV, I built ramps using supported lengths of 2x6 and attached a come-along tool to the parking brake handle in the front seat. I was able to move the ratcheting lever with one hand and steer the generator up the ramps with the other.

—Jim Boyle

Get adjustable moving straps

Moving and lifting straps ("hump straps") make carrying heavy items easier on your back by relying on stronger muscle groups like your legs and shoulders. They also leave your hands free to maneuver awkward items like mattresses. However, they can be tricky to use on stairs because the weight shifts completely to the downhill mover.

Look for moving straps that can be adjusted for different-length objects as well as for different-sized movers. Be careful not to trip on any slack from the straps. Since these straps are rarely padded, they can leave your shoulders sore (but that's better than your back!). The Forearm Forklift, TeamStrap Shoulder Dolly and others are available for $15 to $40 at home centers and online retailers.

—Elisa Bernick, Associate Editor

Take the back off a recliner

Find the back brackets on the outside or inside of the back frame. Lift the locking levers on both sides (you may need to use long-nose pliers) and slide the back straight up to remove it from the recliner. Always lift a recliner from the sides, not by the back or footrest. Tie the footrest in place so it doesn't spring open.

—Elisa Bernick, Associate Editor

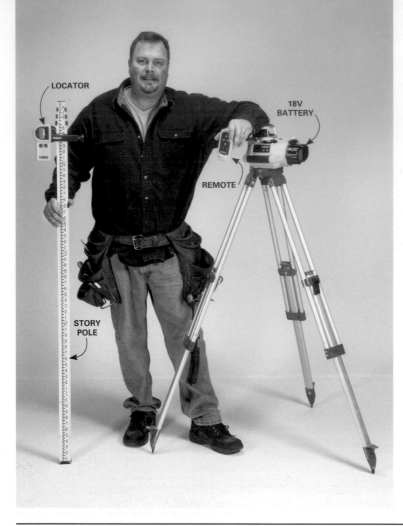

LOCATOR

18V
BATTERY

REMOTE

STORY
POLE

Mark's favorite laser level

If a long, straight line is what you're after, nothing beats a rotary laser level. As a general contractor, I've used mine for hanging cabinets, setting pole barn poles, straightening walls, setting fence posts, leveling floors, hanging suspended ceilings, installing chair rail, leveling footings, stacking block and laying out retaining walls.

I own the DeWalt DW077. It's self-leveling. I just set it up on the wall bracket or tripod and it's ready to go. It can spin 360 degrees, creating a continuous line around the room, or—get this!—it can make one dot on the wall that can be moved to wherever I want using the remote control. There is a beeping locator that can be mounted on a story pole, which works great for leveling floors. This laser can be set on its side to beam a plumb line as well. Sometimes I invent projects just to play with it!

The more accurate the level, the more it will cost you. I got the one shown about five years ago. Today, a similar device costs about $900. There are many less expensive models available. I love my laser level and can't imagine life without it.

—Mark Petersen, Contributing Editor

Dog heaven

These gel-filled mats are super easy on your feet but tough on your wallet. With prices starting at $60 for an 18 x 24-in. mat, GelPro floor mats are for those of you who spend lots of time standing in one place. But if you're one of those folks, you'll have very grateful dogs. There are dozens of size, pattern and color choices available. Go take a look at gelpro.com.

Use plastic wrap, not tape, to secure items

When you're moving things, secure appliance doors, cords, tubing and other items with plastic wrap or moving bands rather than bungee cords or tape, which can leave a residue or damage the finish.

—Elisa Bernick, Associate Editor

3-in-one nail punch

Why fumble around with three tools when one can do the job? Bostitch's 58-500 Nail Set gives you interchangeable 1/32-in. and 2/32-in. nail sets, and the shaft of the tool works as a bit holder extension—nice! You can get one at amazon.com for under $10.

—Mark Petersen, Contributing Editor

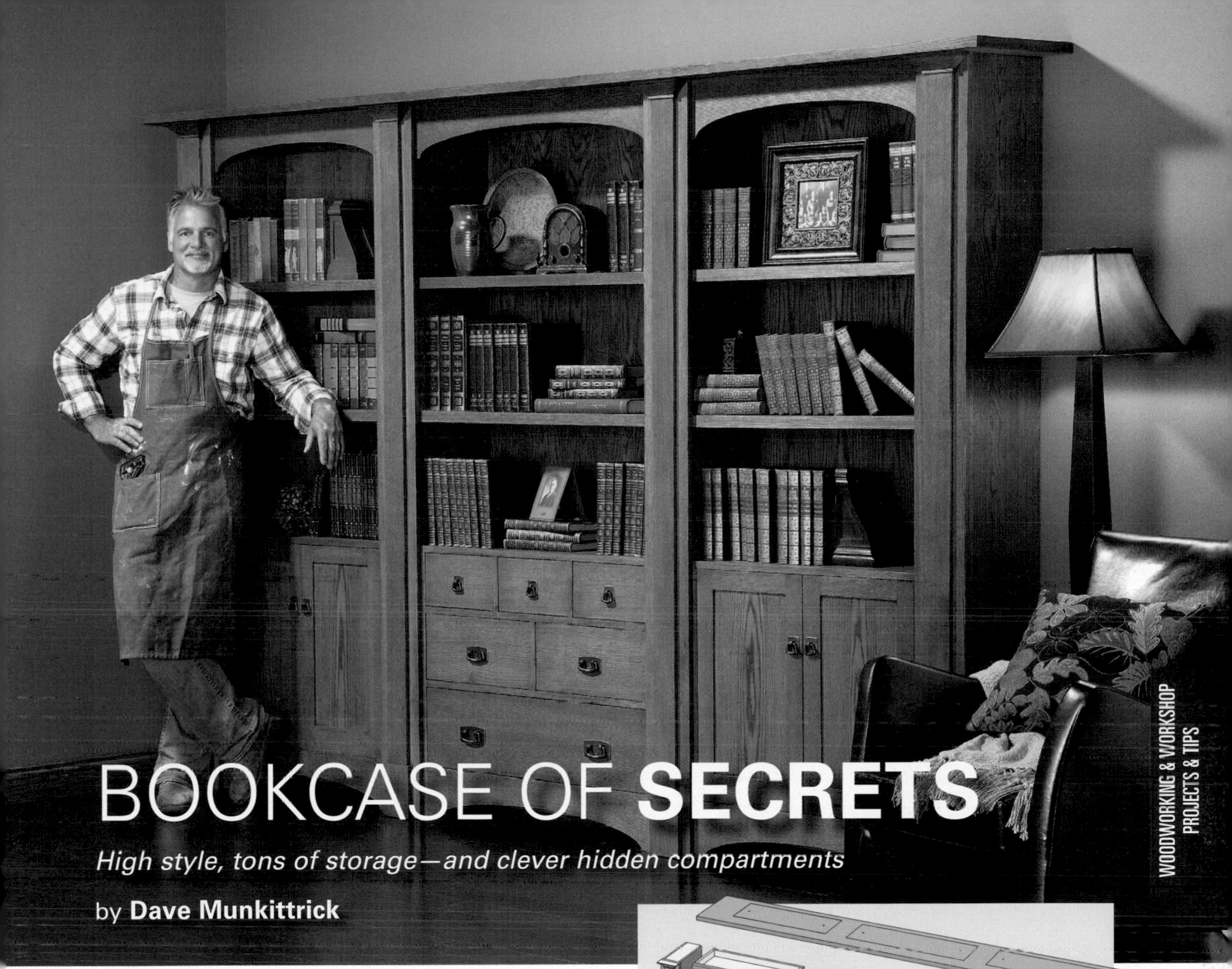

BOOKCASE OF SECRETS

High style, tons of storage—and clever hidden compartments

by **Dave Munkittrick**

C an you keep a secret? This bookcase contains more than meets the eye. Behind the magnificent Arts and Crafts styling, there are 10 hidden compartments. Some are big, some are small, but they're all easy to build, and most of them don't reduce regular storage space at all.

I splurged on the wood and built this bookcase with rift-sawn red oak for a total materials cost of $700. The straight-grain lines of rift-sawn oak give furniture an authentic Arts and Crafts look. But you could use rotary-cut plywood and plain-sawn solid oak and cut your costs by about $225. Either way, it's a bargain price for an heirloom like this— even if you don't have anything to hide.

Build 10 boxes out of plywood

Start with the column box sides (A and B). Rough-cut two sheets of plywood to 80-1/4 in. with a circular saw. Then trim them to their final length of 80 in. using a straightedge and a router fitted with a flush-trim bit. This will give you a perfect edge. Mark the dado locations on the plywood and cut them (**Photo 1**). Note: You'll have to add your own bearing to the plywood bit (see Buyer's Guide, p. 124). Repeat the procedure for the cabinet sides (C), cutting the plywood to

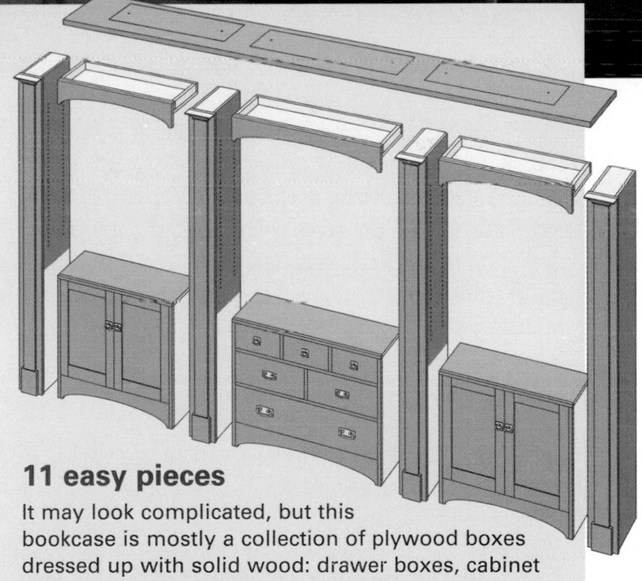

11 easy pieces

It may look complicated, but this bookcase is mostly a collection of plywood boxes dressed up with solid wood: drawer boxes, cabinet boxes...even the columns are nothing more than tall, skinny boxes with decorative faces. The bridges, too, are just shallow boxes with arched fronts. If you can build boxes, you can build this bookcase.

All of the components are separate units, so you can easily disassemble the whole bookcase in a few minutes—that's great for finishing, even better for moving the bookcase into the house.

Secret spaces

Hidden hole

Remove the bottom drawer and lift off the panel to reveal the hiding place.

Overhead hiding place

Each of the top's three lift-off panels covers a shallow box. You'll need a ladder to reach them, so they're best for long-term storage.

Column compartment

The column face is held in place by magnets. Give it a hard tug for instant access. Build just one column this way—or all four.

False-bottom drawer

Flip the drawer over, remove a few screws and slide out the bottom panel.

Drawer nook

A shortened drawer box leaves space behind the drawer. Add a removable panel to hide a concealed cubby.

Hang-up box

The cabinet false rail hides a drop-down box that's supported by magnets.

30-in. lengths first. You can get the four sides for the door cabinets from a single width of plywood. **Note:** The bottom dado on the drawer cabinet is lower than on the door cabinets in order to create the hidden compartment below the lower drawer. With the column and cabinet sides cut and machined, the next step is to lay out and drill the adjustable shelf holes.

Cut the shelf parts for the columns (S and T) and cabinets (F and G) and cut the dadoes and rabbets as shown. Hold off on the cabinet tops (D and E). You want to assemble the cabinet first to finalize the top dimensions. Dry-fit all the parts to make sure everything goes together right. I prefinished the interior parts of the door cabinets before assembly. Tape off the dadoes to keep them free of stain and varnish.

Make sure the cabinets are square before you drive any screws. The drawer cabinet is assembled from the inside out, starting with the shelves and dividers. With the cabinets assembled, you can determine the final measurements for the tops and the upper compartment bottoms (D and E). You'll likely have to adjust the sizes given in the Cutting List. Tiny differences in plywood thickness and dado depth can add up to a cabinet that's a little narrower or wider than the listed dimensions. It's essential that the tops fit perfectly flush to the cabinet sides. **Note:** The bridge bottoms (D and E) are the same size as the cabinet tops and should be cut at the same time. With the tops cut

to final sizes, lay out and cut the dadoes on the underside of the drawer cabinet top. Assemble the cabinets and columns with glue and screws (**Photo 2**). Glue and clamp the tops to the cabinets.

OK, seven boxes down; there are just three to go. Time to build the bridge boxes that do double duty as secret compartments. It's critical to build the bridge boxes so they're exactly the same width and length as the cabinet tops below. Fortunately, that's easy to do since the cabinet tops and the compartment bottoms are identical. Simply add the sides (P, Q and R) to the compartment bottoms. Double-check your work by setting the bridge boxes on top of the assembled cabinets. They should line up perfectly with the cabinet tops.

Add compartments to the cabinets

To build the secret compartment below the bottom drawer, simply cut and rout the compartment sides (HHH) and install them at the bottom of the drawer cabinet with screws. Cut the lid to the compartment (H) and drill a 1-in. finger hole. Ease the edges of the

Mighty mini magnets

Rare earth magnets are puny but powerful. So they make great, invisible fasteners for unusual projects like hidden compartments. Three of our six secret spaces rely on rare earth magnets.

hole with a 1/8-in. round-over bit.

To build the compartments behind the middle drawers: Cut the false backs (FF) and spacers (GGG). Drill a pair of holes for the rare earth magnets toward the end and on the edge of each spacer. Secure the magnets with epoxy. Install the spacers at the back of the cabinet (one reason to leave the cabinet backs off for now). Epoxy four washers on the back of the false back where the magnets make contact. Add a finger hole and you've got two more hiding places.

Cut the two false rails (EEE) that hide the drop-down boxes in the door cabinets and glue the drop-down box lip (FFF) centered on the lower edge on the back. Position the false fronts in the cabinet to act as a stop for the doors (don't forget to consider the thickness of a felt or cork bumper). Fasten with glue and screws.

Build the drop-down boxes (U, V, JJ) from scrap plywood. Embed two rare earth magnets in the top of the back edge. After the epoxy has set, grab some leftover paint and goop up the magnet faces. Set the box in place and push up on the back edge to mark the corresponding holes in the underside of the top. Drill and epoxy in the magnets under the top. Cut and fit the backs for the columns and the cabinets. Prefinish the backs of the two door cabinets before installing them.

To complete the cabinets, cut and fit the hardwood trim (DDD) for the cabinets. Use glue and a brad nailer to fasten the trim. Sand the hardwood flush and smooth.

Complete the columns

Cut the column backers (MM), columns (NN) and column bases (PP). Leave the columns (NN) a little long. Machine the crown (LL); see **Figure B**, p. 122. Assemble the crowns with glue (**Photo 3**). Machine the stock for the crown cap (QQ) and base (RR) and cut to size. You'll want to sand the individual parts to 180-grit before assembly.

Lay out all the column face parts on the column backer.

Figure A
Drawer cabinet details

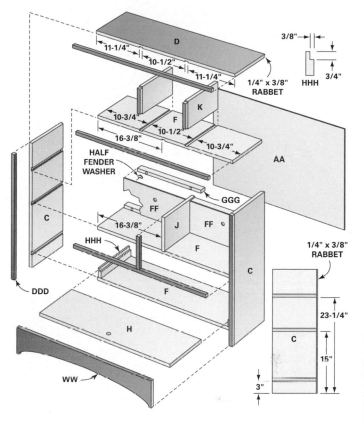

Adjust the final length of the column so all the parts fit perfectly on the backer. Screw the columns and bases to the backer through the back of the column backers. Nail and glue the crown base to the top of the column. Attach the crown with screws from behind and nail the cap in place. You should have four very nice-looking column faces that are ready to mount on the column boxes (**Photo 4**).

Now it's time to add the magnets. For maximum grip, I used pairs of magnets that stuck to each other rather than

1 **Cut four dadoes in one pass.** For the column and cabinet sides, dado the plywood first. Then rip the plywood to width. This saves setup time and guarantees that the dadoes will match up.

2 **Assemble the columns.** Screws and a little glue are fine for most of the assembly; screw heads will be covered up later. But use clamps rather than screws on the outer sides of both end columns.

Figure B Bookcase overview

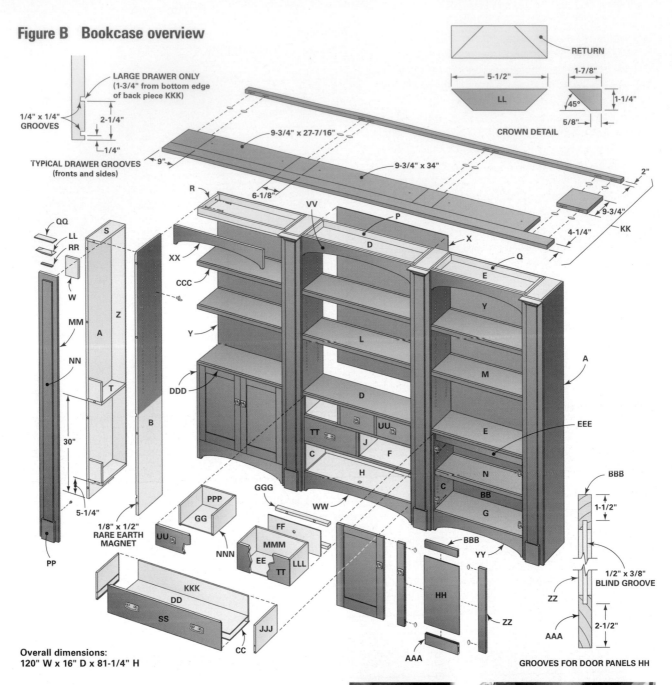

RETURN

5-1/2"
LL

1-7/8"
45°
1-1/4"
5/8"

CROWN DETAIL

LARGE DRAWER ONLY
(1-3/4" from bottom edge
of back piece KKK)

1/4" x 1/4"
GROOVES

2-1/4"

1/4"

TYPICAL DRAWER GROOVES
(fronts and sides)

9"

9-3/4" x 27-7/16"

6-1/8"

9-3/4" x 34"

2"

9-3/4"

4-1/4"

KK

R

VV

P

D

X

Q

QQ

LL

RR

S

W

MM

NN

Z

A

T

XX

CCC

Y

DDD

B

30"

5-1/4"

1/8" x 1/2"
RARE EARTH
MAGNET

PP

E

Y

L

M

D

E

N

C

BB

G

A

EEE

TT

UU

J

C

F

H

PPP

GG

UU

NNN

GGG

FF

MMM

EE

TT

LLL

WW

KKK

DD

SS

JJJ

CC

HH

BBB

YY

ZZ

AAA

BBB

1-1/2"

1/2" x 3/8"
BLIND GROOVE

ZZ

2-1/2"

AAA

GROOVES FOR DOOR PANELS HH

Overall dimensions:
120" W x 16" D x 81-1/4" H

magnets paired with metal plates. Drill a series of holes for 1/2-in. rare earth magnets in the edge of the column box. It's best to do this on a drill press with a Forstner bit so the holes are flat and perpendicular, allowing the magnets to lie perfectly flush with the surface. I spaced four magnets along each edge of the column box and one in the middle of each shelf for a total of 11 magnets. Epoxy the magnets into their holes. Use the paint trick mentioned earlier to mark the location for the magnets in the column backer. Set the column on the box and the paint will leave marks where the other magnets go. Drill magnet holes and epoxy in the magnets, taking care to orient the magnets correctly so they grab the magnets in the column boxes and don't repel them.

If you don't want a secret compartment in a column,

3 **Finger clamp the crowns.** Glue and your fingers are the best way to assemble the small parts of the column crowns. Hold them together for a few seconds, then leave them undisturbed while the glue sets. Any wood glue works, but molding glue bonds faster and won't run too much.

4 **Set the column blocks.** Clamp the column face to the box, then reach in from behind to position and nail the blocks. Add screws to lock them in place. These blocks automatically position and support the removable column face to the column box.

5 **Assemble the whole thing.** Screw through the cabinet boxes into the columns. To install each bridge, clamp it in place and then add screws.

6 **Glue up the top.** Clamp up the top using the access panels as spacers between the blocks. Old business cards work great as spacers around the access panels. Be careful not to glue the panels in place.

simply glue the columns to the column boxes. Position the columns so they overhang the edges of the boxes by 1/4 in. on the sides. Secure with a few brad nails and clamp.

When the columns are complete, join them to the cabinets (**Photo 5**), stand back and admire your work. Then get back to work and install the backs that cover the space between the columns above the cabinets.

Make perfect-fitting top panels

I went all out on the top and made it out of glued-up 1-1/4-in. solid oak (KK). First, glue up the boards to make one solid top. To create tight-fitting access panels with an uninterrupted grain pattern, start with a glued-up blank. Make the blank about an inch oversize in length and 1/2-in. extra in width. Next, rip a 2-in. strip off the back edge and a 4-1/4-in. strip off the front and set them aside. Take the middle section and crosscut the panels and blocks in sequence (see **Figure B**, p. 122). Reassemble the top using the panel cutouts as spacers (**Photo 6**).

After the glue has set, you can remove the panels and trim the edges for a clean fit. The result is a top with access panels that fit perfectly without a lot of fussy fitting. The grain pattern is uninterrupted, which helps keep the panel visibility low.

You could build up 3/4-in. and 1/2-in. plywood to make the top. It's more work, but it will save you some money. To get the 10-ft. length out of 8-ft. plywood, you need to stagger the joints between the 3/4-in. plywood

and the 1/2-in. plywood. Cut one length of each to 6 ft. and the other to 4 ft. and butt-joint them end-to-end with biscuits and glue. Glue the 1/2-in. plywood to the 3/4-in. plywood with the butt joints staggered so the 4-ft. length of 1/2-in. falls under the 6-ft. length of 3/4-in plywood. Use screws to clamp the two pieces together, taking care not to leave any screw heads exposed where the top overhangs the cabinets (use clamps in these areas). Rip and cut the access panels in the same manner as with the hardwood top, then add hardwood trim to cover the plywood edges.

Build the drawers and doors

Cut the door parts (HH, ZZ, AAA and BBB) and assemble with biscuits. Plywood works fine for the panels, although I think you get a better look with real hardwood panels. The drawers are put together with simple rabbet joints. Assemble the drawers and doors with glue and a brad nailer. I recommend reinforcing the drawer joints with a few trim head screws. The screws guarantee the joints won't pull apart, and the trim heads aren't much bigger than a finish nail hole. The Cutting List for the doors and

Making elliptical arches

An ellipse is a type of arch that curves gently in the middle and more sharply near the ends. It's a complex shape, but I have a simple trick for marking out perfect ellipses. First, you'll need 3/4 x 3/4-in. marking sticks that are half the length of each ellipse: 17-1/4 in. (for part VV), 16-1/2 in. (WW), 14-1/4 in. (XX) and 13-1/2 in. (YY). Cut a 1/2-in. notch in the end of each stick and drive a nail 3 in. from the notch. Next, cut 6-in.-wide MDF template blanks, one for each of the four different elliptical rails. It's best if the templates are a few inches longer than the rails. Mark a square line across the center of each template and clamp a guide along the mark.

To mark each ellipse, hold the marking stick edge against the guide stick edge that's clamped to your center mark. With the nail against the template, swing the marker away from the guide while the other end of the stick slides along the guide stick edge and the nail slides along the template. The result will be a perfect half ellipse. Reposition the guide stick on the other side of the center mark and repeat for the other half of the ellipse. Carefully cut the ellipse template with a jigsaw or band saw and smooth it with a file and sandpaper.

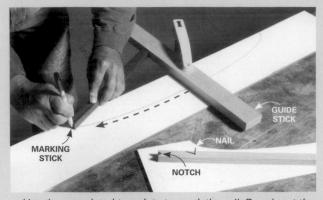

MARKING STICK — NAIL — GUIDE STICK — NOTCH

Use the completed template to mark the rail. Rough-cut the arches, then clamp the template to the rough-cut rail and run a flush-trim router bit along the template to perfect the arch.

You might be tempted to skip the templates and mark the ellipse right on the rails. But trust me, templates are the way to go. It's much easier to perfect the shape of the arch on 1/4-in. MDF than to do it with solid wood. And once the perfect template is made, you'll get perfect finished parts every time.

drawers will give you an exact fit in a perfectly executed cabinet. Measure the openings and adjust your cuts accordingly. Shoot for an exact fit; then plane the door edges for a final fit.

The bottom drawer has a false bottom that hides the last of our secret compartments. There's nothing special about the construction of this drawer other than the fixed false bottom and the extra grooves cut to house it.

The drawer bottoms are sized to stick out past the back of each drawer by 1/4 in. The protruding bottom acts as a drawer stop against the back of the cabinet. This also allows you to easily fine-tune the fit. Simply plane the plywood edge to adjust how far back the drawer sits in the cabinet.

Finish

Take the bookcase apart. Finish-sand everything to 180 grit. I used a Mission Oak stain (see the Buyer's Guide) and topcoated with a wipe-on gel varnish. No need to finish the areas that cover each other such as the outsides of the lower cabinets and the lower parts of the columns.

Enjoy your bookcase and try not to tell everyone about the secret compartments. It's our little secret.

Figure C
Door cabinet details

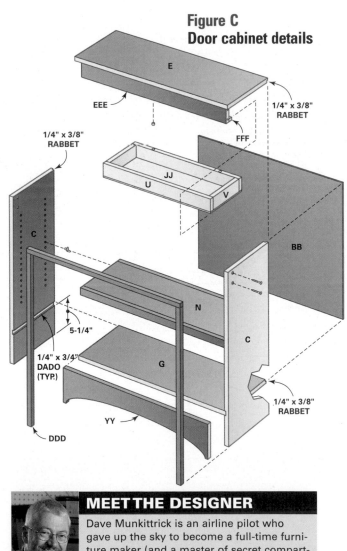

E — EEE — 1/4" x 3/8" RABBET — FFF — 1/4" x 3/8" RABBET — JJ — U — V — C — BB — N — C — 5-1/4" — 1/4" x 3/4" DADO (TYP.) — G — 1/4" x 3/8" RABBET — YY — DDD

MEET THE DESIGNER

Dave Munkittrick is an airline pilot who gave up the sky to become a full-time furniture maker (and a master of secret compartments). It's rumored that his clients include James Bond and Austin Powers.

Figure D Plywood cutting diagram

3/4" PLYWOOD

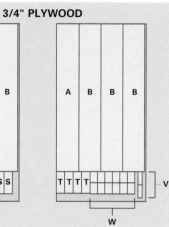
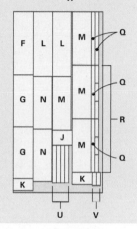
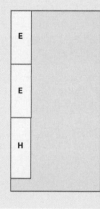
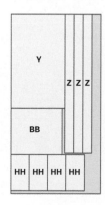

1/4" PLYWOOD

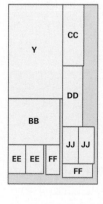

Part	Qty.	Name	Dimension	Notes
3/4" PLYWOOD				
A	2	Outside column side	12" x 80"	
B	6	Column side	11-3/4" x 80"	
C	6	Cabinet side	11" x 30"	
D	2	Drawer cabinet top and center compartment bottom	11" x 34-1/2"	
E	4	Door cabinet top and side compartment bottom	11" x 28-1/2"	
F	3	Drawer cabinet shelves	10-3/4" x 33-1/2"	
G	2	Door cabinet bottom	10-3/4" x 27-1/2"	
H	1	Drawer cabinet compartment lid	10-3/4" x 32-1/4"	
J	1	Middle drawer divider	10-3/4" x 8"	
K	2	Upper drawer divider	10-3/4" x 6-1/2"	
L	2	Adjustable shelf center	10-1/8" x 34-3/8"	
M	4	Adjustable shelf side	10-1/8" x 28-3/8"	
N	2	Adjustable shelf door cabinet	9-7/8" x 26-7/8"	
P	2	Center compartment front/back	2" x 34-1/2"	
Q	4	Side compartment front/back	2" x 28-1/2"	
R	6	Compartment side	2" x 9-1/2"	
S	8	Column top/bottom shelf	4-1/2" x 12"	
T	4	Column middle shelf	4-1/2" x 11-3/4"	
U	4	Drop-down box front/back	2-1/4" x 20"	
V	4	Drop-down box side	2-1/4" x 7"	
W	6	Column hangers	4" x 6"	3 per false compartment
1/4" PLYWOOD				
X	1	Center back	35-1/4" x 50"	
Y	2	Side back	29-1/4" x 50"	
Z	4	Column back	4-3/4" x 74"	
AA	1	Drawer cabinet back	33-3/4" x 27-3/8"	
BB	2	Door cabinet back	27-3/4" x 24-3/4"	
CC	1	Lower drawer bottom	10-1/2" x 32-1/2"	
DD	1	Fixed lower drawer bottom	10-1/4" x 32-1/2"	
EE	2	Middle drawer bottom	9 x 15-5/8"	
FF	1	False back	7-1/2" x 16-1/8"	Trim to fit
GG	3	Small drawer bottom	10 1/2" x 10"	
HH	4	Door panel	9-7/8" x 19-5/8"	
JJ	2	Drop-down box bottom	8-1/2" x 20"	
1-1/4" OAK				
KK	1	Top	16" x 120"	Top overhangs back by 1/4"
LL	1	Crown	2" x 48"	Cut to fit
3/4" OAK				
MM	4	Column backer	6" x 80"	Trim bottom for easy removal
NN	4	Column	1/2" x 3" x 72-1/4"	
PP	4	Column base	4" x 6"	
QQ	4	Crown cap	1/4" x 2" x 6"	
RR	4	Crown base	1/4" x 3/4" x 3-1/2"	
SS	1	Drawer front	9" x 33"	Trim to fit
TT	2	Drawer front	7-1/2" x 16-1/8"	Trim to fit
UU	3	Drawer front	6" x 10-1/2"	Trim to fit
VV	1	Middle rail top	6" x 34-1/2"	
WW	1	Middle rail bottom	6" x 33"	
XX	2	Side rails top	6" x 28-1/2"	
YY	2	Side rails bottom	6" x 27"	
ZZ	8	Door stile	2-1/8" x 24"	
AAA	4	Door rail	3" x 9-1/4"	
BBB	4	Door rail	2" x 9-1/4"	
CCC	1	Shelf edging	1-1/4" x 32'	Cut to fit
DDD	1	Cabinet edging	3/4" x 33'	Cut to fit
EEE	2	False rail	3" x 27"	
FFF	2	Drop-down box lip	1/2" x 3/4" x 20"	
GGG	2	False back spacer	1-1/2" x 16-1/8"	
HHH	2	Drawer cabinet compartment side	2-1/4" x 10-3/4"	
1/2" WOOD				
JJJ	2	Bottom drawer sides	9" x 11"	Trim top edge to fit
KKK	1	Bottom drawer back	8-1/2" x 32-1/2"	Trim top edge to fit
LLL	4	Drawer sides	7-1/2" x 9-1/4"	Trim top edge to fit
MMM	2	Drawer back	7" x 15-5/8"	Trim top edge to fit
NNN	6	Drawer sides	6" x 11"	Trim top edge to fit
PPP	3	Drawer back	5-1/2" x 10-1/2"	Trim top edge to fit

HandyHints

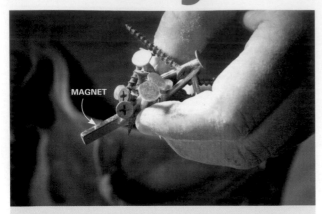

MAGNET

REPORT
COVER SLIDE

SIMPLE SAW BLADE PROTECTORS

To protect your saw blades and prevent injuries, slip plastic sliding bars for report covers over the business end of the saw. These come in a package of six for about $3 and can easily be cut to fit nearly any blade.

Stuart Osedo

TOOL BELT HARDWARE ORGANIZER

While you're working on projects, your tool belt fills up with random screws, washers, nails, and other odds and ends. And when you want to find something in your belt, you have to take your gloves off and rummage around in all that mess.

Here's a simple but helpful timesaver: Toss a magnet into your tool belt. Every small fastener will stick to it, and all you need to do is grab the magnet and pick off whatever you need. You don't even have to take off your gloves. Awesome!

—John Luebbers

DIY FLUTED DOWELS

With the nearest hardware store about 15 miles away, I've learned a few tricks to save on driving. If you need to glue a dowel and you're out of the fluted version, just make your own.

Put a smooth dowel in your vise and drag your hacksaw over it a few times to roughen up the surface. You'll create the grooves that the glue and air need to escape when you drive in the dowel.

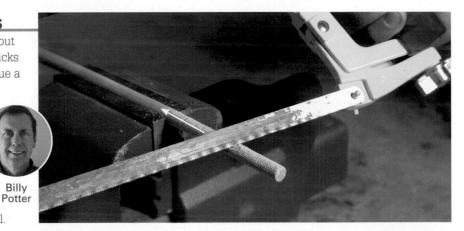

Billy Potter

TOUGHER CARDBOARD BOXES

I like to hang staple boxes on my pegboard, but the cardboard hanging hole on the box eventually rips. To prevent this, I place a layer of duct tape over the top of the box and cut out the hanging hole. The box can now hang on the pegboard and be removed many times before the staples are used up. This idea could be used for any small box with a hanging hole.

Barrett Weadick

METAL SHAVINGS COLLECTOR

A simple way to keep metal fragments and shavings from flying all over when you're drilling is to put a magnet next to the bit. This keeps metal bits off the floor, your vise and your body. When you're done, just clean off the magnet over a trash can. Don't forget to wear eye protection (doctor's orders!).

Joe Emmite, M.D.

RETRIEVING MAGNET

DOUBLE-SIDED TAPE "HANDLE"

TAPE REMOVAL TRICK

Sergo Duclos

If you've ever used double-sided tape on a woodworking project, you know how tough it is to get under the tape edge to pull it away from your project when you're done. Here's a trick I use: I make a tape "handle" by letting the tape hang over the edge of my project a little bit. When it's time to remove the tape, I just tug on the handle and it comes off easily.

COLOR-CODED WRENCHES

I use colored vinyl tape on my wrenches to identify the type. I wrap a strip of blue tape around the handle of my metric wrenches and red tape around the SAEs. I don't cover the whole handle, just a strip of tape once around at one end so I don't cover up the size marking.

Cameron LiDestri

READER PHOTO

ROOM DIVIDER

This handsome, easy-to-build divider helps hide clutter

by **David Radtke**

I was recently "encouraged" to clean up my desk before the holiday guest season began. That's not a job one man could finish in just a few weeks, so I took an easier path and built this room divider to hide the chaos. It did the trick and got me off the hook (for now anyway).

My room divider has three sections, but you can join as many sections as you like. I used white oak and chose really expensive wallpaper to cover the plywood panel, so my materials bill was about $400. You could build it for about $275 using red oak and more reasonable wallpaper. You'll also need a dado blade for your table saw. Prices for those start at about $40.

Thicker looks better

You could make a divider from standard 3/4-in.-thick boards. But I used 1-1/16-in. stock to give it extra heft and stability. This thicker wood is called "five-quarter" because it's 1-1/4 in. thick before it's planed smooth. You won't find it at home centers, but if you have a hardwood lumberyard in your area, it's sure to have it. You may have to pay extra to have it planed. To order online, check out walllumber.com or hearnehardwoods.com.

An adjustable dado blade wobbles as it spins. Turn the center cam to adjust the amount of wobble and the width of the "dado," that is, the groove. You have to remove your saw's blade guard to use a dado blade, so be extra careful.

ZERO-CLEARANCE THROAT PLATE

1 Set up the dado blade. Set the height of the blade using a 3/4-in. block of wood. Set the width of the cut by adjusting the blade, making a test cut and then readjusting. Then position the fence so the cut is centered on the board and test again.

FEATHERBOARD

STILE (A)

2 Cut grooves in the rails and stiles. Mark one side of each part and always cut with the mark facing away from the fence. That way, the grooves will match up perfectly, even if the cut is a hair off center. A featherboard holds the board tight to the fence. Outfeed support is a must.

FENCE CARRIAGE

3 **Mortise the rails.** Build a carriage that rides along the fence to hold the rails upright. You'll need to reposition the fence for this step, but don't change the blade settings.

Make all the parts

Each of the frames has two stiles (A) and two rails (B and C). These parts are held together with tenons that fit snugly into grooves, or "dadoes," cut into the rails and stiles. Before you can cut the grooves, you need to choose the panel materials so you can get the width of the grooves just right. I took a scrap of 1/4-in. plywood and covered both sides with wallpaper to make a sample block to check my groove width. The perfect groove width for my panels was just a skosh over 1/4 in.

To cut grooves, I used an adjustable dado blade in the table saw (also called a "wobble" blade; see photo, p. 128). Plan to spend about a half hour adjusting the width of the cut to get it just right. Depending on the throat plate in your saw, you may need a "zero-clearance" plate for your table saw.

Cut grooves in the edges of the rails and stiles (**Photo 2**). Then mortise the ends of the rails (**Photo 3**). If you've ever made upright cuts like this, you already know how hard—and dangerous—it is without some kind of support. To steady the rails, I made a carriage that straddles the saw fence. Don't forget to adjust the saw fence so that the end grooves will align perfectly with the others. Complete the bottom rail with an arch (**Photo 4**). Complete the stiles by gluing fillets into the grooves.

Next, make the plywood tenons that hold the frame together. Using the same carriage as before, I shaved down scraps of plywood until they fit snugly into the grooves. (You should be able to pull the tenon out with your fingers; if you can't, it's too tight.) After shaving the tenon material to the right thickness, cut it to size (see **Figure A**).

Rip the muntin material on your table saw. The muntin thickness depends on the panel material you choose. I cut my muntins from oak 1x4s and made them 7/16 in. thick so they would be flush with the rails and stiles.

Finishing and assembly

Prefinish the parts to avoid slopping stain or varnish on the

**Figure A
Room Divider**

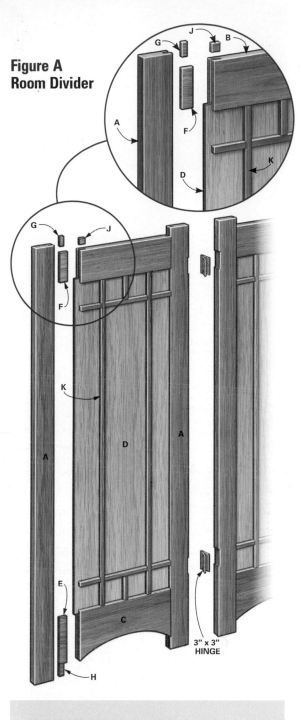

3" x 3" HINGE

MATERIALS LIST

Use the Cutting List as a guide to buying lumber. You'll also need four 3 x 3-in. butt hinges. I finished the wood with Minwax Early American stain and two coats of satin Minwax Wipe-On Poly. The "Nasturtium" pattern wallpaper costs $210 per roll at trustworth.com.

CUTTING LIST

KEY	QTY.	SIZE & DESCRIPTION
A	6	1-1/16" x 3-1/2" x 72" stiles
B	3	1-1/16" x 5-1/2" x 18" top rails
C	3	1-1/16" x 8-1/2" x 18" bottom rails
D	3	1/4" x 19-3/8" x 56" plywood panels
E	6	1/4" x 1-1/2" x 5-1/2" tenons
F	6	1/4" x 1-1/2" x 3-1/2" tenons
G	6	1/4" x 3/4" x 1-3/4" fillets
H	6	1/4" x 3/4" x 2-1/4" fillets
J	8	1/4" x 3/4" x 3/4" fillets
K	6	7/16" x 3/4" x 14' muntin bars (trim to fit)

4 Mark the arch. Drill a pencil hole near one end of a stick and nail the other end to a wood scrap. Draw an arch across the lower rail, cut, and then sand the arch smooth.

5 Wallpaper the panels. Cut the plywood panels to size and prime both sides. When you paste on the wallpaper, let it overhang the panel and trim off the excess.

6 Put it all together. Glue both rails to one stile, then insert the panel. Work the panel into the dadoes carefully to prevent wallpaper "roll back." Finally, add the other stile, make sure the whole assembly is square and clamp it together.

7 Add the muntins. Glue decorative muntins to the panel. For longer muntins, you may need a weight to hold them down until the glue sets. Don't distort the panel with too much weight.

panels. Be careful to keep finish out of the grooves, it will weaken the glue bond.

Here's the assembly process I followed: Glue the tenons to one stile (A) and then apply glue to the rails, tap these pieces together and carefully insert the panel. Next glue the tenons to the opposite ends of the rails, then align the remaining stile. Carefully persuade the panel into the groove and then draw the joints together with clamps. While the glue is setting, cut the muntin strips and glue them to the face of the panel (Photo 7).

Mark the hinge locations and chisel the mortises to the depth of the hinge plate thickness. Pay attention to the direction of the hinges; they're opposite from the left section to the right section. Once the hinges are screwed in place, apply felt strips to the bottoms of the rails and you're ready to set up your room divider.

The golden rule of glue-up

Before you grab the glue bottle, test-assemble the whole project. You don't want to discover mistakes or misfits after glue is applied.

MEET THE DESIGNER

David Radtke is a designer, cabinetmaker, woodworker and writer. A former Senior Editor for The Family Handyman, David splits his time between his table saw and his computer.

Panel possibilities

Each section of the divider is simply a wood frame that encloses a panel. Dave covered his panel with wallpaper, but there are lots of other options:

Wood on wood. The simplest panel option is 1/4-in. plywood, finished to match the frame. You could also choose a contrasting wood finish

Fabric. Cover the panel with fabric to match upholstery or curtains. Lightly coat 1/8-in. hardboard with spray adhesive (3M Super 77 is one brand) and then carefully lay the fabric over it.

Window film. Apply decorative window film to clear acrylic panels. You'll find both at home centers. For a larger film selection, go to lighteffects.com or decorativefilm.com.

SUPER SIMPLE BOOKCASE

A veteran woodworker and a beginner team up to re-create a classic

by **Dave Munkittrick**

This is the perfect first-time furniture project—simple, useful and satisfying.

My neighbor, CT, asked me to help him build a bookcase he found in an old Stickley furniture catalog. I love Craftsman furniture and CT is a great neighbor. How could I refuse? We sat down to do a little research and figure out the details. CT wanted a slightly larger bookcase, so we stretched the width from 22 in. to 36.

I told CT we could build it in his garage with nothing more than a table saw, a drill and a pocket hole jig. If you don't own a pocket hole jig, you owe it to yourself to buy one. Pocket screws aren't as strong as most other types of joinery, but they are plenty strong for this bookcase, and you can't beat their speed and simplicity. CT agreed, especially when he found out that for $40 he could buy a complete pocket hole system. For tips on using pocket screws, go to familyhandyman.com and search for "pocket screws." You'll also need at least four pipe clamps for this project, which will cost about $60 altogether.

Wood selection matters

At the home center, we took our time picking through the oak boards. We wanted straight, flat

Build it yourself and save $151,900! This bookcase is inspired by a Gustav Stickley model that sold for $12 in 1910. One of the original Stickley models recently sold for $152,000, but you can build ours for about $100.

What it takes

Time: 12 hours. This is a great weekend project. Our building time was about eight hours, plus a few hours more for final sanding and finishing.

Cost: $100. That includes wood, glue, screws and finishes. We used oak boards and plywood. If you choose another species, such as cherry or maple, expect to spend at least $40 more.

Skill level: Beginning woodworker. This is a great project for anyone who's done some woodworking and is ready to tackle their first real furniture project.

1 Add edging to the sides. Cut the plywood box parts to size, then glue strips of wood to the bottom edges of the box sides. This edging keeps the plywood veneer from chipping. Trim off the excess edging with a handsaw and sand it flush with the plywood. Take care not to sand through the thin veneer.

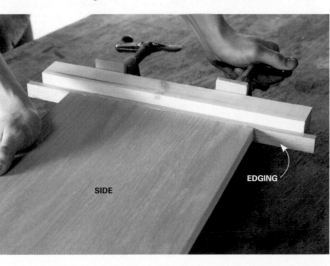

SIDE

EDGING

boards, of course, but we also looked closely at grain pattern. Novice woodworkers usually skip this tedious process, but they shouldn't. It has a big impact on the final look of the project. For the legs, we examined the end grain and chose boards with grain that ran diagonally across the ends (see Photo 4). This "rift sawn" wood has straight grain on both the face and the edge of the board.

("Plain sawn" boards typically have wilder grain on the face.) Straight grain will give the legs a look that suits the Stickley style. Also, glue joints disappear in straight grain wood, so the legs—which are made from sandwiched boards—look better. For that same reason, we chose boards with straight grain along the edges to form the bookcase top (see Photo 11).

2 Drill pocket holes. Pocket hole jigs are super easy to use: Place the jig where you want the holes; clamp and drill. The stepped bit bores a pocket hole and a pilot hole at the same time. The holes on the ends are for attaching the top to the sides. The holes along the front and back are used to attach the box to the face frame.

3 Assemble the box. Drive in the pocket screws with a drill. To avoid stripping the screws in plywood and softwoods, switch to a screwdriver for the final tightening. Long clamps make assembly easier, but they aren't absolutely necessary.

4 Glue up the leg blanks. Sandwich two 1x4s together and later cut the legs from this stock. Use scrap wood "cauls" to distribute clamping pressure evenly.

5 Mark the arches. Make an "arch bow"—simply a 3/16-in.-thick strip of wood with slots cut into both ends. Hook a knotted string in one slot, tighten the string to bend the bow and tie off the other end.

Build a box and add face frames

After cutting the plywood box parts to size (see the Cutting List), we added the 3/8-in.-thick edging (J) to protect the bottom of the cabinet sides (A; **Photo 1**). We applied the same edging (H) to the plywood shelves (C). Then we drilled the pocket holes in the box top and bottom (B; **Photo 2**). After that, we drilled holes for adjustable shelf supports in the plywood sides and—finally—we assembled the box (**Photo 3**).

With the box assembled, we turned our attention to building two identical face frames. (Since the bookcase has no back, it needed two face frames.) Unlike a standard face frame, which has vertical stiles, our face frame has legs (E) made from two layers of 3/4-in.-thick boards. We glued up the leg blanks (**Photo 4**), ripped both blanks into two legs and sanded out the saw marks.

Like many other beginning woodworkers, CT figured that curves were complicated, so he was a little intimidated by the arched upper rails (F). But I showed him a neat trick for marking out a shallow arch (**Photo 5**). His curved cut (**Photo 6**) wasn't perfect, but a little sanding smoothed it out (**Photo 7**).

With the rails and legs complete, we were ready to drill pocket holes in the rails and assemble the face frames (**Photo 8**). It's easy to make mistakes during face frame assembly, so—before driving any screws—we clamped the frames together, then set them on the box to make sure everything was aligned correctly. We used similar caution when we finally attached the face frames to the box: We dry-fitted the face frames (**Photo 9**) before we glued and clamped them into place (**Photo 10**).

Top it off and finish up

CT figured that making the top (D) was a simple matter of edge-gluing two boards together (**Photo 11**). That's mostly true, but there are a few tricks that make it easier. First, always do a complete dry run by clamping up the boards without glue. That will alert you to any clamping or alignment problems before it's too late. Second, start with boards that are an inch or so longer than the final top. It's

Figure A   Bookcase

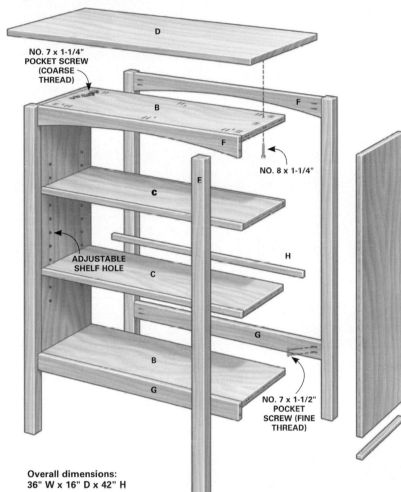

NO. 7 x 1-1/4"
POCKET SCREW
(COARSE
THREAD)

D

B

F

F

NO. 8 x 1-1/4"

E

C

H

ADJUSTABLE
SHELF HOLE

C

G

B

G

NO. 7 x 1-1/2"
POCKET
SCREW (FINE
THREAD)

Overall dimensions:
36" W x 16" D x 42" H

MATERIALS LIST

ITEM	QTY.
3/4" oak plywood	4' x 8'
1x4 solid oak	24'
1x10 solid oak	6'
Wood glue, pocket screws, stain, polyurethane, adjustable shelf supports	

CUTTING LIST

MATERIAL	KEY	QTY.	DIMENSION	NOTES
3/4" Oak Plywood	A	2	10-1/2" x 32"	Sides
	B	2	10-1/2" x 29-3/4"	Top and bottom
	C	2	9-1/2" x 29-5/8"	Adjustable shelves
3/4" Oak	D	1	16" x 36"	Top
	E	4	1-1/2" x 1-1/2" x 41-1/4"	Legs (double up 3/4" stock)
	F	2	2-1/2" x 29"	Arched rails
	G	2	2" x 29"	Bottom rails
	H	4	1/2" x 29-5/8"	Edging for adjustable shelves
	J	2	3/8" x 10-1/2"	Bottom edge sides

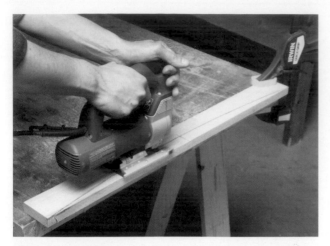

6 Cut the arches. For a smooth cut, use a fine-tooth blade and move slowly, putting only light forward pressure on the saw. If your saw is variable speed, cut at full speed. If the saw has orbital action, switch it off.

7 Sand the arches. Smooth the arches with an orbital sander. Keep the sander moving so you don't sand too deep in one spot and create a wave in the curve.

8 Assemble the face frame. Clamp the face frame together and drive in pocket screws. Pocket screws rarely strip out in hardwood, so you can skip the screwdriver and use only a drill.

FACE FRAME

9 Dry-fit the face frames. Align the face frames, pocket-screw them to the box and check the fit. If your alignment is a bit off, you can drill new pocket holes and reattach the frames. If the fit is right, you're ready to remove the face frames and add glue.

10 Glue on the face frames. Apply a light bead of glue over the box edges and screw on the face frames as before. There are no screws fastening the legs to the box sides, so you'll need to clamp them.

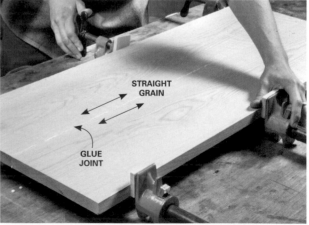

STRAIGHT GRAIN

GLUE JOINT

11 Glue up the top. Edge-glue the boards together to form the top. Choose boards that have straight grain lines along one edge and place those edges together. A glue joint with straight grain on both sides is almost invisible.

12 **Drill slotted screw holes.** Drill screw holes in the shelf box to fasten the bookcase top. Rock the bit back and forth to bore elongated slots that will allow the top to swell with changes in humidity.

13 **Screw on the top from below.** Drive the screws snug, but not so tight that they won't allow for seasonal wood movement. Remove the top for sanding and finishing.

much easier to trim the boards later than to fuss with edge alignment during glue-up. Finally, to ensure that the tops of the boards meet flat and flush, use pocket screws on the underside of the top. A couple of pocket screws won't provide enough pressure to substitute for clamps, but they will hold the board flush while you crank on the clamps.

When the top was trimmed to size and sanded, CT drilled elongated holes (**Photo 12**) and screwed on the top (**Photo 13**). When I asked him to remove the top, he gave me a look that said, "What's the point of that?" I had two answers: Finishing is always easier when furniture is disassembled, and more important, both sides of the top

need to be finished. Wood absorbs and releases moisture as humidity changes. Wood finishes slow that process. So wood with a finish on only one side will end up with differing moisture levels in the finished and unfinished sides. That leads to warping.

So we finished both sides of the top (and the rest of the bookcase) with a coat of General Finishes Mission stain ($14 a pint at rockler.com) followed by polyurethane. That's it. Not bad for a weekend of woodworking. I wonder how much CT's bookcase will be worth in a hundred years....

GreatGoofs

Wood vibrations

I love my Craftsman portable planer. I feed rough, ugly boards in and beautiful boards come out. But until recently, I had never clamped it to my worktable. I'd just reposition it as it vibrated around the table. My technique changed recently when I fed in a 6-ft. board and turned around to grab the next board. While my back was turned, the exiting board caught the planer's power cord. As the board exited the planer, the cord stayed taut and the planer pushed itself to the edge of the table. I turned around just in time to watch the planer tip over the edge, fall to the floor and keep right on planing while upside down. I still love my planer, but now it gets clamped!

—Ken Scharpenberg

BEST
TAPE MEASURES

Advice from guys who use their tape measures all day, every day

by **Gary Wentz, Senior Editor**

Our all-around favorite: Stanley FatMax

We love this tape for its combination of great "stand-out" and sheer toughness. It's easy to read, feels good in the hand and isn't quite as bulky as some of the other wide, pro-grade tapes. The FatMax line includes lengths from 16 to 100 ft., which cost from $18 to $30.

Ryan Haskins, Field Editor

"FatMax tapes are the best I've ever used. I'm a framer and I get about six months of use out of a FatMax. I destroy other tapes in a matter of weeks."

The Family Handyman
EDITORS' CHOICE

Field Editors love it, too

When asked about their favorites, our Field Editors named Stanley's FatMax more than all the other tapes combined.

Mini tape

If you like to carry a tape at all times, this is the one for you. It's just over 1/2 in. thick. And unlike most tiny tapes, it's not a cheap gimmick that will soon fall apart. The underside of the blade has a diameter scale like the one on p. 138. To get one, search online for "Stanley 33-115" ($5).

The best tape for any kind of job

Shop work

For woodworking and tinkering in the shop, there's rarely any reason to go bigger than a 16-ft. tape. It's small and light, and it slips comfortably into a pocket or shop apron. Get one for less than $10.

Big projects

A tape in the 16- to 30-ft. range is best for remodeling jobs. Most of us like the upscale versions with wider blades, better standout and a bigger hook (about $25).

Long-distance measuring

An "open reel" tape is perfect for long measurements. There's no spring or enclosure, so it won't get choked with dirt or sand. Unlike metal blades, the fiberglass tape won't kink or break when you step on it. And the big crank winds in the tape fast. A 100-ft. model costs less than $20.

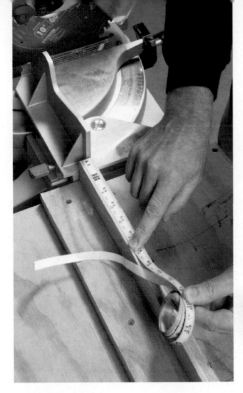

Sticky tape

Bet there's a place in your shop for a peel-and-stick tape measure. Just remember that there are two kinds: left-to-right and right-to-left (like the one shown here). Search online for "adhesive backed tape measure" to find various lengths ($7 and up).

Big hooks are better

They grab better and catch on all four sides of the hook. But they can also catch where you don't want them to, like on your tool belt. And they're clumsy for measuring into corners. Still, the benefits outweigh the hassles, and big hooks are better for most types of work.

A built-in pickup tool

Tiny, powerful "rare earth" magnets turn your tape hook into a handy grabber, a nice feature at no extra cost. But it's not for those who like to carry their tape in a nail pouch. Every time you grab your tape, a cluster of nails comes along with it. You'll find magnetic hooks on Husky, Kobalt, Lufkin and other brands.

WOODWORKING & WORKSHOP PROJECTS & TIPS

"Stand-out" counts

The greater the "stand-out"—the distance a tape can extend without crumpling—the greater the measuring reach. But even for shorter measurements, a long-reach tape is easier to use. Because the blade is stiffer, you can handle it faster and with less care than you could a flimsy tape.

Most pro-grade tapes list the stand-out on the packaging. We found most of those claims to be accurate and sometimes even understated. Manufacturers make the blade a lot stiffer by making it just a bit wider. Most blades in the 16-ft. or over category are 1 in. wide. Stiffer blades are 1/16 in. to 1/4 in. wider than that.

Some tapes make you squint

Some tapes are marked in 1/16-in. increments, some in 1/32-in. increments, and some have a combination of both. For most jobs, 16ths are precise enough—and a lot easier to read.

Tape wreckers

Nothing wrecks a tape measure faster than working in dirt and sand. The innards get jammed up and the blade won't slide in or out. So reserve a shabby old measuring tape for down-in-the-dirt jobs.

Fat tapes need a fat holster

I bought my first wide-blade, long-reach tape a few years ago and fell in love instantly. But it didn't fit into my old tape holder, and I couldn't find a bigger holster at home centers. So I hunted online and ordered one supposedly designed for fat tapes. My tape did fit, but I almost needed a hammer to drive it in and pliers to yank it out. Finally, I found this holder, which comfortably handles every 25-ft. fat tape I know of except the Husky and Kobalt models. Search online for "clc 464" to find several sources ($7).

—Gary Wentz, Senior Editor

Remove the belt clip

Lots of pros immediately unscrew the clip when they get a new tape. A clipless tape slips smoothly in and out of your tool belt.

The hook is supposed to be sloppy

We've heard that some folks hammer the hook rivets to tighten them. Bad idea. The hook needs to slide in just a little when you push it against something for an inside measurement and slide out when you hook onto something. That movement compensates for the thickness of the hook itself. It's smart design, not a manufacturing defect. This extra-thick magnetic hook has enlongated slots to allow for extra movement.

Diameter tape

Wrap it around anything round and instead of the circumference, you get the diameter. Even Pythagoras couldn't do it that fast. Search online for "diameter tape measure" ($10 and up).

Center-finding tape

Just measure the overall length with the upper scale, then go to that same measurement on the lower scale to find the halfway point. No need to divide fractions! Search online for "self centering tape measure" to find lots of models ($10 and up).

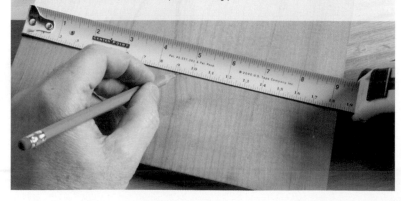

Mysterious marks

You already know that the highlighted numbers (16, 32, 48...) are for laying out studs, joists or rafters every 16 in. But what's the deal with those little diamonds or triangles? They're "truss marks" for 19.2-in. layouts (which save on framing materials). Never heard of that? Don't worry. Lots of carpenters haven't either.

REFINISH FURNITURE
WITHOUT STRIPPING

Less time, less effort, less mess, better results

by **Jeff Gorton, Associate Editor**

Stripping furniture is a messy, time-consuming process. And sometimes the results aren't as great as you had hoped. Fortunately, you don't always have to resort to stripping to restore your furniture to its original luster.

To show you an easier alternative, we enlisted Kevin Southwick, a furniture restoration specialist. We'll show you Kevin's tips for cleaning, repairing and restoring finishes without all the messy chemical strippers and tedious sanding. You'll save tons of time. And since you'll preserve the patina and character of the original finish, your furniture will retain the beauty of an antique.

One word of caution, though: If you think your piece of furniture is a valuable antique, consult an expert before you do anything.

MEET AN EXPERT

Kevin Southwick specializes in the conservation and restoration of antiques and in custom wood finishes. He also consults in these areas. Kevin's expertise is the result of more than 20 years' experience working with and learning about wood finishes and furniture repair and refinishing.

Assess the finish with mineral spirits

Before you start any repairs or touch-up, wipe on mineral spirits to help you decide what your next steps should be. The mineral spirits temporarily saturates the finish to reveal how the piece of furniture will look with nothing more than a coat of wipe-on clear finish. Don't worry; this won't harm the finish. If it looks good, all you have to do is clean the surface and apply an oil-based wipe-on finish. If the surface looks bad even when wetted with mineral spirits, you'll have to take other measures to restore the finish. We show some of those in the following steps.

Clean it up

A thorough cleaning is an important first step in any furniture renewal project. Removing decades of dirt and grime often restores much of the original luster. Kevin says it's hard to believe, but it's perfectly OK to wash furniture with soap and water.

Kevin recommends liquid Ivory dish soap mixed with water. Mix in the same proportion you would to wash dishes. Dip a sponge into the solution, wring it out, and use it to gently scrub the surface. A paintbrush works great for cleaning carvings and moldings. When you're done scrubbing with the soapy water, rinse the surface with a wrung-out sponge and clear water. Then dry it with a clean towel.

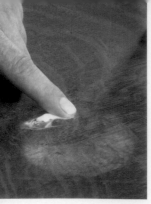

Fix white rings

White rings can be easy to get rid of, or they can be a real nightmare. First, slather the ring with petroleum jelly and let it sit overnight. The oil from the petroleum jelly will often penetrate the finish and remove the ring or at least make it less visible.

If that doesn't work, you can try a product such as Homax White Ring Remover ($5 at Amazon) or Liberon Ring Remover (about $22 at Rockler, Woodcraft or Amazon). They often work but may change the sheen. If these fixes don't work, consult a pro to see what your other options are.

Scrape paint without damaging the finish

Paint spatters are common on old furniture, and most of the time you can remove them easily without damaging the finish. Here's a trick we learned from Kevin to turn an ordinary straightedge razor into a delicate paint scraper. First, wrap a layer of masking tape around each end of the blade, and then bend the blade slightly so it's curved.

The masking tape holds the blade slightly off the surface so you can knock off paint spatters without the blade even touching the wood. Hold the blade perpendicular to the surface. The tape also keeps you from accidentally gouging the wood with the sharp corner of the blade. The curved blade allows you to adjust the depth of the scraper. If you tilt the blade a little, the curved center section will come closer to the surface to allow for removing really thin layers of paint.

Replace missing wood with epoxy

If you discover missing veneer, chipped wood or a damaged molding, you can fix it easily with epoxy putty. Kevin showed us the process he uses, and the resulting repair is so realistic that it's hard to spot. When it's hardened, the epoxy is light colored and about the density of wood. You can shape, sand and stain it like wood  too, so it blends right in. Quickwood and KwikWood are two brands of this Tootsie Roll–shaped epoxy. You'll find it at home centers and specialty woodworking stores for about $9 a tube.

To use this type of epoxy, you slice off a piece with a razor blade or utility knife and knead it in your gloved hand. When the two parts are completely blended to a consistent color and the epoxy putty starts to get sticky, it's ready to use. You'll have about five or 10 minutes to apply the epoxy to the repair before it starts to harden. That's why you should only slice off as much as you can use quickly.

Photo 1 shows how to replace missing veneer. Here are a few things you can do before the putty starts to harden to reduce the amount of sanding and shaping later. First, smooth and shape the epoxy with your finger (Photo 2). Wet your finger with water first to prevent the epoxy from sticking. Then use the edge of a straightedge razor to scrape the surface almost level with the surrounding veneer. If you're repairing wood with an open grain, like oak, add grain details by making little slices with a razor while the epoxy is soft (Photo 3).

After the epoxy hardens completely, which usually takes a few hours, you can sand and stain the repair. Kevin sticks self-adhesive sandpaper to tongue depressors or craft sticks to make precision sanding blocks (Photo 4). You can also use spray adhesive or even plain wood glue to attach the sandpaper.

Blend the repair into the surrounding veneer by painting on gel stain to match the color and pattern of the existing grain. You could use stain touch-up markers, but Kevin prefers gel stain because it's thick enough to act like paint, and can be wiped off with a rag dampened in mineral spirits if you goof up or want to start over.

Choose two colors of stain that match the light and dark areas of the wood. Put a dab of both on a scrap of wood and create a range of colors by blending a bit of the two. Now you can use an artist's brush to create the grain (Photo 5). If the sheen of the patch doesn't match the rest of the wood when the stain dries, you can recoat the entire surface with wipe-on finish to even it out.

1 Fill in the damage with epoxy. When the epoxy putty is thoroughly mixed, press it into the area to be repaired.

2 Smooth the putty. Use your wetted finger to smooth the putty. Press the putty until it's level with the surrounding veneer.

Restore the color with gel stain

It's amazing what a coat of gel stain can do to restore a piece of furniture—and you don't need to strip the old finish. Kevin used gel stain on this round oak table, which had a worn and faded finish. He loaded a soft cloth with stain and worked it into the surface, then wiped if off with a clean cloth. It was a surprising transformation. Gel stain won't eliminate dark water stains or cover bad defects, but it will hide fine scratches and color in areas where the finish has worn away.

There are other products, but Kevin prefers gel stain because he finds it easier to control the color and leave a thicker coat if needed. Also, since it doesn't soak in as readily as thinner stains, gel stain is somewhat reversible. Before it dries, you can remove it with mineral spirits if you don't like the results. Gel stains offer some protection, but for a more durable finish or a more even sheen, let the stain dry overnight and then apply a coat of wipe-on finish as shown below right.

Fill small cracks

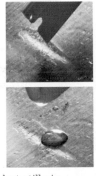

If you find nail holes or tiny cracks after applying the final finish, fill them with colored wax fill sticks, wax repair sticks or fill pencils, found at home centers and paint stores.

The directions tell you to rub the stick over the defect. But Kevin recommends breaking off a chunk and warming it in your hands. Shape it to fit the flaw and press it in with a smooth tool. He uses a 3/8-in. dowel with an angle on the end. For cracks, make a thin wafer, slide it into the crack and then work the wax in both directions to fill. Buff with a soft cloth.

3 Add wood grain. On open-grain wood like this oak, use a razor blade to add grain marks.

4 Sand the epoxy. Sand carefully to avoid removing the surrounding finish. Make a detail sander by gluing sandpaper to a thin strip of wood.

5 Stain the epoxy to match. Stain the dry patch with gel stain to match the color and pattern of the grain. Match the stain color to the light and dark areas of the wood.

Get rid of dents

You can often get rid of *small* dents by wetting them to make the crushed wood fibers swell back to their original shape. Moisture must penetrate the wood for this to work; finishes prevent this, so Kevin makes many tiny slits with a razor blade to allow the water to penetrate. Use the corner of the blade, keeping it parallel to the grain direction. Fill the dent with water and let it dry. If the dent is less deep but still visible, repeat the process. As with most repairs shown here, the repaired surface may need a coat of wipe-on finish.

Renew the luster with wipe-on finish

The final step is to wipe on a coat of finish. After you clean your furniture piece and do any repairs and stain touch-up, wiping on a coat of finish will restore the sheen and protect the surface. Any wipe-on finish works—Minwax Wipe-on Poly is a common brand (about $12 a pint). But Kevin prefers a wipe-on gel finish like General Finishes Gel Topcoat Wipe On Urethane (about $14 a pint). It's thick, so it's easy to put on with a rag. One coat is usually all you need to rejuvenate an existing finish. To find a retail store near you that sells General Finishes Gel Topcoat, use the store locator at generalfinishes.com.

To apply wipe-on finish, put some on a clean rag and apply it in a swirling motion like you would with car wax. Then wipe off excess finish, going in the direction of the grain. Let the finish dry overnight and you'll be ready to proudly display your furniture restoration project.

5 GREAT SAWHORSES

No matter how you work, you'll find something here to fit your style

by **Mark Petersen, Contributing Editor**

It's tough to imagine a DIYer without a trusty pair of sawhorses. We all have our favorites, whether they're store-bought or homemade. No one design is ideal for every job. That's why we're showcasing five different sawhorses: three from our editors here at *The Family Handyman* and two from our Field Editors.

THE DIY FOLD-UP

LIGHTWEIGHT CLASSIC

ADJUSTABLE LEGS

SUPER-STRONG, EASY TO BUILD

COMPACT WORKHORSE

A QUICK-AND-DIRTY SAWHORSE THAT'S **ROCK-SOLID**

Framing carpenters usually build these horses when they show up at a job site. They leave them behind for the other subcontractors to use, then build new ones at their next job. It's not unusual for the new homeowner to inherit a pair and hold on to them for years.

You'll need two 12-ft. 2x4s and one 10-ft. 2x4. Using 16d nails or 3-in. screws, assemble the three boards that make up the I-beam. Attach the legs, using a framing square to square the legs to the beam. Attach the rails last. You're done, so get to work.

36"

34"

22"

33"

21"

ALL BOARDS ARE 2x4S

Mark's favorite

"I've probably built 50 of these. It's a simple design, strong and super easy to build."

—Mark Petersen, Contributing Editor

Features: Inexpensive, easy to build, super strong
Cost: $12 each
Time: 10 to 15 minutes each (using a pneumatic nail gun)
Skill level: Beginner

Features: Inexpensive, elegant, light, stackable, strong
Cost: $12 each
Time: One hour each
Skill Level: Intermediate

A TRUE CLASSIC THAT WILL LAST A LIFETIME—OR MORE

Set your circular saw to cut at a 13-degree bevel, and cut the legs to length at a 13-degree angle. Mark each piece as you cut it.

Set each sawhorse upright and set something heavy on it so all the legs are sitting nice and flat. Attach the gussets with four 1-5/8-in. screws.

Here's a design that's been around for a hundred years—maybe longer. It's low, so you can use your knee to hold down your work. The compound miters make this one a little trickier to build than the others, but if you take one component at a time and label them as you go, in a couple of hours you'll have a pair of sawhorses that your *own* grandkids will be proud to replicate someday.

We simplified this one a little bit. On the version Ken made, the legs are mortised into the edge of a non-tapered top board. To make this horse, you need one 8-ft. 2x6 and two 8-ft. 1x6s.

■ **Top:** Cut the top to length first, then taper the edges on a table or circular saw. All the angles on this horse are 13 degrees. (If you're the superstitious sort, cut your angles at 12.99 degrees.)
■ **Legs:** It helps to cut the legs close to their actual size beforehand so you can hold them up and visualize the direction of the cut and the orientation of the bevel. After cutting the legs to size, reset your circular saw to 90 degrees and taper the legs. Mark the taper line 3-1/2 in. over on the bottom of the leg up to the bottom of the gusset. Lay the top board upside down on a flat surface and attach each leg with three 2-in. screws.
■ **Gussets:** Trim the top and bottom edges of the gusset boards with parallel 13-degree angles. Mark one gusset using the sawhorse and copy the other three from that template.

Ken's favorite

"I still have the first pair of these horses that I built 30 years ago. I copied the design from the ones my grand-father built 30 years before that."

—Ken Collier, Editor in Chief

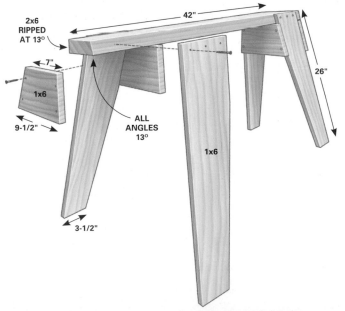

2x6 RIPPED AT 13°
42"
7"
1x6
26"
9-1/2"
ALL ANGLES 13°
1x6
3-1/2"

Features: Foldable, includes a shelf, fun to build
Cost: $40 each
Time: One hour each
Skill Level: Beginner to intermediate

Cut two blocks of wood to temporarily hold the shelf in place while you fasten the hinged side of the shelf to the legs.

Jeb's favorite

"The foldable shelf adds stability, and it's a great place to store tools and fasteners up off the ground while doing a project. I had a blast building these!"

—Jeb, Field Editor

A FOLDING HORSE WITH A **BUILT-IN SHELF**

Some horses have a shelf and some fold up, but Jeb's design combines both features. And he's right—these horses *are* fun to build. To make a pair, you'll need a 4 x 4-ft. sheet of 3/4-in. plywood, one 8-ft. 2x6, one 8-ft. 2x4, two 12-ft. 2x4s and eight hinges.

■ **Legs:** After cutting the top 2x6 to length, cut both sides of each leg at a 15-degree angle. Make sure the angles are parallel. Fasten hinges to the ends of two of the legs, then attach those legs by fastening the hinges to the top piece. Attach the other two legs with 3-in. screws.

■ **Shelf:** Cut the 2x4 that supports one side of the shelf. Mark a line 8 in. up from the bottom of the leg, line up the bottom of the 2x4 with that line, and attach it with two 3-in. screws on each side. Cut the shelf to size and notch the two corners using a jigsaw. Fasten the hinges to the shelf, then use two 11-1/8-in. blocks of wood to temporarily hold the shelf in place while you fasten the hinged side of the shelf to the legs. Cut a 23-3/4-in. x 1-1/2-in. strip of plywood to overlap the 2x4 shelf brace. Attach it with wood glue and 1-1/4-in. screws. You may have to trim it a bit before fastening.

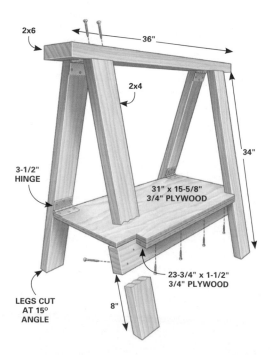

2x6
36"
2x4
34"
3-1/2" HINGE
31" x 15-5/8" 3/4" PLYWOOD
23-3/4" x 1-1/2" 3/4" PLYWOOD
LEGS CUT AT 15° ANGLE
8"

Features: Inexpensive, foldable, strong
Cost: As low as $14 each, plus the cost of the top board

SPACE-SAVING
SAWHORSES

These metal foldable horses can be hung on a wall or stacked in a corner. And if you have to drag horses from one job to another, these are the ones for you. But be careful not to pinch a finger folding them up.

Travis is particularly fond of the EBCO brand—he claims to own a dozen of them.

If you want to avoid scratching the floors, get the protective feet EBCO makes for its horses. A set of four costs $7 at ebcoproducts.com.

Travis's favorite
"I don't know why anyone would buy or build another kind of sawhorse. These are strong and cheap, and they hardly take up any room when they're folded up. Screw a 2x6 on the top and you're good to go."

—Travis Larson, Senior Editor

HORSES **LOADED**
WITH FEATURES

We asked our Field Editors to pick their favorite horse, and the most popular by far was the FatMax. The top has notches, making it a great place to hold sacrificial 2x4s when you're cutting up plywood and other sheet goods. Each leg is adjustable, which is pretty handy when you're working on uneven ground. They have a built-in shelf and fold up relatively flat, making them perfect for storing on the wall.

Features: Foldable, includes a shelf, adjustable legs
Cost: The model shown can be found online starting at about $50

Steve's favorite
"Hard to believe any homemade horse could compete with the FatMax. They're light, foldable, height-adjustable and have notches for holding two-by cross braces. I can't imagine not having them."

—Steve Yaeger, Field Editor

FOLD-UP WORKBENCH

Extra work surface when you need it; extra parking space when you don't

by **Mark Petersen, Contributing Editor**

What it takes

Time: One day, not including the paint and varnish

Cost: $135, including the hardware but not the finish

Skill level: Beginner to intermediate

Tools: Circular saw, drill and jigsaw

The last time I stopped in at my sister's house, my brother-in-law was on the garage floor putting together a tricycle for his grandson. They had recently moved into a new house, and apparently his last workbench hadn't made the trip. I decided to build him a new one.

Space was a major consideration. I wanted to build a bench big enough to be useful, but there was only a few feet between the garage wall and the front of their parked cars. Money was also a concern—I didn't want to spend a lot of it. He is, after all, my brother-in-law. Finally, I wanted something easy and fun to build. I came up with an inexpensive design with a top that will work fine for smaller jobs. It has an additional top that folds up for those larger projects...like assembling a tricycle.

Build the top and bottom

Cut the 3/4-in. plywood parts to size following the cutting diagrams (p. 149). Cut a 15-in. x 8-ft. strip out of the 1/4-in. plywood to use as drawer bottoms. The leftover is the perfect width for the back (E); it just needs to be ripped down to length. Don't cut the drawer fronts until after the workbench carcass is assembled.

Cut the 2x4s that make up the top and bottom frames (F and G). Assemble them with two 3-in. screws into each end. The studs I used were made from Douglas fir, which is strong but brittle, so to prevent splitting, I predrilled the screw holes with a 1/8-in. bit. Fasten the plywood top and bottom (A and C) to the frames with 1-5/8-in. screws. I countersunk the screws on the top so I could fill them with wood filler. I used wood glue in addition to screws throughout this project.

Attach the sides

Lay the top upside down and attach the sides (B) with six 1-5/8-in. screws. Flip the sides and top upside down and set it on the flattest surface available, then attach the bottom with 1-5/8-in. screws as well. Try to position the wood with the fewest flaws toward the front (Photo 1).

Fasten the shelf and drawer divider

Cut a couple of scrap 2x4s to the same height as your drawer divider (D). Use the divider on one side and the 2x4 scraps on the other as guides to achieve the proper height for your shelf (C). Predrill 1/8-in. holes through the plywood into the shelf before installing the four 1-5/8-in. screws (see Photo 2). Use a framing square to mark the location of the drawer divider. Predrill holes through the plywood and into the divider before securing it in place with four 1-5/8-in. screws on both the top and bottom.

Attach the back

Use a framing square to make sure everything is all squared up before you fasten the back (E). If you don't have a framing square, you can measure diagonally from top to bottom both ways. If the numbers aren't the same, tweak it one way or the other until they are. Don't glue the back on—you'll want to be able to remove it when it's

time to paint and stain. Predrill the holes, then fasten the back with 1-1/4-in. trim screws.

Build your drawers

Make your drawer guides (K) out of 1x6s. Rip them down to 7/8 in. and align them all so the drawers will rest on the larger side. Rip down a sacrificial chunk of plywood to 5-7/8 in. to use as a spacer to achieve the proper height for the drawer guides (Photo 3). Screw the guides on with 1-1/4-in. trim screws. Don't forget the glue; screws alone won't be sufficient to hold a drawer full of heavy tools.

There is enough plywood left over on this project to build all the drawer frames, but 1x6s happen to be the perfect size. So for an extra $15, you don't have to rip down a bunch more plywood. Build the drawer boxes so there is at least a 1/8-in. gap on each side of the drawer. Use 1-5/8-in. screws to assemble the frames and 1-1/4-in. screws to attach the bottom.

Install the folding top

Flip the bench upside down, and butt the folding top (A) tight up against the permanent one. To ensure that the

1 **Assemble the main components**. Lay the top upside down and attach the sides with six 1-5/8-in. screws. Then flip the whole thing over and attach the bottom. Position all the wood so the best sides are facing the outside and top.

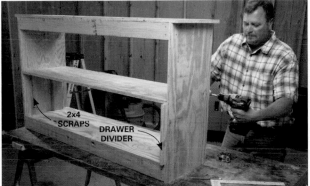

2 **Add a shelf**. Temporarily support the shelf using the drawer divider and a couple of 2x4 scraps. To avoid splitting the plywood shelf, predrill holes through the sides and into the shelf before fastening with screws.

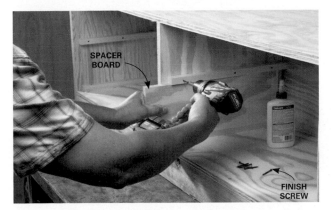

3 **Install the drawer guides**. Install the bottom drawer guides first, and then cut a scrap of plywood to act as a spacer for the upper guides. Fasten the guides with glue and trim-head screws.

4 **Position drawer fronts perfectly**. With the drawer box in place, position the front with shims. Fasten the pulls with 1-1/4-in. screws. Those screws will hold the front in place so you can pull the drawer out and add more screws from inside.

Figure A Simple workbench

Overall Dimensions:
60-1/2" wide x 34-3/4" high x 32" deep (or 16" deep, folded)

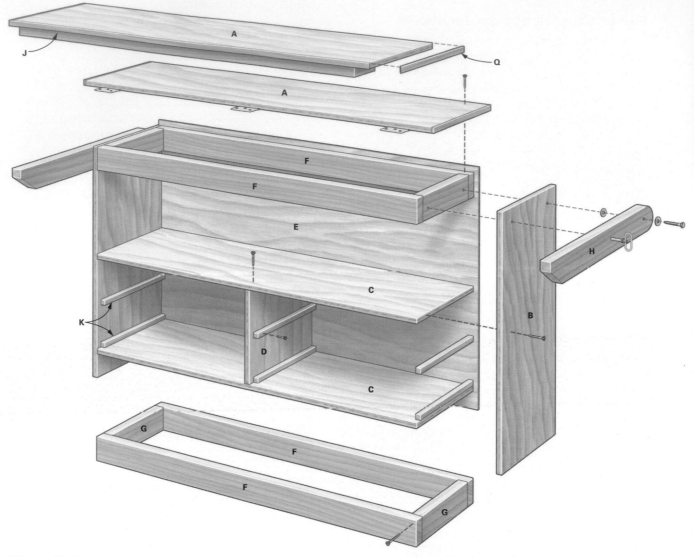

Figure B Drawer construction

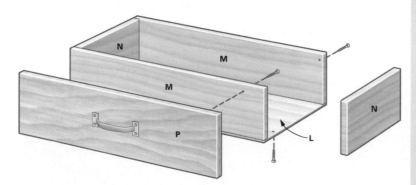

MATERIALS LIST

ITEM	QTY.
4' x 8' x 3/4" BC plywood	2
4' x 8' x 1/4" BC plywood	1
2x4 x 8' studs	5
1x6 x 8' No. 2 pine	4
1/4" x 3/4" x 8' pine screen mold	2
3-1/2" door hinges	3
3" self-drilling exterior grade wood screws	1 lb.
1-5/8" self-drilling exterior grade wood screws	1 lb.
1-1/4" trim screws	1 lb.
3/8" x 4-1/2" lag screws	2
3/8" fender washers	4
1/2" hitch pins	2
Drawer pulls	4
Bottle of wood glue	1
Primer	1 qt.
Enamel paint	1 qt.
Polyurethane	1 qt.

FOLDING TOP

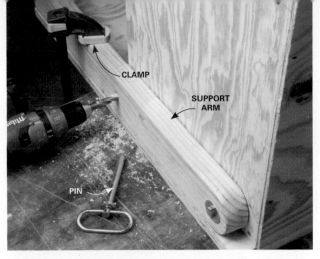

CLAMP

SUPPORT ARM

PIN

5 **Install the folding top.** Flip the bench upside down and push the folding top tightly up to it. Use 3/4-in. screws to connect the hinge to the bench top so they don't poke all the way through.

6 **Drill the pin hole.** Make sure the folding top is clamped securely to the support arm before you drill a hole for the hitch pin. When drilling a hole this big, it's easier to start with a pilot hole about half the size.

screws start straight, mark the hinge screw locations with a pencil, and use a nail set to create a starter hole. Use 3/4-in. screws to fasten the hinges to the folding top—the ones that come with the hinges will likely poke through.

Cut and assemble the support arms

After cutting the support arms (H) to length, use a compass to mark a half-circle on one end of the arms, and then trim them with a jigsaw. Cut a 45-degree angle on the other side. With the bench still upside down and the support arm clamped down about 1 in. in from the back of the bench, predrill a 1/4-in. hole for the lag/pivot screw. Start the hole at the center of the circle you made at the end of the arm. Drill through the arm and into the bench.

Next, install the lag screws with a washer on both sides of each arm. Check to see that they swing back and forth freely. You may have to trim a little off if they rub on the bench top. When you drill holes for the hitch pins, make sure you avoid the 3-in. screws that hold the top frame together (Photo 6).

Fasten the brace board and screen mold

Glue, clamp and screw on the benchtop brace board (J). The brace board should be at least 1/4 in. shorter than the opening of the area above the shelf. If you countersink 3/8-in. holes in the bottom of the brace, 1-5/8-in. screws will work from the bottom up. Screen molding (Q) helps protect the exposed plywood edges of the bench tops. Install the molding with the folding top up. Leave a small gap between the two tops so the molding doesn't bind when the top is folded down. Use glue and brad nails, or use a trim gun if you have one.

Finishing

To finish the carcass, I used a primer formulated for raw wood, and enamel paint for durability. Paint the bottom to prevent moisture from wicking up into the raw wood. I used satin polyurethane for the tops and drawer fronts, and also on areas the drawers come in contact with (painted parts tend to stick together). If the drawers start to bind, try a coating of shellac on the drawers and guides.

Cutting Diagrams
1/4" plywood diagram not shown

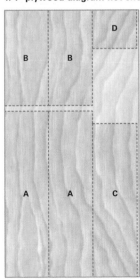

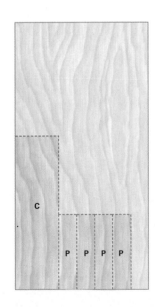

CUTTING LIST

KEY	QTY.	SIZE & DESCRIPTION
A	2	60" x 15-3/4" bench tops
B	2	34" x 15-3/4" sides
C	2	55-1/2" x 15-3/4" bottom and shelf
D	1	13-1/4" x 15-3/4" drawer divider
E	1	57" x 32-7/8" x 1/4" back
F	4	55-1/2" x 1-1/2" x 3-1/2" front/back of frames
G	4	12-3/4" x 1-1/2" x 3-1/2" frame sides
H	2	30-1/2" x 1-1/2" x 3-1/2" support arms
J	1	55-1/4" x 1-1/2" x 3-1/2" benchtop brace
K	8	15" x 3/4"x 7/8" drawer guides
L	4	15" x 27-1/4" x 1/4" drawer bottoms
M	8	27-1/4" x 3/4" x 5-1/2" drawer front/back
N	8	13-1/2" x 3/4" x 5-1/2" drawer sides
P	4	27-1/4" x 6-1/2" plywood drawer fronts
Q		Screen mold/plywood edging cut to fit

Using Tools

MAGNETIC DRIVERS FOR TIGHT PLACES

I fix my own appliances, and most of them are held together with hex-head sheet metal screws. I've tried using a socket set, but usually the space was so limited that I couldn't turn the ratchet. Even if I could get the screw out, I had to stick chewing gum into the socket to hold the screw so I could reinstall it. That's why I gave up on sockets and switched to these magnetic nut drivers (available for less than $5 each in the tool department at home centers). I just slap them into my battery-powered screwdriver and zip the screws in and out. For hard-to-reach areas, I add a quick-change locking extension (Irwin No. 4935704; $9 at amazon.com).

—Rick Muscoplat, Contributing Editor

CUSTOM CORD WRAPS

I make my own cord wraps using old bungee cords and synthetic wine corks. I drill two holes in the cork, thread cord through the holes and tie off the ends. You can make them as long or as short as you want. They're very light-weight and work great for securing air hoses and other things too.

Chris Conway

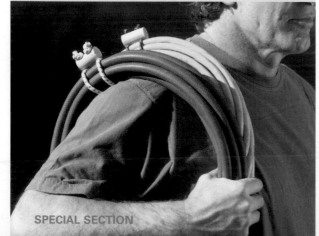

PORTABLE TOOL BATTERY SMARTS

Lithium ion (Li-ion) batteries are expensive. So get with the program and follow these care tips to get the longest life and best performance out of them.

- Li-ion batteries can handle only 800 to 1,000 charges. Don't recharge a battery if you've used it for just a few minutes.
- Don't leave them in the car—either in the cabin or the trunk. Heat (above 140 degrees F) and sub-zero cold can reduce battery life by 15 percent.
- Storing a battery in direct sunlight can really heat it up, so shield it from the sun.
- Don't store a discharged battery that has less than one-half charge. Give it a full charge before storing it.
- If your tool was sold with two batteries and you're a part-time user, stick the extra one in the refrigerator. It'll last for years and you'll have a new one to use when the first one dies.

BEST OIL FOR AN AIR COMPRESSOR

If you're tempted to use motor oil in your air compressor, don't; even if you use high-quality oil, it's the wrong stuff. Motor oil manufacturers add a detergent additive to clean up the contamination caused by the combustion process. Since there's no combustion going on inside your air compressor, you don't need detergent. And you don't want it.

Here's why. Home air compressors rely on "splash lubrication" to throw the oil onto all the internal parts. But all that splashing causes detergent to generate foam (think dishwashing detergent). Foam doesn't cool or lubricate very well, so metal parts can overheat and fail prematurely.

Finally, motor oil has the wrong properties. You want oil that's thicker and clings to piston rings and valves. Air compressors depend on that heavier film to improve sealing power and develop maximum pumping capacity. For all those reasons, you should dump the motor oil and refill with the non-detergent compressor oil recommended by your compressor manufacturer.

FIX YOUR BALKY AIR COMPRESSOR

If your compressor starts up fine on the first start of the day, but stalls and makes a loud humming sound on subsequent tries, you've got a bum "unloader" valve. The unloader valve is what makes the "psssssst" sound when the motor shuts off after reaching operating pressure. It's actually venting the residual pressure from the compressor head so the motor doesn't have to work as hard on the next startup.

The unloader valve is usually built into the pressure switch assembly. Contact the compressor manufacturer to buy a new assembly. Or, remove the cover from the switch (unplug the compressor first) and locate the pressure switch part number. Then do an Internet search for that part. I found a complete four-port pressure switch assembly replacement for this compressor for $20 (at amazon.com). Here's how to replace it.

Start by unplugging the compressor. Then open the drain valve at the bottom of the tank to depressurize it. Next, remove the 1/4-in. line going to the unloader valve (**Photo 1**). Then use a slip-joint pliers or small pipe wrench to remove the quick-connect fitting, pressure regulator and gauge from the pressure switch.

Disconnect the wires from the pressure switch (**Photo 2**). Then remove the old switch. Coat the pipe threads with pipe dope and install the new switch (**Photo 3**). Finally, apply pipe dope to all the plumbing parts and reassemble.

1 **Disconnect the unloader valve.** Slap two open-end wrenches on the compression fitting and loosen the nut on the air line. Pull it out of the fitting.

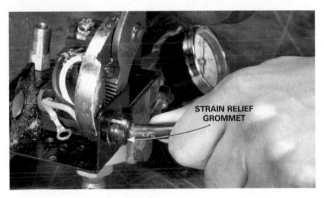

2 **Remove the wiring.** Disconnect the hot, neutral and ground wires from the old switch. Then squeeze the strain relief grommet with pliers and remove the cord.

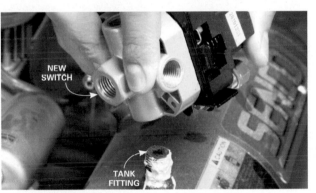

3 **Install the new switch.** Spin on the new switch. Tighten the switch with a wrench and hold the stub pipe from the tank with a pliers.

JEFF TALKS UTILITY KNIVES

Over the years, I've tried dozens of "new and improved" utility knife designs, but I keep coming back to this classic Stanley knife (model 10-399). There are two things I want in a utility knife: easy, quick blade changing and a super-secure blade. And this knife is perfect on both counts. Plus, it's got a nice curved shape that allows you to cut shingles without scraping your knuckles. Granted, you can't retract the blade. But I don't care. As far as I'm concerned, this knife is perfect, and it's definitely my favorite. The only downside: It's a little hard to find. If your local hardware store doesn't have one, you can order it online for less than $8 at amazon.com.

—Jeff Gorton, Associate Editor

UsingTools
7-PLUS WAYS TO USE A **RIP HAMMER**

Hammers aren't just for nails anymore

by **Travis Larson, Senior Editor**

Most carpenters will tell you a hammer is for driving nails. But watch them work and you'll see that they hardly ever whack nails. Air nailers—fast, lightweight, reliable and cheap—have changed all that. But that doesn't mean carpenters don't sling hammers around anymore. They're still indispensable for an incredible number of tasks, including driving the occasional nail.

The vast majority of carpenters prefer hammers with a straight "rip" claw over "claw" hammers, which have curved claws. That's because they use the ripping end nearly as much as the pounding end. At least I do. Here are just a few of my hammer feats over the years, most of them accomplished with the rip end of my trusty framing hammer.

Lumber splitter

Need a 2x2 when all you have are 2x4s? Or need to clean out a crude dado? Or hack off a projecting piece of framing for the drywall to fit flat? Grab your rip hammer and whale away.

OFF THE WALL

BACK SCRATCHER
Don't try this with your nail gun!!

Measuring stick

Most of my electrician buddies don't like tape measures, so I guess that's why they use their hammers to position outlet boxes. A hammer's length from the floor to the bottom of the box is about right. It's not so important how high the boxes are, just that they're all the same height.

Weapon of mass destruction

Anytime there's demo work on my plate, I grab my flat bar, recip saw, sledgehammer and, of course, my rip hammer. I use the claw to pull off corner beads, drive through plywood, pry studs apart—just about anything that needs destruction. If I had to, I could demo a whole house with a ripping hammer. (Or at least I could in my 20s.)

Caulking gun for airheads

Can't tell you how many times I've forgotten a caulking gun and needed a little dab or two to seal up a hole. That's when I shove the handle down the tube and force out some caulk with my "hammer gun."

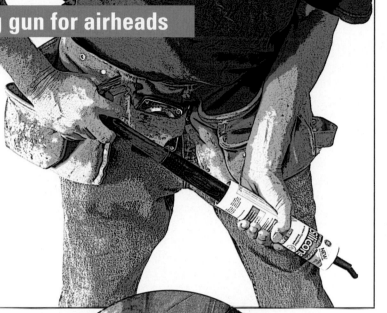

LIFESAVER
Say you find yourself sliding down the sheathing of a new roof. On your way to the precipice, you have the presence of mind to pull out your hammer and slam the claw through the plywood to arrest your fall. Sound far-fetched? Well, I have two friends who have pulled off this stunt. Of course, if they had any brains, they wouldn't have been in that slippery situation in the first place.

Blade straightener

About every third time I use a recip saw, the blade gets jammed and bent. So I grab my hammer and straighten it out with the claw. You could also lay the blade flat on a 2x4 and beat it.

So who in the heck uses a claw hammer?

Everything a claw hammer can do, a rip hammer can do better. And there are many things you couldn't do with a claw hammer—like most of these tips! So what good are they? Claw fans argue that they excel at pulling nails. So what? I pull nails all the time with my ripper. If I need more leverage or working room, I slip a chunk of wood under the hammerhead. But usually that's not even necessary.

I do actually own a claw hammer. Maybe I'll sharpen the claw and use it for a fish gaff.

Hole digger

Sometimes I think I've spent half my life on extension ladders. In spite of that, I've never taken a fall. That's because I've always made sure the ladder feet were anchored in little pockets dug into the ground, especially in the winter. Didn't matter if the ground was frozen or not; the rip claw on my hammer would dig through anything. It also works great for prying rocks out of the hole when you're digging.

Icebreaker

I live in Minnesnowta. And with our infamous winters come ice dams, sometimes *monster* ice dams. I'm an old hand at dealing with them, and I always use my rip claw for the job. I've broken up ice dams that were the size of bathtubs. It's just the right tool to chunk up the bergs without wrecking the roof.

UsingTools

REBUILD YOUR RATCHET

Got a ratchet that's jammed, rusted or won't switch directions? Don't toss it, rebuild it. In most cases, you can slap yours back into shape with just a good cleaning and new grease. But if you've broken a spring or a pawl, you'll need to buy a rebuilding kit. A rebuild kit for most major brands costs about $10. To find one for yours, enter the ratchet brand and model number in a search engine, or try ebay.com.

Before you buy a kit, disassemble the ratchet to assess its condition. Use a combination snap-ring pliers (one brand is Tekton No. 3578; about $7 from amazon.com) to remove the internal or external snap ring from the ratchet head (**Photo 1**). Or use a small flat-blade screwdriver to remove a spiral snap ring (**Photo 2**). If your ratchet doesn't use snap rings, it'll come apart with either a hex wrench or a screwdriver.

Throw a towel over the ratchet (to capture flying springs) and slide the entire ratchet assembly out of the head. Clean the parts with brake cleaner and an old toothbrush. Remove any rust with a rust removal chemical. If the spring ends are intact and the pawl teeth are sharp, you can reuse them. If not, buy a rebuild kit. Then apply a light coating of wheel bearing grease to all the parts. Don't use engine oil; it'll just drip out. And don't pack the head with grease—that'll prevent the pawl from reversing. Then reassemble (**Photo 3**).

RATCHET REBUILDING KIT

RATCHET LUBE CHICAGO, IL 60632

FORWARD/ REVERSE SPRING

RATCHET PAWL

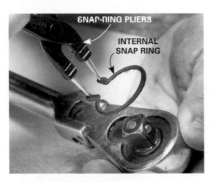

SNAP-RING PLIERS

INTERNAL SNAP RING

1 Remove an internal/external snap ring. Jam the prongs of the snap ring pliers into the holes on the snap ring. Then compress the internal snap ring and lift it out of the retaining slot. Change the pliers over to external mode to expand an external snap ring.

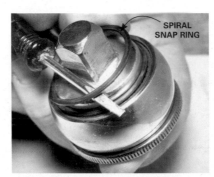

SPIRAL SNAP RING

2 Remove a spiral snap ring. Locate the clipped end of the spiral snap ring and twist it out and up with a small flat-blade screwdriver. Then "unwind" the snap ring in a counterclockwise direction. Reverse the procedure to reinstall.

3 Grease and reassemble. Compress the pawl assembly with your fingers and slide the entire ratchet into the head. Rotate it in both directions to check the pawl's operation and spread the grease. Then reinstall the snap ring or screws and double-check the operation.

THE RIGHT OIL FOR A BENCH GRINDER

If you're nursing an old bench grinder and need to oil it, pick up oil that's especially for electric motors. One brand is 3-In-One electric motor oil ($3 at home centers).

Just don't use automotive motor oil! It's too "thin" for electric motors. Plus, it contains detergent. If the excess oil seeps onto the motor windings, it might dissolve the insulation and fry the motor.

3-IN-ONE

SPECIAL BLEND FOR 1/4 HP MOTORS OR LARGER

MOTOR OIL

SAE 20

LOOK MA, NO BRUSHES

Many new drills and impact drivers have motors powered by microprocessors instead of the carbon brush blocks that drag against the motor armatures. Brushless motors will most likely grow in popularity, and for good reason. A brushless tool creates less friction, allowing it to run cooler, which results in more power and as much as a 50 percent longer run-time. Oh, yeah, it's also quieter and lasts longer. What's not to love? You will pay about a 15 percent premium for brushless technology, but the benefits make that an easy pill to swallow.

5 Exterior Repairs & Improvements

IN THIS CHAPTER

HomeCare&Repair

TIPS, FIXES & GEAR FOR A TROUBLE-FREE HOME

FOUR FIXES FOR A NOISY GARAGE DOOR

When a garage door makes noise, it's usually just screaming for a bit of TLC. We'll show you some fixes to quiet down any garage door. And, if you have a tuck-under or attached garage, we'll show you how to reduce the vibrations and noise that transfer to the living space.

Test the noise level by opening the door after each fix and quit when things are quiet enough for you.

Before you get started, go to Home Depot and pick up a Prime Flo garage door lubrication kit for $7. You'll get all the lubricants you need for this job. Also pick up rollers if you need them for Fix #4.

Fix #1
Isolate the opener

If you have an attached or tuck-under garage and your opener seems loud inside the house, try this step.

Mechanically isolate the opener from the garage rafters/trusses with rubber pads. Cut rubber pads out of an old tire, or buy specially made rubber/cork anti-vibration pads. (Four 5-1/2- x 5-1/2- x 3/8-in. pads are $13 at amazon.com; search for "anti vibration pads." You'll need two packages, for a total of eight pads.) You'll be adding about an inch in thickness, so you'll need four longer lag screws and four fender washers.

Add anti-vibration pads. Slide one anti-vibration pad between the mounting bracket and the ceiling, and the second pad under the bracket. Then slip a fender washer onto the new lag screw and drive it into the rafter with a socket wrench or impact driver. Repeat on all four corners of the opener bracket.

156   EXTERIOR REPAIRS & IMPROVEMENTS

Fix #2
Tighten the chain and lube the opener

A loose garage door opener chain makes loud slapping sounds and causes jerky door movements that smack the rollers against the track. So start by tightening the chain (find the procedure in your owner's manual).

If you have a track drive opener, the next step is to lubricate the opener track with grease. If you have a screw drive opener, grease the threads.

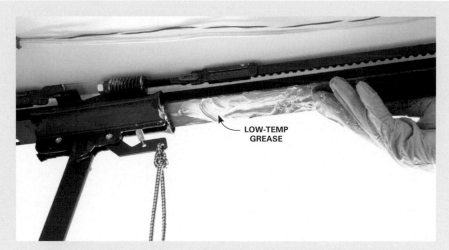

LOW-TEMP GREASE

Grease the track. Squeeze a large dollop of grease onto your gloved hand and wipe it onto the track. Operate the opener several times to spread the grease along the track and into the trolley.

Fix #3
Lube the hardware

Next, quiet all the garage door's moving parts with garage door lube spray. It works much better than spray-on oils because it stays in place and dries to a greaselike consistency. The grease also does a better job of quieting moving parts. Repeat this step every six months.

CARDBOARD SPLASH GUARD

TORSION SPRING

Lube everything that moves. Spray the roller shafts and hinges first. Wipe off the drippy excess. Then slip a piece of cardboard behind the torsion springs and soak them, too.

Fix #4
Install quieter rollers

If your garage door has steel track rollers, they're part of your noise problem. Buy eight "quiet" nylon rollers. They're equipped with bearings and cost a few bucks more than nylon "bearingless" rollers or nylon rollers without end caps, but they're quieter, roll smoother and last longer. You can find them at home centers and online at garage-doors-and-parts.com.

Swap out the steel rollers for the new nylon ones (one at a time). If your door uses torsion springs mounted on the header above the door, do NOT attempt to replace the rollers in the two bottom brackets. Those brackets are under constant spring tension and can cause serious injury if you unbolt them. That's a job for a pro.

Install new rollers. Remove the hinge retaining nuts and tilt the hinge/bracket toward you. Swap out the rollers and reverse the procedure to reinstall. Then reinstall the nuts and snug them up with a wrench (but don't overtighten).

EXTERIOR REPAIRS & IMPROVEMENTS

HomeCare&Repair

TIPS FOR REPLACING WINDOW AND DOOR SCREEN

It's easy to replace the screen fabric in an aluminum frame. What's hard is figuring out which diameter spline to buy and how tight the fabric should be stretched. No problem—here's how to conquer both of those issues.

Let's start with spline basics. Don't reuse the old spline unless it's fairly new. It's probably dried and brittle, so install new spline when you install new fabric. New spline is more pliable and will slip into the channel easier and hold the fabric tighter. Besides, it's cheap.

There are nine different sizes of spline (yikes!), but most home centers only carry the four most common sizes. Forget about measuring the spline channel width. Just bring a small section of the old spline with you and visually match it to the new spline. If none of the options are dead-on, buy the two closest sizes. Then test-fit each one using a small patch of new screen. The spline should take just a bit of effort to snap into the frame. If you have to use a lot of muscle, the spline is too large.

You may be tempted to buy aluminum fabric. Don't. It's harder to install and is overkill for residential applications. Instead, take your old screen fabric with you to find new screen that matches the color and mesh size. That way it'll match your other screens. Then buy a concave spline roller (less than $5) and a roll of screen fabric.

Cut the screen 1 in. larger than the opening. Then clip off a corner of the fabric and place it over a corner of the aluminum frame. Press the spline and fabric into the channel and continue rolling it into the long edge of the screen (**Photo 1**). Round the corner (don't cut the spline at the corners), and use the same technique along the second edge of the screen frame. Next, place a heavy object in the center of the screen fabric (**Photo 2**) and finish installing the screen. Note: Don't overstretch the screen trying to get it "banjo" tight. That'll bend the frame. Finish the job by trimming off the excess screen (**Photo 3**).

1 **Roll in the screen and spline.** Align the screen squarely to the frame along the longest edge. Lay the spline directly over the channel ahead of the roller. Lightly stretch the screen away from the starting corner as you roll the spline into place.

CONCAVE ROLLER

2 **Depress the center with a heavy object.** Load a brick in the center of the screen to create the proper amount of slack. Then continue installing the fabric along the third and fourth sides of the screen frame. Remove the brick.

3 **Cut off the excess screen.** Use a brand new utility blade and position the knife at a steep angle against the frame. Then trim off the excess screen.

REPLACE A BALKY PATIO SCREEN DOOR

Most patio doors come with really crummy sliding screen doors. They're constantly out of adjustment and the wheels always break. If you're tired of trying to tweak it, or somebody has walked into it and bent it, now's the time to upgrade to a premium door. Premium screen doors are made from extruded aluminum, so they don't flex like the cheapo rolled aluminum styles. And they only cost about $120 ($20 more than an original replacement version).

Several online companies custom-cut them to fit your door (two sources are qualitywindowscreen.com and apexproducts.com). The door ships disassembled (to save on shipping), so you'll have to assemble the mitered corners and install the screen yourself. But that's a very simple task.

Here's another tip. If you have a pet that likes to paw at the patio door screen, order the new door with pet-safe screen fabric. It's amazingly resilient when it comes to pet claws.

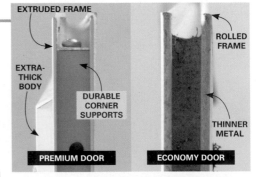

EXTRUDED FRAME

EXTRA-THICK BODY

DURABLE CORNER SUPPORTS

ROLLED FRAME

THINNER METAL

PREMIUM DOOR   ECONOMY DOOR

The difference between premium and economy screen doors. Premium screen doors are extruded rather than rolled and have thicker metal and extremely rigid corners. High-quality wheels make the door slide easier.

RECAP
CONCRETE STEPS

Rebuild damaged edges and corners to make your steps look like new

by **Rick Muscoplat, Contributing Editor**

EXTERIOR REPAIRS & IMPROVEMENTS

oncrete steps break up, especially in northern climates. Water soaks into the concrete, freezes and breaks off the outside corners. Once that starts, the damage spreads along the front edge of the step, eventually turning the step into a ramp. That's not only ugly but mighty dangerous.

The best repair for severe corner and front edge breakage—short of completely replacing the steps—is to "recap" them. You break away the damaged areas, rebuild them with new concrete and then coat your entire steps to give them a uniform look. It takes about two days altogether and costs about $225 for tools and materials.

Bust off the old surface

Start by rigging up your circular saw and grinder with water supply lines (Photo 1). All it takes is a few bucks' worth of sprinkler system parts from any home center to fabricate a water-cooling and dust-reduction system. Secure the assembly to the saw with hook-and-loop tape. Build another spray unit (with only one nozzle) for your angle grinder.

Set the circular saw blade to full depth and adjust the water flow. Then don your safety gear (goggles, hearing protection, knee pads and leather gloves) and connect your saw/grinder to a GFCI extension cord. Cut a grid pattern into the steps (Photo 2) and bust off the surface (Photo 3). You must remove at least 3/4 in. of concrete (3/4 in. is the minimum thickness for a cap). But a thicker cap is stronger, so try to remove 1-1/2 in. of concrete or more.

Switch to the angle grinder to cut the remaining concrete where the stair tread meets the riser (Photo 4). Once you've removed the entire stair tread, run the circular saw lengthwise down the front and side edges of the step. Break off the faces with the maul and chisel.

Repair or replace?

The best way to fix concrete steps is to demolish the old ones and pour new ones. No repair lasts forever. And replacement is the only real fix for steps that are sinking or have deep cracks. But if your steps are level and have only the usual damage that's a few inches deep, you can save yourself a ton of money and/or labor by patching or recapping them.

Patching works well for small, shallow chips and cracks (less than 1/4 in. deep). Simply fill them with premixed concrete patching material. To patch cracked corners, chisel them out to a depth of at least 3/4 in. Then drill holes and drive in concrete screws as anchors, apply a bonding adhesive and fill with crack-resistant concrete. The patch won't match the color or texture of the steps, so you may want to recoat all the steps with concrete resurfacer for a uniform look.

If the cracks or voids extend over large areas of your steps, forget about patching. Go ahead and cap the steps following the procedure shown here.

CAUTION: Plug your saw into an extension cord with built-in GFCI protection—or risk electrocution.

TEE   IRRIGATION TUBING   ELBOW   VALVE

1 **Turn your saw into a wet saw.** Rig up a water line using irrigation system parts. Water keeps the blade cool and eliminates dust. In addition to the parts shown here, you'll need an adapter to connect the tubing to a garden hose.

2 **Slice up the damaged area.** Cut the stair tread into a 4- to 5-in. grid pattern. Sawing concrete is no fun, but the more cuts you make, the easier it will be to break off the step's surface.

3 **Break out the blocks.** Aim the chisel at the same depth as the saw cuts and whack away. The squares of concrete created by your saw cuts will pop off neatly (well, usually).

Tools and materials

Everything you need for this project is available at home centers.

- Segmented diamond blades for a circular saw and grinder.
- Irrigation system tubing, valves, elbows, tee and hose adapter. Don't forget the GFCI extension cord!
- Concrete mixing tub, wood float, steel trowel and edger.
- Concrete bonding adhesive. We used Quikrete No. 9902.
- Concrete mix. A "crack-resistant" mix is best. We used three bags of Quikrete No. 1006.
- Resurfacer. We used Quikrete No. 1131.

Pour a new cap

Hose down the steps and let them dry. Then coat the chipped-out areas with concrete bonding adhesive.

Build a concrete form to match the original height of the step. Locate the front of the form about 1 in. out from the old face of the step. If that extra inch will cause the step to overhang the sidewalk, place a strip of 1/2-in.-thick foam under the form to create a gap between the step and the sidewalk. The gap will allow the sidewalk to rise during a freeze.

Next, mix the crack-resistant concrete and fill the form (**Photo 5**). Then finish the concrete (**Photo 6**). Remove the form after 24 hours.

Wait a week and then apply the resurfacer. Mix it in small batches. Then wet all the steps with a water spray bottle and apply the resurfacer (**Photo 7**).

RISER

STAIR TREAD

4 **Cut into the corner.** Your saw can't reach into the corner where the stair tread and riser meet. So cut with a grinder and chisel out the concrete. Add a spray system to your grinder similar to the one on your saw.

5 **Fill the form.** Work the concrete into the front of the form with your shovel or a stick. When the form is completely full, screed off the excess concrete.

WOOD FLOAT

6 **Finish the concrete.** Skim the surface with a wood float. When the mix hardens a little, round the edges with a concrete edger and smooth it with a steel trowel. Don't overwork the concrete or you'll weaken the surface.

7 **Resurface the whole thing.** Resurfacer hides the mismatch between old and new concrete and masks small imperfections. Pour it on and spread it with a masonry brush.

HOUSE WRAP SMARTS

These tips and techniques help avoid code violations and problems down the road

by **Mark Petersen, Contributing Editor**

House wrap is not a lot of fun to install, but with today's emphasis on energy efficiency, it's here to stay.

In recent years, there have been several changes in the building codes that apply to house wrap installation (none of which makes it any easier to put up, unfortunately), and building inspectors have been rigorously enforcing these new codes. Here are a bunch of installation tips and techniques to speed up your installation and help keep the inspector off your back.

Cut to workable sizes

A windy day can make house wrap installation a frustrating experience at best. So cut full rolls down to more manageable sizes with a circular saw. Most saws won't cut all the way through a full roll, so cut as deep as you can, then twist the roll until the cut is complete. Smaller rolls means more tape on the horizontal seams, but the labor saving is worth the extra trouble and expense.

No more staples allowed

The good old days of using a hammer tacker to install house wrap are gone forever. Today, most house wrap manufacturers require their product to be installed with cap nails or cap staples. This change definitely slows down the process, but on the upside, capped fasteners hold house wrap to the wall up to 25 times better than staples. Using them will assure you of a good night's sleep on those windy nights knowing the house wrap you installed last week is not blowing all over the neighborhood.

CAPPED FASTENERS

Meet the "Stinger"
Yes, you can hand-nail capped fasteners, but it'll take you forever. Pick up a Stinger Cap Staple Hammer for $50. It works like a hammer tacker, only it sinks capped nails instead of staples. There is a learning curve to using the Stinger, and the caps and staples aren't cheap ($31 for a box of 12 rolls), but it beats the heck out of hand-nailing cap nails.

Tack, straighten, fasten

When starting a new row, don't fasten the whole vertical length of the wrap right away. Get the roll into position, and attach a few fasteners in the center of the paper. This will allow you to roll out several feet and still be able to adjust the roll up and down without creating wrinkles. Wrinkles not only look sloppy but can also trap water.

Save time—buy 3-in. tape

Years ago, only vertical seams required tape, but no longer. Now every seam must be taped, and most manufacturers recommend that a minimum of 1 in. of the tape be sealed to each side of the seam—that's hard to accomplish using 2-in. tape! Instead, buy 3-in. rolls. If your house wrap supplier doesn't stock 3-in. tape, it should be able to order it. If not, like practically everything else, it's available online.

3" TAPE

2" TAPE

Don't buy bargain house wrap

"Perm rate" is the rate at which a house wrap allows water vapor to pass through it. Bargain house wraps often have low perm rates and they should be avoided. In cold climates, this is especially true for older homes with little or no moisture barriers. Moisture will escape through the wall cavity and sheathing, and if the house wrap doesn't allow it to pass through fast enough, it will condense and accumulate in the form of frost and ice. When the ice thaws, you'll end up with wet sheathing and/or wall cavities—not good.

Bargain house wraps have perm ratings in the 8 to 12 range. Instead, choose a quality house wrap like Tyvek, with a perm rating of 54.

Overlap seams 6 in. or more

Overlap all seams at least 6 in. And make sure to think like you're shingling. Work from the bottom up so that higher rows overlap lower ones.

OVERLAP OF 6" OR MORE

Don't cut out window openings!

The way we used to deal with window openings was to roll right over them, cut them out, then move on down the wall. It was quick, but there's a much better way.

After the opening is covered, make one cut with your knife straight up and down in the center. Next, cut the house wrap flush at the top and bottom of the opening, creating two flaps. Wrap the flaps inside the building, past the jack stud, before cutting off the excess. At the top, slice several inches up and away at an angle, and hold the flap up with a piece of tape (it will be folded back down and taped after the window is installed).

The opening is now ready for pan flashing and a window. This method will meet the requirements of most window manufacturers, and best of all, the inspector will be happy.

Talk to your subs

If you're the general contractor, make sure there's an extra roll of house wrap at the job site for the framers, electricians and any other sub who's going to be attaching objects to the wall. (Include instructions for installing it!) Soffit stringers, trim boards and electrical meters all need house wrap behind them.

Use flexible flashing on existing windows and doors

If you're installing house wrap around existing windows and doors, most building inspectors require those windows and doors to be sealed directly to the house wrap. This means you have to roll a butyl-style tape up onto the edge of the brick mold or window itself. This can be a tedious operation, especially if you're working with a super-sticky tape. Here's a suggestion. Don't peel off the window tape backing all at once; do just one section at a time.

Prime wood siding

Water tends to condense on house wrap, much more so than it would if there was just wood sheathing behind the siding. That water will penetrate wood siding and lift off the finish. So it's more important than ever to prime the back side of wood siding before it's installed.

Every wall penetration needs tape

It's not only seams that need taping—everything that penetrates a wall needs it too! Regular house wrap tape is usually sufficient.

Here's how to deal with a pipe. Cut out around it as closely as you can, then make two angled cuts up and away from the top of the pipe. Tape the flap up to keep it out of the way. and then starting at the bottom, tape the pipe to the wall. Finally, fold down the flap and tape it up.

Leave a chunk in the middle

House wrap is easy enough to cut with a sharp utility knife, but cutting a smaller piece off the roll can be a pain. Cutting the first half always goes slick, but when you get to the last little bit, it tends to crumple up. You can avoid this by starting in the middle and cutting one half, then the other. Leave a small section of wrap intact, and cut off the other half. Then simply tear the piece away from the roll.

Patch large holes and tears

Inevitably you'll have to deal with a tear in your beautiful handiwork. Small holes and tears can be repaired with tape, but larger ones require a patch. Here's how to do it. Make a horizontal slice in the house wrap just above the damaged area and slide in a patch, making sure to cover the hole by 2 in. in every direction. Tape up the seams and get back to work.

PRO **CAULKING TIPS**

Choosing and using caulk and tools

by **Mark Petersen, Contributing Editor**

I've emptied at least 5,000 tubes of caulk in my career—that's a bead about 20 miles long! I've filled in gaps so flawlessly that the caulk was virtually imperceptible, but there have been plenty of times that I've globbed things up pretty good.

To help you get a top-notch caulking job with a lot less frustration, I'm going to share a few tips I've learned along the way.

POKER
CRADLE
RATCHET
HOOK

My favorite gun

The most expensive gun on the rack isn't necessarily the best. Here's what I look for: I like a gun with a cradle. Tubes seem to fall out of the guns with the rails. I prefer guns with ratchet action rather than friction action. I won't even consider a gun that doesn't have a hook. Forget about gun-mounted tube cutters—I've yet to see one of them do a good job. I use a utility knife. And if all other things are equal, buy the gun with the longer tube poker. Some aren't long enough to work on every kind of tube.

Cut tips off straight

You probably learned to cut the tip at an angle. That works OK in some situations, but an angled tip limits the position the caulking gun has to be in. With a straight tip, I can swivel the gun out of the way of obstacles, and I'm able to caulk right up to an inside corner. And if you have various-size gaps to fill, cut the tip small and do the small gaps first, then cut it bigger for the larger gaps. I guarantee it won't work the other way around.

Choose the right caulk for the job

The selection in the caulk aisle at home centers is mind-boggling, but actually choosing the right one is pretty simple. Most of the caulk on store shelves is basically one of four types: elastomeric, polyurethane, latex or silicone. Here's how I make the right choice:

1. Siding, windows and doors: Polyurethane is my hands-down favorite. It's paintable. It doesn't shrink. It stays flexible. It adheres better than silicone, and it doesn't attract dust and dirt the way silicone does.

2. Roofing: I like an elastomeric or rubberized product. This stuff won't dry out in extreme conditions, and it sticks to everything.

3. Interior trim: If I'm sealing gaps and nail holes in trim that's going to be painted, I always use latex. It cleans up easily and dries fast. It's also easy to tool—and cheap.

4. Kitchen and bath: This is where silicone products shine. Silicone tools well. It can be purchased with antimicrobial additives, and can be easily removed and replaced when it gets grungy.

Ride the smooth side

When one of the surfaces I'm caulking is rougher than the other, I always try to ride the tip on the smoother surface (the brick mold in this case). If you ride the middle or the rough surface (siding), the caulking will duplicate the bumps, sometimes in an exaggerated way.

Mark's tooling tips

I'm not a huge fan of tooling. I try to get the bead right the first time. But sometimes it's a necessary evil. Elastomeric and polyurethanes don't tool well—a finger dipped in soapy water is your best bet. Latex is easily tooled, and even if you screw it up, you can wipe it off with a wet rag and start over. The only time I tape off an area is when I'm using a silicone product, and the only time I use a tool other than my finger is when I'm working with tape.

The DAP Pro Caulk Tool Kit (No. 09125) shown above is available at home centers for less than $10. And if you get your bead close to the way you want it, my best advice is to leave it alone. It seems the more I mess with a bead, the uglier it gets.

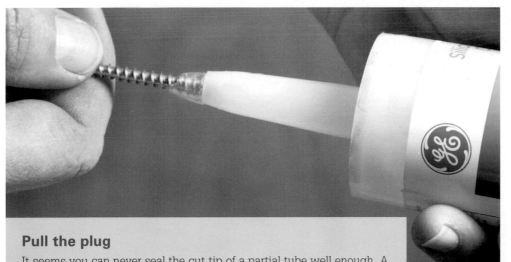

Pull the plug

It seems you can never seal the cut tip of a partial tube well enough. A plug usually forms in the tip. Try using a large screw with aggressive threads to remove the plug. This tip works best with silicone products.

Choose the right color

When you're caulking gaps between prefinished siding and trim, use the color of the siding. When working with stained or natural wood, choose a color a little darker than the wood. A darker color will blend in with the knots and other imperfections.

Don't use your wrists

Every golfer knows that the best way to keep a putter moving in a straight line and at a consistent speed is to control it with the upper body. It's the same with caulking. Use your upper body, or even your legs, to move the tube along, not your wrists.

Salvage a wet tube

The new guy left the case of caulking out in the rain again (it's always the new guy). Those soggy tubes are now going to split open under pressure. Before that happens, wrap some duct tape around the tube. I've also salvaged tubes with house wrap tape, masking tape, stretch wrap, shipping tape—it all works. Just use whatever's handy.

Meet in the middle

When you have a long bead to run and you can't get it done in one shot, don't start again where you left off. Instead, start at the other end and meet in the middle. It's hard to continue a bead once you've stopped without creating a glob. I also try to keep the meeting place somewhere other than eye level.

Push, don't pull

I always try to push the caulk into the gap rather than drag it over the gap. This greatly increases the odds the caulk will adhere to both surfaces because it forces caulk into the gap—pulling doesn't. One exception to this rule is when both surfaces are flush. When caulking flush surfaces, if you try to push the tip too hard, it will skate all over the place, and you'll have a big mess on your hands.

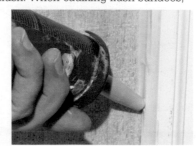

The after-mess

Some tubes have air in them and "burp" at the worst possible moment. Some continue to run after you set them aside. The bottom line: There's going to be cleanup. Use mineral spirits to clean up elastomeric and polyurethane. Latex cleans up great with just a wet rag. Silicone is another story. It seems to get on everything. My only tip for cleaning up silicone is that when it does get all over your gloves (and it will), just consider the waterproofing it provides as a bonus.

LOW-UPKEEP MAILBOX

The strength of wood and the convenience of PVC!

by **Mark Petersen, Contributing Editor**

L ast winter, my teenage son ran over our mailbox. He blamed it on an antilock-brakes malfunction. It wasn't a huge loss, however; the destroyed mailbox had been looking pretty shabby. And since painting and staining are not my favorite things to do, I took the opportunity to build a low-maintenance version.

I found all the materials I needed at my nearest home center. The PVC post sleeves can be a little tricky to work with, but PVC boards are easy to cut and fasten with regular woodworking tools. PVC doesn't tear out, split or splinter.

The whole project cost under $120. Building it took about four hours, which included shopping but not digging the post hole—I made my son do that.

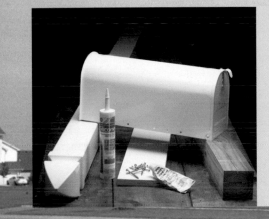

An old-time design with modern materials

PVC is great to work with because it's consistent and forgiving. It's easy to sand and shape. It cuts without tearing. You can screw right next to the edge without splitting it, and once two boards are cemented together, they literally become one. And best of all, PVC will never require paint or stain.

EXTERIOR REPAIRS & IMPROVEMENTS

Start with a trip to the post office

Don't assume the dimensions I used will work for you. The height, distance from the curb and newspaper box requirements may be different in your area. The dimensions for this box are based on a pamphlet I picked up at my local post office. The USPS recommends that a post be buried no more than 24 in. It's safer if the post gives way if someone runs into it.

Cutting the parts

A 6-ft. fence post sleeve leaves virtually no extra length for cutting mistakes. Start your 45-degree cut as close to the end as possible; a 20-in. angle bracket will leave you a 52-in. post sleeve. Cut into the sleeve slowly; thinner plastic can shatter if you cut too aggressively, especially when it's cold. After cutting the angle bracket sleeve, use it as

a template to mark the wood angle bracket. Once again, start your cut as close to the end as possible. An 8-ft. post with 20 in. cut off will leave you with 2 ft. of post to bury in the ground.

The two newspaper box sides (J) only need to be cut to length, but don't assume the factory ends are square—they're usually not. Trim just as much as necessary to make a true 90-degree end. After cutting the top (H) and bottom (G) to length, you'll need to cut them to width. Start by removing 1/4 in. from one side of each board to remove the rounded edges. The leftover scrap from the top should be about 1-1/8 in. wide. Save that piece to make the mailbox base.

I used the lid of a 1-gallon ice cream container as a template to mark the curves on the sides. But any circle with an 8- to 9-in. diameter will work (**Figure B**, p. 175).

Once all the curves are cut, clamp the two sides together and sand the curves smooth so the pieces are identical.

The mailbox I used required a 17-1/2-in. x 6-1/8-in. base. Your mailbox might be different. The total length of the base is not the same as the length of the mailbox—it has to be about 1 in. shorter to allow the door to open. Cement the scraps (E and F) together to form a base board that fits your mailbox.

I cut kerfs in the bottom of the newspaper box (G) to allow water to drain. Set your table saw blade at a height of 1/4 in. and set your fence 1/2 in. from the blade. Run the board through, then flip it around and do the same on the other side. Then run both sides of the board through at 1 in. and then again at 1-1/2 in. The middle kerf should be centered at 2 in., but you may want to double-check and line the last kerf up manually. I practiced on a sacrificial board.

Assemble the newspaper box

Use PVC-vinyl-fence cement to assemble the newspaper

box. The cement is a little runny, so be prepared to wipe off the excess after clamping.

Clamp the box together, bottom side up. Hold both the top (H) and the bottom (G) out flush with the curves on the front of the sides (J), as shown in **Photo 2**. The bottom is shorter than the top at the back of the box. This gap allows water to escape.

Putting it all together

If your 4x4 post is twisted on one end, use the straight portion above ground. Slide the PVC sleeve over the post, leaving it flush at the top. Attach the wood angle bracket. Slide on the angle bracket sleeve (**Photo 3**).

Once the newspaper box is in place, clamp a framing square onto the post to ensure a true 90 degrees (**Photo 4**). Don't worry about splitting the small areas between the kerfs—PVC is much more forgiving than wood.

Screw the mailbox base to the newspaper box flush with the front edge of the box. Use your 1-5/8-in. screws,

1 **Cut the side curves.** A dull blade actually works better than a sharp blade, which tends to grab and shake the PVC as it cuts. Cut one side of the newspaper box, then use it as a template to mark the other side.

DULL WOOD BLADE

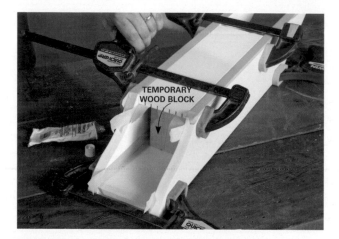

TEMPORARY WOOD BLOCK

2 **Assemble the box, bottom side up.** Dry-fit the entire newspaper box before you apply any cement. Cut a couple of 4-in. blocks to hold the bottom (G) at the right height. Tape along the joints to catch excess cement. Work fast—the cement won't wait.

SCREWS APPROVED FOR TREATED LUMBER

3 **Screw on the wood angle bracket.** Most post sleeves aren't perfectly square, but slightly rectangular with one side a hair wider than the other. Attach the bracket to the narrow side. The newspaper box will slide on easier that way.

3/4" ACCESS HOLE

4" BIT HOLDER

NEWSPAPER BOX

4 **Fasten the newspaper box.** Bore two 3/4-in. access holes in the top of the box. You will need a magnetic bit holder at least 4 in. long to reach the screws that attach the box to the angle bracket.

and be sure to screw down into the sides or your screws will poke through into the box. Attach the mailbox to the base. Slide it all the way forward to allow room for the door to open (Photo 5).

Apply the cement to the cap, not the post—it's less messy. I used a pretty basic fence post cap, but feel free to decorate your post with a fancier cap, maybe one with a built-in solar light.

There will be a little play in the vinyl angle bracket sleeve. Use a putty knife to slip a bit of cement underneath each end of the sleeve in order to seal it to the newspaper box and post. Caulk both sides of the angle bracket with white exterior-grade caulk. Silicone is the easiest to work with. You're done!

MATERIALS LIST

ITEM	QTY.
Mailbox	1
8' x 4x4 treated post	1
6' x 4x4 PVC/vinyl fence post sleeve	1
10' x 1x6 PVC trim	1
Vinyl fence post cap	1
Tube of PVC-vinyl-fence cement	1
Tube of white exterior-grade silicone	1
Box of 1-5/8" screws approved for treated lumber	1
Box of 3" screws approved for treated lumber	1
White hinged screw cover	4
Black hinged screw cover	4

5 Mount the mailbox Leave a gap under the mailbox door so it can open without binding against the base (E). Hinged screw covers snap shut and hide the screw heads for a clean look.

**Figure A
Mailbox post**

E & F

GAP TO LET WATER OUT

1-5/8" SCREWS

H

G

1-5/8" SCREWS

J

B

D

3" SCREWS

A

24" UNDERGROUND

C

**Figure B
Newspaper box sides**

2-3/4" 2-3/4"

CUTTING LIST

KEY	QTY.	SIZE & DESCRIPTION
A	1	52" x 4" x 4" post sleeve
B	1	20" x 4" x 4" angle bracket sleeve
C	1	76" x 3-1/2" x 3-1/2" wood post
D	1	20" (long side) x 4" x 4" wood angle bracket
E	1	17-1/2" x 3/4" x 1-1/8" mailbox base
F	1	17-1/2" x 3/4" x 5" mailbox base (glue to part E)
G	1	14" x 3/4" x 4" newspaper box bottom (with kerf cuts)
H	1	20" x 3/4" x 4" newspaper box top
J	2	30" x 3/4" x 5-1/2" newspaper box sides

BANISH **BUGS** & CRACK DOWN ON **CRITTERS**

Don't go batty trying to fend off unwanted intruders!

by **Elisa Bernick, Associate Editor**

GETTY

Do you have bats in your attic or ants in your pantry? Are mosquitos, moles and wasps driving you nuts? Check out these great ideas from critter control experts and Field Editors to get rid of your worst pests, both inside your house and out in the yard.

You think you have problems?

I dived into our pool and came face to face with a baby brown snake, the second most lethal snake in the world. Getting ready to strike, it hissed at me and I leapt out of the pool faster than I had dived in! We got it out of the pool, and my wife grabbed a spade and chopped the snake into three pieces with one swing! Three hours later, as she showed my son the snake pieces, it lifted its head and hissed at him. An old man explained this, saying, 'Snakes only die once the sun goes down.'

GETTY

—Lee Dashiell, Associate Editor, *Handyman* Australia

The right bait is the key

Field Editor Michael Finfrock has lots of experience live-trapping rodents and small mammals.

"In the past seven years, I have trapped well over 50 small animals." Finfrock says his success comes down to researching appropriate baits and trapping methods for each particular animal. Local extension services, the "critter library" on havahart.com, and state DNRs provide detailed trapping and baiting information on their Web sites. In many areas, it's illegal to relocate nuisance animals, so check with local authorities. Also, according to wildlife experts, more than 50 percent of relocated animals don't survive because they don't have an established shelter, food source or territory.

To live-trap a ground hog (aka a woodchuck), bait the trap with cantaloupe—the more rotten, the better.

Lights and sprinkler deter raccoons and foxes

We have chickens in our backyard, so we have a problem with foxes

and raccoons. I installed an electric fence, which helped, but the biggest success was a motion-activated light on the chicken coop along with a motion-activated sprinkler. It works quite well.

—Hans Ocken, Field Editor

GETTY

The Contech CR0101 Scarecrow Motion Activated Sprinkler shown is available for $50 at home centers and online.

Healthy turf fends off burrowing wasps

Field Editor Jill Bucolo writes, "I have one heck of a yard nightmare... huge mounds of dirt in our yard filled with huge—and I mean huge—Jurassic-size cicada killer wasps. Their tunnels have killed the grass, and they come back every year."

These large wasps live in all states east of the Rockies. Male cicada killer wasps are aggressive, but they don't have stingers. The females do but will sting only if they feel threatened. These wasps, which feed cicadas to their young, typically nest in disturbed, sandy areas and rarely infest healthy turf.

Adequate lime, fertilizer and frequent watering promote a thick growth of turf and can usually eliminate a cicada killer wasp infestation in one or two seasons. Mulch heavily around flower beds and shrubs to cover sandy soil. For severe infestations, call in an exterminator.

Control crickets with DIY sticky traps

A lot of cricket-like bugs had taken up residence in my basement. I'm concerned about chemicals in bug sprays, so I came up with this simple trap—duct tape. I set out a long strip of duct tape sticky side up in my basement. When I returned a couple of days later, I found it had about 15 to 20 bugs attached. Since then, I have set tape out several times with the same results.

—Matt Langford

Editors' Note: To permanently banish crickets, seal entrances by caulking around basement windows. Also dehumidify your basement—crickets like damp areas.

Repel ants with mint

Discourage ants from entering your home by planting a mint barrier around your foundation, says Field Editor Wayne Piaskowski.

"Over the past three years I've tried ant bombs, spraying their nests out in the yard. I even physically dug up a stubborn colony near the street that was three feet deep and wide. The mint that I've planted around the house seems to be helping a lot."

Bleach gets rid of drain flies

Tiny drain flies are harmless but can gather in huge numbers in your house. They're sometimes mistaken for fruit flies, but they actually live on the gunky slime in your drainpipes. Field Editor Lindsay McLeod told us about a recent plague of drain flies in her basement.

"An exterminator would have charged $65 to come investigate plus the cost of exterminating. Instead, I poured a teaspoon of bleach down the basement drain and the flies started pouring out! Gross! So I poured a little more bleach in, blocked the drain hole, waited an hour and presto! No more drain flies!"

If the bleach doesn't work, experts suggest starving the flies by cleaning the gunky slime out of the drain with a long-handled brush.

Holy mole-y!

Even the "experts" don't agree on what works for moles, so we can't give you any magic bullets. But some of our readers have real-world success stories to tell:

"Get rid of the grubs that are their food source," suggests Field Editor Jerry Young. "Use a good **grub insecticide** in the spring and again in July and you'll starve out the moles."

"I tried all of the typical mole products and remedies and finally the **Wire Tek Easy-Set Mole Eliminator Trap** did the trick," says Field Editor Ed Stawicki. "It traps the moles with a 'scissor-effect.' Very effective." The Mole Eliminator is about $35 at amazon.com.

Ed Stawicki, Field Editor

"The **Mole Chaser** worked for me," says Field Editor Scott Craig. "It's a foot-long metal cylinder that vibrates underground intermittently and causes the moles to find a new home." Mole chaser stakes are available in several models for $12 and up at home centers and online.

Scott Craig, Field Editor

Several Field Editors recommend the **Victor Out O' Sight Mole Trap** ($12 at home centers and online). Visit amazon.com and type in this product's name and you'll find tons of helpful advice, tips and tricks posted by customers who have used this trap successfully.

VICTOR OUT O' SIGHT MOLE TRAP

DIY critter trap

Craig Taylor, Field Editor

I've captured and relocated armadillos, a raccoon, water moccasins, pine snakes, rats, you name it. My trap of choice is a big, empty 32-gallon plastic trash can. Lay the can on its side and to the critter it looks like a dark tunnel to hide in. Force them in with a stick, flip the can upright, put the lid on and transfer. For the armadillos, I've placed the trash can over them and slid a flat board underneath and flipped the whole thing upright.

Carpenter ants can wreak havoc

After college, I moved into my blind grandfather's decrepit house to care for him. I kept seeing big ants in the kitchen, but ant bait did nothing and my grandfather insisted the ants were from the houseplants I'd brought with me. One afternoon, I walked into the kitchen and headed for the ancient refrigerator.

Suddenly, I noticed strange movements on the walls. I looked around and there were literally hundreds of winged carpenter ants covering the walls, counters and ceiling of the kitchen. It was a scene from a horror movie. Turns out carpenter ants had been nesting behind the refrigerator for years and had tunneled through nearly every bit of wood. The entire back of the house was being held together by lath and stucco.

—Elisa Bernick, Associate Editor

Mosquitos don't care for pesto

Basil smells good to us, but not to mosquitos. Plant several bunches in pots around your patio to stay swat-free (and enjoy some good eating, too, as you harvest the leaves).

A better mousetrap

I propped a soda bottle up at about a 20-degree angle and baited it with peanut butter. A day later I had a very scared mouse trapped in my bottle. He was relocated to a field more suited to his skill set.

John Williams,
Field Editor

A swipe of vegetable oil around the inside of the lip will prevent the mouse from "slipping" away.

Gel ant bait targets tough areas

Chemical ant baits are most effective for grease-eating and sweet-eating ant species. The key is to allow the ants to eat the bait and take it back to kill the entire colony, which may take several weeks. Gel ant baits let you apply bait in hard-to-reach areas such as behind appliances and in cracks and crevices (keep all chemical baits away from pets and kids).

New expanding foam has pest barrier

Great Stuff expanding foam seals small holes and cracks. The newest product—Great Stuff Pestblock ($10 at home centers)—contains a bitter ingredient (but not a pesticide) that discourages insect pests and rodents from gnawing on the insulating foam to gain entry to your home.

Remove bird feeders to prevent nighttime visitors

We live on 20 acres in the mountains of northern New Mexico and have regular visits by elk, deer, coyotes and bear when I forget to take my bird feeders in at night.

—Joe Stehling, Field Editor

Keep ants at bay

To repel ants, set whole bay leaves around kitchen food canisters and sprinkle crushed bay leaves along windowsills.

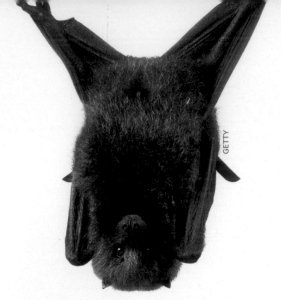

GETTY

Banish bats with an exclusion door

When Field Editor Chris Phelps counted 70 bats exiting his attic one evening, he knew he had a problem. He quickly discovered the solution—a bat exclusion door—

Chris Phelps,
Field Editor

which lets bats out but won't let them back in. One type of "exclusion door" is a piece of netting that hangs a foot below the bats' exit point. You tape the netting along the top and sides but leave the bottom free. The bats will slip out the open bottom, but won't be able to fly back in.

"We installed the door," says Phelps, "and within a week the bats were gone. I sealed the hole to keep them out permanently. We also built a couple of bat houses since bats eat mosquitos."

Bat exclusion door: Bats can exit but can't return

Natural citronella

Lemongrass contains citronella. Repel mosquitos by growing it in clumps around your deck. You can also mash up the inner leaves and rub the juice on your skin.

GreatGoofs®

Holy intruder!

I built a permanent roof over my patio a couple of years ago. Recently I noticed water stains on the inside wall directly below the step flashing that sealed the new roof to the house siding. So I climbed up there to track down the leak. I looked for holes, checked for flashing that had slipped out of place and even flooded the area with a hose. No dice. Then I climbed a ladder and held my head close to the wall behind a rafter to see if any light was shining through to reveal a hole. Inches away and staring right back at me was a bat. And directly below him were his urine stains.

—Ed Lejchar

MODERN STONE

Pro tips for installing veneer stone

by **Jeff Gorton, Associate Editor**

If the words "cultured stone" conjure up images of a fake that you can spot a mile away, then you need to take a look at modern manufactured veneer stone. Today's versions look so good that you'll be hard-pressed to tell them from actual stone. And since manufactured stone is cheaper and lighter than the real thing, it's a great DIY choice for any stone veneer project.

There are several national brands of manufactured stone—including Eldorado, Coronado and Cultured Stone—and they all provide detailed installation instructions on their Web sites. But we were sure that a professional would have tons of great tips and advice, so we enlisted Marcus Schilling, a third-generation mason, to show us how he installs stone veneer.

You can use manufactured stone indoors or out, but exterior applications require special attention to details of waterproofing and flashing. Before installing exterior stone veneer, talk to your local building inspector to see what's required in your area. We'll show you tips for installing manufactured stone indoors; however, most of the tips also apply to exterior applications.

Stone veneer in a nutshell

Before we launch into the tips, it's helpful for you to have a general idea of the installation process. Almost all stone veneer installations start with a layer or two of building paper, covered by properly installed dimpled and galvanized wire lath. The next step is to cover the lath with a 1/2-in. layer of Type S mortar, which is "scratched" while it's still wet to allow the stone to cling better. After this "scratch coat" dries overnight, the stone is applied with the same type of mortar. If you're using stone intended to look like it's dry-stacked—that is, no mortar between the stones—you're done. Otherwise you'll finish the job by grouting the joints between the stones with mortar.

MEET A PRO

Marcus Schilling was introduced to the world of masonry when he was only about 7 years old. He helped his dad with all sorts of stone-mason tasks, including carrying small stones and cleaning up at the end of the day. And he loved it from the start. His grandpa was a stonemason. His grandpa taught his dad, and his dad taught Marcus and his brothers. And now Marcus is teaching his sons—and us!—the craft of setting stones and laying bricks.

Easy way to cut wire lath

Wire lath can be unruly, and the cut edges are sharp. So anything you can do to keep the stuff under control while you're cutting it is a big bonus. Here's a tip from Marcus on how to make long cuts. Lay the wire lath on some long boards. Measure from the edge of the lath to the edge of the board on each end so the desired cutting line is lined up with the edge of the board. Then secure the lath temporarily with a few staples. Now use the edge of the board as a guide to make the cut. Marcus uses cordless metal shears, but tin snips or aviation snips will also work.

More tips for working with lath:

- Wear gloves and safety glasses.
- Cut wire lath with large tin snips, power metal shears or a diamond blade mounted in an angle grinder.
- Prebend lath at inside corners. Bend it over a board before putting it in place.
- Make sure the lath is installed so it feels rough when your hand is going up, and smooth going down.

You don't need a special tool to scratch the mortar

Grooving or scratching the wet mortar provides a better bond for sticking on the stones. You can buy a special rakelike tool for this, but Marcus prefers to use a 3/16-in. square-notched tile mastic trowel. They're cheap and easy to find at home centers and hardware stores. Simply drag it across the wet mortar to make horizontal stripes.

Tip

When installing "dry-stack" stones, use a colored mortar or dye the mortar to match the stones.

Speedy troweling

Marcus swears this is the fastest way to get the mud on the wall. Prop up your mud board about 16 in. high and within easy reach. Load it with mortar. Then use your London trowel as shown to transfer the mortar from the mud board to your trowel. Pull the trowel up the wall to embed the mortar in the lath.

What mortar should I use?

You'll find recipes for mixing your own mortar in the stone manufacturer's instructions, but Marcus uses premixed Type S mortar that's labeled for use with veneer stone. Special additives are already included—all you add is water. Look for it at masonry suppliers or ask about it when you buy your stone.

Disguise the cut ends of stones

Occasionally you'll have to cut stones to fit. Marcus uses a 10-in. chop saw equipped with a dry-cut diamond blade. But if you're doing only one job, you can get by with a diamond blade mounted in an angle grinder. Regardless of the tool you use, you'll want to disguise or hide the cut ends. After cutting a stone, Marcus cuts angles on the corners to make them look more natural. You can also use a tile nipper or horse-hoof trimmer to chip away at the sharp edge left by cutting. Marcus chooses thin stones to cut if possible. Then he hides the cut edge against a thicker stone.

And if he's using mortar that's dyed to match the stone, as you would in a dry-stack installation, Marcus butters the end of the stone so it blends in better.

Stick on the stone like a pro

Marcus makes a swipe across the entire back of the stone with the trowel first to create a good bond for the mortar bed. Then he wipes mortar from the trowel all around the perimeter. This creates a little hollow spot in the middle that will act as a suction cup to hold the stone in place until the mortar hardens. The key is to put on enough mortar to create about a 1/2-in.-thick layer when the stone is pressed against the scratch coat. If any mortar oozes out around the edges, knock it off with the trowel so it doesn't get in the way of grouting.

Cut off the tip of the grout bag

Grout bags come with either metal or plastic tips. Marcus prefers the plastic tips for grouting stone. He cuts the tip to create an opening that's about 5/8 in. in diameter to allow proper mortar flow. Marcus says a common mistake is to mix grouting mortar too stiff. Make sure the mortar is loose enough to ooze from the tip without having to squeeze the bag.

Fill the joints completely

Marcus says he often encounters hollow grout joints on work done by beginners. Be careful to fill the joints full from back to front as you're grouting. Joints that are hollow underneath will fall out later. Keep the tip pressed deep into the joints so they get filled from the back to the front of the stone.

You don't need a special tuckpointing trowel

Marcus finishes the joints using a 3/8-in.-wide tuckpointing trowel that he's cut off to about 5 in. long. He says most masons prefer the shorter length because it gives them much better control. But he says a carpenter's pencil is a great alternative. It's the perfect size and shape for striking your grout joints. Let the grout set up until it's firm to the touch but not hard; usually this is about 20 to 30 minutes. Then rake the pencil over the grout to smooth and shape it. Finish up by brushing off any loose mortar with a soft masonry brush.

Rinse the bag to avoid clogs

Marcus recommends rinsing out the bag after every third bagful of grout. Otherwise sand builds up along the edge, clogs the tip and makes grouting difficult. Just fill the empty bag with water and rub it back and forth to dislodge the caked-on grout.

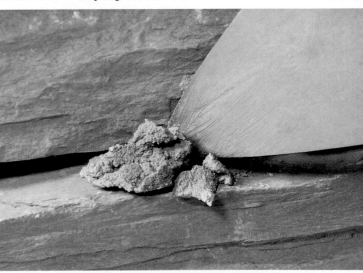

Wait! Don't wipe off that wet mortar

When you spill a glob of mortar on the stone, which is almost certain to happen, leave it alone. Let the mortar set up about 30 minutes. Then flick the partially hardened mortar off with the tip of the trowel. Dab the remaining residue with a damp rag to remove it.

WORKING WITH
FIBER CEMENT BOARD

To install it, you just need a few special tools and tricks

by **Mark Petersen, Contributing Editor**

Hold the starter 1/4 in. down

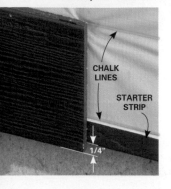

Find your most beat-up pieces of siding and rip them down into 1-1/4-in. starter strips. These strips, installed at the bottom, will make your first row of siding angle out to match the rest of the rows. Snap a line 1 in. above the bottom of the wall sheathing as a guide. Install these fragile starter strips with a 15-gauge trim gun. Snap another line for the bottom row of siding, positioning it so it will hang down an additional 1/4 in. from the starter.

CHALK LINES

STARTER STRIP

1/4"

Flash the butt joints

Caulking butt joints is unnecessary, and some manufacturers prohibit it. However, you should flash behind the joints. You can use metal, house wrap or any other approved WRB (weather-resistant barrier), but Jaime prefers to use 30-lb. felt paper. It's easy to work with and cheap, and it isn't noticeable if a seam happens to open up a little. Tack it to the wall so it doesn't get knocked out of place when you install the second piece of siding.

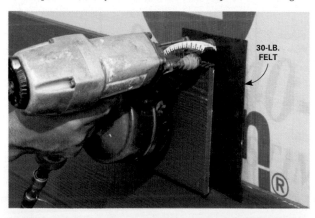

30-LB. FELT

MEET AN EXPERT

Jaime Venzor has been in the siding business for more than 15 years. He started out installing mostly vinyl, but now 80 percent of his work is fiber cement. Here he shares some tips that helped earned his good reputation with his customers.

Cut the planks with a circular saw

Tons of fiber cement cutting gadgets are available, but most jobs can be handled with just a steady eye and a standard circular saw fitted with a fiber cement blade. If you plan to hang a lot of fiber cement, though, you'll want a chop saw with a proper blade that will allow you to cut several pieces at once. You can buy fiber cement blades sized to fit any saw style or size for $20 and up at most home centers. When you're cutting this stuff, a dust mask is the bare minimum protection, and this is not a casual warning: The silica dust generated by cutting fiber cement can be bad news for your health!

Painted vs. primed

We decided to use a prefinished product in this story, but the other way to go is simple primed siding. That material is primed and ready for you to paint. Here are some facts to consider when making your decision.

■ **The advantages of primed:** Primed products cost 50 percent less than prefinished products. On-site painting looks better up close because the touch-up paint and caulked areas aren't as noticeable. Primed products are easier and less expensive to install.

■ **The advantages of prefinished:** The color on a prefinished product won't fade nearly as fast. Some finishes come with a 15-year warranty. But the best part of using a prefinished product is that after installation, you're done and not faced with painting an entire house.

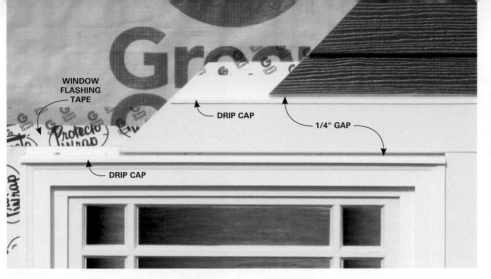

WINDOW FLASHING TAPE

DRIP CAP

1/4" GAP

DRIP CAP

Windows need drip cap and a gap on top

Whether or not you're installing trim boards around your windows, you'll need to install a drip cap over the window. You'll also need to leave a 1/4-in. gap (no caulking) between the top of the window and the plank or trim board directly above it. This is to allow any water that may have gotten behind the siding to weep out. Tape the drip cap to the wall, but don't tape all the way to the bottom of the drip cap because it will be visible through the 1/4-in. gap. The top trim board will also need its own drip cap and 1/4-in. gap. Treat the tops of doors the same way.

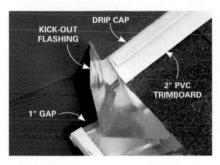

KICK-OUT FLASHING

DRIP CAP

2" PVC TRIMBOARD

1" GAP

Don't skip the kick-out flashing

Kick-out flashing is essential for preventing water from running down a roof and behind the siding on an adjacent wall. You'll fail your inspection if the inspector doesn't see it on your job. It's a pain to work around, but it helps if you don't nail the flashing tight until you have your siding cut to size. It's much easier to get a proper fit for a plank if you can shift the flashing beneath it.

It's a two-man job without siding gauges

Fiber cement siding is heavy and breaks if it's bent too much. Installing this stuff by yourself is tough, but it's possible with the aid of siding gauges. These tools not only create the proper reveal (the part of the siding that shows) between rows but also actually hold the planks in place while you nail. Even if you do just one fiber cement job, siding gauges are worth the money. A pair of the SA902 Gecko Gauges shown here costs about $85 at amazon.com, but cheaper versions are available. Most gauges are adjustable to accommodate reveals from 5 to 8 in.

Nailing basics

Fiber cement siding can be hand-nailed, but because it's so much harder and more brittle than wood, you have to predrill holes near any edge. You can save yourself a bunch of time by using a pneumatic coil siding nail gun. Unfortunately, a siding gun will set you back twice as much as a 15-gauge trim gun, and it's only half as versatile, so if installing fiber cement isn't your full-time gig, you may want to rent one (about $110 a week). Every manufacturer has specific nailing guidelines, but here are some basic rules:

■ Use 6d galvanized or stainless siding nails and install them no more than 16 in. apart.

■ Nail lengths should be chosen so they penetrate a minimum of 1-1/4 in. into the solid wood (wood sheathings like OSB and plywood count toward the 1-1/4 in., but "soft" sheathings like fiber board and foam don't).

■ Don't drive nails into the siding at an angle.

■ Fastener heads should be snugged up against the siding, not driven into the surface.

■ The end of each plank making up a butt joint needs to be fastened to a stud.

■ Nail butt joints last. That way you can tweak the ends of each plank so the bottom edges line up perfectly.

The lowdown on clearances

Fiber cement siding is not bulletproof—it will deteriorate if exposed to water for a long time. It's imperative that you honor the proper spacing between the siding and the roof surfaces and between the siding and the horizontal surfaces, such as the ground or cement slabs and decks. Check with your specific manufacturer before you start. Here are some general guidelines for the amount of space to leave:

- 1/8 in. to 1/4 in. between siding and trim
- 1/4 in. between siding and horizontal flashing
- 1 in. between the gutter and an adjacent wall
- 2 in. between siding and roofing, decks, patios, driveways, steps and walkways (using PVC trim boards is a good way to accomplish these clearances)
- 6 in. between the siding and the ground.

15-GAUGE TRIM GUN

OUTSIDE CORNER

Vinyl mounting blocks work best

Most fiber cement manufacturers make mounting blocks for lights, electrical receptacles, A/C lines, PVC venting, etc. Jaime prefers to use the vinyl mounting blocks typically used with vinyl siding. They're cheaper and easy to install, and you can cut the proper-size hole in a plastic mounting block with a utility knife or a snips. With fiber cement blocks, you have to use a jigsaw or a hole saw.

MountMaster is one brand of blocks sold at Lowe's and many lumberyards. It's available in more than 25 colors, but you can order paintable blocks if you want an exact match with your siding or trim.

VINYL MOUNTING BLOCK

Preassemble the corners

It's a lot easier to preassemble corners on a flat surface. Jaime uses 2-1/4-in. galvanized nails in his 15-gauge trim gun. He uses the same size nails to install the corners on the wall. Don't use a framing gun or try to hand-nail the corners together; that's a good way to break the trim boards. Also, the trim nails look better where nails will be exposed, especially on a prefinished corner board. So, if you don't have a 15-gauge trim gun, what a perfect "opportunity" to go buy one ($115 and up at home centers).

PAINT DAUBER

1/4" GAP

Paint, prime or caulk all cut edges

Every time you cut a plank, you create an exposed surface that has no primer or paint to protect it from the elements. If a cut edge is going to butt up against a corner post or trim board, it gets caulked. If the cut edge is part of a butt joint in the middle of the wall, it needs to be painted (try to use factory edges on all butt joints). Planks that have been cut to fit over windows and doors also need paint. Order paint kits and caulking to match both the trim and the siding colors. Your siding supplier should have access to both. Painting kits cost $15 to $20.

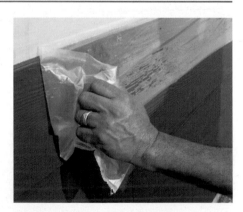

Remove the plastic last

Prefinished fiber cement boards come with a protective plastic coating. To protect the paint from getting scratched during installation, leave the plastic on and make your cuts right through it. Peel away the plastic after the board has been fastened to the wall.

GreatGoofs®

Southern snow removal

As a Southern girl, I didn't have much experience with snow removal. So when I moved north and got married, I decided it was high time I learned. One snowy morning, I told my husband I wanted to learn how to snow-blow. We went outside and he showed me how to move the blower side-to-side and make turns. He made one pass to get me started and then went back to shoveling. I eagerly got behind the blower and started down the driveway. It was a lot harder than I expected, and it took everything in me to get down to the end of the driveway. On the way back, I was just about exhausted and sweating up a storm. I kept wondering why it looked easy when my husband did it. When I FINALLY reached the top, my husband was waiting for me. "What the heck am I doing wrong?" I asked him. "Old people can do this!" My husband just smiled, put it in gear and the thing took off on its own. I didn't know I had to engage the self-propel lever.

—Carrie Wilkinson

Popping caulk

The soffit by the garage had come loose, so I hooked up my nail gun to the air compressor, got on a stepladder and nailed the piece back up. While I was at it, I decided to caulk the joint as well. I put a new tube of caulk in my air-driven caulk gun, got on the ladder and placed the nozzle in the corner of the gable.

I pulled the trigger and in about one microsecond the tube exploded and covered me, the garage, the shrubs and my car with caulk. I had forgotten to readjust the air pressure setting when I changed from my nail gun to the caulk gun, and I hit that tube of caulk with about 100 psi instead of what should have been about 20 psi. I can tell you one thing: Caulk is a bear to get out of your hair.

—John B. Vollmer

SPECIAL SECTION

Storage &Organizing

CHALKBOARD SOLUTIONS

Chalkboard paint is great for creating reusable labels on metal bins, jars, drawers and a ton of other things. When you change the contents of a drawer or jar, you just wipe off the chalk and rewrite the label.

Chalkboard paint is available in spray-on and brush-on versions for $8 to $15 at home centers and hardware stores.

You can apply chalkboard paint directly to most nonporous surfaces. Or make your own adhesive and magnetic labels by covering mailing labels and refrigerator magnets with chalkboard paint.

—Merrilee Post

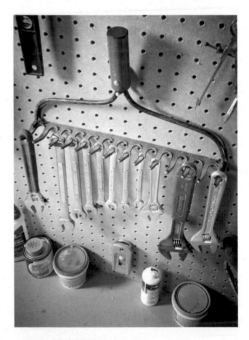

Chalkboard sticky labels. You can also buy already-painted self-adhesive labels at amazon.com and other online retailers. Search for "chalkboard stickers."

SELF-ADHESIVE LABELS

PRINTABLE MAGNETIC LABELS

I have terrible handwriting, so I love making magnetic labels with my home printer. Just create the labels on your computer, put the magnet sheets in your printer, hit "print" and cut them up. They're great on metal file drawers and tool chests. When you reorganize, just move the labels around or add new ones.

—Jordan Van Moorleghem

Editor's Note: Avery Magnet Sheets, which are compatible with ink-jet printers, are available in five-sheet packs for $10 at office supply stores and online retailers.

GARDEN RAKE RECYCLING

Don't put your old rake out to pasture. Put the rake to use in your workshop instead. Just cut off the handle and hang it on the wall or on your pegboard. It's a handy place to store wrenches and other tools.

—Roy Dupont

BUILD SHALLOW DRAWERS

I have a pretty organized shop with lots of drawers, and here's my tip. If you're going to build drawers, build lots of shallow ones and very few deep ones. Here's why. Just about everything you store for a shop is fairly thin—hand tools, blades, fasteners, sandpaper, etc. If you have a ton of shallow drawers, you can dedicate each one by category. Plus, it's easier to find what you need when it's not buried under 8 inches of other junk in the same drawer.

—Travis Larson, Senior Editor

TRAVIS LARSON

ADD A CABINET SHELF

Almost everyone has wasted space in their kitchen cabinets. This is especially true in upper cabinets where you house glasses and coffee cups. Take advantage of every inch of room by setting shelf pegs close together to gain extra flat storage for trays, placemats and cutting boards.

REINFORCING FLAT-PACK FURNITURE

Flat-pack furniture is the type that comes in a flat box and requires assembly. Some brands are better than others, but cheaper versions can get wobbly or fall apart the first time you move them. That doesn't always mean the furniture is a total loss. With some 2x2s and 1x2s, screws and a bit of glue, you can reinforce and save the piece to live another day. It's the connections that generally fail because the particleboard just isn't as strong as real wood. Use any or all of these tips to strengthen the connections and help your furniture last.

STRENGTHENING TIPS

- Choose 2x2s that are straight. No twists.
- Use construction adhesive or polyurethane glue wherever finished surfaces meet each other or meet raw wood.
- Use wood glue for joining raw wood surfaces.
- Use screws with matching finish washers for exposed screws.
- If the whole piece is wobbly, disassemble the whole piece to remove the back. Then use glue instead of nails to reattach the back.
- Bar clamps will many of the fixes much easier.

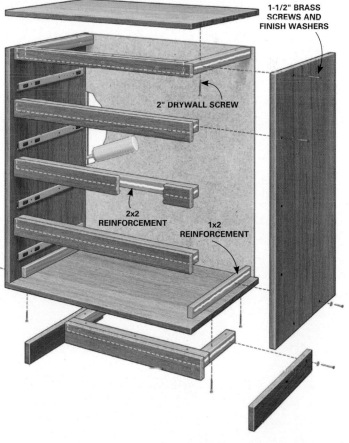

1-1/2" BRASS SCREWS AND FINISH WASHERS

2" DRYWALL SCREW

2x2 REINFORCEMENT

1x2 REINFORCEMENT

Storage&Organizing

LABEL MAKER MANIA

There should be a 12-step program for people like me who become addicted to their label makers. It started when I innocently labeled our tool cabinet drawers. I did our power strip next, and now I just can't stop. The confusing light switches in our entryway—labeled. The kitchen items we take to potluck dinners—labeled with our last name. File folders, the fuse box, pantry jars, tools the neighbors borrow, power adapters—stop me before I label again!

—Tomkin Lee

Editor's Note: Label makers cost $30 to $130 at office supply and discount stores. Several of our Field Editors love the Brother P-Touch PT-2030 (about $35).

FLEXIBLE T-RACK STORAGE

Here's a hanging T-rack that combines two different types of storage space. One side is a typical U-shaped rack for storing pipe and other items that might roll off. The other side is a horizontal rack that allows you to load and unload lumber and molding from the side, instead of from the ends. This is very useful in garages and basements where space is tight.

James E. Rohen

TAPE MEASURES ALWAYS WITHIN REACH

I have a dozen tape measures, but there was never one around when I needed it. So I bought a bunch of electrical junction boxes (50¢ apiece) and nailed them up in strategic locations—next to the miter saw, the table saw, on my workbench, in the garden shed—and put a tape measure and pencil in each one. No more searching for a tape in the middle of a project.

—Gary Wentz, Senior Editor

BIN INDEX

Like a lot of other people, my wife and I love large plastic bins. But remembering what's inside each bin is tough, and reading a small label is nearly impossible when your bins are stored high on garage shelves. We solved both problems by labeling our bins with large numbers. Each number corresponds to a page in a binder that lists the contents of each bin. It's simple to change the list, and it's a heck of a lot easier to find what you need by checking the binder than by rummaging through each bin.

—Gerald Naumann

Editor's Note: When it comes to bin I.D. tags, we like adhesive storage pouches that let you slip index cards in and out easily. You can find these at office supply stores or online retailers. One such product is the NACKit at onlineorganizing.com.

PUT A LAZY SUSAN IN YOUR FRIDGE

If your refrigerator is like mine, the door shelves are filled with salad dressing and mustard and the rest of the condiments get lost behind leftovers on the top shelf. Keep everything in plain view by storing overflow condiments on a lazy Susan on one of your fridge shelves. One spin and that small jar of capers will be a cinch to spot.

—Elisa Bernick, Associate Editor

2-IN-1 TARP STORAGE

As the owner of three ATVs, I use large tarps and bungee cords to protect them from the weather. When they're not in use, I store the tarps on lengths of 2-in. PVC pipe with two PVC end caps. I stick a cap on one end, put my bungee cords inside the pipe, snug on the top cap and roll the tarp around the length of pipe. Things stay orderly, and it's a lot easier to roll a tarp around the pipe than to try to fold it.

—Gregory Jones

WIRE DISPENSER

A plastic crate is a great place to store anything on a spool. Just slip the spools onto a piece of metal conduit and secure the conduit with washers and bolts. There's even space below the spools for tools or scraps of wire.

—John Collins

Storage&Organizing

WIRE SHELVING MADE EASIER

Wire shelving is popular because of its price, flexibility and ease of installation. Wire shelving can be designed to meet almost any need at a fraction of the cost of a custom built-in system. And while installing wire shelving isn't quite a no-brainer, you don't need to be a master carpenter or own a fully equipped cabinet shop to get it done. We picked the brain of a pro for these tips to help you on your next installation.

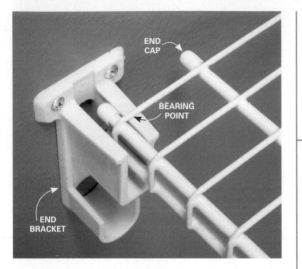

MEET A PRO

Over the past 15 years, Tim Bischke has hung wire shelves in thousands of closets. His jobs have ranged from simple one-shelf reach-in closets to elaborate walk-in wardrobe sanctuaries. When you've hung that many shelves, you can't help but know what you're doing.

A bolt cutter works best

Cut your shelving with a bolt cutter. It's quick and easy, and it makes a clean cut. To make room for the cutter, Tim uses his feet to hold the shelving off the ground.

Measure an inch short

When cutting the shelf, measure wall to wall, and subtract an inch. This allows for the thickness of the end brackets plus a little wiggle room. It's the top, thinner wire that actually supports the shelf, and one wire per end is enough. Cutting exact lengths will only earn you wall scratches and a trip back to the cutting station.

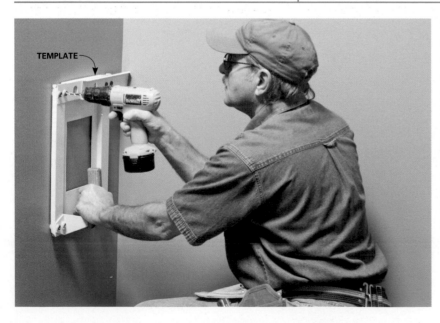

Use a template on the end brackets

Tim's first template was nothing more than a 1x3 with a couple of holes drilled in it. He rested a torpedo level on top of the board and marked the end bracket locations with a pencil. The template he's using here has a built-in level and allows him to drill the holes without marking them first. At $190, this is for guys who do lots of closet shelving. But if that's you, it's a great investment. You can order one from your local Closet Maid dealer.

BUBBLE STICK

Lay it out with a bubble stick

Tim uses a bubble stick rather than a level. A bubble stick is like a ruler and a level rolled into one. Holding a level against the wall with one hand can be frustrating. Levels are rigid, and they pivot out of place when resting on a stud that's bowed out a bit. A bubble stick has a little flex, so it can ride the imperfections of the wall yet still deliver a straight line. You can get one at acehardware.com for less than $10.

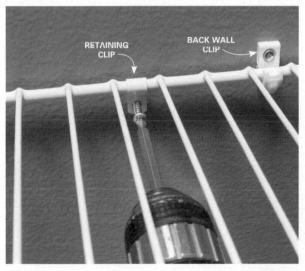

RETAINING CLIP

BACK WALL CLIP

Space the angle brackets evenly

Tim considers aesthetics when installing his angle brackets. If a shelf only needs one bracket, he'll find the stud closest to the center. If two or three brackets are required, he'll try to space them evenly, making sure that at least one bracket toward the center is hitting a stud.

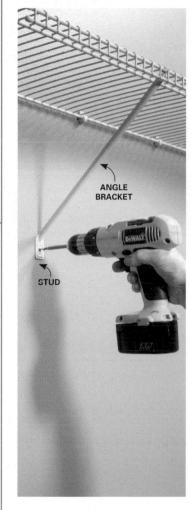

ANGLE BRACKET

STUD

Avoid upheaval

Back wall clips are designed to support the shelf, but if there are a bunch of clothes hanging on the front of the shelf with nothing on top to weigh them down, the back of the shelf can lift. To keep the shelf in place, Tim installs a retaining clip in a stud near the middle of the shelf. One clip toward the middle of an 8-ft. shelf is plenty.

Pegboard prevents tipping

When Tim installs wire shelving in pantries, he likes to cap the top of the shelves with white 1/4-in. pegboard. This stops the skinnier items from tipping over. He uses white zip ties to hold the pegboard in place. A 4 x 8-ft. sheet costs less than $20 at most home centers, which makes it an inexpensive option.

PEGBOARD

Storage&Organizing

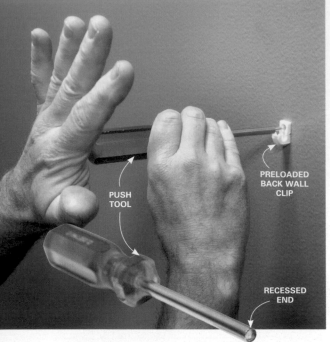

Back wall clips don't need to hit studs

It may go against your every instinct, but hitting a stud when you're installing the back wall clips slows the process down and isn't necessary. After marking their locations, Tim drills a 1/4-in. hole and pops the preloaded pushpin in with a push tool. He loves his push tool. It has a little indentation in the tip that won't slip off the pin when it's being set in the drywall. The occasional wall clips that do land on studs need to be fastened with a screw instead of a pin. You can order a push tool from your local Closet Maid dealer. It should cost less than $25. Use the dealer locator at closetmaid.com.

PUSH TOOL

PRELOADED BACK WALL CLIP

RECESSED END

Buy extra pieces

Even if you're just planning to build one closet shelf, have extra parts on hand. It takes a lot less time to return a few wall clips than it does to stop working to make a special trip to the store for just one. And plans change, so if you or your customer decides to add a section of shelving, you'll be prepared.

Leave the heavy stuff for the garage

Tim primarily works with Closet Maid's standard wire shelving, sold at home centers. Most manufacturers make a heavier-duty product for garage storage, but Tim feels that the regular stuff is plenty strong for the average bedroom or hall closet. However, if your customer's closet is going to store a bowling ball collection, you may want to consider upgrading. The materials for the closet shown here (approximately 22 ft. of shelving and rod) cost about $150.

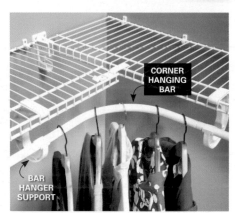

CORNER HANGING BAR

BAR HANGER SUPPORT

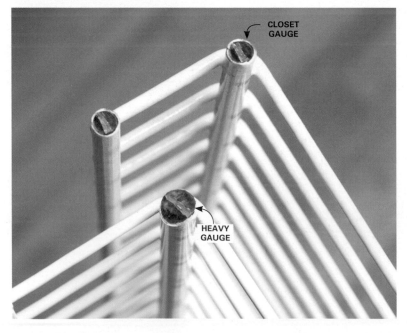

CLOSET GAUGE

HEAVY GAUGE

Hanger sliding freedom

One common complaint about wire shelving is that it restricts the movement of the hangers because the hangers are stuck between the shelves. That's why Tim always offers the upgrade of a hanger rod. Most manufacturers make some version of one. A hanger rod allows clothes to be slid from one end of the closet to the other, even past an inside corner. This upgrade will add about 30 percent to the cost of the materials on a standard shelf design. Make sure the type of shelving you buy will work with the hanging rod hardware you plan to use.

AN **ORGANIZED** CLOSET

Easy-to-build boxes suit any situation

by **David Radtke**

A few months ago, I finally got the bug to organize our closets. I got dizzy wading through Web sites and visiting stores. There was a shelf for this, a rack for that... So I put pencil to paper and devised a simpler system that was easy to build, easy to customize and a money-saver besides. I was so happy with it that I used the same system in my home office, too.

Money, materials and tools

Materials for the boxes shown cost about $250, and I spent an additional $40 on closet hardware. I used 3/4-in. birch plywood because it's strong and thick enough to accept screws. It also finishes well, and the simple grain and warm color look good with just about any décor.

A 4 x 8-ft. sheet costs about $45. Here's a rule of thumb for estimating the plywood you'll need: One sheet will get you two large boxes or four small boxes, plus some leftover parts. If you don't have a pickup, have the plywood ripped

into roughly 16-in.-wide pieces at the home center and then rip it to 15 in. at home.

Before you start cutting up box parts, check the thickness of your plywood. Most "3/4-in." plywood is actually 23/32 in. thick, and the measurements given in the Cutting Lists are based on that. If your plywood is thicker or thinner, you'll have to adjust your box part sizes. The measurements given also account for the typical thickness of iron-on edge band.

A simple jig for perfect crosscuts

To make this closet system work, you need to cut lots of box parts to exact, identical lengths. This plywood jig makes that toolproof. Build the jig and you'll find lots of other uses for it. I use mine whenever I'm building bookcases, cabinets or shelves.

If your saw is out of whack, you won't get accurate cuts. So do a quick inspection: Measure from the front and back of the blade to the edge of the saw's shoe to make sure the blade runs parallel to the shoe. Then grab a square and make sure the blade is set at 90 degrees to the shoe. Install a 40-tooth carbide blade for clean cuts.

Take your time when you build and install the carriage assembly. First, screw the guide to the carriage. Then run your saw along the guide; that will trim the carriage to suit your saw. When you mount the carriage on the rails, use a framing square to make sure the carriage is perfectly perpendicular to the rails. I added a stick-on measuring tape to my jig. One last note: Be sure to set the saw depth so it

1 **Cut a bunch of box parts.** This simple jig lets you churn out precise, identical box parts fast. Raise the stop block on a 1/4-in. spacer so dust build-up doesn't throw off the accuracy.

SPACER

MEET A PRO

David Radtke is a designer, cabinetmaker, woodworker and writer. A former Senior Editor for The Family Handyman, David splits his time between his table saw and his computer.

Storage&Organizing

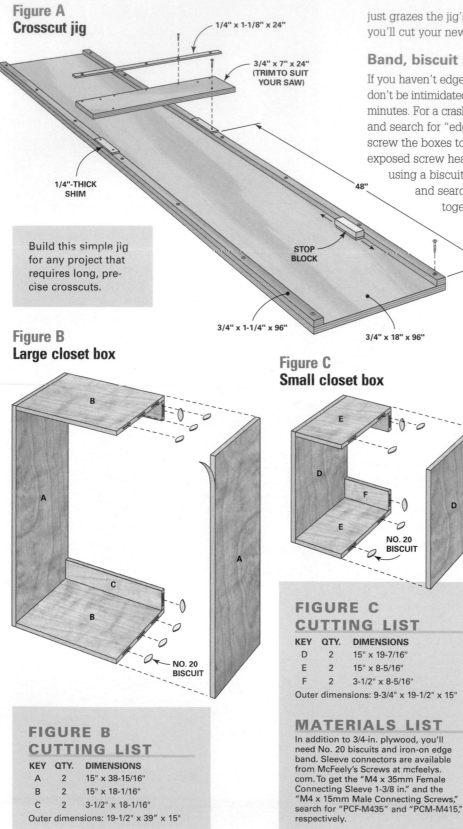

Figure A
Crosscut jig

1/4" x 1-1/8" x 24"

3/4" x 7" x 24"
(TRIM TO SUIT
YOUR SAW)

1/4"-THICK
SHIM

48"

STOP
BLOCK

3/4" x 1-1/4" x 96"

3/4" x 18" x 96"

Build this simple jig
for any project that
requires long, pre-
cise crosscuts.

Figure B
Large closet box

B

A

A

C

B

A

NO. 20
BISCUIT

FIGURE B
CUTTING LIST

KEY	QTY.	DIMENSIONS
A	2	15" x 38-15/16"
B	2	15" x 18-1/16"
C	2	3-1/2" x 18-1/16"

Outer dimensions: 19-1/2" x 39" x 15"

Figure C
Small closet box

E

D

F

E

D

NO. 20
BISCUIT

FIGURE C
CUTTING LIST

KEY	QTY.	DIMENSIONS
D	2	15" x 19-7/16"
E	2	15" x 8-5/16"
F	2	3-1/2" x 8-5/16"

Outer dimensions: 9-3/4" x 19-1/2" x 15"

MATERIALS LIST

In addition to 3/4-in. plywood, you'll
need No. 20 biscuits and iron-on edge
band. Sleeve connectors are available
from McFeely's Screws at mcfeelys.
com. To get the "M4 x 35mm Female
Connecting Sleeve 1-3/8 in." and the
"M4 x 15mm Male Connecting Screws,"
search for "PCF-M435" and "PCM-M415,"
respectively.

---

just grazes the jig's base. If you set the saw too deep,
you'll cut your new jig in half.

Band, biscuit and assemble

If you haven't edge-banded plywood before (**Photo 2**),
don't be intimidated; it's a skill you can master in a few
minutes. For a crash course, go to familyhandyman.com
and search for "edge banding." You could glue and
screw the boxes together, but I used biscuits to avoid
exposed screw heads (**Photo 3**). For a full article on
using a biscuit joiner, go to familyhandyman.com
and search for "biscuit." Clamp each box
together (**Photo 4**) with a clamp at
each corner and check the box
with a framing square. It
should automatically
square itself if you've made
accurate square cuts. Let
the glue set for at least
an hour before removing
the clamps.

Finish and install

Finishing the boxes could
be frustrating: Birch tends
to get blotchy when
stained, and brushing on
a clear finish inside boxes
is slow, fussy work. I side-
stepped both problems
by applying two coats of
Watco Golden Oak fin-
ish. It's a penetrating oil
that leaves only a light
film on the surface, so you
don't have to worry about
brush marks. And the light
color minimizes blotch-
ing. Minwax Wipe-On Poly
would work well too. Use a
brush to apply either finish
and then wipe it with a lint-
free cloth.

Once the finish is dry,
join the boxes together
(**Photo 5**). I used sleeve
connectors (see the
Materials List) because
they look a lot better than
exposed screws. Just
remember to use a Pozidriv
screw tip to tighten the

connectors. It may look like a Phillips, but it's slightly different. Pozidriv screw tips are available at home centers and hardware stores. You'll also need a 3/16-in. or 5mm drill bit.

To simplify mounting the boxes to the closet wall, install a ledger (**Photo 6**) on the wall studs about 8 in. from the floor. The 8-in. elevation keeps the boxes off the floor and provides usable space below. Make the support from long plywood scraps. The elevated ledge will support the assemblies while you get them placed and then screwed to the wall studs. Drive 2-1/2-in. screws through the box backs and the studs. If a box doesn't land on studs, use drywall anchors such as E-Z Ancors.

Once you have all the boxes secured to the wall, you can add closet rods (centered about 11-1/2 in. from the back wall) and other organizers like tie racks and belt hangers and screw them directly into the 3/4-in. plywood construction.

2 **Edge-band the parts.** Cover the visible edges with iron-on edge band. Band only the front edges of the short parts (B, E). On the long parts (A, D), band three edges.

IRON-ON EDGE BANDING

SUPPORT BOARD

3 **Cut the biscuit slots.** Clamp a support board flush with the edge to keep the biscuit joiner from rocking as you cut.

This box system is also great for laundry rooms, garages, entryways... You can even stack the boxes to form furniture such as bookshelves or nightstands.

4 **Assemble boxes.** A cheap disposable paintbrush makes a good spreader. Keep a damp rag handy to wipe off excess glue.

5 **Join the boxes.** Gang the boxes together with screws or special sleeve connectors at the front and back.

SLEEVE CONNECTORS

Endless combinations!

Here's the key to this whole system: The large box is twice as tall as the small box, and the height of each box is equal to twice its width. That means you can combine them in dozens of different configurations. For more versatility, you can drill holes and add adjustable shelf supports to any of the boxes.

6 **Support the units with a cleat.** A level cleat screwed to studs makes aligning and installing the box units a lot easier. Assemble the cleat from leftover plywood scraps.

Storage&Organizing

FOAM WEATHER STRIPPING

DIY DRAWER DIVIDERS

Here's an easy way to make your own inexpensive drawer organizers. Attach thin strips of adhesive-backed foam weather stripping to the inside of your drawers (either to the sides or to the front and back, depending on which way you want your drawers divided). Then set 1/4-in. plywood strips into the drawer with the ends pressed against the weather stripping. Add as many dividers as you need, and voilà—a perfectly organized drawer.

PUT A LAZY SUSAN NEXT TO YOUR STOVE

Having to reach into a cabinet or drawer for frequently used oils, vinegars and sauces is a recipe for frustration. Instead, store them on an attractive lazy Susan on the counter next to your stove. Top it with a plastic mat for easy cleaning. No more frantic searches in the middle of cooking dinner (and all those condiments in full view will make you look like an expert cook!).

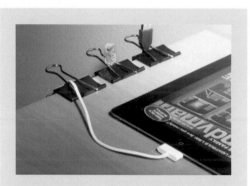

BINDER-CLIP CABLE CATCHER

If you haven't run across this particular cable-organizing tip yet, it's time you did, because it's dirt simple and pure genius. Clamp a binder clip to the edge of your desk to holster USB cables. No more cables slipping behind your desk into the dusty darkness below.

KEEP YOUR SPRAY BOTTLES IN LINE

It can be hard to keep spray bottles from falling over and making a mess under your bathroom and kitchen sink. To keep them upright, hang them from a short tension rod (about $12 at discount stores) in your cabinet.

A BETTER HOSE WRANGLER

There are lots of different products for tying up cords and hoses, including bungees, hook-and-loop straps and cable ties. They all work pretty well. But then we ran into Kwiktwist foam ties (under $10 per pair at online retailers and home centers) and thought they were unique for a couple of reasons. Unlike bungees, they won't stretch or scratch things; they're longer (32 in.) than most cable ties; and the ends are threaded. You can connect several of them and bundle up or hang larger objects like lawn chairs, bikes and ladders. Each tie holds up to 100 lbs.

SKINNY LAUNDRY ROOM CART

A lot of laundry rooms have a narrow wasted space either next to or between the washing machine and dryer, and it's usually a hideout for socks and lint. To take advantage of this space, build a simple plywood cart on fixed casters to hold detergents and other laundry supplies.

STORAGE ABOVE WINDOWS AND DOORS

The empty wall space above doors and windows is organizational gold! Hang a shelf there and use it for bathroom towels, toiletries, books, files, tablecloths—the list is endless.

ORGANIZING TIPS

Do a bit at a time

"When it comes to organizing, a few minutes of clutter-clearing each week takes far less time than attacking an area once a year or even once a month."

—Elizabeth Larkin, home organizing expert

Open your mail over your recycling bin

That way, you'll be less tempted to save unimportant things for later "when you have time." You'll keep what's really important and immediately recycle the rest.

Keep a virtual shopping list

I often found myself at a home center wandering around thinking, "I know I need something else…" but I could never remember what it was. Now I keep an open "notes" tab on my iPhone with a shopping list. I add items to my notes whenever I think of it, and then when I'm at the store, I have my latest and complete list.

Paul Kupprat, Field Editor

Storage&Organizing

REEL-EASY EXTENSION CORD MANAGEMENT

The Cordpro has been around for a few years now, and it remains ridiculously popular in online discussion boards. The gadget organizes a cord, hose or cable into two separate flexible chambers, one for each half. This allows you to access either end independently, so you only unwind what you need and the rest stays coiled.

There are lightweight and heavy-duty versions and a new holiday light version available. Prices range from $8 to $35. Visit cordpro.com.

INSTANT LABELS FOR PARTS DRAWERS

Plastic drawers let you see the nails or screws inside, but you can't always tell their size. Here's a simple solution: Cut the labels off fastener boxes and tape them inside the front of each drawer. You'll know exactly where everything is located at a glance.

—Brett Meineke

TURN-OF-THE-CENTURY OFFICE SUPPLY HOLDER

Screw hose clamps to a board and mount it on the wall in your home office. Secure mason jars in the hose clamps to create clever storage for office supplies such as stamps, paper clips and string. The clear jars let you immediately see where everything is. This is also a great idea for bathrooms and workshops.

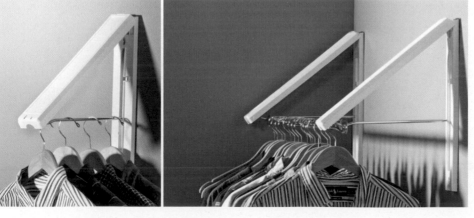

CLOTHES STORAGE

Folding hanger rods collapse against the wall when they're not in use, saving valuable space in tiny rooms. They're great for wet clothes and hunting gear. The Arrow Hanger single- and double-hanger versions shown ($19 and $45) are available at amazon.com and other online retailers.

6 Outdoor Structures, Landscaping & Gardening

IN THIS CHAPTER

HandyHints®

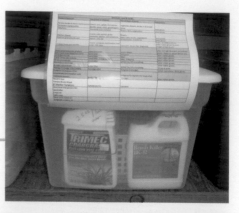

FENCE POST REMOVAL

I've tried a lot of different methods for removing 4x4 fence posts sunk in concrete, but this is the easiest one I've found. Screw a piece of scrap 2x4 to the post a couple of inches from the ground, put a landscape timber alongside as a fulcrum, and use a long metal bar as a lever. Just stand on the bar, and the post and concrete footing will usually pop right out of the ground.

—Mike Barnes

LAWN CHEMICAL INVENTORY

I kept buying duplicates of fungicides and weed killers because I never knew what we already had. Not only that, we have so many I could never remember how to use them all (and reading the small print on the labels is no fun). So I put all our lawn chemicals into a plastic bin, made a simple spreadsheet on the computer and attached it to the front of the bin. Now I can easily see what we have and how to use it.

READER PHOTOS (2)

—Karen Merkel

DIGGING POSTHOLES IN SANDY SOIL

Randy
Schmitt

When you're digging postholes in hard-packed sandy soil, removing the last bits of dirt at the bottom of the deep hole can be tough. It's time to grab your shop vacuum. Loosen the soil and shape the hole as usual with a clamshell posthole digger. Then attach a long, straight extension tube to your shop vacuum hose and suck up the loose soil at the bottom of the hole.

SEED I.D.

Steve Virgilio

When you sow new seeds in the spring, it's hard to remember exactly where they're planted before they sprout. That's a problem when putting in other seeds and plants and even for watering, especially if you plant in curved rows. To make my rows easy to find, I sprinkle a little play sand over the seeds as I plant them. The seeds sprout right through the sand, I know exactly where to water, and the sand helps keep the weeds down while providing good drainage.

LARGE-PRINT LAWN GUIDE

I use a hose end sprayer for liquids and a broadcast spreader for granular lawn treatments. When it's time to apply herbicides and fertilizers, it takes me 10 minutes to hunt down my glasses so I can read the tiny print that tells me the correct application rates. This year I wrote the information in large print on my spreader and hose end sprayer. Now when I lose my glasses, at least I know they're not in the garden shed! —Jeff Cox

SPOT-WATERING TIP FOR GRASS SEED

When you need to water newly seeded patches throughout your lawn, it can be tough to remember where you've spread the seed. Give yourself a visual reminder by lightly topping the new grass seed with hamster bedding. It will keep the newly seeded areas moist, the grass will grow right through the bedding and you'll immediately see where you need to water.

—Mike Donacik

LAWN CHEMICAL OVERSPRAY PREVENTION

To protect my shrubs and flowers when I'm using a weed killer such as Roundup, I came up with this nifty technique. I take the sprayer head off my spray wand, tape a funnel to the wand and then replace the sprayer head. The funnel directs the weed killer where I want it and protects everything else from overspray.

—Bill Brinkman

Bob Riedel

PROTECT SPRINKLER HEADS IN THE ROCKS...

Many of my sprinkler system heads are surrounded by landscape rocks. To keep the rocks from interfering with the sprinkler heads, especially when they're coming down, I protect them with PVC pipe. I cut the PVC pipe into 6-in. lengths and push it into the ground around the heads so the pipe sticks up a little bit higher than the rocks.

...AND IN THE LAWN

I've had to replace numerous sprinkler heads over the years after running over them in the grass with my lawn mower. To solve the problem, I stuck short lengths of 4-in. PVC pipe around each head so they stick up about an inch higher than the sprinkler heads. I haven't had to replace a sprinkler head since, and it's also helped keep leaves and grass clippings from building up around the heads.

Matthew Campanile

HandyHints®

Brenda Barnes

UMBRELLA STAND/PLANTER

I needed a stand for the large shade umbrella I bought for our patio, but all the ones I could find were designed for use under a patio table. Then I had a brilliant idea. I bought a large resin flowerpot and filled it about a third full with concrete.

CONCRETE   PVC

While the concrete was wet, I inserted a short length of PVC pipe that was just slightly larger in diameter than the umbrella pole. I covered the bottom of the pipe with duct tape so it wouldn't fill with concrete. Then I drilled a few drainage holes above the concrete, filled the pot with potting soil and planted some shade-loving plants. Now I have a windproof umbrella stand and a beautiful pot of flowers in one!

WATER TUBE

READER PHOTO

POISON YOUR IVY, NOT YOUR SHRUB

Here's a clever way to get rid of twining briars and nuisance vines without damaging your shrubs. Buy a few floral water tubes (available at floral supply companies and nurseries) or just reuse the tubes that come with individual roses. Fill the floral tube with a little herbicide (like Roundup) and replace the rubber cap to keep out pets and rain. Stick the tube in the ground and then stick the tip of the vine into the tube. The vine will "drink up" the weed killer down to its roots and die within a few days.

Judi Collins

WEATHERPROOF PLANT LABELS

Here's an easy way to keep a paper seed packet from getting destroyed by wind and rain out in your garden: Slip a small zipper-type plastic bag over the packet, with the bag upside down so the rain doesn't get in.

—Rev. John Henault

DEPOSITS MADE HERE

OUTDOOR DOGGY DOO-DOO HOLDER

If you're a dog owner, getting rid of all those little bags of doggy doo-doo can be a pain. They get lost in the snow if you set them outside, and if you toss them directly in your outdoor garbage can, they fall to the bottom and get stuck until spring (yuck!). We use an old mailbox mounted on a post as our doo-doo collector. We stick a small shopping bag inside, toss in the little collection bags all week long and then tie up the larger bag and toss it in the garbage can.

—Brian Kiviat

STONE WATERFALL

This simple-to-build water feature adds a lot of charm to your yard

by **Jeff Gorton, Associate Editor**

There are a thousand ways to build a backyard fountain. But if you're looking for simplicity, you can't beat this approach. You basically dig a hole in the ground, line it with rubber membrane and cover it with a stack of rocks. The waterfall looks beautiful, but the best part is the sound. If you close your eyes, it's easy to imagine yourself sitting next to a gurgling creek in the middle of the woods.

Once the materials were in hand, the project took less than a day. We were a little surprised at how much digging there was, considering the size of the reservoir. But this was the only tough part. Stacking the stone was fun. We had to rearrange the stones a few times, but in the end the water flowed nicely over the edges and created just the effect we wanted.

Gather your supplies ahead of time

We've provided a Materials List (p. 206) so you'll know what to shop for. Check local landscape suppliers and home centers to find the stone, pump and pond liner. You can also order a pump online. One source is discount-pumps.biz. A home center or lumberyard will have the treated lumber, rebar, hardware cloth and miscellaneous hardware you'll need. We spent about $150 for 700 lbs. of bluestone and $125 on the remaining items.

Pick out your stones

You'll need a minivan or truck to haul this much stone, or you'll have to make several trips with your car. At the stone yard, start by finding a large, flat stone for the base. Ours was about 24 in. across. Then stack stones on top in an arrangement you like. When you think you've got enough, add a few more for good measure. Don't forget to pick up three or four 5-gallon buckets full of crushed stone for the base. For this we used gray stones that ranged from 2 to 2-1/2 in. in diameter.

Dig the hole and build the frame

Using 2x8s like we did, you'll need a hole that's about 8 in. deep. In our garden, stone walls limited the size of our reservoir to about 30 in. across, but if you have room, make it bigger. The bigger the reservoir, the less often you'll have to fill it with water.

The first step is to cut the 2x8s to length and nail or screw them together. Use stainless steel or corrosion-resistant screws. Set the frame in the hole and level it (**Photo 1**). Then spread a 1-in. layer of sand over the bottom. Cut a square of pond liner about 2 ft. wider and longer than the inside dimensions of the frame and lay it in place. Fold the pond liner to fit the inside corners and let the extra drape down the outside of the frame. From the leftover material, cut a 20-in. square of pond liner and lay it in the center as padding for the two concrete blocks. Then set the two concrete blocks into place and wiggle them into the sand until the tops are level with the edges of the frame. The blocks will support the weight of the stones.

Next cut pieces of 1/2-in. rebar to span the reservoir. A hacksaw will work, but it's slow going. An angle grinder with a metal-cutting disc is a better option. Attach the rebar with 1/2-in. copper plumbing straps (**Photo 2**). When you're done, cover the rebar with galvanized 1/4-in. hardware cloth. Bend the hardware cloth down around the outside edges of the box to hold it in place and hide sharp edges.

Cut an access hole in the hardware cloth about 8 in. square and between two lengths of rebar. Once again, fold the edges of the hardware cloth down to hide sharp edges. Use this hole to

1 **Dig a hole and lay in a wooden frame.** Add or remove dirt from under the frame to level it. Remove rocks, dirt chunks and other debris from the dirt and rake it roughly level. Pour a 1/2- to 1-in. layer of sand over the dirt and level it out.

2 **Line the frame and add rebar.** Lay the pond liner in the frame and fold the corners. Set the two concrete blocks in the center. Attach lengths of rebar about every 8 in. Complete the reservoir by adding a layer of hardware cloth.

Figure A
Waterfall details

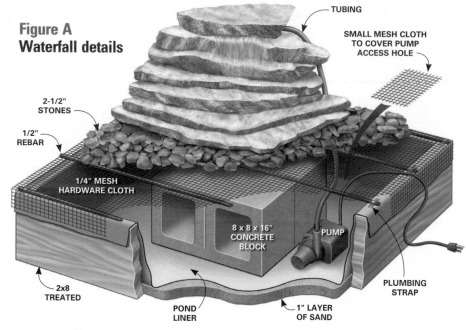

TUBING

SMALL MESH CLOTH TO COVER PUMP ACCESS HOLE

2-1/2" STONES

1/2" REBAR

1/4" MESH HARDWARE CLOTH

8 x 8 x 16" CONCRETE BLOCK

PUMP

2x8 TREATED

POND LINER

1" LAYER OF SAND

PLUMBING STRAP

MATERIALS LIST

- 600 to 700 lbs. of flat stone
- Three 5-gallon buckets of crushed stone
- Two 60-lb. bags of sand
- Five 3- or 4-ft. lengths of 1/2-in. rebar
- Two 8 x 8 x 16-in. concrete blocks
- Pond liner (depending on the size of your reservoir)
- Ten 1/2-in. copper plumbing straps
- 12 corrosion-resistant 3-in. screws

- 20 corrosion-resistant 1-1/2-in. screws
- Two 2x8s, 8 ft. or longer (depending on the size of your reservoir)
- Water feature pump (see "Buying the Pump," p. 207)
- Three or 4 ft. of plastic tubing—match the tubing size to the outlet on your pump
- One small stainless steel band clamp
- One or two blocks of duct seal putty— you'll usually find this in the electrical department.

3 **Build the waterfall.** Spread a layer of gravel over the hardware cloth. Then start stacking the stone. Pour water over the stones occasionally to see how it's flowing.

install the pump. Cut another piece of hardware cloth to set over the hole so you can cover it with gravel. You'll use this access hole to clean out the reservoir occasionally and to remove the pump in the winter if you live in a cold climate.

Stack the stone

Now for the fun part—building the waterfall. Spread the stone out near the reservoir so you can choose the size and shape you want. Start the stack with your large base stone. Stack a few stones, then pour some water over them to see how it flows (Photo 3). You can adjust the position of the stone, or choose a different one, until you get a flow pattern you like.

Install the pump and watch the water flow

Connect the pump to a length of tubing with a hose clamp. Allow enough tubing to reach from the bottom of the reservoir to the top center of the stone stack. Set the pump in the reservoir and route the tubing to the top in the least conspicuous place. Photo C at right shows how we held the tubing in place and directed the water to the front of the waterfall with duct seal

Buying the pump

We made the mistake of starting off with a pump that was too small and were unhappy with the amount of water flowing. We recommend a pump with a flow rate of at least 300 gallons per hour and a "lift" or "head" of at least 6 ft.

If you don't have a GFCI outlet within reach of the pump cord, consider buying a low-voltage pump instead. It'll cost a little more because in addition to the pump you have to purchase a transformer (about $35), but that's a small price to pay to avoid digging a deep trench.

Buy low-voltage pumps online at discount-pumps.biz, or ask at the local landscape supplier. You can mount the transformer near the outlet and run low-voltage wire to the pump. Low-voltage wire only needs to be buried a few inches. Running new wiring for a 120-volt pump requires an electrical permit and a much deeper trench.

putty. The duct seal putty also prevents the tubing from being crushed by the top stone.

Now for the moment of truth. Fill the reservoir with water and plug in the pump. It may take a few seconds at first for the pump to start moving the water. When it does, see how it flows and make final adjustments by shimming the stones (Photo B at right).

Keep an eye on the waterfall for the first day or two to get a feel for how often you have to refill the reservoir. On hot, windy days, it may run low quickly. In cold climates, remember to bring the pump inside before winter so it isn't damaged by freezing.

Fine-tuning techniques

If the water isn't flowing the way you'd like, here are a few tips to try. You can cause the water to drip rather than follow the underside of the stone by cutting a drip groove (**Photo A**). If the water isn't running in the right direction, shim under the stone to tilt it and redirect the water flow (**Photo B**). You can also create a dam with duct seal putty (**Photo C**) to block or change the water flow.

A **Cut a drip groove for better flow.** Create a better waterfall effect by cutting a groove on the underside of flat stones. The groove causes the water to drip rather than flow back along the underside of the stone.

B **Shim with small stones.** Redirect the water by tilting the stones with small shims. Just lift the stone and wedge the shim underneath.

C **Reroute water with a dam.** Make a dam out of duct seal putty to prevent water from rolling off the back of the waterfall. Here we also used the putty to secure the tubing between the top two stones.

GARDEN BENCH

A curved seat makes it comfortable; biscuit joinery makes it simple and strong

by **Jeff Gorton, Associate Editor**

I built this bench four years ago. Since then, it's been used and abused as a prop on photo shoots, and sat on and commented on by staff and passersby. The first thing they all notice is the design—simple but handsome. Then, as soon they sit down, they're all surprised by how comfortable it is.

Finally, everyone admires my amazing woodworking skills. But the truth is, this bench is just plain easy to build. I used only biscuits and screws, the simplest types of joinery. Still, the bench is surprisingly strong. It's been hauled around, knocked around and used as a mini scaffold—and once it even fell out of a moving pickup. But it's still solid.

Round up the tools and materials

I spent about $95 for the lumber for this bench. You may have to buy more lumber to get knot-free pieces, so your cost may vary. You'll find everything you need to build this bench at your local home center or lumberyard. Refer to the Materials List on p. 210, then choose the lumber carefully to avoid large knots.

In addition to the lumber, screws and wood plugs, you'll need No. 20 wood biscuits and a special tool called a plate or biscuit joiner to cut the biscuit slots. You can buy a good-quality biscuit joiner for $100 to $170. You'll also need some clamps, a table saw and a router fitted with a 1/4-in. round-over bit.

Cut, drill and slot the parts

Start by inspecting your boards and planning the cuts to take advantage of the knot-free sections. Use a table saw to rip the boards to the right width. For crisp, clean edges, rip about 1/4 in. from the edge of the boards before you rip them to the final width. To work around knots, you may have to rough-cut some of the boards to approximate length before ripping them. When you're done ripping, cut the parts to length. We used a 1/4-in. round-over bit and router to ease the edges of the seat boards. It's a great task for a router table setup if you have one.

Next, measure and mark the center of all the screw holes and drill 3/8-in.-deep holes for the 1/2-in. wood plugs. I used a Forstner bit to create clean, flat-bottom holes. The final step in preparing the parts for assembly is cutting the biscuit slots. If you've read my previous plate joiner story, you know I'm a proponent of a technique I call the bench reference method. Rather than use the adjustable fence to position the slots, you simply place your workpiece and the base of the biscuit joiner against the bench top and cut the slot. To find the story, go to familyhandyman.com and search for "biscuit joints."

The only downside to this method is that the slot isn't always centered on the part, so you have to pay close attention to orientation as you cut the slots and assemble the bench. You'll see how I use masking tape to keep track of the orientation. Photos 2 – 5 show the plate-joining techniques I used to cut slots in the parts.

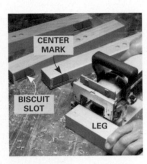

1 Drill plug recesses. Use a 1/2-in. Forstner bit to drill recesses for the screws. Later you'll fill them with wood plugs to hide the screws. You can easily control the depth of the hole by drilling until the top of the cutter is flush with the surface.

2 Cut biscuit slots for the seat rails. Mark the centers of the biscuit slots on masking tape. Then, with the plug recesses facing up, cut the slots in the narrow sides of the legs. Keep the plate joiner and leg tight to the bench top as you cut. Use tape to avoid marks on the wood and to keep track of the orientation of the pieces.

3 Position slots for the long rails with a spacer. Orient the leg so the previously cut slot is facing up, and cut a slot on the side opposite the plug holes. Use a spacer to position the slot so the long rail will be centered on the leg when it's installed.

4 Cut slots in the rail ends. Mark the centers of the curved seat rails and long rails on masking tape. The tape also helps you keep track of the orientation of the slots.

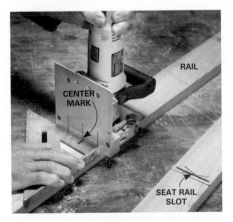

5 Cut slots in the long rails. Position the long rails with the masking tape facing down. Use a Speed Square as a guide for cutting biscuit slots for the intermediate rails. Align the square with the edge mark for the seat rail. Make a center mark on the square as a reference for lining up the plate joiner.

6 Join the seat rails and legs with biscuits. Put a biscuit in the slot and dry-fit the leg and seat rail to make sure the rail is oriented correctly. It should be centered on the leg. Then spread glue in the slots and on the biscuit and press the leg and the seat rail together.

MATERIALS LIST

ITEM	QTY.
2x4 x 8' cedar*	1
5/4x6 x 10' cedar decking*	2
1x6 x 6' cedar*	4
No. 20 biscuits	12
1-lb. box of 2-1/2" deck screws	1
1-lb. box of 1-5/8" deck screws	1
8-oz. bottle of exterior wood glue	1
1/2" flat-top wood plugs	40
Quart of exterior wood finish	1

You may need extra if you want all knot-free parts.

CUTTING LIST

KEY	QTY.	SIZE & DESCRIPTION
A	4	16" x 1-1/2" x 2" legs
B	4	13" x 1" x 3" seat rails (curved top)
C	2	13" x 1" x 2" lower rails
D	2	54" x 1" x 3" rails
E	1	55" x 1" x 2" brace
F	4	10-1/2" x 1" x 3" leg braces (curved)
G	4	6" x 1" x 2" corner braces
H	7	60" x 3/4" x 2-1/8" seat slats

7 **Complete the leg assembly.** Use a spacer to support the lower rail. Then drive screws through the legs into the rail.

1/2" SPACER

8 **Connect the seat rails with biscuits.** Join the two long rails with the two intermediate seat rails with biscuits and glue. Clamp them and let the glue set about 30 minutes.

Figure A   Garden bench

Overall dimensions: 60" long, 16-1/2" wide, 16-3/4" tall

Part F
Detail

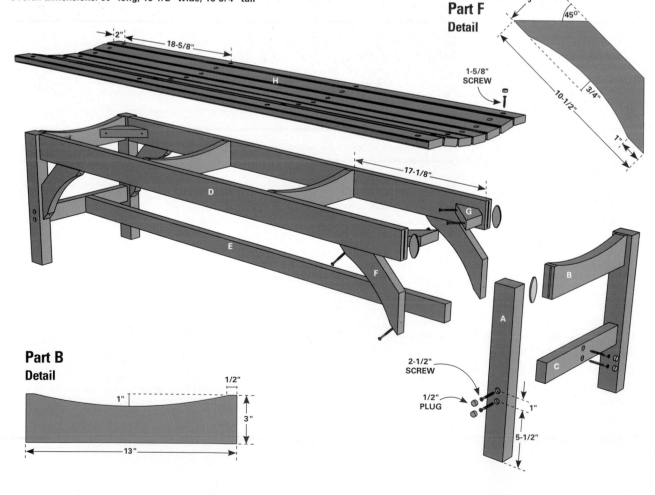

Part B
Detail

9 **Join the leg and seat assemblies.** Connect the leg assembies to the seat assembly with biscuits and clamp them together. Then attach the brace with screws.

LEG ASSEMBLY

BRACE

SEAT ASSEMBLY

Assemble the bench with biscuits and screws

Photos 6 – 11 show the assembly steps. Biscuits connect the legs to the rails for extra strength. Spread exterior wood glue in the slots and on the biscuits. Then clamp the parts until the glue sets. Use 2-1/2-in. deck screws to attach the legs to the braces (Photos 7 and 9). If you aren't using self-drilling screws, drill pilot holes to avoid splitting the parts. Attach the top slats to the frame with 1-5/8-in. deck screws. I plugged the screw holes with 1/2-in. flat-top birch plugs, but if you own a drill press, you can make your own cedar plugs using a 1/2-in. plug cutter.

I finished the bench with Cabot Australian Timber Oil. This penetrating oil finish leaves the wood looking natural, but it has to be reapplied every year. For a glossy, more permanent finish, you could use Sikkens Cetol SRD or spar varnish.

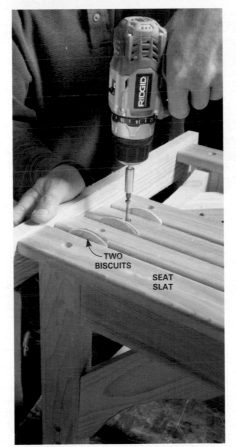

TWO BISCUITS

SEAT SLAT

10 **Screw on the seat slats.** Start by attaching the two outside slats. Then center the middle slat and attach it with screws. Next, position the remaining slats so there's an even space (two biscuits wide) between them. Use a board to align the slat ends.

11 **Hide the screws with wood plugs.** Glue flat-top wood plugs into the plug recesses. Use a cutoff dowel or a small block of wood to pound them flush.

TREE HOUSE
TIPS & IDEAS

Advice for building, attaching and furnishing your home in the treetops

by **Elisa Bernick, Associate Editor**

Climbing trees has always been part of human history, allowing us to escape floods, saber-toothed tigers and intruders (especially parents with chores in mind). Building tree houses has long been part of human history, too. In that spirit, we've gathered tree house building tips, project ideas and photos from *TFH* readers and professional tree house builders. Maybe something here will inspire you to build the tree house of your dreams, for the special kids in your life or as a way to escape from modern day saber-toothed tigers and chore-requesting spouses. Enjoy!

VERTICAL HORIZONS

Tree house building tips

OUT'N'ABOUT

Site considerations

■ Choose a healthy, long-lived hardwood for maximum support, with load-bearing branches at least 8 in. in diameter (larger if the species is a softwood).

■ The best trees include maple, oak, fir, beech and hemlock.

■ You don't have to build it very high, just high enough so nobody gets a bump on the head when walking underneath it.

Keep weight and stability in mind

■ Build the platform as close to the trunk as possible and add diagonal bracing for extra strength to support uneven loads.

■ Put the load over the base of the tree, not on one side.

■ For heavy tree houses, consider spreading the weight among several trees.

■ A tree house will act as a sail in strong winds, which can add a large load to the tree's roots. In high-wind areas, build your tree house in the lower third of the tree.

"You get a different perspective when you're up in a tree. First of all, nobody can find you because nobody ever looks up. And when you're up there, you're able to look up, down and all around—it's another world up there."

—Michael Garnier,
professional tree house builder

VERTICAL HORIZONS

212   **OUTDOOR STRUCTURES, LANDSCAPING & GARDENING**

CRAIG MACLEAN

Don't restrict tree growth

- Don't constrict branches with rope, straps or wire. This can strangle the tree.
- Add spacers between the beams and the tree to allow movement.
- Use extra-long large bolts. This leaves most of the shaft exposed so you can mount items on the ends and lets the tree grow over the shaft (see "Use the Right Fasteners," p. 215).
- Allow a 2-in. gap around the tree if it passes through the floor and a 3-in. gap if it passes through the roof (photo left).

To accommodate tree movement and growth, allow gaps around any branches or trunks that penetrate the tree house.

References you may find useful

Books

Treehouses: The Art and Craft of Living Out on a Limb and *Home Tree Home* by Peter Nelson

Build Your Own Treehouse by Maurice Barkley

Web links

- thetreehouseguide.com
- treehouses.com
- treehousesupplies.com
- treetopbuilders.net

"I built a tree house for my kids in our backyard. It was tricky getting the roof in place and, of course, nothing is square. They drew the wall design on regular paper, and we transferred the pictures to the walls, using a grid method. We replace the old pictures with new ones each year."

—Sean Milroy

When building on one main trunk, level the main platform by cantilevering the beams and supporting them from below.

SEAN MILROY

TREE HOUSE TIPS & IDEAS   **213**

Level the floor

It's much easier to build the rest of the structure if the floor is level and can support the entire weight of the tree house. Consider these methods:

- Lay beams across the branches and shim until level.
- Run the beams between trunks of several different trees.
- Cantilever the beams out from a single trunk and support them from above or below.

To keep a large tree house stable, center the load over the trunk and spread the weight among several branches.

"I wanted my kids to experience the same fun I had in my tree house as a kid but without the risk of killing themselves—like I nearly did."

—Brenton LaFleur

Build sections on the ground and hoist them into position

Tree houses are heavier than they might look. It's often easier and safer to fabricate the main sections on the ground and then hoist them into position (**photo right**). If branches penetrate areas of the treehouse, complete the construction up in the trees (**photo below right**).

"I built it in my driveway and used a friend's backhoe to lift it up on the joists I'd hung in the trees. The morning of 'the big lift' was quite exciting. We served bagels and coffee in the driveway for people who came to watch."

—Mike Whitaker

"I assembled the platform and house on the ground, then disassembled them. After attaching the supports to the trees, I lifted the platform piece by piece and assembled it on the supports. An extra set of hands was needed only to raise the four walls and two roof sections. Final assembly took place in the trees."

—Bob Lackey

NATE MAANE

Kids can build treehouses too

"I am 13 years old and I've been building this fort for a few years now. I've had no help from adults at all. I've got a toolbox full of tools, plus I have a DeWalt drill and a jigsaw with a laser. I really want the world to know about my fort. Remember, I'm only 13 and I built this myself. If you don't believe me, you can e-mail my mom."

—Nate Maane

Use the right fasteners

■ Don't run bolts through the tree. Lag bolts cause less tree damage than through bolts.

■ Don't use too many fasteners. One large bolt is better than many screws or nails. You get the same strength but with fewer puncture wounds to the tree.

■ Whenever possible, perch your tree house on top of fasteners rather than pinning beams to the tree. This gives the tree room to move and grow.

■ Even for smaller, lighter tree houses where the load is spread over three or four attachment points, consider using 1-in.- or 1-1/4-in.-diameter lag bolts.

■ You can order floating brackets and tree house fasteners from specialty suppliers such as garnierlimb.com or treehousesupplies.com or special-order them from home centers. These bolts are pricey (about $100 each) and often require special tools. But they allow the tree more room to grow (they can support heavy loads up to 5 in. from the tree) and they hold more weight than normal bolts.

MICHAEL GARNIER

Allow for flexible supports, especially if you use more than one tree, so that trees can move in the wind. Special floating brackets allow the tree to sway.

Large, strong custom bolts can support tree house beams with only one puncture point in the tree. These specialty tree house fasteners (known as TABs or GLs) are worth considering if you want your tree house to last more than a few years, you want to keep tree damage to a minimum and the tree house you're building is large.

MICHAEL GARNIER

MICHAEL GARNIER

Minimize tree damage by perching beams and braces on top of specialty fasteners instead of pinning them to the tree.

Tree house tourism destinations

Type "tree house hotels" and "tree house destinations" into your browser, and you'll be dazzled by the number of amazing tree houses you can visit all over the world. Here are a few close to home:

Vertical Horizons Tree House Paradise, a B & B tree house resort located in southern Oregon. Three state-of-the-art tree house guest quarters. Also offers tree climbing as well as salmon run and mushroom-picking expeditions. treehouseparadise.com

Out'n'About Treehouse Treesort in Takilma, Oregon. Michael Garnier's B & B tree house complex with 13 custom guest tree houses including Treezebo, Serendipitree and Pleasantree. Garnier also offers tree house building workshops, a zip-line course, a canopy walk and more. treehouses.com

Mystrees. A large backyard village of seven child-size tree houses connected by seven rope bridges and created by tree house architect Maurice Barkley. Each is designed to spark a child's imagination. Mystrees is located near Rochester, New York. mystrees.com

Vertical Horizons

Out'n'About

Mystrees

Checklist of cool accessories (to buy or make)

Zip lines
Rope swings, ladders and bridges
Speaking tube
Periscope
Clothesline pulley with bucket
  between tree house and kitchen
  for frequent snacks (or to lower to
  the ground to fetch provisions)
Pirates' treasure chest
Flag
Binoculars
Tennis ball/potato launcher
Water cannon
Fire pole or slide
Trap door
Solar-powered lights or lanterns
Fold-down benches and tables

The dark side of tree houses

Building a tree house is a wonderfully whimsical and romantic idea. But it's important to go into it with your eyes open. Keep the following issues in mind before building:

Tree damage
Tree houses do damage trees. Foot traffic compresses the soil, which is bad for the roots. Adding weight in the branches can also stress the tree roots, and fasteners can cause infection. Most trees will survive this abuse, but think twice before you build in a treasured tree.
  To minimize tree damage:
- Consider using one or two supports to take stress off the tree.
- Make the fewest punctures necessary to support the tree house safely. Any damage to the bark of the tree is a potential entry point for disease and bacteria.
- Don't put fasteners too close together, which can weaken that section of the tree. Use at least 3/4-in. bolts spaced at least 18 in. apart vertically and 12 in. apart horizontally.
- Avoid slinging cables and ropes over branches. They cut through the bark as the structure moves.

Neighborhood concerns and municipal regulations
Do you need a building permit? It depends on local laws and the nature of your tree house. If you're considering building one that will be visible to your neighbors, discuss it with them in advance to avoid problems. Often, a municipality becomes involved after a neighbor complains. Stay away from boundary lines and don't build your tree house where it will infringe on a neighbor's privacy.

Injuries
Kids can get hurt playing in a tree house. Don't build higher than 8 ft. and make sure to build safe, strong rails. Also, nobody should be in a tree house in high winds or lightning.

PEBBLE MOSAIC
STEPPERS

Collect some river rock and make your own unique stepping-stone path

by **Jeff Gorton, Associate Editor**

Alice Medley loves to create works of art from the pebbles she collects. And she was generous enough to invite us into her garage workshop to show us how to make these beautiful pebble mosaic stepping-stones. She uses a "dry-set" technique that makes it easy to change or adjust the pattern as you go without having to dig the stones out of wet mortar.

In addition to showing you how to make these stepping-stones, we've included plans for an ingenious reusable wooden mold that Alice purchased from a North Woods carpenter. The initial investment for this project—about $50—gets you the plywood, a bag of mortar, pigment and muriatic acid. It's enough material to make about seven or eight stepping-stones. After that, each one will cost you less than a dollar.

Build the mold

A small sheet of 3/4-in. plywood and some 1-1/4-in. screws are all you'll need to build the mold. Cut out the pieces according to the Cutting List. **Figure A** (p. 218) shows how the parts go together. When you're done, brush linseed or vegetable oil on the mold to protect it from moisture.

Start by collecting the stones

Alice collects her stones on the north shore of Lake Superior. You'll find similar stones in most parts of the country. Look for them in river and creek beds or along lakeshores. Wherever you find them, make sure you have permission and that it's legal to collect them. Another possible source is your local landscape supplier or wherever landscaping stone is sold.

Alice likes to sort them by color. She's got buckets and cans full of red, gray, white, brown and speckled

MEET AN EXPERT

Alice Medley started out using more traditional mosaic materials like tile and glass for her outdoor art projects. Then she discovered she could marry her love of stones with her love of mosaics. Alice learned this dry-mortar technique from Laura Stone, a stone mosaic artist from Minnesota. Alice has also created a 4-ft.-diameter, built-in-place pad for her backyard fire kettle using the same technique and is waiting to see how it holds up through harsh Minnesota winters.

1 Assemble the mold. This plywood mold goes together quickly and comes apart easily after the mortar hardens. And you can use it again and again.

2 Spread dry mortar in the mold. Fill the plastic-lined mold to about 3/4 in. from the top with dry Type S mortar. Level it with your gloved hand. It doesn't have to be perfectly flat.

3 Arrange stones in a pattern. The only rule is to keep the stones close together so they touch and stand up and are not laid flat.

MATERIALS LIST

- Collection of small stones
- One bag of Type S mortar mix
- 2' x 2' square piece of 6-mil poly
- 48" x 48" x ¾" plywood
- Forty 1-1/4" corrosion-resistant screws
- Optional items: mortar pigment or colored grout, muriatic acid and stone sealer

Figure A
Stepping-stone mold
(forms 12" square steppers)

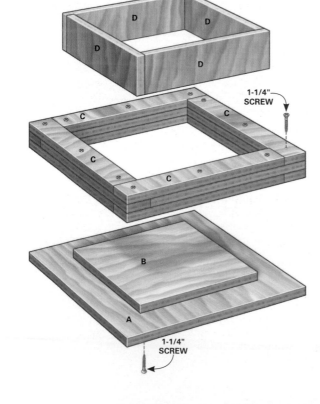

stones. Keeping them sorted makes it a lot easier for her to find the right one as she creates a pattern.

Assemble the stepping-stone

Photos 1 – 4 show the assembly steps. Alice likes to add a little brown pigment to the dry Type S mortar mix to give the stepping-stones a mellower look. You'll find cement pigments and Type S mortar at home centers and masonry suppliers. Or you can cheat like Alice does and just mix in a little colored ceramic tile grout. Make sure to wear rubber gloves to protect your skin from the mortar, which can cause skin burns.

Some of Alice's vast collection of rocks.

You don't have to plan your pattern ahead of time. Alice says she has a design in mind and just starts arranging the stones. It's easier to start along the edges or in a corner and work toward the center, though. You'll have less fitting to do as you fill in the last few stones. Keep the stones close together and oriented with the long axis up and down. While it's tempting, Alice cautions against laying a stone flat. She says it doesn't look as good as you think it will and is more likely to pop out later. When you're done tamping the stones into the dry mortar, inspect the space between the stones to see if there are spots that require more mortar. They should be buried at least halfway. Fill sparse areas with more mortar. Dust any dry mortar off the stones with a small brush.

The trickiest part of the process is wetting the mortar (Photo 5). We can't tell you exactly how much water to add, but it's better to sprinkle on several small doses than to get

CUTTING LIST

KEY	QTY.	SIZE & DESCRIPTION
A	1	18" x 18" x 3/4" subbase
B	1	12" x 12" x 3/4" base
C	12	2-1/4" x 15-3/4" x 3/4" frame
D	4	3-1/4" x 12-3/4" x 3/4" sides

Tip

"You can just pull out the rocks and wipe the slate clean if you don't like the design."

—Alice Medley

4 **Tamp the stones to level the tops.** Lay a board across the stones and pound on it with a rubber mallet to embed the stones in the dry mortar and set the tops level with each other.

impatient and risk adding too much. Alice says the key is to alternate between wetting the top and tapping on the mold with the rubber mallet until it seems like not all of the water is being absorbed and bubbles quit appearing (**Photo 6**). Expect to spend about 45 minutes sprinkling and tapping.

When the mortar is thoroughly dampened, set the completed stepping-stone in a shady spot and cover it with a damp cloth and plastic. Wait at least 48 hours before removing the mold.

After you remove the mold from the stepping-stone (**Photo 7**), brush the stone off to remove any loose mortar and rinse it with clear water. If, after drying, the embedded stones have a film of mortar on them, clean them off with muriatic acid diluted according to the instructions on the container. Remember, always add acid to water, not the other way around, and wear rubber gloves and safety glasses.

To enhance the color of the stones, coat them with stone sealer. Alice recommends Sparks Stone Glamor sealer. You can find it online at sparkssw.com for about $20 per quart. Other brands will also work. You'll find stone sealers at home centers; masonry, landscape and tile suppliers; and online.

5 **Sprinkle the stone.** Adjust your spray wand or sprayer to the finest spray setting and sprinkle water over the completed stepping-stone to wet the mortar.

6 **Tap on the mold.** Tap on the mold with the mallet to remove air and help the water penetrate. Continue sprinkling and tapping until it seems like no more water will be absorbed by the mortar.

7 **Pull off the mold.** Allow the stepping-stone to harden and cure for at least two days. Then carefully flip it over and remove the mold. Clean it with water and then acid if needed.

OUTDOOR STRUCTURES, LANDSCAPING & GARDENING

PEBBLE MOSAIC STEPPERS   **219**

BUILD A MODERN DECK

Pro tips for using low-upkeep materials

by **Mark Petersen, Contributing Editor**

BOB

MATT

RANDY

Your deck should be a place to relax, not a painful reminder of those looming weekends you're going to spend sanding, painting and staining. So if you're in the planning stages for a new deck, consider alternatives to wood.

You can build yourself a low-maintenance deck using the same tools as you would a wood deck, and similar techniques. But there are differences between low-maintenance and wood products. We asked our pros for some tips to help DIYers avoid expensive mistakes.

MEET OUR EXPERTS

We asked Randy Moe from Decks Unlimited, and Bob Januik and Matt Norden from Precision Decks, for some tips on working with low-maintenance deck materials. Altogether, these guys have built more than 1,000 decks, using every material imaginable. Ten years ago, about half their jobs were wood. Today they install low-maintenance materials on three out of four.

Beware of dark colors

Boards with dark colors can get blistering hot when the sun is beating down on them. If you like to go barefoot, consider a lighter color.

Check your joist spacing

If you're planning to replace old wood decking with PVC or composite, measure the joist spacing first. Most deck joists are centered 16 in. apart, which is the maximum span for most low-maintenance decking. If you plan to install your decking at a 45-degree angle, your joists may need to be 12 in. apart. You may also have to install more stair stringers. Check your product specs, and talk to your local building official before you buy.

Flatten the joists to avoid a wavy deck

Most PVC and composite products aren't as rigid as wood, so they don't bridge imperfections in the framing as well. If some of your joists are higher than others, you might end up with a wavy surface. Our pros stretch a string across the deck joists to detect high spots and then plane them down with a power hand planer. This might seem like a pain, but it takes less than an hour and pays off with a better-looking deck.

Avoid random splices

If your deck is 24 ft. long, don't use random-length boards and butt-joint them together. Install a splice board to create two 12-ft. x 12-ft. spaces instead. Your deck will look better and you'll avoid the frustration of trying to splice the decking over joists. A splice board will also require extra framing. Do it the same way you would for the perimeter boards (one extra joist and a 2x6 on its side between the outside joist and the extra joist).

SPLICE BOARD

Hide the ends

Many PVC and composite decking products are not the same color all the way through, so you'll want to cover the ends. One solution is to "picture frame" the deck by installing deck boards around the perimeter. A picture frame creates a professional look but does require some additional framing. One way to support the perimeter boards is to add an extra joist 5-1/2 in. away from the outside joist and then install a 2x6 on its side between the two joists.

EXTRA JOIST

2x6

Protect joists from rot

Pressure-treated lumber is rot-resistant, not rot-proof. Two places our pros often see deterioration are along the top edge, where the decking traps moisture, and in between two joists that have been sandwiched together. Rolling butyl tape over the top of the joists will add years to your deck's framing. Choose a dark-colored tape; shiny silver and white are noticeable between the gaps. A 4-in. x 75-ft. roll will cost you about $20 at a home center.

BUTYL TAPE

Stair rails made simple

Stair railings are one of the trickiest parts of any deck project. Some aluminum manufacturers offer a preassembled railing that racks to whatever angle you need. Just measure the distance between the posts, transfer the proper angle and cut to length. If your rails fit into a sleeve, you can cut them with a hacksaw, recip saw or circular saw. If your rail ends will be exposed, you may want to invest in an aluminum blade for your chop saw. Either way, clean up the ends with a file so you don't scratch things up during installation.

PLUG

Hide the screws

When it comes to fastening PVC or composite decking, all three of our pros like the Cortex concealed fastening system. You just countersink the screws using the special bit included with the kit, and hammer in a plug that's made of the exact same material as the decking. Screw holes virtually disappear, and damaged boards are easy to remove if you have to. A box of 350 costs about $80 at Home Depot.

Mix and match

You don't have to stick with one type of product or one look for the entire deck. Our pros mix and match all the time: composite posts with aluminum rails, composite rails with aluminum spindles. And don't be afraid to think outside the box when it comes to color. You can install perimeter boards the same color as the railing. Choose a post color that's different from the railing. Have the spindles be a different color than the posts and rails. The possibilities are endless.

COMPOSITE

ALUMINUM

Connectors make railings easier

Creating a tight fit between a composite post and a rail is difficult—even pros struggle with it. Railing connectors make it easy. This connector, made by Deckorator, is screwed onto the end of the rail before being attached to the post. It comes in five colors. You can buy these connectors from the same place you get your decking, or order them at amazon.com for less than $10 a pair.

RAILING CONNECTOR

Dress up an ugly post

If your deck is more than a couple of feet off the ground, you may want to wrap the posts in PVC to match the rest of the deck. You'll need two 1x6s and two 1x8s for each post. Our pros avoid material thinner than 3/4 in. because PVC expands and contracts more than wood, and it's hard to keep the seams together using thinner material. Pin the boards in place with a trim gun before screwing them together.

Dark, round spindles improve your view

Do you know why horse fences are usually white? It's because dark ones are harder for horses to see. The same principle applies to deck railings and people. If you want an unobstructed view, dark spindles are the way to go.

And round is better than square. A 3/4-in.-diameter round spindle stays 3/4 in. no matter what direction it's viewed from, but a 3/4-in. square spindle grows to more than an inch when you view it at an angle.

Want a flat, solid, strong deck?

If you covet a new deck that's absolutely billiard-table flat, won't show waves in the decking, and doesn't feature ugly green wood from the underside, you have to take a look at Elevations, the new steel joist system from Trex. It's not only flat on top but also better looking from underneath. And if you want a curved edge or two, you can cut a series of saw kerfs in the rim joist flanges and give your deck a dramatic look. (Take our advice: don't try to do that with 2x10s!)

Elevations deck joists can span longer distances than wood joists, which means fewer beams, posts and footings. Translation: big labor and material savings. With Elevations framing, you can span just under 14 ft. plus a 4-ft. cantilever (the part of the deck that hangs over the beam). Eighteen feet is pretty impressive for just one beam. The only bad news is that it costs $2 to $4 more per square foot than treated. Choose from 12-, 16- and 20-ft. lengths at your favorite home center or lumberyard. If it's not in stock, it can usually be special-ordered.

But wait, there's more! Trex offers RainEscape, a deck drainage system that nests between the joists. If you want dry space below your deck for all of that comfy overstuffed furniture, RainEscape has got you covered. Read all about it at trex.com.

—Travis Larson, Senior Editor

GROW A
GREAT LAWN

The 6 magic bullets—and more!

by **Travis Larson, Senior Editor**

Travis Larson, Senior Editor

As the in-house turf "expert" at Handyman for the past 15 years, I've spent a huge amount of time talking with world-class grass gurus and learning the science of lawns. And I've spent even more time clearing and converting my half-acre of rough, overgrown horse pasture to a Pebble Beach–quality lawn.

My final conclusion is this: Getting great grass is surprisingly simple and easy. If you're willing to learn some basic facts and put in just a few hours of light labor every summer, you can have a lush lawn. Here's how.

1 Water deeply, but not often

If you water frequently and for short periods, the grass roots have no reason to grow deep. Those shallow roots can't reach deep soil nutrients or deliver the water when you skip a watering. Instead, water deeply enough to penetrate the soil 4 to 6 in. Do the test below for a few waterings to get a sense of how long and how often. It'll depend on weather conditions and your soil type.

Heavy soils should be watered less often and less heavily but for longer periods of time. Sandy soils, on the other hand, can handle heavy, fast watering but dry out more quickly. In hot, dry weather, you may have to water every two to three days.

Determine how long you need to water. Water for 30 minutes. Then plunge a spade into the soil and pry out a wedge to see how far the water has penetrated. Four to 6 in. deep is ideal. Not deep enough? Water longer. Once you know how long to water, use a water timer and you'll know what to set it for every time.

2 Attack broadleaf weeds in mild weather

You need to kill weeds when they're growing. That's because the herbicide is absorbed through the leaves and then sent throughout the rest of the plant. When the weather is too cool, the weed isn't growing and the herbicide won't be absorbed, so the chemical isn't as effective. Too hot and the herbicide will stress the grass. The product directions will give you the best temperature range. Apply herbicides when rain isn't forecast; a soaking will just rinse off the herbicide before it can do any good.

3 Kill crabgrass before it sprouts

Crabgrass preventers (aka preemergence treatments) do one thing and one thing only. They prevent crabgrass (and any other seed) from sprouting. Once crabgrass sprouts, it's too late.

Here's the key. Apply preventer between the second and the third mowings. Because crabgrass starts sprouting a few weeks after the grass greens up, that's generally just the right time.

4 Don't cut the grass too short

Every grass type has an optimal cutting height. And you're better off on the high side of that height. Here are a few reasons. The grass blade is the food factory of the plant. Short blades just can't generate as much food as long blades. Long blades also shade and cool the soil. That means weed seeds are less likely to sprout, and you won't have to water as often because water won't evaporate as fast.

Not sure what type of grass you have? Take a sample to a garden center for help. Or go to scotts.com and click on "grass type identifier" at the bottom of the page. Compare your sample with the ones shown.

224 OUTDOOR STRUCTURES, LANDSCAPING & GARDENING

⑤ Don't skip the fall fertilizing

Before the lawn goes to sleep for the winter, you should feed it well. Even after the grass seems to go dormant, the roots are soaking up nutrients and storing energy for the next growing season. Surprisingly, it's much more important to fertilize in the fall than in the spring, when most people do it. Like watering, this is one of the most important favors you can do for your lawn.

⑥ Test the soil pH level

Grass grows best when it's growing in the "pH happy zone." If the soil is too acidic or too alkaline, the grass won't thrive even if you do everything else right. So collect one tablespoon-size sample a couple of inches under the sod in three different places in your yard and take the three samples in for testing. Some garden centers offer the service, or search online for "soil testing" to find a place to send it.

You're after a pH between 6 and 7.2. If it's too high, you'll treat the lawn with iron sulfate or sulphur; too low and you'll use pelletized limestone. Whoever does the testing will tell you what and how much to use to fix the pH. Applying the treatment is as easy as walking around the yard with a spreader.

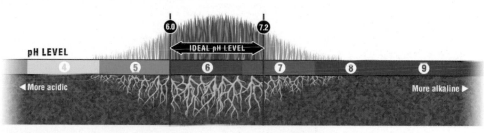

5 ways to make it all easier, simpler and cheaper

1. Use a broadcast spreader—not a drop spreader. Drop spreaders (the type that drops granules straight down) are notoriously tricky to use. You're bound to end up with stripes or checkerboard patterns on your grass. You're much better off with a broadcast spreader, which spews out the granules at random for much more consistent coverage.

2. Don't treat your whole lawn for just a few weeds. That's expensive, a hassle and ecologically unsound. If you have only a few weeds, pull them by hand or spray each one with a pump-up sprayer.

3. Use a hose-end sprayer to kill a yard full of weeds. It's faster and more effective to dispense concentrated liquid broadleaf killers than to use granular broadleaf killers. You just add the herbicide, dial in the right concentration on the sprayer lid and walk around the yard misting all the weeds. You can treat an average yard in less than 20 minutes.

4. Reseed in the late summer/early fall. Whether you're seeding a small patch or a whole yard, you're going to be much more successful if you wait for the cooler, damper weather of late summer or early fall. It's almost impossible to get seed to survive during the dog days of summer. It's simply too hot and dry. You'll most likely just waste your time and expensive seed.

5. Use concentrates whenever you can. For most liquids, you can buy concentrates and mix your own treatment with water. You'll save about 70 percent of the cost of premixed. Be sure to mix only as much as you can use within a week or two. Minerals in tap water will reduce the potency of the chemicals in just a short time.

12 pearls of lawn wisdom

1. Don't mow wet grass. You'll leave giant clumps of sodden clippings where they'll smother the grass beneath. Not only that, it'll carpet the underside of your mower deck with a thick mat.

2. Set your spreader at half the recommended dosage and treat the lawn twice from opposite directions. It'll take twice as much work on your part, but you'll get a more consistent distribution.

3. Fill the spreader on the driveway, not over the grass. Or at least spread a tarp on the grass to catch spillage. Otherwise, if you have an accident you'll have a nice, big dead spot in your lawn.

4. Accept that you can't grow grass everywhere. If you've struggled to grow grass in a shady spot, at some point give it up and mulch, use a shade-tolerant ground cover or plan yourself a patio.

5. Give crabgrass a second dose of crabgrass preventer. About one month after your first treatment, apply a second to prevent the seeds that survived the first treatment from germinating.

6. Rinse out your spreader every time, especially after using fertilizer. Fertilizer is essentially a type of salt. And it eats up any metal parts it finds.

7. Aerate in the fall if you have heavy loam or clay soil. (No need if you have sand.) Just before you fertilize, rent an aerator and aerate the lawn from both directions. It will help loosen the soil and allow the fertilizer to penetrate deep into the soil.

8. Give your lawn a good flat-top for winter. Just this one time each year, set your lawn mower to 1-1/2 to 2 in. and clip it off. That'll help retard mold during the winter.

9. Water new seed lightly and twice a day or more. If you can't be bothered to keep the soil moist over new seed, don't bother seeding. Dampen the soil even more often during hot, windy weather. Keep watering for at least two weeks and don't miss any days.

10. Rake up downed leaves in the fall or those soggy leaves will suffocate the new sprouts in the spring and leave dead spots all over your lawn.

11. Choose "slow-release" fertilizers. Rather than feeding the lawn all at once, this type provides nutrients over a longer period. These fertilizers cost a bit more but are well worth the added expense.

12. Don't apply too much seed. You should try to achieve a concentration of about 15 seeds per square inch. If you exceed this, you'll have an over-populated lawn with too many plants competing for nutrients and sunlight.

5 ways to wreck your yard

1. Dethatch when it's not needed. Dethatching involves flailing away at your lawn with a powerful, engine-driven steel rake. If that sounds scary, imagine how your grass feels! The idea is to rake up the old woody stems resting at the base of the grass leaves. Dethatching does this, but at great cost to your lawn because it tears up not only the grass but also the roots. It's rarely a good idea. If you have thatch, it's probably because you've been underwatering, overfertilizing and/or consistently mowing when the grass is overgrown.

2. Overfertilize! Yep, just skip the directions and pour it on. You'll kill your whole yard in no time. And if you don't kill it outright, it'll turn yellow and take weeks to heal itself.

3. Catch the clippings. OK, maybe it won't actually wreck your lawn, but you're not doing it any favors either. Let the clippings lie. They'll release nutrients into the soil and form a mulch to help keep in soil moisture.

4. Ignore the directions on lawn treatments. They are SO important! It's not only the concentration for fluids or the spreader setting for granules. Pay attention to the details like the rain forecast and what temperature ranges the treatments require. Skip them and you'll either wreck your lawn or waste your time and money.

5. Mow with dull blades. Dull mower blades rip through the leaves, which stresses the plant. Instead, you want to slice grass off cleanly. You can always tell a lawn that's been mowed with a dull blade because it looks brown on the top. Get on your hands and knees and you can actually see the damage.

DULL BLADE (DON'T USE!)

SHARP BLADE

UPGRADE YOUR GAS GRILL TO **ELECTRONIC IGNITION**

If you're tired of replacing worn-out piezo starters, try this fix

by **Rick Muscoplat, Contributing Editor**

It's supposed to be simple: Push the spark igniter on your gas grill and you're fired up and ready for steak. But after a few years, those piezo-style igniters stop working. They bind up and refuse to "click," or they click but don't produce a spark. Rather than replace them every few years with the same trouble-prone style, why not upgrade to a battery-powered spark generator?

You can buy a new-style spark generator and electrode for less than $20 at some home centers and online (one online source is grillparts.com). You'll probably have to mount it in a different location. That'll mean abandoning the old piezo unit and drilling a new hole. If you're OK with that, grab your drill, bits and a rotary tool and get to work. The entire project takes about one hour from start to fire. Here's how.

First, connect the wires from the existing electrode to the new spark generator and press the button. If you get a spark, the old electrode is good and can stay put. If you don't get a spark (and the battery is installed properly), you'll have to replace the old electrode as well.

Next, find a new location for the generator that's within reach of the electrode wires. Make sure the new generator won't interfere with the gas valves or supply line. Then drill the hole (**Photo 1**).

The spark generator we bought had side tangs and snap clips to hold it in place. To accommodate those locking features, just cut side grooves in the freshly drilled hole with a rotary tool and a cutoff wheel (**Photo 2**). Then insert the new spark generator, drop in a new battery, and twist on the push button cap. Connect the electrode wires (**Photo 3**). Test the unit and get ready to grill.

GROOVES

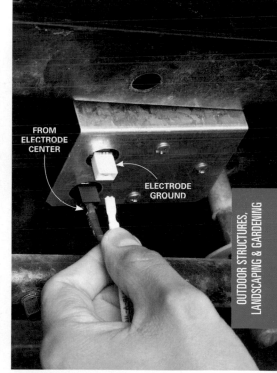

FROM ELECTRODE CENTER

ELECTRODE GROUND

OUTDOOR STRUCTURES, LANDSCAPING & GARDENING

1 Make a hole. Drill a starter hole and double-check for fit and clearance. Then drill the larger hole with a metal-cutting hole saw.

2 Grind grooves. Dial your rotary tool up to high speed and use a cutting wheel to cut grooves 180 degrees apart.

3 Connect the electrode wires. Connect the center electrode wire to the positive (+) terminal on the spark generator. Then connect the other wire to the negative (-) terminal.

DEALING WITH LEAVES

*Field Editors' tips
for fall cleanup*

by **Gary Wentz,
Senior Editor**

You've probably been raking leaves since you were a kid. And you might figure that there's nothing left to learn. That's what Vern and I thought too. But when we asked *The Family Handyman*'s crew of Field Editors for advice, we got this heap of tips for saving time and labor. Take a few minutes to read these pages to save yourself hours of work in the fall.

Vern Johnson, Art Director, doesn't need to rake—all the leaves fall right into his gutters.

Bag 'em

We have a BIG yard and lots of trees. So I bag the leaves with my mower. It does a nice job of shredding the leaves, so they're ready to become compost or mulch.

Gary Dowley, Field Editor

Rake picks

Lots of Field Editors told us about their favorite rakes. The most popular rakes are beloved just for their size—a big rake makes the job smaller. Most home centers carry rakes up to 30 in. wide.

Other Field Editors swear by "no-clog" rakes—the tines don't skewer leaves, so you don't have to stop and unclog the rake. Several manufacturers make them, also in widths up to 30 in.

Gary Wentz is a Senior Editor at *TFH* and the CEO of lawn care at home.

A tarp beats a trailer

Instead of bagging or hauling leaves, I rake them onto a tarp, which I drag into the woods. It's even easier if you get your kids to do it!

Mark Ripplinger,
Field Editor

Mulch 'em

A mulching mower shreds leaves into tiny flakes that settle into the turf and decompose into natural fertilizer. You might have to go over some areas two or three times to completely chop up the leaves. Still, it's fast and easy and it makes the grass happy.

Cameron
LiDestri,
Field Editor

Vacuum in tight spots

A leaf blower/vacuum sucks up leaves fast, especially around shrubs, in flower beds and in other hard-to-rake areas. You might think that the bag would need to be emptied every five minutes, but the vac minces the leaves and packs a mountain of them into just a few bags.

Dave Switzer,
Field Editor

GreatGoofs

No-mow mister nice guy

All winter long whenever it snowed, our next-door neighbor Ron came out with his snow blower and cleared off our 225-ft.-long driveway. He even did it at night! So this spring when his grass reached an unprecedented height and was almost ready to drop its seed, I thought I would return his kindness and surprise him by mowing it while he was at work. Several other neighbors stopped by to encourage me as I gamely pushed the mower through the knee-high grass. Ron, returning home from work, came running across the yard with tears in his eyes. Turns out he'd been waiting for the grass to reseed itself.

—Alex Jones

SHED PLUS SHELTER

Easy access, storage galore and a protective porch

by **Jeff Gorton, Associate Editor**

This shed has a large sliding door on one end to access the 8 x 16-ft. storage area, three windows for lots of light and a front entry door for extra convenience. But the best feature is the large covered porch where you can work on projects or just hang out in the shade with friends. The front half of the roof is supported by 6x6 posts and 2x10 beams. We continued the post-and-beam look on the rest of the shed, using the 2x10 beams to support the wide roof overhangs. We used inexpensive standard framing lumber for the beams and corner boards, and coated it with a super-durable finish to give it a rich, rustic appearance. The windows are aluminum storm windows. The front door is a steel entry door purchased at a home center.

What it takes

Time: Four or five weekends. With a few helpers, you'll get the framing up in a long weekend. Then you can work at your own pace to finish up.

Cost: $3,800, not including the slab. We spent $70 per 4 x 8-ft. sheet of the rough plywood and $60 each for the cedar posts. You could save a few hundred dollars by substituting smooth plywood and standard wood posts.

Skill level: Intermediate to advanced. Building this shed doesn't require furniture-making skills, but experience with framing and roofing will help.

Before you start building

At least a month before you plan to build, check with your local building department to see if a permit is required. You may have to supply a survey to show where the shed is located on the property. We hired a concrete contractor to pour the slab, but if you decide to tackle this part of the project yourself, you can find instructions on our Web site. Go to familyhandyman.com and search for "concrete slab." A few days before you plan to dig, call 811 for instructions on how to locate buried utility lines.

You'll save time and get a better job if you prefinish the beams, trim and grooved plywood for the overhang ceiling. Then all you have to do is touch up the cut ends after the parts are installed. We used Sikkens Cetol Log and Siding finish for the posts, beams and corner trim. It's expensive but looks great and is very durable. Then we put two coats of clear exterior finish on the cedar plywood siding and the grooved roof plywood (**Photo 8**).

In this article, we'll show you the important steps of how to build the shed. For more details on wall and roof framing and information on how to build the sliding doors, go to familyhandyman. com/2012shed

Build the walls

Start by measuring 3-1/2 in. from the outside edge of the slab on the back and sides and snapping chalk lines to mark the interior edge of the bottom plate. Then measure from the back line to mark the location of the front bottom plate and snap a line. Now measure between the pairs of opposite lines to make sure they're parallel, and measure diagonally from corner to corner (where the chalk lines intersect). The diagonal measurements should be equal. If not, the slab is not square and you should cheat the lines as needed until the diagonal measurements are equal. If you skip this step, you risk fighting with an out-of-square building for the entire project. With chalk lines snapped, you can cut the 2x4 plates to length and mark the stud and window and door openings on them according to the plans. Go to **familyhandyman.com/2012shed** for more details.

Cost, time and tools

You can find most of the materials for this shed at your local home center or lumberyard. But you'll have to special-order the windows and the sliding door hardware. See the Materials List at **familyhandyman. com/2012shed** for ordering information.

As with any larger construction project, you'll need a set of standard carpentry tools plus a circular saw and drill. We used a framing nail gun to speed up the wall and roof framing and a miter saw for the exterior trim work, but hammers and a circular saw will do the job. You'll have to rip boards for the windowsill and some of the other trim parts. A table saw works best for this.

1 Stand and brace the walls. Build the walls flat on the slab and then stand them up. Plumb the corners with a level and nail diagonal braces to the walls. Straighten the top plate by stretching a string over spacer blocks at each end. Gauge the straightness with a third block. When the top plate is straight, nail the brace.

2 Mark the post notches. Temporarily position and brace the posts. Then use one of the beams as a giant straightedge to mark the post notches. Align the beam with the top plate of the side wall, tack it into place and mark the post. Do the same thing on the other end. Then snap a chalk line between the two marks to mark the inner posts.

Drill holes in the treated bottom plates for the anchor bolts. Then build the walls. Lay the plates for the back wall on the slab and spread the studs between them, aligning them with the marks. Nail the plates to the studs. Stand the back wall—you'll have to lift it over the anchor bolts—and support it with temporary braces on each end. Align the bottom plate with the chalk line and tighten the anchor bolts.

Build, stand and temporarily brace the front wall. Then build the side walls. When all of the walls are up, nail the corners together and nail the second top plates to the back and side walls, overlapping the plates at the corners. Finally, check the corners with a level to make sure they're plumb, and nail diagonal braces across the studs on the inside to hold them in place. Also straighten the top plates using a taut string and braces (**Photo 1**).

Nail the plywood siding to the back wall. We used Roseburg Forest Products' Breckenridge 5/8-in.-thick plywood without any grooves, but you could substitute any good-looking exterior plywood. To cut costs, we substituted 5/8-in. oriented strand board in the area under the windows that would be covered by siding.

Stand the front posts and beams

The front half of the roof is supported by four 6x6 cedar posts that are notched to accept both 2x10 beams. **Photo 2** shows how we set them up for marking the location of the notches. Rest the bottom of the posts on the metal post brackets and temporarily brace them. We used screws for all the temporary bracing because they're easy to put in and take out. Use one of the 2x10 beams to mark the end post as shown in the photo. Do the same thing on the opposite end, and then snap a chalk line between the marks to mark the center for notching.

Number the posts so you get them back in the right spot. Then take them down and cut the notches (**Photo 3**). Finish up by putting the posts back in place. Use a level to plumb the posts and brace them with pairs of 2x4s. Then cut the front 2x10 beams to length and mark the post locations on them. Line the posts up with the marks and screw the posts and beams together (**Photo 4**).

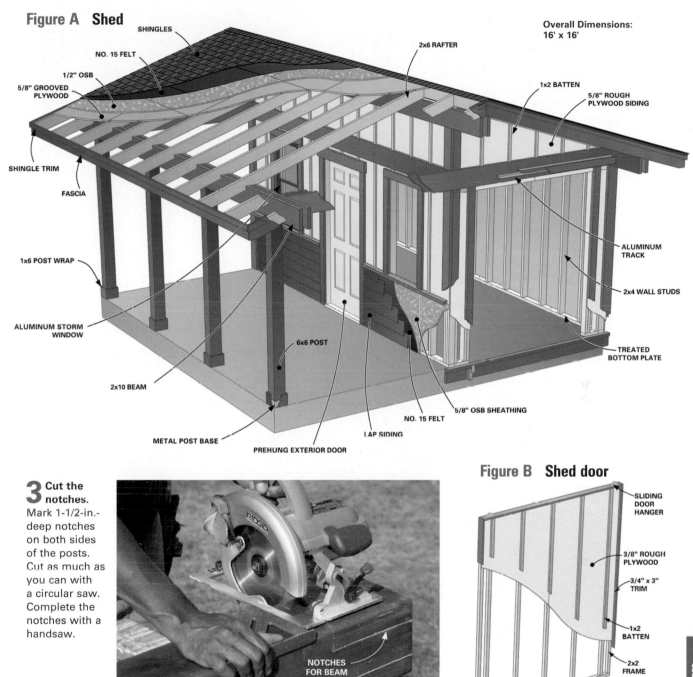

Figure A Shed

SHINGLES
NO. 15 FELT
1/2" OSB
5/8" GROOVED PLYWOOD
SHINGLE TRIM
FASCIA
1x6 POST WRAP
ALUMINUM STORM WINDOW
2x10 BEAM
METAL POST BASE
PREHUNG EXTERIOR DOOR
6x6 POST
LAP SIDING
NO. 15 FELT
5/8" OSB SHEATHING
2x6 RAFTER
1x2 BATTEN
5/8" ROUGH PLYWOOD SIDING
ALUMINUM TRACK
2x4 WALL STUDS
TREATED BOTTOM PLATE

Overall Dimensions: 16' x 16'

3 **Cut the notches.** Mark 1-1/2-in.-deep notches on both sides of the posts. Cut as much as you can with a circular saw. Complete the notches with a handsaw.

NOTCHES FOR BEAM

Figure B Shed door

SLIDING DOOR HANGER
3/8" ROUGH PLYWOOD
3/4" x 3" TRIM
1x2 BATTEN
2x2 FRAME

Frame the roof

Cut the 2x6 rafters according to the dimensions online at familyhandyman.com/2012shed. Mark the 2x6 ridge, the top plate of the back wall and the top of the front beam with the rafter locations. The rafters are 2-ft. on center. Nail or screw the ridge to the top of the front wall. Check the plans online for the exact position of the ridge. Also cut and attach the 2x10 beam that runs along the top of the back wall, making sure it protrudes 2 ft. on each end. Now you're ready to install the rafters (**Photo 5**). We used 3-in. screws to attach the rafters, but 16d framing nails will also work.

Complete the wall frame and siding

With the roof frame in place, you can fill in the short studs on each end wall. Start by cutting angles on the ends of the top plate and screwing or nailing it to the underside of the rafter. Then mark the location of the studs (**Photo 6**). Measure and cut the studs and nail them in.

Finish the walls by nailing the cedar plywood siding to the top of the front and side walls. You can cut the window and door openings before or after installing the plywood siding.

Complete the beams

The remaining beams are decorative. One snugs to the underside of the rafters on the front wall. Two more run between the front and the back beams. After these are in place, add the 2-1/2-in. spacers (**Photo 7**) and the decorative second half of all the beams. Finally, cut a 2x10 to fit horizontally between the side beams, above the door and windows, and nail it to the front wall.

Sheathe the roof

For a more finished-looking ceiling, we installed 4 x 8-ft. sheets of 8-in.-on-center grooved pine siding, face side down, over the rafters (**Photo 8**). Then we covered this with a layer of 1/2-in. OSB so the roofing nails wouldn't poke through.

Build the sliding door

Screw 2x2s together to form the frame for the sliding door according to the details online. Then nail 3/8-in.-thick

4 Set the beams. Stand the posts and brace them. Mark the post locations on the first beam. Align the posts with the marks and connect them with screws. Screw the second beam to the other side of the posts.

5 Install the rafters. Cut the ridge to length and mark the rafter locations on it. Also mark the rafter locations on the front beam and the top plate of the back wall.

cedar plywood to the 2x2s and wrap the perimeter with 1x4s ripped to 3 in. Nail the 1x4s flush with the back of the 2x2s so they protrude past the siding. The 1x4s will cover the ends of the battens.

We used Johnson Hardware's heavy-duty bypass door hardware to support the exterior sliding door. The parts are easy to order online (see the Materials List online), and the three-wheel hangers operate smoothly. Attach the 2x4 track support to the 2x10 beam with 1/4-in. x 5-in. lag screws. Then screw the tracks to the underside of the 2x4, spacing them about 1/4 in. from the beam (**Photo 9**).

Mount the hanger brackets to the top of the door (**Photo 10**). Slide the wheel assemblies into the track and screw a block of wood into the open end of the track to prevent the door from rolling off the end. Then hang the door on the track by clipping the wheel assemblies into the hanger brackets.

Close the gap between the bottom of the door and the concrete slab by attaching a sill with polyurethane construction adhesive and concrete screws (see plans online). Then, to prevent the door from swinging out, screw a bent steel "bar holder" (search online for "zinc open bar holder") onto a spacer block that allows enough clearance for the door to slide. Finish the installation by covering the track and mounting board with a 1x4 trim board.

Install the entry door and windows

We bought a standard 3-ft.-wide steel entry door from a home center, removed the molding and installed it in the front wall. For more information on how to install a door, go to familyhandyman.com and search for "door install." Install the front door and windowsill before mounting the windows. Nail 1-in. x 4-in. trim boards to the sides of the front door and use a 2x6 for the top trim. We cut the window and door trim from 1-in.-thick cedar decking.

Make the angled sill piece by ripping a 10-degree bevel on the front and back edge of a 2x4. Notch the sill pieces to protrude 1 in. into the window openings. Then mark where they intersect at the outside corner and cut the miters (**Photo 11**). Be sure to tilt the sill at a 10-degree

6 **Fill in the gable-end studs.** Cut angles on the top plate and screw it to the underside of the rafter. Make marks every 16 in. Measure and cut the studs and nail them in.

7 **Add the false beams.** Screw 2-1/2-in. spacer blocks to the protruding beam ends. Then screw or nail on the false beam.

8 **Sheathe the roof—twice!** Sheathe the roof with a layer of decorative grooved plywood so the underside of the roof looks good from below. Then add another layer of OSB so the roofing nails don't pop through.

angle in your miter saw when you're cutting the miters. Do this by pressing the beveled side tight to the fence.

The custom-size aluminum storm windows we used have 1-in.-thick expandable U-shaped channels around the perimeter for mounting. We nailed 1x2s to the sides and top of the framed openings, 1 in. back from the face of the siding and screwed the windows to these (**Photo 14**). If you use storm windows with thin mounting flanges, relocate these nailing strips to 1/8 in. behind the face of the siding. See the Materials List online for window-ordering details.

Finish the exterior

The corners are covered with 2x6 SPF lumber to look like

posts. The front corners are a little tricky because the 2x6s have to be cut to fit onto the angled sill. The easiest solution is to rip the 2x6s to form a 45-degree bevel on one long edge. Then cut the 10-degree angle on the bottom (where they sit on the sill) and join the bevels to form the corner.

You can start roofing anytime after you've finished installing the fascia trim (**Photo 12**). It's a good idea to cover the roof with roofing paper as soon as possible to keep everything dry. Then shingle the roof (**Photo 13**) and cover the ridge with ridge shingles. For information on how to install shingles, go to familyhandyman.com and search for "roofing."

We installed 1/2-in. x 7-1/4-in. rough-cedar lap siding

9 **Hang the door track.** Attach a track support to the beam with 1/4 x 5-in. lag screws to support the track. Then screw the aluminum track to the support.

10 **Mount the hangers.** Screw the hanger brackets to the top of the sliding door. Slide the three-wheel hangers into the track. Lift the door to the track and connect the hangers to the hanger brackets.

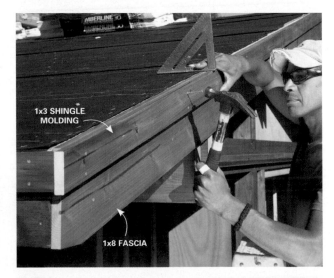

11 **Wrap the front and side with a sill.** Cut 10-degree bevels on 2x4s to form the angled sill. Notch the sills to fit into the window opening. Then mark for the miters where they intersect at the outside corner. Cut the miters and nail the sill to the wall, making sure it runs level.

12 **Trim the roof.** Install the 1x8 fascia boards and the 1x3 shingle molding. Make sure the 1x3 shingle molding is lined up with the roof surface.

STAGGERED ENDS

(Photo 15) under the windows and finished the cedar plywood siding with 1x2 battens nailed to the studs every 16 in. Cover the OSB with No. 15 building paper before you install the siding. If you use the same size siding, you'll have six courses with 5-1/2 in. of the siding exposed on each course. Start by ripping the top piece of siding to 5-1/2 in. and using the leftover strip as a starter under the first course. Align it with the bottom edge of the bottom plate and nail it on. Then nail the first course of siding over this. Continue with the remaining pieces, overlapping them to leave 5-1/2 in. of the previous course exposed.

Touch up the paint and stain and install the door hardware and you're ready to pull up some chairs to enjoy your new hangout.

13 Nail on the shingles. Staple roofing felt over the sheathing, overlapping the seams about 3 in. Then nail on the shingles according to the manufacturer's instructions. Cover the ridge with ridge shingles.

14 Install the windows. Nail 1x2 stops to the top and sides of the openings. Set the window in the opening and slide the expandable U-shaped channels tight to the framing. Screw through the channels into the stops to secure the windows.

ALUMINUM STORM WINDOW

1x2 STOP

SILL

5-1/2"

LAP SIDING

15 Install siding below the windows. Make chalk lines to indicate the top edge of each row of siding. Line the siding up with the lines and nail it to the studs. Leave a 1/16-in. gap at each end and fill them with caulk later.

Handy Hints

Trim shims in a jiffy with an oscillating tool

Matt Kelly, Field Editor

When you install a door, the usual way to trim the shims is to score them with a utility knife and then snap them off. It's a slow way to go, and half the time, you push the shims out of place. Other times, they don't break off cleanly. But I discovered that my oscillating tool does the job perfectly. Quick, clean, no hassles.

OUTDOOR STRUCTURES, LANDSCAPING & GARDENING

THE ART OF FELLING A TREE

An expert shows you how to make it fall where you want it

by **Travis Larson, Senior Editor**

It would be hard to name a more dangerous DIY project than felling a big tree. There's the obvious risk of getting crushed by a falling tree, but you could also have your melon crushed if a big limb shook loose from above. Trees can twist as they fall and make all kinds of other unexpected moves. Add a chain saw to the mix, and—well, you get the idea. It's not a job for the careless, the reckless or the faint-of-heart.

There are some commonsense precautions you should take and techniques you should employ to make tree felling as safe as possible. We'll share those with you. We'll also tell you how to analyze the situation so you'll know when it's best to call in a pro.

Aside from a chain saw, a stiff dose of common sense and a bit of courage, you'll need a few things to properly fell a tree. They include safety gear (see "The Right Stuff," at right) and two plastic felling wedges to keep your saw from getting pinched in cuts on larger trees. You can find everything you'll need at any outdoor power equipment store that carries chain saws. Don't bother looking for these items at home centers.

MEET AN EXPERT

Bob Tacke has been involved in the chain saw industry for 30 years and has taught dozens of safety classes. He teamed up with us for this story, as he has over the past 12 years. Thanks, Bob!

The right stuff

Safety isn't a throwaway word when it comes to felling trees and running chain saws. You must take it seriously. There are a few absolutely essential safety gear items you need to wear for any chain saw work.

■ **Loggers helmet** ($60): The helmet protects you from falling branches, a major cause of logging injuries. Earmuffs and a face screen protect your ears and eyes. Safety glasses keep the dust out—you don't want something in your eye in the middle of dropping a 4-ft.-diameter cottonwood.

■ **Kevlar chaps** ($75): Kevlar fibers will stop a chain instantly should you happen to drop the bar against your leg. It's the best logging safety device developed in the past 30 years, and it's a rare (and foolish) pro who doesn't wear them.

■ **Felling wedges** ($15): These wedges will prevent your saw from getting pinched during a cut.

Estimate the felling zone

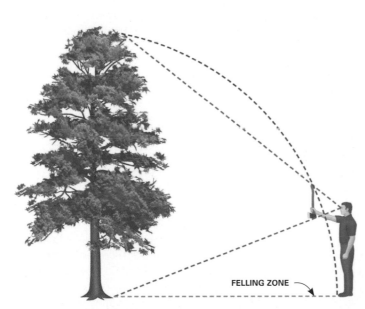

FELLING ZONE

Trees are taller than you think and reach farther on the ground than you'd expect (maybe all the way to your shed). You can estimate where a tree will fall by using the "ax handle trick." Hold an ax handle at arm's length, close one eye, and back away from or move toward the tree until the top of the ax is even with the treetop and the bottom even with the base. Your feet should be about where the treetop will rest after falling. It's just an estimate, though, so allow extra room if there's something it might fall on!

Clear a cutting zone

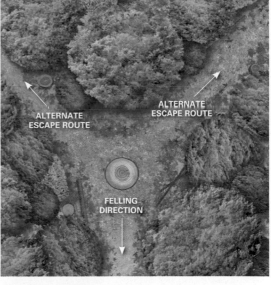

ALTERNATE ESCAPE ROUTE

ALTERNATE ESCAPE ROUTE

FELLING DIRECTION

Even when you're sure which way the tree is going to fall, you're still not ready to fell it. Cut away any brush around the trunk and clear two escape routes on the "non-falling" side of the tree. They should be about 45 degrees away from each other in opposite directions. The last thing you want is to trip while walking away from a falling tree.

Anatomy of a proper notch

The rule of thumb is to make the depth of the notch one-fifth of the tree trunk's diameter. The goal is to make the angles as shown in the diagram (or as close as you can). The felling cut should meet the point of the notch. When the tree starts to fall, the hinge will help guide the tree to fall in the desired direction.

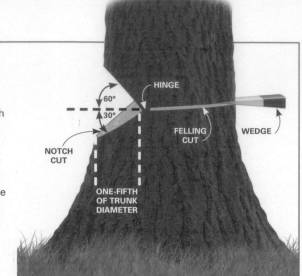

HINGE

60°

30°

FELLING CUT

WEDGE

NOTCH CUT

ONE-FIFTH OF TRUNK DIAMETER

Size up the tree

Start by studying the crown of the tree. Look for dead branches that are broken but attached, or actually broken off and supported by other branches. Don't even think about cutting down the tree yourself if you see any danger upstairs. You're bound to knock a branch loose and have it fall on you.

Next look at the lean and the branch loading. If it's obviously leaning in one direction or heavily loaded with branches on one side, that's the way it's going to fall. Forget the myth that a pro can drop a tree on top of an empty beer can. If it's perfectly straight and evenly loaded—maybe he'll get close. But if it's loaded or leaning, he won't have a chance.

Are there any buildings, fences, power lines or other things you care about in the felling zone? If so, skip the felling and call a pro.

NOTCH LOCATION

Plan the notch

You're going to be cutting a notch on the "fall" side of the trunk. Sight along the handle and adjust the saw until it's pointing toward your fall direction. The spot where the bar touches the bark will be the center of the notch. Before cutting, lay out the notch by marking with chalk or by scoring the bark with the chain saw. Make the notch at a comfortable working height. (You can always shorten the stump later.)

Cut the notch

Make the top cut first and then the bottom. When you're making the bottom cut, adjust your hand to control the throttle with your thumb. If you meet the top notch perfectly, the wedge will drop out of the notch. But most likely you'll have to extend the cuts from either the top or the bottom so the wedge can drop free.

NOTCH

FELLING CUT

FELLING CUT

Use wedges on big trees

If you have a tree that's more than 18 in. in diameter, go ahead and make your notch cut and begin the felling cut. Stop cutting as soon as you've penetrated far enough to pound wedges behind the bar. Leave the bar in the cut with the saw running, but lock the chain brake and tap in the wedges. Then finish the cut. Wedges will keep the saw from getting pinched in the cut if the tree leans back.

Tree-dropping wisdom

- Never cut on a breezy day.
- You'll have an easier time cutting up a fallen tree if you do it when the leaves are missing.
- Grab the chain saw handle with an encircling thumb on your right hand and never release it during a cut.
- Stay away from hollowed-out trees, especially if they're big. They are extremely unpredictable and dangerous to fell.
- Gas up the saw before beginning a cut. Never run out of gas halfway through a cut.
- Once you start working, don't stop until the tree is down. You don't want the tree to fall while you're taking a break.

Make the felling cut

Score a line connecting the apex of the notch on both sides for a cutting guide. The back cut should be parallel and even with the apex of the notch. Then make the felling cut. The instant the tree begins leaning, pull the saw free, set the chain brake and walk away along one of your escape routes, keeping an eye on the tree so you can react if it doesn't fall the way you planned. Never take your eye off a falling tree.

A lookout might save your life

You'll be a lot safer if you have a trusted assistant standing a few feet behind you, watching the top of the tree for falling branches and letting you know when the tree starts to fall. Have your assistant tap you on the shoulder with a stick to alert you when it's time to vacate the area. If it's early in the cut and you get the tap, leave the saw and walk away immediately. That means a branch is falling. Near the end of the cut, a tap means the tree is beginning its descent.

YARD & GARDEN
TOOLS & TIPS

Work smarter and get better results with these tips and ideas

by **TFH Editors**

Loosen a stuck throttle cable

If your lawn mower's throttle cable is hard to move or stuck, here's a fix. Disconnect both ends of the cable from the mower. You'll probably have to remove a bolt and disassemble the lever assembly near the handle to get the cable out. Take a digital photo to help you put it back together when you're done.

At the engine end, loosen the clamp that holds the cable to the engine and unhook the cable from the carburetor. Pour penetrating oil into the cable (**Photo 1**). Grab the inner cable with pliers and work it up and down to loosen it. When the cable moves freely and all the penetrating oil has drained out, squirt silicone lubricant into the funnel to keep the cable sliding freely. Reinstall the cable (**Photo 2**).

1 **Soak with penetrating oil.** Stick the end of the cable into a funnel and wrap electrical tape around it to create a seal. Spray or pour penetrating oil into the funnel. Position the opposite end of the cable over a small container to catch the penetrating oil as it drips out. Then lubricate the cable.

2 **Reinstall the cable and adjust the choke.** Remove the air cleaner assembly so you can see the choke plate. With the throttle control lever in the "choke" position, pull on the outer jacket of the cable near the clamp until the choke plate opens. Tighten the clamp with the cable in this position. Reassemble the air cleaner.

What's the best gas to use in lawn equipment?

"If you can find and afford nonoxygenated gas, it's the way to go," says our favorite motorhead, Rick Muscoplat.

According to Muscoplat, nonoxygenated gas doesn't absorb moisture as quickly as oxygenated gas (which contains ethanol), so you won't have as many carburetor corrosion problems. "Unfortunately," says Muscoplat, "non-oxy gas isn't available everywhere. Often you can only find it at marinas, where you'll pay two or more bucks more per gallon than for regular gas."

Whichever gas you use, Muscoplat suggests adding a fuel stabilizer, such as Sta-Bil. Another product is Advanced Formula Fuel Treatment & Stabilizer, from Briggs & Stratton, which claims it will keep fuel fresh for three years. Lawn equipment that you plan to store for an extended period should be prepped according to the manufacturer's instructions. Search online for "nonoxygenated gas" to find stations that sell it..

Long-handled shears

To cut tree branches that are just out of reach, extend the range of your lopping shears and gain leverage with this easy trick. Slip lengths of PVC pipe over the handles, tape them in place and you'll have shears that reach out a few more feet for pruning.

—Terry Raudio

Lawn mower oil-change tip

Most late-model lawn mowers don't come with a bottom oil drain plug. So you have to tip the entire lawn mower on its side and drain the oil out of the oil filler tube at the top of the engine. Before you do that, unscrew the gas cap and lay a plastic bag over the gas tank opening. Then screw on the cap. The bag prevents gas from leaking out of the gas cap vent. Here's another tip: Always tilt the mower on the side opposite the air cleaner so you don't drain gas out of the carburetor at the same time.

Chain saw sharpening made easier

When you're sharpening your chain saw, it's easy to get confused about which teeth you've sharpened and which ones you haven't as you pull the chain around the bar. To prevent confusion, just mark each tooth with a permanent marker after you've sharpened it.

—Zach Ross

CHOOSING A GAS-POWERED **CHAIN SAW**

Before you buy a chain saw, here are some features to consider.

1. Engine size is measured in cubic centimeters (cc) or cubic inches. In general, the bigger the number, the more powerful the engine. Most homeowners will do fine with a saw in the 32 cc to 45 cc range.

2. A bigger bar isn't necessarily better. For most home-owners, a 16-in. bar is plenty. Longer bars can get in the way and increase the likelihood of dangerous kickback.

3. In general, more expensive saws have better compo-nents and will last longer, but most DIYers will never wear out even a less expensive saw.

4. Safety gear isn't optional. You need a helmet with a face shield, hearing protection, leather gloves and special chain saw chaps. Expect to spend about $120 total for these items.

5. In many cases, you can buy the same saw with or without special features like tool-free chain tensioning. You can save money by forgoing a little convenience.

6. If you're not experienced with chain saws, consider buying from a full-service dealer that can help you set up the saw and show you how to start it. For safety tips, go to familyhandyman.com and search for "chain saw."

Choke and on/off switch

Starting a cold chain saw requires closing the choke and increasing the throttle speed. To stop the saw, you switch it off. Some saws combine all these functions in one switch. Others have separate on/off and choke switches.

We prefer the type of switch found on the Husqvarna and Jonsered saws because it's large enough to operate easily with gloves on, pushing down on the switch stops the engine, and the switch automatically returns to the "run" position. You don't have to switch the saw back on to start it again. This helps prevent accidentally flooding the engine by trying to restart it with the switch off.

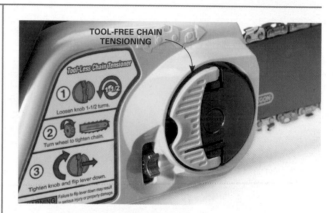

TOOL-FREE CHAIN TENSIONING

Tool-free chain tensioning

The chain on your saw has to be tensioned correctly. If it's too loose or too tight, it can damage the bar and present a safety hazard. Without tool-free tensioning, adjusting the chain tension requires a wrench and screwdriver. With this innovation, you don't need either.

Systems vary slightly among saws, but in general, the nuts that secure the bar to the saw's body have been replaced by a mechanism built into the clutch cover. You loosen the bar by hand and then turn a knurled wheel of some sort to adjust the chain tension. We like this feature and think it's worth spending a few extra dollars for.

CHOKE AND ON/OFF SWITCH

Easy-start systems

The bigger the engine, the harder it is to pull the starter cord, unless there's some feature built in to reduce the starter cord tension. One innovative solution changes the spring mecha-nism in the recoil (the part that rewinds the starter cord) to make it easier to pull. Stihl's Easy2Start system, which uses this mechanism, is surprisingly easy to pull, and works great. Other manufacturers have easy-start recoils too, but the dif-ference isn't as dramatic.

Another design that reduces starting effort opens a tem-porary hole in the cylinder to reduce compression, making it easier to pull the starter cord. Look for this decompression valve feature on larger chain saws.

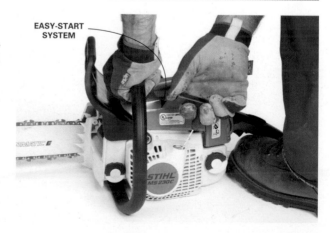

EASY-START SYSTEM

Features to look for

Air purge
Most quality saws have a translucent, rubbery bulb that you press five or six times before you start the cold engine. It's called an air purge or a primer bulb because it replaces the air in the gas line with fuel. This reduces the number of times you have to pull the starter cord, saving wear and tear on the saw and your arm.

Fuel gauge
On some saws, you can see the level of the fuel in the tank without removing the cap.

Easy-to-remove fuel and oil caps
Stihl chain saws have fuel and oil caps that you remove by flipping up a handle and twisting a quarter turn. Other saws include a raised "handle" that allows a better grip. Both are nice features.

Air precleaner system
Many of the more expensive saws have a precleaner system that throws out most of the larger dust particles before they reach the air filter. This reduces air filter maintenance and improves engine performance.

Anti-vibration
All but the cheapest chain saws have springs or rubber bushings that separate the handle assembly from the rest of the saw to reduce the amount of vibration you feel. The more expensive the saw, the more robust the springs or bushings are. We could feel the difference between the saws that didn't have any springs or bushings and those that did.

Easy-access air filter
Every chain saw has an air filter connected to the carburetor, and if it gets clogged, your saw will waste gas, pollute more and perhaps run poorly. If you can access the air filter easily, without having to pull out a screwdriver, you're more likely to keep it clean. Stihl saws have one of the easiest covers to remove.

Carbide-toothed chain

A dull chain cuts slowly, but worse, it can damage the chain and the bar as well as put extra strain on the saw. It only takes a fraction of a second to dull the blade if you touch the ground with the chain, saw dirty wood or hit a nail.

A chain with carbide tips, like the one you'll find on the Stihl MS 230 C-BE, can withstand encounters with dirt and nails and still be sharp enough to keep cutting. You'll pay an extra $50 or so for this feature, but if you cut dirty wood, need to cut stumps close to the ground, or cut a lot of "urban wood" that's likely to have nails embedded in it, then this may be money well spent.

The downside is that you can't easily sharpen a carbide chain yourself, and even sharpening shops may not have the equipment to do it. Before you buy a carbide-tipped chain, or a chain saw that includes one, find out if you can get it sharpened and how much it will cost.

CARBIDE TOOTH

STEEL TOOTH

Gearhead's guide to what's under the hood

Ever wonder why one chain saw costs 30 percent more than another comparably sized saw? Here's a list of the features you'll find on more expensive saws:

- Two- or three-piece crankshaft vs. five-piece cranks means less vibration and longer life.
- Forged rather than stamped connecting rods. Forged rods are stronger.
- Centrifugal precleaner built into the flywheel means better airflow for better engine performance.
- Chrome-impregnated vs. chrome-plated cylinders. Chrome-impregnated cylinders have microscopic pores that help lubricate the piston.

SKINNY SAW

FAT SAW

Body width
Pros who work with chain saws all day prefer compact saws. More expensive saws like the Husqvarnas, Jonsereds and Stihls have narrower bodies than some of the cheaper ones. The narrower body makes the saws easier to carry and to maneuver in tight spots.

What's the best weed barrier to use under a tree?

You have two good choices—an organic mulch or a high-quality landscape fabric. (Don't use black plastic. It doesn't allow rain to reach plant roots, and it traps water vapor, which facilitates the growth of mold and mildew.)

Use an organic mulch or high-quality landscape fabric. Don't use black plastic.

HSP PHOTO

An organic mulch such as shredded bark, in a layer several inches deep, will help control weeds. It will also decompose over time, which will add organic matter to the soil and make your tree happier. However, you'll have to add more organic mulch every couple of years.

Landscape fabric, when protected from sunlight, decomposes more slowly than organic mulch and doesn't need to be replaced as often. However, the type of landscape fabric makes a difference. Hold the fabric up to the light and make sure the pores in the fabric are small enough to prevent weeds from growing through the barrier. Also, a good-quality landscape fabric is one you can't tear or stretch easily. It should feel stiff, not flimsy and limp.

STAMPED BRASS FITTING

CRUSH-PROOF CAST BRASS FITTINGS

What's the best garden hose?

The best garden hose doesn't kink or leak, lasts forever, is exactly the right length and weight for your needs and isn't too expensive.

In other words, the best doesn't exist. But happily, high-quality hoses do exist, and they all share a few characteristics. They might be 100 percent rubber or made of a rubber/vinyl composite material, but the label will clearly state that the hose is both heavy-duty and flexible. They have heavy-duty crush-proof cast brass fittings that, unlike stamped brass fittings, won't get deformed when you drive over them, and they come with a lengthy warranty period (usually a lifetime). They're also not cheap. Expect to pay $35 to $50 for a good 50-ft. garden hose.

CHEAP VINYL

HEAVY-DUTY RUBBER/VINYL MIX

HEAVY-DUTY, REINFORCED 100% RUBBER

What's the best grass to grow under trees?

Growing grass under shade trees isn't easy, but one key to success is choosing the right shade grass species and planting method for your region.

In cool-season areas (check the zone map at lawngrasses.com/info/climate-map.html), you'll get a better result using seed rather than sod. Sod is grown in wide-open fields under conditions that favor sun-loving grasses. Choose red and tall fescues for shady areas in Northern zones. Garden centers will have grass seed mixes formulated for shade. Late summer and mid-spring are the best times to establish cool-season grasses in shady areas.

In warm-season areas, St. Augustine grass is probably your best choice for moderate shade. Unfortunately, this species is not currently available as seed, so the only way to plant it is with plugs, sod or sprigs (a significantly more expensive proposition). St. Augustine grass has limited cold and drought tolerance.

GRASS SEED

GRO·FORMULA #1622

DENSE SHADE
NET WT 6 LB (2.267 Kg)

GRASS PLUGS

Shade seed and fescue mixtures work best in cool-season areas. St. Augustine grass plugs are your best bet in warm-season areas.

To help ensure success with shade grasses:

■ Don't skimp on the prep work. You'll need to rototill before planting and keep the area watered and weed free to give the grass time to fill in.

■ Selectively prune tree limbs to allow more light to reach the turf and improve turf quality.

7 Vehicles & Garages

IN THIS CHAPTER

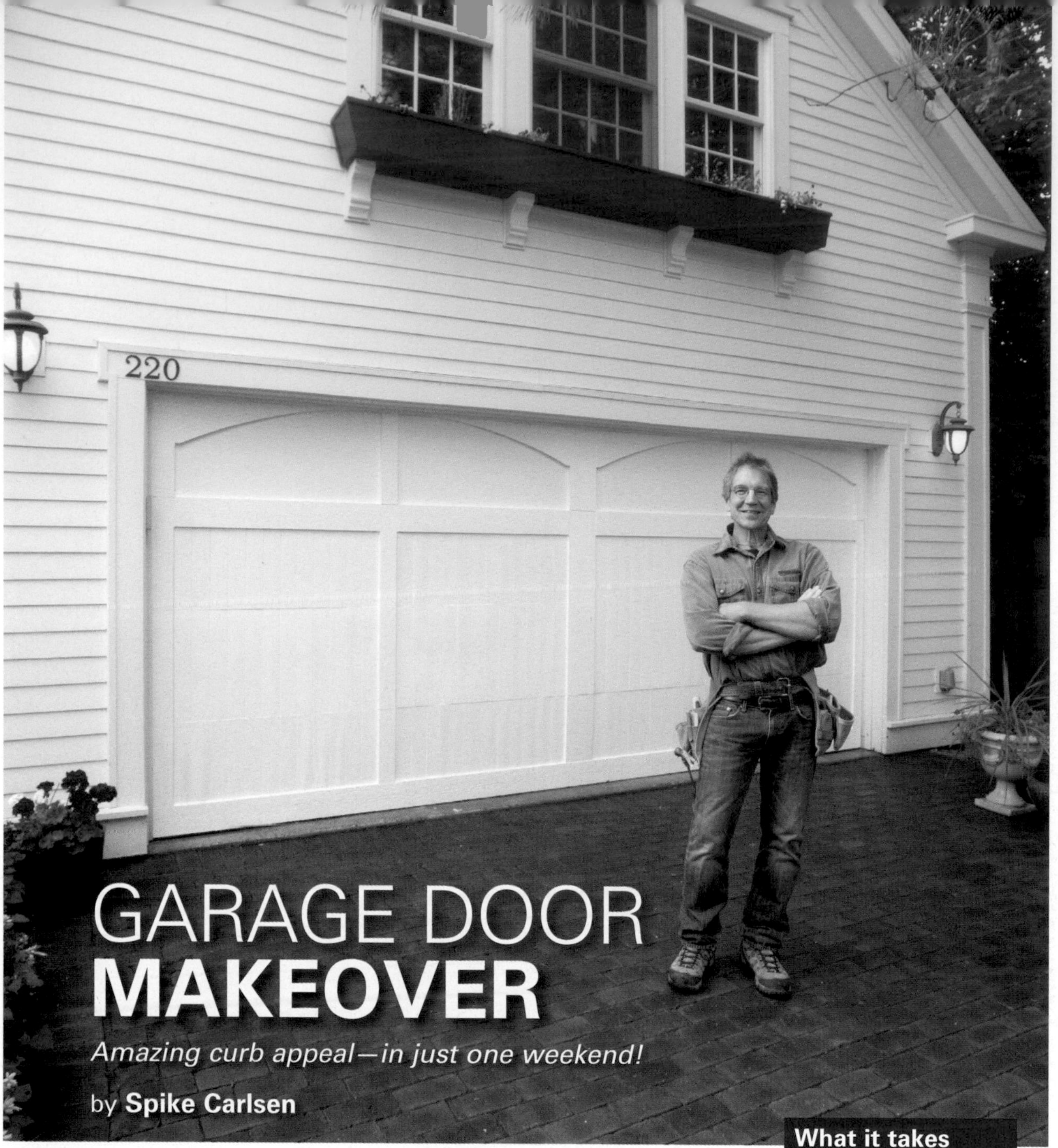

GARAGE DOOR MAKEOVER

Amazing curb appeal—in just one weekend!

by **Spike Carlsen**

Our Greek Revival house stood garageless for the first 150 years of its life, so I knew when it came time to add one, it had to honor the character of the old girl. I also knew I had a bad case of sticker shock after shopping for a carriage house–style overhead door. Wood doors of the style I was looking for started at $2,800 and climbed to three times that amount. So I did what any self-respecting do-it-yourselfer would do: I built my own. And I did it using an inexpensive hardboard door, cedar boards and tongue-and-groove paneling.

You can use the techniques shown to customize a new door or update an old one. **Note:** The design shown on the following pages isn't exactly like my door shown above. I changed some details, especially about the arch.

Tools and materials

Since most "off the shelf" doors these days are metal or fiberglass, you may have to special-order your hardboard door through a home center, lumberyard or garage door dealer. Do your homework: I had some quotes as high as $800—more than twice what I paid.

I purchased cedar boards, rough sawn on one face and smooth on the other, for the rails and stiles, and

What it takes

Time: One weekend. You can complete the woodwork in one day and paint the next.

Cost: About $600. That's about $350 for the garage door, plus $250 for other materials. Pro door installation costs about $300.

Skill level: Beginner to intermediate.

Tools: Miter saw, pneumatic brad nailer and jigsaw.

1/4-in. x 4-in. x 8-ft. cedar tongue-and-groove material—often used for interior wainscoting or closet lining—for the recessed slats. Choose material that's straight with a minimum of knots. Cedar is ideal because it's lightweight and naturally rot resistant. In some parts of the country, you may need to special-order it.

Use a pneumatic finish nailer. This will allow you to work twice as fast as hand nailing, and since the nail heads leave only tiny dents, the primer and paint will fill them, saving you hours of nail setting, puttying and sanding. The nails are important, but it's the adhesive that holds the boards flat and secure for the long haul. I used heavy-duty "subfloor" adhesive for that task. The caulk is equally important since it keeps moisture from getting between the boards and the door. I used white silicone caulk—itself a tenacious adhesive—for that job. Some silicone caulk isn't paintable—and it's usually available in a limited number of colors. If you can't find a silicone caulk that matches the paint color of your door, buy a "paintable" version.

To ensure accurate cuts, beg, borrow or steal a power miter saw.

Structural and safety considerations

I actually built and installed my garage door 10 years ago—and haven't had a lick of trouble since. Before you launch into your project, keep these factors in mind:

1. When you modify a door, you'll most likely void the manufacturer's warranty, so create watertight seals wherever you can.

Rail and stile layout

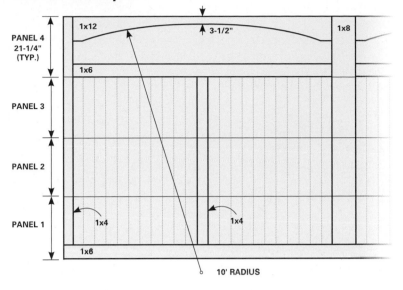

2. Since you're adding 3/4 in. of thickness to the door, the vertical garage door tracks will need to be set back from the opening an extra 3/4 in. You may need oversize jamb brackets for the job.

3. Your door will be 40 to 60 lbs. heavier once the wood overlay is added. Figure out the total weight of your door and install springs and a garage door opener rated for that weight.

4. Make certain each of the four hardboard door panels has a heavy-duty horizontal reinforcement bar along the back to prevent bowing. Those bars are installed when the door is hung.

5. If you're working with an existing door, make certain it's in good shape. Remove any loose or flaking paint so the glue and caulk have a solid surface to adhere to.

Hanging a garage door is tricky—and potentially dangerous—work. I suggest you do what I did: Have a professional hang the door. A pro will know how to install the door, the track and the opener safely. Plan to talk *before* you start your project to get additional input into the work you're doing.

1 Mark out the layout. Lock the panels together with 1x3 cleats and drywall screws. Snap chalk lines to indicate the edges of the rails and stiles. The four "openings" between the stiles should be of equal width.

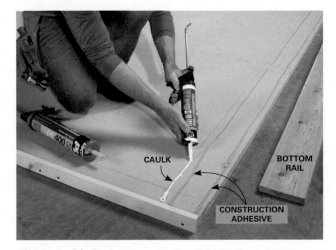

2 Start with the bottom rail. Run beads of construction adhesive and caulk before nailing on the rails and stiles. The caulk locks out moisture along the edges while the adhesive provides long-term holding power.

VEHICLES & GARAGES

Start with a game plan and a sketch

We designed our 16-ft.-wide door to resemble a pair of smaller carriage house doors, but you could come up with other designs. You can increase or decrease the number of vertical stiles, install a straight top rail instead of an arched one, or install crisscross battens for a barn-door look.

Measure the height and width of each door panel, as well as the overall height and width of the assembled garage door, and sketch it out on graph paper. Draw in the rails and stiles and how they meet so you have a solid game plan.

Position your four garage panels on the floor. Make sure they're in the proper order (if they're new, they'll be marked top, middle, middle, bottom) and that the edge grooves overlap properly. Temporarily secure them to one another using 1x3 cleats and drywall screws (Photo 1). Transfer the measurements from your graph paper to the door, then snap chalk lines to indicate the edges of all the rails and stiles.

I first snapped lines for the horizontal rails, then the lines for the two 1x4 outer stiles and the 1x8 center stile. I measured between the edge stiles and the center stile to find that center point, then snapped lines for the

intermediate stiles (Photo 1). When I was done, the four spaces between the stiles were identical in width.

Install the rails, stiles and slats

Apply two beads of heavy-duty construction adhesive and a bead of silicone caulk to secure the bottom rail (Photo 2). Install the caulk bead so it's just "kissing" the bottom of the chalk line; that way the caulk will smoosh out a little to help create a watertight seal along the top of the board. Set the bottom rail in place, rough side up, and secure it with nails every 12 inches.

Next install the edge, center and intermediate stiles (Photo 3). Their ends should be even with the seams between the door panels. Use your chalk lines as guides for laying down beads of construction adhesive and caulk prior to installing each board. Also run beads of silicone caulk at the outer edges to create a good seal. Install the 1x6 rails at the top of panel 3.

Draw the arches onto the 1x12 top rails (Photo 4) using a screw as a center point and a tape measure as a giant compass. Cut the arch using a jigsaw and smooth the edges by hand or by power-sanding. Install the arches using construction adhesive and silicone caulk.

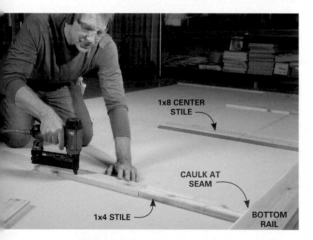

3 **Install the stiles.** Apply silicone caulk to the ends of the stiles before butting them against the rails. Use nails sparingly; just enough to hold the parts in place until the construction adhesive cures.

1x8 CENTER STILE

CAULK AT SEAM

1x4 STILE

BOTTOM RAIL

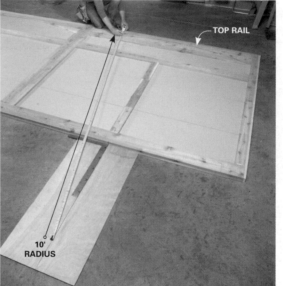

TOP RAIL

10' RADIUS

4 **Mark arches on the top rails.** Center a scrap of plywood below the door and drive in a screw to act as a pivot point. Hook on your tape measure, hold your pencil at the desired radius and "swing" an arch across the top rail. In this case, the 10-ft. mark on the tape provided the perfect radius. Cut the arch with a jigsaw.

BUMP BLOCK

5 **Get identical lengths without measuring.** Determine the exact length of the slats for each panel, then clamp down a bump block to cut them to identical lengths.

INDIVIDUAL SLATS

1/4" TONGUE-AND-GROOVE TEST PANEL

EQUAL SPACING

6 **Lay out slats for symmetry.** Temporarily fit tongue-and-groove slats together, then center this "test panel" in the opening. Mark the two end slats, then cut them to width for the installation.

Measure the height for the tongue-and-groove slats for panel 1. Mark one of the slats to length, position it on the miter saw, then install a "bump block" so all the slats you cut for panel 1 will be identical lengths (**Photo 5**).

Nest a dozen or so precut pieces side-by-side to create the test panel shown in **Photo 6**. Center it in the opening, then mark the two end slats so the slats will be centered during the actual installation. Rip the first piece to width as indicated by your mark, then install it with the tongue facing out. Continue installing the other pieces (**Photo 7**). Rip the last piece to the exact width so it butts tightly against the other stile. Install all the pieces in panel 1, then move up to the second panel. Your "starter pieces" in each section of each panel should be identical.

Finishing up

Once all your slats are installed, apply more silicone caulk where they butt to the stiles and rails (**Photo 8**). Remove the 1x3 cleats holding the panels together, place the panels on sawhorses and prime all the exposed edges and surfaces with a thick coat of stain-blocking exterior primer. Really work it into the exposed end grain of the slats to prevent moisture from wicking in. Once the primer has dried, apply two coats of good exterior paint, again paying special attention to the exposed ends of the slats, rails and stiles.

Call your friendly neighborhood garage door person to hang your new creation. Expect to pay $300 to $500 for installation of the door and an opener.

7 Install the slats. Run triple beads of construction adhesive and a single bead of silicone caulk at the top of the door panel, then nail the slats into place, one by one.

CAULK
CONSTRUCTION ADHESIVE
STARTER SLATS OF IDENTICAL WIDTH

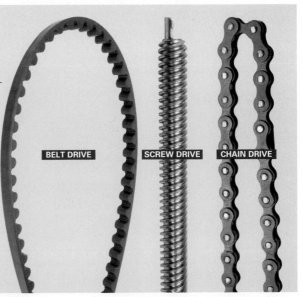

8 Caulk the slats. Apply additional caulk where the slats butt into the rails and stiles.

CAULK

MEET AN EXPERT

Spike Carlsen is a former editor at _The Family Handyman_ and is the author of three books: _A Splintered History of Wood_, _Ridiculously Simple Furniture Projects_ and _Woodworking FAQ_.

Choosing a quiet garage door opener

A belt-drive opener is the quietest. The lifting mechanism is a rubber belt, often steel reinforced, which makes a heck of a lot less noise than a chain drive. It also tends to cost more (but not that much more) than other options. Next quietest is a screw-drive opener, which has few moving parts and requires little maintenance. It's slightly cheaper and slightly easier to install than a belt-drive unit (but both are fairly straightforward for a skilled DIYer). Chain-drive openers are the noisiest and also the least expensive type of opener.

BELT DRIVE   SCREW DRIVE   CHAIN DRIVE

PHOTOS: GENIE (4)

VEHICLES & GARAGES

HandyHints®

LUG WRENCH TWOFER

Changing a flat tire isn't fun, and spending any extra time on the side of the road increases the safety hazard. Make this task a little bit easier with these two tips: Mark the correct socket for your vehicle with electrical tape. If you use the same wrench for different vehicles (or your boat), color-code the appropriate sockets. The second tip is to cover the unused socket arms with foam pipe insulation. This will make the whole ordeal easier on your hands.

Nat Silber

NO-SLIDE CARGO

Here's a great idea for keeping grocery bags, tools and equipment from shifting around in the back of your pickup or SUV. Use an adjustable shower curtain rod to keep everything in place. You can move it to wherever you need it, and it keeps everything right where you put it.

—Steve Herrin

DUCT TAPE DRINK HOLDER

I keep a roll of duct tape on the center floorboard in my truck. It works great as a cup holder and it's just sticky enough to stay put. When I need the roll, I know right where to find it.

—Charles Crocker

DUCT TAPE

VINEGAR-AND-ICE TWOFER

Are squeaky window wipers driving you crazy? Solve the problem by rubbing your wiper blades with vinegar. It'll prevent streaking and silence your blades, at least for a while.

—Tom Flanagan

Heavy frost warnings tonight? Fill a spray bottle with three parts vinegar and one part water. Right before it gets dark outside, shake the mixture well and

VINEGAR/ WATER SOLUTION

spray it evenly on your car windows. The acetic acid in the vinegar will prevent water from freezing on your windows overnight.

—Kevin Sullivan

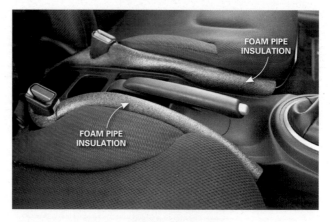

FOAM PIPE INSULATION

FOAM PIPE INSULATION

LOST ITEM PREVENTION

I was always losing things between the front seat of my car and the center console. I stuffed towels in the space, but it wasn't exactly attractive. Then I came up with this solution: Cut a length of foam pipe insulation. Reinforce a section about 3 in. from one end with duct tape and cut a hole through it big enough to accommodate the seat belt buckle. Slip the foam insulation over the buckle and stuff it down between the seats and trim off any excess. No more lost keys, pens or quarters.

—John Rusnacko

NOT YOUR FATHER'S MOTOR OIL

Oil technology has changed over the years; get up-to-date with these tips

by **Rick Muscoplat, Contributing Editor**

4 big synthetic oil myths

Myth #1: You have to flush the engine before you can run synthetic oil in it.
False. You should NEVER flush your engine. All carmakers warn against this practice.

Myth #2: Synthetic oil causes leaks
False. This was true 25 years ago. Not anymore. Current formulations contain seal conditioners to prevent leaks.

Myth #3: Once you switch to synthetic, you can't go back to regular oil.
False. No truth whatsoever to this one.

Myth #4: Since synthetic oil flows better when cold, I can ignore the manufacturer's recommendations for 5W-20 and use 10W-30.
False. Heavier-weight oil reduces fuel efficiency and can mess up valve timing mechanisms. Stick with the manufacturer's oil weight recommendations.

An oil filter that goes the distance

Many carmakers recommend 10,000 miles between oil changes. Genuine factory oil filters last that long, but most filters at the auto parts store last only 3,000 miles. Now you've got an affordable option: the Purolator Synthetic oil filter, which is rated for 10,000 miles. The filter's built with 100 percent fully synthetic filter media (no paper), quality metal end caps, and a silicone anti-drainback valve. And, it has a rough-textured finish so you can tighten it with your greasy hands. It's available online and at some auto parts stores for about $13.

Racing oil is for racing

Ever heard someone brag about running racing oil in a muscle car? Well, the joke's on them, because racing oil isn't meant for daily or even occasional driving. In fact, running racing oil in a non-track vehicle can increase the likelihood of sludge buildup in the engine. And, it can damage the $1,200 catalytic converter.

Racing oil contains three times more antiwear and friction reducing additives (for less wear and more horsepower) than ordinary oil. To make room for that spiked dose, the manufacturers yank the detergent, anticorrosive, antifoam and dispersant additives—precisely the additives you need most to keep your street engine running clean for 3,000 miles. The bottom line: Racing oil is for racing only, get it?

VALVOLINE

Racing oil tidbits

- Race teams use lower-viscosity oil with more friction modifiers to qualify. Then they change to a higher-viscosity oil for the race.
- Racing teams go through racing oil at the rate of about 2,130 qts. of oil per car, per season.
  - In a typical NASCAR race, oil temps can run as high as 320 degrees F.
  - Pit crews bring about 60 qts. of oil to every race.
  - Teams analyze the oil after every race. They check for viscosity change, the level of metals worn away, oxidation (indicates how the oil held up to heat) and additive depletion.

VEHICLES & GARAGES

DIY CAR REPAIR & SERVICE

Save big money by performing these DIY-friendly repairs and checks yourself

by **Rick Muscoplat, Contributing Editor**

Check your brakes

You can check the condition of your brakes yourself in two steps. First find a safe area to test your brakes and check for brake pedal pulsation. Brake to a stop from about 30 mph. The pedal should feel smooth with no pulsation at all. Then try braking at highway speeds. If you get pulsation, the rotors are "warped" and must be machined or replaced.

With the engine cold, remove a front wheel. Then use a compass and a tape measure to check the brake pad thickness (**Photo 1**). A new brake pad is about 1/2 in. thick. Replace the pads when they get down to 1/8 in. Compare the readings top to bottom; they shouldn't vary by more than 1/16 in. If they do, the caliper isn't releasing properly and must be serviced. Finally, check the rotor disc for grooves (**Photo 2**).

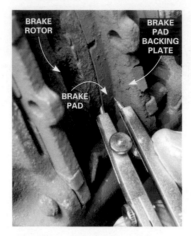

1 Check the pad thickness. Measure the pad thickness by placing the compass points between the backing plate and the rotor. Measure the thickness at both the top and the bottom of the pad.

2 Check the rotor's condition. Run your fingernail across the rotor surface. If your nail catches in deep grooves, the rotors should be machined or replaced as a pair.

Replace wimpy gas lifts

Worn gas lifts can fail any time of the year. But they really lose their "oomph" when the mercury heads toward freezing. Why risk brain injury (beyond what you've already achieved) from a falling hatch when you can fix the problem yourself for less than $50. The job takes less than 20 minutes and requires only a small flat-blade screwdriver, a 1/4-in. drive metric socket set and a buddy to hold the hatch.

Buy a pair of gas lifts (always replace them as a pair) at an auto parts store or online. Have your buddy support the hatch, hood or trunk lid or buy a lift support clamp (one choice is Lisle 44870, about $11 from amazon.com) if you plan to do the job yourself (**Photo 1**). **Caution:** Don't rely on a 2x4 to hold the hatch open during this repair. You'll have to wiggle the hatch up and down slightly to disengage the ball and socket end of the lift. That can cause the 2x4 to disengage and the hatch to fall.

Remove the top portion of the gas lift first. Use a socket and a ratchet to remove the bolted-in-place variety; a screwdriver for the more common C-clip style (**Photo 2**). Then perform the same procedure on the bottom connection.

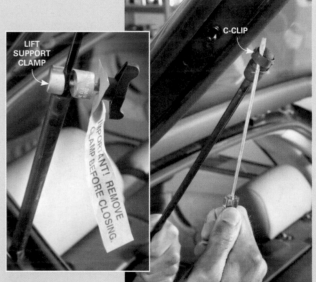

1 Support the hatch. Lock the hatch in place with a lift support clamp. Or have a friend hold the hatch up while you remove the gas lift.

2 Disengage the lift. Jam a small flat-blade screwdriver into the depression in the center of the C-clip. Then pull the gas lift off the ball stud. Reverse the procedure to connect the new lift.

Install a remote starter

Remote starters are downright cheap these days. You can get one with some pretty cool features for about $70 (Bulldog RS82B from sears.com is one choice). If you can read a wiring diagram, are patient enough to use a test light before you connect wires and are willing to take the time to make really good splices, you can install a remote starter yourself and save about $125.

If your vehicle has an antitheft system, make sure the remote start unit includes all the necessary components. Some "inexpensive" brands require additional (and costly) antitheft bypass modules. The Bulldog RS82B unit shown here works with most antitheft systems and comes with a computer-safe test light and wire splicing supplies.

Download the free wiring diagram for your specific vehicle from the manufacturer's Web site (in this case, bulldogsecurity.com). Follow the instructions. When finished, you can program the unit to work with your key fob remote.

If you want more high-tech features, get Bulldog Security's Deluxe 500 model (about $160). You'll get a two-way LCD transmitter/receiver with a half mile range. The starter sends a confirmation signal back to the receiver letting you know the engine has started. And the in-car temp sensor reads cabin temperature and transmits that to the screen as well. The deluxe unit also includes remote keyless entry, so you can ditch the factory remote.

Ask the mechanic

I have a squealing drive belt. How do I fix it?

A squealing belt is a sign of improper belt tension, a misaligned or worn pulley, a worn belt or a sluggish idler roller bearing. Since most late-model vehicles use a spring-loaded self-tensioning mechanism, check that first. Attach a socket or ratchet to the tensioner and rotate it. It should turn smoothly and return to its original position on its own. If you feel any binding or have to manually move it back into position, it's worn out. Replace it. If the tensioner checks out, use an automotive stethoscope to identify the source of the squeal. Just remove the probe from the end of the stethoscope and hold it next to each belt-driven component while you run the engine. Then listen for the squealing sound. Replace the noisy component.

Never use "belt dressing" to silence a squealing belt. The sticky spray never fixes the root cause of the squeal. Worse yet, the sticky goo collects road dust and sand and grinds up the belt and pulleys. That'll cost you far more when the squeal returns.

Brake job tips for advanced handymen

If you do your own brake jobs, chances are you've switched to the newer ceramic-style brake pads. They're much cleaner and quieter than semimetallic pads. But they don't dissipate heat as well, and that high heat can degrade the grease in caliper and pad slides. So it's critical that you use synthetic high-temp grease to lubricate the caliper pins, pad abutments and pad slide hardware.

Now there's a new type of grease made especially for ceramic brake pads (one choice is Permatex No. 24125 Ceramic Extreme Brake Lubricant; $15 for 8 oz. at amazon.com). The high-temp lube contains ground-up ceramic particles that act like ball bearings to ensure proper caliper and pad movement. Apply it to all slide areas as shown.

SLIDE PIN BOOT

ABUTMENT

Grease things up. Wipe ceramic grease onto brake pad abutments, pad slide hardware and inside the caliper's slide pin boots.

TEST & REPLACE YOUR **ALTERNATOR**

If the charging light is lit on your dashboard or your battery won't stay charged, chances are you've got a bum alternator. I'll show you how to test yours without removing it from the vehicle and how to replace it if it's bad. This hour of work will save you about $100 in labor, and even more if you're a smart buyer (see "Alternator Buying Tip," below left). You'll need a digital multimeter to perform the test, and you'll probably need a battery charger to bring the battery up to full charge.

Test it first

Start by testing the battery's engine-off voltage (**Photo 1**). Then refer to the battery voltage chart below to find your battery's "state-of-charge." If the battery is less than 50 percent charged, you'll have to charge it up to 100 percent with a battery charger before testing the alternator.

After you remove the battery charger, turn on the headlights (engine off) for four minutes. Then shut off the lights, start the engine and test the battery voltage again. If the alternator is good, you'll get a voltage reading of 13.5 to 14.5 volts. If it's not that high, turn on the headlights and the blower motor and raise the engine speed to about 2,000 rpm. If the reading still doesn't hit the mark,

Battery voltage and temperature tells state-of-charge				
	80°	60°	30°	0°
100%	12.65	12.63	12.59	12.51
75%	12.45	12.43	12.39	12.32
50%	12.24	12.22	12.18	12.10
25%	12.06	12.04	11.99	11.92
0%	11.89	11.87	11.82	11.75

1 **Connect the multimeter to the battery.** Set the multimeter knob to DC volts (20 or less). Then touch the red lead to the positive battery post and the black lead to the negative post. Note the voltage reading.

Alternator buying tip

The economy has been really hard on original equipment auto parts manufacturers. Instead of selling only to the carmakers, some manufacturers now sell brand new alternators through online stores. In many cases, you can buy a new alternator with a lifetime warranty for 30 percent less than the cost of a rebuilt. So if you can live without your car for a couple of days, buy online. To find a seller, enter "Visteon alternator" in your search engine.

let the engine run for five minutes and repeat the test. If it fails this time, replace the alternator. If the alternator does produce the correct voltage, move on to the diode test.

The diodes are the electronic part of the alternator that convert AC voltage to DC. Switch your multimeter to the lowest AC setting and reattach the test leads to the battery. With the engine running, you shouldn't see any AC voltage. If you do, you've got a bad diode and you need a new alternator.

Replace the alternator

Start the alternator swap-out by disconnecting both battery cables from the battery. Then remove the wires and cables from the back of the alternator (**Photo 2**). Next, remove the alternator belt (**Photo 3**). Then remove the two alternator retaining bolts. The bolts are really long and you'll be cranking for a long time. If there was ever a time to invest in an air-powered ratchet, this is it. The bolts are usually different lengths, so note where each bolt came from. With the bolts removed, lift out the old alternator and drop in the new one. Then reverse the procedure to reinstall.

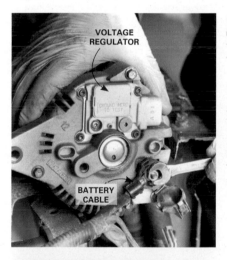

VOLTAGE REGULATOR

BATTERY CABLE

2 Disconnect the cables from the alternator. Depress the latch clip on the electrical connector going to the voltage regulator and wiggle it out. Then loosen the locknut to the "BAT" cable and remove the ring terminal.

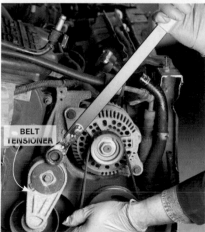

BELT TENSIONER

3 Replace the alternator. Rotate the belt tensioner (if equipped) or loosen the tensioning bolt near the alternator. Then slide the belt off the alternator pulley. Replace the alternator.

Fix your power door locks yourself and save $90

Power door locks fail quite often on late-model Ford vehicles. They're controlled by a computer, but most often it's the actuator itself that's failed—not the computer. So if you press the lock/unlock button and hear clicking or see that the lock is moving, but not enough to open the door, the actuator is fried. A new actuator costs about $50, and you can save about $75 in shop labor if you do the job yourself. Along with ordinary screwdrivers and sockets, you'll need a few inexpensive special tools: a door handle remover for crank windows (about $7 from any auto parts store) and a flat-blade offset screwdriver.

Buy a new actuator online (silverstatefordparts.com) or from your local Ford dealer. Then remove the interior door trim panel (consult a shop manual for screw and snap locations). It's hard to see in these photos, but the trick involves using a flat-blade screwdriver to pry the old actuator off the latch while you depress the actuator locking tab with the flat blade of the offset screwdriver. You'll be working blind behind the door structure, so examine the new part to get a feel for how the locking tab works.

OFFSET SCREWDRIVER

LOCKING TAB

BACK OF ACTUATOR

Depress the locking tab, pry and then slide the actuator off. Force the flat blade of the offset screwdriver into the plastic locking tab to depress it. Then jam another flat-blade screwdriver between the latch and the actuator and pry. The actuator will slide off two "rails."

Find a vacuum leak

A vacuum leak can cause a rough idle, high rpm or poor gas mileage, and can even trigger a check-engine light. Pros find leaks by filling the engine with smoke and looking for wisps of it. But you can search for leaks on your own with an ordinary spray bottle using this technique.

Start the engine and spray. Scope out all the vacuum lines under the hood. Then start the engine and spray each connection with a light stream of water. If a connection sucks in the water, you've found your leak.

Buy new headlights for less than used. Check out online prices for new headlights before you try a DIY fix on your old unit or call a junkyard. To install the new one, unscrew or unclip the old assembly and pop in the new.

Cracked, crazed or leaking headlights

If your headlight is cracked, fills with water or gets all fogged up, don't waste your time trying to fix it with silicone. That won't last. Instead, buy a new headlight assembly. I bought this new headlight assembly for my neighbor's Ford Ranger for just $21 online—and that price included a new bulb.

There may be several headlight styles for the year of your vehicle; they vary based on the trim package (LE, SE, SPORT, XT, etc.). So gather all that information before you start shopping. Then go to rockauto.com, amazon.com or another online auto parts site to find the best price.

Web links: Expand your engine knowledge

- Go to animatedengines.com. Then click on one of 21 different engine types to see an animation of how they work.

Gap new spark plugs

Spark plugs don't come gapped for your particular engine. For the best performance, you must gap the plug to the engine manufacturer's specs. If you're buying a plug for a small engine, ask the parts store to look up the gap size info for you. If the plugs are for your vehicle, find the info in the owner's manual. Then adjust the gap as shown.

1 Check the gap with a gap gauge. Find the "gapping wire" that matches the recommended gap. Then slide it between the center and side electrodes. When the gap is correct, the gauge should drag slightly going in and out. If the gap is too large or the wire won't fit, adjust the side electrode.

2 Bend the side electrode. Hook the side electrode with the gauge's bending arm. Then pivot the arm in or out in small increments to open or close the gap. Recheck with the gauge until you get a snug fit.

Economy parts are no bargain

When you go to the auto parts store for replacement parts, the salesclerk will usually quote the price for "economy" grade parts. They're cheaper but not nearly the same quality as "professional grade" parts. Unless you're planning to junk the car in a year or so, you're better off spending more for the better parts.

I learned this lesson the hard way on my minivan with 200,000 miles on the clock. I bought "economy" tie rod ends. Big mistake. The suckers wore out in less than a year, forcing me to replace them again. This time around, I bought "professional grade" parts and paid for another alignment, making the economy parts a losing proposition. Thinking that experience was a fluke, I tried again with economy wheel bearings. Same result. Now I won't touch economy parts.

PREMIUM PART

ECONOMY PART

Learn from my mistakes. Whether you're doing the repair yourself or having a shop do it, if you expect the repair to last longer than a year, insist on professional-grade parts. They cost far less in the long run.

—Rick Muscoplat

Remove paint scratches

It's no secret that car paint scratches easily. All you have to do is set a grocery bag on your roof, hood or trunk lid and then slide it off. Result? Instant scratches. But don't freak out. You might be able to repair these minor scratches yourself in less than an hour and for less than $30. To see if your scratches qualify for this DIY repair, run your fingernail across the scratch. If your nail glides across the scratch without catching in it, it's a minor scratch that'll polish out. But if the scratch catches your fingernail, it's a job for a body shop.

If your scratch qualifies, pick up 3,000-grit sandpaper, rubbing and polishing compound, and polishing pads. You'll also need a portable drill or dual action (DA) polisher unit. You can buy most of the components off-the-shelf at any auto parts store. Or, you can buy a complete scratch removal kit (one choice is the 3M Scratch Removal System No. 39071; about $16 from amazon.com). Here's the procedure.

3,000-GRIT SANDPAPER

POLISHING COMPOUND PAD

1 Sand the scratch. Wet the scratch and sandpaper and lightly sand until the finish looks dull and the scratch is no longer obvious. Then clean the surface with a microfiber towel.

2 Apply compound. Squirt rubbing compound onto the polishing pad and spread it around with the pad. Then run the polisher or drill at 1,200 rpm until you get a light haze. Follow up with polishing compound to restore the shine.

Replace a broken wheel stud

If you're just like everyone else, you've tightened the lug nuts on your car without using a torque wrench. You're an "all the muscle you can put into it" kind of guy, and now you're staring at a broken stud. You can fix this yourself in about an hour and for less than $50. You'll need to buy a tie rod end remover (OTC No. 7315A, about $40 at amazon.com), or rent one from an auto parts store. Then buy a new stud and two new lug nuts (yes, two of them). Next, stop at the hardware store and get a handful of washers with a hole diameter slightly larger than the threaded portion of the stud.

Above all, don't hammer out the broken stud. That's the worst thing you can do! The hammer blows can wreck your wheel bearings and turn this into a $125 repair bill.

Instead, squeeze the broken stud out with the remover tool (**Photo 1**). It's staked into the hub, so the tough part is getting it to budge. Once it moves, the rest is easy. Rotate the hub until you find a deep recess so you can angle the stud into the hole. Then pull it through. Next, place a bunch of washers over the stud and spin on the lug nut. Crank down on the lug nut to pull the staked portion of the new stud into the hub (**Photo 2**).

By this point, you've probably stretched the threads or damaged the bevel. So toss the nut (they're cheap). If you can't fit the new stud into the hub, you may have to remove the brake dust shield (drill out the rivets and replace them with stainless steel screws, nuts and thread-locking adhesive).

BROKEN STUD

STUD REMOVER

1 Pull the broken stud. Place the remover around the head of the stud, behind the hub. Center the driving screw over the broken stud and tighten it with a ratchet until the stud pops out the back.

NEW STUD

WASHERS

LUG NUT

2 Pull in the new stud. Stop tightening when the head of the stud sits flush with the back of the hub. Install the second lug nut (the one you didn't toss) on the new stud—it'll go on easier. Tighten with a torque wrench.

THE ULTIMATE WALL SYSTEM

Flexible garage storage that you can build with just a circular saw and a drill

by **Jeff Gorton, Associate Editor**

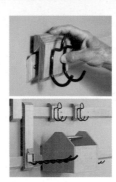

The problem with organizing garages is that there are so many different kinds of things to store that it's overwhelming trying to decide how to do it. But with this system, you don't have to worry about the ultimate positioning of all your hooks and shelves because **you can rearrange them at will**. And you don't have to plan ahead for future storage needs either. You can **easily add on to the system** just by assembling more hangers and rearranging the existing ones. Once the beveled strips are attached, you never have to locate a stud or use drywall anchors to hang hooks or other hardware. Just screw them to an appropriate-size

wood-cleat hanger and put them up wherever you want.

The system consists of beveled strips that are screwed to the wall studs, and custom-made wooden hangers that lock onto the strips. We built everything with utility plywood, which costs about $45 a sheet. You can cut enough strips from a 4 x 8-ft. sheet to cover a 12-ft.-long wall. And you can assemble enough hangers, tool totes and other miscellaneous holders from another 4 x 8 sheet to get a good start on organizing your garage. See the Materials List on p. 263 for other items you may need. We used four sheets of plywood to build everything you see in the photo.

See the Materials List on p. 263 for other items you may need.

What it takes

Time: 2 or 3 days. Expect to spend the weekend cutting and mounting the strips and building some hangers.

Cost: $100 and up. Your cost will vary depending on how much wall you want to cover and how many accessories you build. The materials for the wall shown here cost $275.

Skill level: Beginner to intermediate. If you have a few basic carpentry skills like measuring, leveling and using a circular saw, you'll have no trouble with this project.

Tools: Circular saw and a drill.

It would be a little quicker to cut the parts using a table saw and a miter saw, but you don't need these tools; we'll show you how to safely and accurately cut all the parts using just a circular saw. You'll be surprised at how quickly and easily you can cut the parts with the help of a few simple saw guides. But before you start, make sure you have a sharp blade for your circular saw. To make clean, splinter-free cuts in plywood, we spent $15 on a 40-tooth carbide blade. In addition to a circular saw and drill, you'll need a hammer, level, tape measure, pair of clamps, chalk line with dust-off chalk, and small and large rafter squares.

Screw the strips to the wall

Cut the strips from a sheet of plywood. **Photo 1** shows how. You won't be able to cut the narrow beveled strips from the last 10 or 12 in. of the plywood sheet with this guide. Instead, use the remaining wide strip for the totes or other wider parts.

Next, to ensure that the strips are straight and level and that all the screws hit the center of the studs, make a grid of chalk lines. Start by drawing a level line to mark the bottom of the lowest strip (**Photo 2**). Then make marks every 12 in. above the line and connect the marks with chalk lines (**Photo 3**). Use special dust-off chalk—it's easily erasable.

Next, locate the center of a stud. Use a stud finder or knock on the wall until you feel and hear a solid spot. Then zero in on the center by probing with a nail (**Photo 4**). Do this above the lines, where the nail holes will be covered by the strips. Find both edges of the stud with the nail. Then mark the center. In most cases, studs are 16 in. apart, and you can measure from this first center mark to

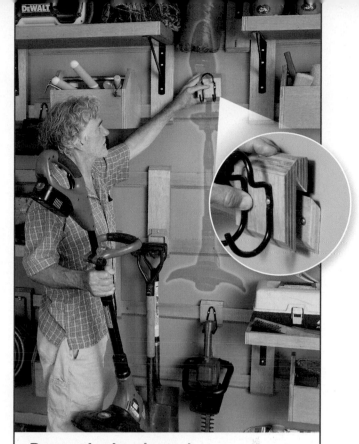

Reorganize in minutes!

Rearrange, reorganize, add on, make room for new stuff. It's as easy as lifting off the hangers and putting them somewhere else. There's nothing complicated about this storage system. The matching bevels and gravity hold the hangers securely until you want to move them. And you can build the whole system with just two power tools—a circular saw and a drill. What could be simpler!

SAW GUIDE

BEVELED STRIP

2-1/2"

1 **Cut beveled strips.** Start by positioning the beveled guide 1 in. from the edge and cutting a strip with a bevel on one edge. You can use this to make hangers. Then make a series of marks 2-1/2 in. apart on each end of the sheet. Line up the saw guide (p. 262) with the marks to cut the beveled strips.

LEVEL

STRAIGHT BOARD

2 **Mark a level line.** Measure up from the floor 9 in. and make a mark. Use a straight board and a level to draw a level line.

BUILD THESE GUIDES TO MAKE CUTTING EASY!

Saw guide for perfect cuts

To make the saw guide, start by marking a line and cutting a 5-in.-wide strip from the edge of an uncut sheet of plywood (**Photo 1**). You could simply clamp this straightedge to the plywood as a saw guide, but then you would have to compensate for the distance from the guide to the saw blade every time. **Photo 2** shows how to build a guide that you can line up with the cutting mark, a technique that is

quicker and more accurate. To see a video on how to build this saw guide, download the September iPad edition.

Make another guide just like this one, except set the saw to cut 90 degrees when you cut off the excess 1/4-in. plywood. You can use the opposite edge of the same sheet of plywood for the straight edge. Use this guide for non-beveled cuts.

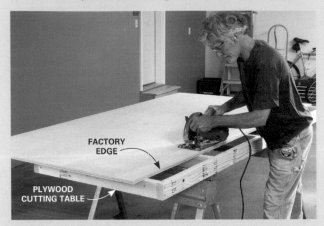

FACTORY EDGE

PLYWOOD CUTTING TABLE

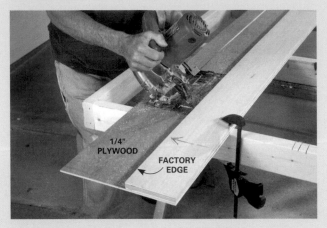

1/4" PLYWOOD

FACTORY EDGE

1 **Make a straightedge.** Saw off the factory edge of a sheet of plywood to use as a straightedge. It doesn't matter if you don't saw perfectly straight because you'll only use the factory edge. Draw arrows toward the factory edge to identify it.

2 **Build the guide.** Attach a 12-in.-wide strip of 1/4-in. plywood to the straightedge with short screws. Make sure to face the factory edge of the straightedge toward the excess base material. Then, with the saw set to a 45-degree bevel, run the saw's bed along the straightedge to cut off the excess base. Make a second guide using the opposite edge of the 4 x 8 sheet of plywood, only set the saw to cut 90 degrees.

Use these simple crosscut guides to cut the small parts

Both of these crosscut guides are simple: All you need to do is glue a 1-3/8-in.-wide strip of plywood or MDF to a wider strip. Set the workpiece on the guide, clamp on a rafter square and run your saw along the square to get straight,

precise cuts. This works for plain cuts or 45-degree bevels. It's best to have two widths and two sizes of rafter squares for different size parts.

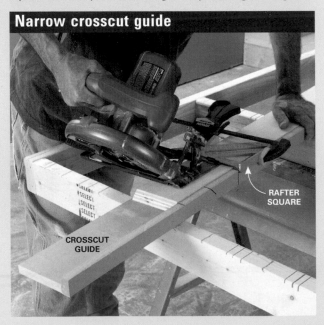

Narrow crosscut guide

RAFTER SQUARE

CROSSCUT GUIDE

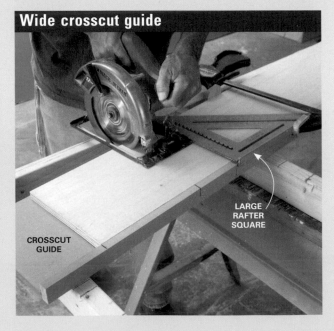

Wide crosscut guide

LARGE RAFTER SQUARE

CROSSCUT GUIDE

find the remaining studs. Whatever method you use, probe with a nail at each stud to make sure you hit solid wood. Make marks for the center of the studs at the top and bottom and connect the marks with chalk lines. With the grid done, it's easy to align and attach the strips (Photo 5).

Cut out the parts for the hangers

With the saw guides, it's fast and easy to make long, table saw–quality cuts in plywood. But what about all those small parts? One problem with cutting small parts freehand is that it's hard to keep the cuts square. Another is that the cutoff pieces tend to fall away just before the cut is finished, creating a little torn-off section. You can solve both these problems, and make marks for repeatable cuts, by building two crosscut guides (p. 262). We bought a 2 x 4-ft. piece of MDF at the home center, but you can use any flat scraps of plywood.

Start by cutting two fence strips 1-3/8 in. wide by 3 or 4 ft. long. Then cut a 4-1/2-in.-wide strip and a 9-1/2-in.- wide strip for the base pieces. Use your straightedge saw guide to make these cuts. Glue and clamp the fence parts to the base pieces. Or you can glue and screw them. If you use screws, remove them after the glue sets.

The sidebar on the bottom of p. 262 shows how to use the crosscut guides. When you make the first cut, mark the location of the square on the crosscut guide. To make several parts that are the same length, measure from the saw kerf in the work support and make a mark. Line up the end of the material with this mark and align the clamp with the clamp mark.

continued on next page

MATERIALS LIST

Here's what we used. Adjust the quantities for your project.

ITEM	QTY.
2' x 4' x 3/4" MDF (crosscut guides)	1
2' x 8' x 1/4" plywood or hardboard (saw guide base)	1
4' x 8' x 3/4" plywood	4
No. 4 x 3/4" wood screws (to attach 1/4" plywood to straightedge for guide)	20
7/8" pan-head screws (to attach hardware to cleats)	100
1-1/4" construction screws (to attach cleats to hangers)	100
1-3/4" construction screws (optional—for cabinets)*	100
2-3/4" construction screws* (to attach cleats to wall)	175
8-oz. bottle of wood glue	1
3/4" copper tubing (optional)	
Hooks and other hardware**	

*We used GRK No. 8 Cabinet Screws. Go to grkfasteners.com to find a retailer or online source.

** We used the Everbilt Hook Assortment Pack, Flip-Up Tool Holder and Flip-Up Bike Holder, which are available at Home Depot.

3 **Mark the cleat locations with chalk lines.** Measure up from the level line and make marks every 12 in. Do this on both ends. Then snap chalk lines between the marks. Use dust-off chalk, which won't leave permanent stains on the wall.

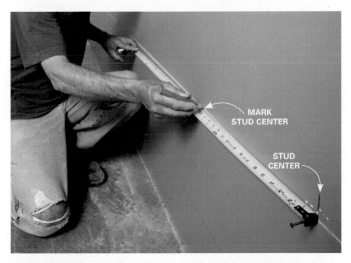

4 **Mark the center of the studs.** Locate a stud with a finder or the knuckle-knocking method. Then probe with a nail until you find both edges of the stud. Mark the center of the stud. Measure from this mark—most studs are 16 in. center-to-center—to find the remaining stud centers. Double-check by probing with a nail at each mark. Repeat this process at the uppermost chalk line and connect the marks with chalk lines.

5 **Screw the strips to the studs.** Line up the bottom of the strips with the lines and drive a screw into each stud. We used washer-head cabinet screws, but any type of screw will work.

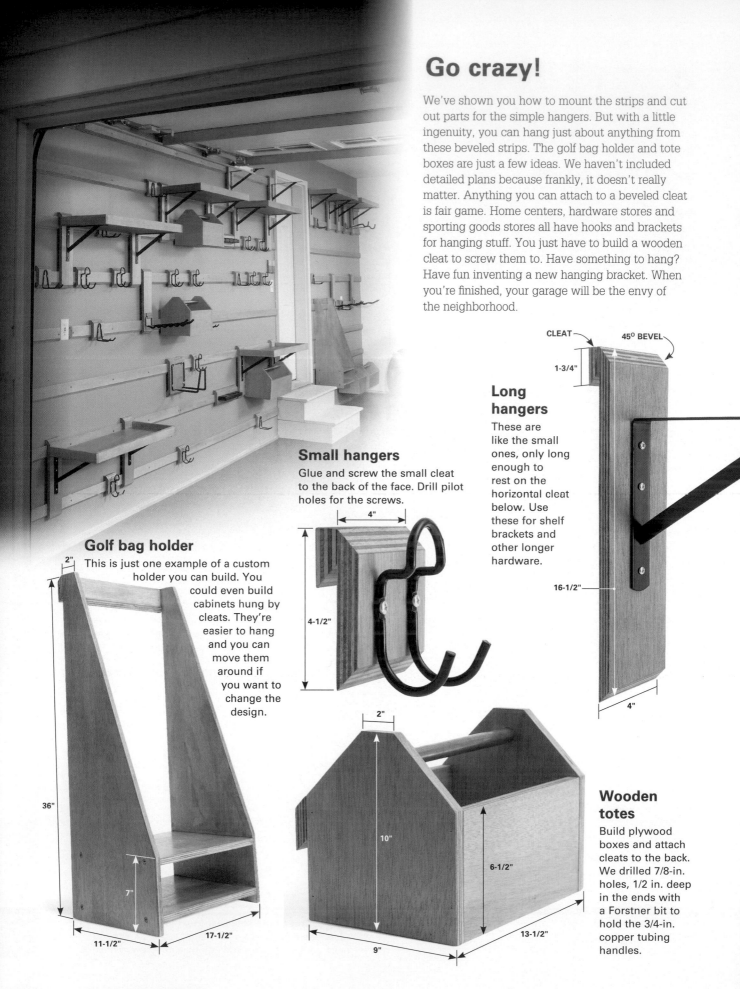

Go crazy!

We've shown you how to mount the strips and cut out parts for the simple hangers. But with a little ingenuity, you can hang just about anything from these beveled strips. The golf bag holder and tote boxes are just a few ideas. We haven't included detailed plans because frankly, it doesn't really matter. Anything you can attach to a beveled cleat is fair game. Home centers, hardware stores and sporting goods stores all have hooks and brackets for hanging stuff. You just have to build a wooden cleat to screw them to. Have something to hang? Have fun inventing a new hanging bracket. When you're finished, your garage will be the envy of the neighborhood.

CLEAT 45° BEVEL

1-3/4"

Long hangers

These are like the small ones, only long enough to rest on the horizontal cleat below. Use these for shelf brackets and other longer hardware.

16-1/2"

4"

Small hangers

Glue and screw the small cleat to the back of the face. Drill pilot holes for the screws.

4"

4-1/2"

Golf bag holder

This is just one example of a custom holder you can build. You could even build cabinets hung by cleats. They're easier to hang and you can move them around if you want to change the design.

2"

36"

7"

11-1/2"

17-1/2"

2"

10"

6-1/2"

9"

13-1/2"

Wooden totes

Build plywood boxes and attach cleats to the back. We drilled 7/8-in. holes, 1/2 in. deep in the ends with a Forstner bit to hold the 3/4-in. copper tubing handles.

4x4 CENTRAL

Stay safe when you travel off-road

by **Joe Burnside**

Off-road survival gear

You may have thought about the fun of off-roading when you bought your 4x4, but have you done any? Well, now's the time to make plans for a weekend with your buddies. But first you'll have to stock up on the mandatory gear. Here's what you'll need.

Safety gear:

Remember, you're going to be *away* from civilization on this trip. So equip your rig with a fully stocked first aid kit, a fire extinguisher, a toolbox with sockets, wrenches, pliers, etc., a full-size spare (no doughnuts allowed), a lug wrench, a spare tire crank and plenty of water, especially if you're in the desert! And don't forget the GPS unit. Real men do need directions—sometimes.

Recovery gear:

Face it: you're going to get stuck. So bring these items to get yourself unstuck:

■ **Shovel:** Full size is best, but a compact folding shovel is better than no shovel at all.

■ **Hi-lift jack or bottle jack:** Use it to jack the vehicle high enough to fill the rut with dirt or rocks and drive your way out. The jack that came with the 4x4 won't give you enough lift height.

■ **Recovery and extension straps and shackles:** You need to be prepared to get pulled free or pull someone else free. These straps and shackles are probably the most important accessory of all, next to water.

Tire gear:

Depending on the terrain, you may need to add or remove tire pressure. And you should expect tire punctures. So be

JOE BURNSIDE

prepared to fix them. Here's what you'll need.

■ **Tire plugging kit** for fixing a flat in the wilderness. (You'll have to get a permanent fix back home.)

■ **Air compressor or CO2 tank:** Forget the hand and foot pumps. You need a high-quality air compressor with battery cable clamps and a long cord. Or bring a fully charged CO2 tank.

Then grab your gear, grab a friend, and explore the backcountry and byroads near you. Happy trails.

Joe's a Field Editor with a passion for everything related to trucks. In his spare time, Joe reviews truck products for 8-Lug magazine. Find Joe's product reviews at 8-lug.com.

4WD OR AWD? MAYBE NEITHER!

My wife is adamant that we buy either a 4WD or AWD vehicle (all her friends have them). They cost more to buy and get lower gas mileage. I need a counterargument that will win her over.

People often think 4WD and AWD vehicles provide much better all-around winter performance. Not true. Sure, 4WD or AWD may give you more "pulling power" to get out of deep snow. But they're no better for stopping or cornering.

Here's what I'd do (and actually did do this year). Buy the 2WD version of the vehicle she wants. With the money you save, buy four new wheels and four top-of-

the-line winter tires. The winter tires will provide better traction during acceleration than the stock all-season tires. And four winter tires will provide significantly better stopping power on both snow and ice. Plus, winter tires provide better stability in turns. That's what I put on my vehicles, and I've never been stuck once—and I live in snow country (MN). Just swap in the summer wheels and tires when the snow melts.

CAR ADDITIVES
THAT WORK

A professional's guide to the very best products

by **Larry Carley**

Walk down the additives aisle at any auto parts store, and you'll see a few hundred products all claiming to increase your gas mileage and convert your daily driver into a race car. Other "miracle in a bottle"–type products claim to seal your leaking engine, fix your transmission or restore an old, tired engine to "like new" condition. Do they work? Some do. But most are a waste of money. I'll walk you through the maze of products and separate fact from, well, snake oil. Let's start with the most effective additive—fuel injector cleaner.

Fuel additives

All gasoline contains fuel injector cleaner. But Top Tier gasoline (marked on the pump at the gas station) contains a higher dose of it. So my first piece of advice is to spend a few cents more per gallon and fill your tank with Top Tier gas. If you can't find a station that carries Top Tier gas (search for one at toptiergas.com) and you make a lot of short runs or drive in stop-and-go traffic, you may get better gas mileage and improve engine performance by adding a fuel system cleaner to your tank. Chevron Techron and CRC Guaranteed to Pass fuel system cleaners cost less than $13 and do a very good job. There's no need to spend more than that on a fuel system cleaner. Just add a bottle to your tank once every 3,000 miles and your engine will thank you.

If you drive a diesel, Marvel Diesel Supplement or STP Diesel Fuel Treatment will clean the fuel system and lubricate the injectors. They'll also reduce the risk of fuel waxing during cold weather.

Fuel system cleaners that work. Read the bottle instructions for dosing amounts. Add the cleaners directly to the fuel tank.

MEET AN EXPERT

Larry Carley is the technical editor for prestigious professional automotive publications like Engine Builder, Brake and Front End, Tomorrow's Technician and ImportCar. With more than 2,500 automotive articles under his belt, Larry is well suited to offer advice on additives. Larry owns and maintains a comprehensive automotive Web site for DIYers. Visit his site at aa1car.com.

Head gasket sealers

If you constantly have to top off your coolant but can't find any sign of an external leak, you probably have a leaking head gasket. Skip the inexpensive ($15 or less) head gasket sealers (they require at least two full days of water-flushing procedures). Instead, spend the extra bucks for Bar's Leaks HG-1 Head Gasket & Cooling Sealant ($50) or K&W FiberLock Head Gasket & Block Repair (No. 401224-6; $36).

There's an important caveat to using any head gasket sealer. Your engine must be able to run for about 20 minutes without overheating or losing its coolant. If your engine overheats right away or loses coolant too fast, forget about a head gasket sealer—the cylinder head is probably warped. That'll require machine shop service and a new gasket. If the head gasket sealer works, you don't need to add new sealer when you change your coolant.

Seal a head gasket. Pour the head gasket sealer directly into the radiator and run the engine for the specified period shown on the label.

Cooling system

If you notice coolant puddles on your driveway, check for a cracked radiator or heater hose or a loose hose clamp. Repair that first. Next, check for a leaking core plug (also called a freeze plug). Core plugs are cheap and easy to replace if you can access the area easily.

But if it turns out your leak is coming from your radiator, heater core or an inaccessible core plug, try adding a cooling system sealer product like Bar's Leaks No. PLT11 or Gunk C312 ($5 at auto parts stores). If the product seals the leak, great. If not, you haven't lost much money. Just remember to add another dose of sealer next time you change your coolant. If sealer doesn't work, you'll have to bite the bullet and replace the leaking component.

If your vehicle is overheating, forget about pouring in an additive (such as a wetting agent) to stop the overheating. None of them work. You'll waste your money and risk permanent engine damage (a minimum $1,000 repair) simply by driving around waiting to see if the additive works. Just fork over the dough to fix the underlying cooling problem.

Another product to avoid is water pump lubricant. Fresh coolant does a fine job of lubricating the water pump.

Seal the cooling system. Add stop leak products directly to the radiator. If your vehicle doesn't have a radiator cap, remove the upper hose, siphon out some coolant and pour it into the radiator with a funnel.

Your older engine needs a wear additive. Older engines need additional wear protection. Pour in a zinc-enriched additive at each oil change.

Oil additives

Skip any oil additives unless you have an old car (early '80s or older). Those engines were built with high-friction flat tappet lifters, so they need a boost of antiwear additive with ZDDP (zinc dialkyl dithio phosphate). Supplemental ZDDP additives cost less than $15 a bottle. Shop for brands like ZDDP Plus or Hy-Per Lube Zinc. Don't use ZDDP additives with a post-'80s engine—extra ZDDP can damage your catalytic converter.

Hoping to restore your worn engine to "like new" condition with a restorative additive? Dream on—it's just not going to happen. The same holds true for oil treatments that contain Teflon or other ingredients that claim to reduce friction and wear. Save your cash for something more beneficial, such as regular oil and filter changes.

Transmission additives

If your transmission is slow to shift or reluctant to go into gear, and has plenty of fluid, it's most likely ready to give up the ghost. If you're a gambler, you can try a transmission "fix-in-bottle" additive. It may buy you a few more months of driving (at best). But don't think you've fixed the problem. Your transmission is going to fail and probably sooner rather than later.

If your transmission shifts well but leaks fluid, you can add a transmission leak stop product. They work by swelling the seals to slow the leak. But they're not a permanent fix. Eventually you'll have to replace the leaky seals or gaskets.

For older transmissions with no shifting problems, add a bottle of a fluid conditioner like LubeGard, Prolong or Lucas Transmission Fix (about $10). It bolsters the performance of older nonsynthetic transmission fluids. You don't need a conditioner if you're driving a late-model vehicle with the newer long-life synthetic transmission fluids like Mercon V, Dexron VI or Chrysler ATF+4.

Transmission additive for older vehicles. To extend the life of an older but fully functional transmission, pour in a bottle of transmission fluid conditioner.

VEHICLES & GARAGES

7 TRICKS TO
START A DEAD ENGINE

3 symptoms, 7 solutions to get you on the road—fast

by **Rick Muscoplat, Contributing Editor**

Most people don't keep a set of mechanic's tools in their trunk. So when you get stranded with a dead engine, you feel pretty helpless. But don't give up right away. I've compiled a list of tricks you can try, and none of them require tools. They're arranged by symptom, and you've got nothing to lose by trying them. Of course, they won't fix the root problem, but one of them just might get the engine started so you can head to the nearest mechanic to have the problem fixed.

SYMPTOM:
Starter goes click

This can be caused by a weak battery, dirty battery terminals, a worn starter motor or a stuck solenoid. Here are a few tricks to try:

1. Cycle the key

Turn on the dome light and watch it while you try to start the engine. If the light goes out, it's a sign the battery is really weak—almost dead. To heat up the battery, terminals and starter, try the "key cycling" trick (**Photo 1**). But if the dome light stayed bright when you turned the key, move on to the next trick.

2. Tap on the battery terminals

There's no way to clean corroded battery terminals when you're stranded without tools. But you can try to move or at least jar the terminals enough to make better contact (**Photo 2**).

3. Smack the starter

If you have access to the starter motor, try smacking it with the tire iron from your car jack. Sometimes, the electrical contacts get stuck and can be freed by tapping on them.

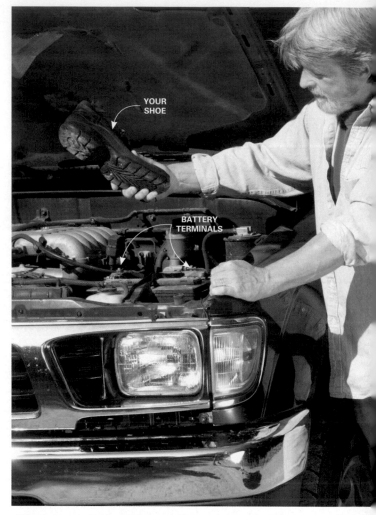

YOUR SHOE

BATTERY TERMINALS

2 **Bang terminals with a shoe.** Smack each battery terminal with the heel of a shoe to rotate it slightly around the battery post. Then try starting the engine.

SYMPTOM:
No click when you turn the key

4. Shift the shifter

With your foot on the brake, move the shift lever to the neutral position and try starting the engine. If that doesn't work, move it back to "Park" and try it again. Moving the shifter sometimes reestablishes electrical contact inside the transmission range selector (also known as the neutral safety switch).

1 **Cycle the key.** Turn the key to the start position repeatedly about 10 times in a row. Stop and wait five minutes. Then try to start the engine.

SYMPTOM: Engine cranks but won't fire up

5. Swap relays

With the radio off, turn the key to the "Run" position and listen for a two-second buzzing sound. That's the fuel pump priming the injection system. If you don't hear any sound, the fuel pump relay may be bad or the pump may be on its last legs. First, find the location of the fuel pump relay in your owner's manual or on the legend of the under-hood fuse box cover. Then locate another relay with the same part number and swap it with the fuel pump (Photo 3). Try starting the engine afterward. If it still won't fire, beat on the fuel tank with your shoe to jar the fuel pump motor (Photo 4).

6. Unflood a flooded engine

If you smell gas, the engine is flooded. Press the accelerator pedal to the floor and hold it there while you crank the engine.

7. Trick the computer

A vacuum leak or funky temperature sensor can result in an air/fuel mixture that's too lean to start a cold engine. If you've tried all the other tricks shown here and it still won't start, press the accelerator halfway and try to start the engine. That'll tell the computer to add more fuel.

3 **Swap relays.** Yank the fuel pump relay straight up. Then align the pins on the replacement relay and push it straight into the socket.

4 **Smack the fuel tank.** Hit the bottom of the fuel tank several times with the heel of your shoe. Then try starting the vehicle.

Own a Ford? Read this!

My wife managed to sideswipe a tree on a recent Saturday morning. That's when I got the call for help: "It won't start." I hopped in the truck and headed over. There she was, sitting in the dead Explorer on the shoulder of the road. There was damage along the entire passenger side, but nothing that would kill an engine. We had it towed into a garage, but the mechanics couldn't get to it for three days. The following Monday, "Dr. Rick" and I were discussing the lead story in Car & Garage this month: "Start a dead engine."

After he went through all his tips, I asked, "Are there any oddball ones you've left out?" "Oh yeah," Rick said. "Most Fords have an automatic fuel pump shutoff switch to prevent fire if the car's in an accident. If that's tripped, the car won't start." What?

"Yeah, it'll shut down even if somebody just bumps you in a parking lot." I asked him how you reset it. "You just push a little button in the toe kick panel on the passenger side."

Really? That afternoon, the wife and I went to the mechanic's parking lot, where I pushed the reset button. Like magic, the car started instantly. A little visit with Rick on Saturday would have saved me a $100 towing charge. At least we saved on some labor, I guess.

—Travis Larson, Senior Editor

Memo from Rick: Those reset buttons are in different places. Check your owner's manual.

HOW TO BUY TIRES

Cut through the confusion with these tips

by **Rick Muscoplat, Contributing Editor**

Nobody likes buying tires. The choices are mind-boggling, and the tire ratings and tread designs confusing. I'll be honest with you: I don't have any "insider secrets" on how to save big bucks on tires. Tires, all of 'em, are expensive—period. But I can give you some tips on how to pick the right tires for your vehicle. And I'll warn you away from the most common tire-buying mistakes. When you're done reading, you'll still have to drop a ton of dough on new tires. But you'll be less intimidated by the process and more confident about picking the right tires for your vehicle.

First things first: Get the original specs

Don't assume the tires on your car are the right size. Instead, buy tires based on the original factory specs. Find the specs on a sticker right on the driver's door or door pillar. Jot down the tire size and the load and speed rating. Don't get talked into buying the wrong tire. If the tire store doesn't stock the recommended tire, ask the staff to order it for you. Installing the wrong size can affect speedometer readings and cause shifting problems.

Set your top priorities

The most common mistake tire buyers make is to choose tires based solely on price. Here's a better way to approach the tire-buying process. Start by ranking the following tire features in order of importance to you: **traction, tread wear, noise, handling/ride comfort and warranty.** Shop for tires based on your top three priorities. However, if you're on a really tight budget, you may have to settle for your top priority and ditch the rest.

The U.S. Department of Transportation mandates tire testing to arrive at traction, temperature and tread wear ratings. Other tire features, such as appearance and warranty, come down to personal preference.

Ranking your priorities is a great first step if you're buying a set of four tires. But, if you're buying only two tires, it's a whole new ballgame. In that case, you have to buy two new tires that match the "keeper" tires. Buy new tires with a tread design that's as close as possible to that of the

Your homework assignment
(to be completed before shopping)

Sure, the tire salesman may claim he "put these babies" on his wife's car. But c'mon, what kind of recommendation is that? If you want objective data, go to tirerack.com. Tire Rack conducts its own tests and posts the results online. And it posts actual customer tire reviews. You can read it all by clicking the "Tire Reviews" tab at the left side of the home page. It's free and you don't have to register to get that information. Of course, Tire Rack would like to sell you your next set of tires. But even if you don't get yours from the site, it's a great place to do your research.

two old tires. Match the traction ratings as well. Mismatching new and old tires can cause uneven braking and instability in turns.

Once you pick out the two new tires, make sure the dealer mounts them on the rear of the vehicle (even if it's front-wheel drive). New rubber on the rear greatly reduces the likelihood of rear-end fishtailing during acceleration and hard stops.

Continue reading on page 272 for more tire-buying advice.

Noise

You want the most aggressive tread design for best performance in snow. But that same aggressive design will make more noise at highway speeds. If you do a lot of highway driving and noise bothers you, shop for a "Touring" style tire. They're designed for a quieter ride.

Temperature

This rating tells you how fast the tire can run under load while still dissipating heat at an acceptable level. It's a pretty worthless rating for most consumers. An "A" tire will cost more and won't get you any better performance under normal street driving conditions. "B" or "C" tires work fine for most drivers.

Handling/ ride comfort

Tires with high tread wear ratings and high performance tires are usually made with harder rubber, so they're far more responsive to minor steering changes—especially at higher speeds. But the tradeoff is you'll have a harsher ride. If you don't mind losing an occasional dental filling, go for those tires. Otherwise, pick a tire that provides a more comfortable ride.

Traction

The traction rating tells you how well the tire's rubber compound generates traction on wet pavement. The ratings are AA, A, B, C. "AA" is the best traction. "C" is the worst. Buy an "AA" tire if you drive in the rain or on snow or ice. If money is tight, drop down to an "A." If you rarely encounter those conditions or want to spend less, drop down to a "B." Only buy a "C" tire if you drive full time on bone-dry roads.

WEEK 44   YEAR 2010

"Born-on" date for tires

When you're shopping for tires, you might want to check the manufacturing date, but it's not as critical as some believe.

Tire makers routinely manufacture odd-size or low-sales-volume tires in batches and store them under controlled warehouse conditions until they're ordered by the store. So it's possible for you to get two-year-old "new" tires from the tire store. As long as the tires were stored in the warehouse and not in a tire rack out in the sunlight, those two-year-old tires are just fine. You'll probably wear them out before they reach their 10-year life span. However, if you're uncomfortable with their age, find a store with fresher stock.

To decipher the age of a tire, find the embossed letters and numbers on the tire's sidewall that start with "DOT." Then locate the last four numbers. If you can't find numbers after the "DOT" marking, look on the other side of the tire. The first two numbers designate the week of manufacture; the second two numbers, the year.

Tread wear

The tread wear rating gives you a rough idea of how long the tread will last when compared with a test-track "base tire." So a tire rated "400" should last four times longer than the "100" base tire. But each manufacturer uses its own formula to extrapolate tread wear from the test. So use tread wear ratings to compare different tire models from a single manufacturer. Don't compare tread wear ratings across manufacturers. If you just need new rubber on your commuter clunker and don't expect the vehicle to last long, you can save money by buying a "100" tire. But if you have the cash and want the maximum tread life, buy a "500" (or greater) tire.

TREADWEAR 500 TRACTION AA TEMPERATURE A

VEHICLES & GARAGES

The straight scoop on directional tires

You may have heard someone talking about "directional" tires, which need to be rotated in a certain pattern. If you thought it was just your buddy's hyped-up imagination, read on. The tread on these tires really is designed to provide maximum traction and hydroplane resistance when rotated in a certain direction. Some directional tires have a V-shaped tread pattern, but not all. A directional tire will have an arrow embossed in the sidewall showing the direction of rotation. You can rotate a directional tire front to back and vice versa, but you cannot swap them from side to side.

COMPLETE
TIRE PRESSURE
SENSOR

FITS INSIDE
WHEEL

NEW GASKET,
WASHER AND
NUT GO HERE

Sensor inside

Do I really need to rebuild tire pressure sensors?

I bought new tires, and the tire store wants to charge me $9 each to rebuild the tire pressure sensors. Do they really wear out to the point of needing a rebuild? Or is this a scam?

It's legit. No shop wants to risk damaging four $100 tire pressure sensors while changing your tires. So the technician unscrews each one from the wheel and lets it drop inside the wheel before dismounting the old tire. Once the sensor's gasket is disturbed, it can't be reused. To guarantee a leak-free seal on the reinstall, the shop uses a new gasket, washer and retaining nut. Then a special torque wrench is used to tighten the nut. So you're paying for the parts and labor.

REBUILD KIT
COMPONENTS

NUT

WASHER

GASKET

The best strategies for buying tires

Buying online can save money. But there are some downsides to consider. First, shipping can take up to a week. Next, you'll have to make sure an adult is home to sign for the tires (the driver won't leave them without a signature or with a kid). Then you'll have to pack the tires into your vehicle and pay a local shop to mount them.

So here's an online shopping tip: Try to find an Internet seller that has arrangements with a local shop near you. That way the shop will accept the shipment and mount the tires for a set fee.

If you don't want the hassle of buying tires online or you need them right away, shop at a local tire store. I prefer tire stores over warehouse clubs because the sales clerks know more about tires. Tell the salesperson your top priorities and your budget. Next, pick out two or three tires that match your criteria. Then ask the salesclerk to quote you "out-the-door" prices for each selection (cost of tires plus all taxes, lifetime mounting and balancing, tire pressure sensor rebuilding charges, and tire disposal costs). Most salespeople include the cost of the road hazard warranty in the out-the-door price. If you don't want the warranty, say so up front. For more on this topic, search for "buying tires" at familyhandyman.com.

AUTOMOTIVE GEAR

Backup alarms sound the alert

We're not telling you to install a backup alarm, throw your vehicle into reverse and "damn the torpedoes." But a backup alarm can help avoid accidents by alerting others that you're about to back up. Backup alarms come in two styles: as a replacement bulb for your existing backup lights and as a freestanding alarm to mount under your vehicle.

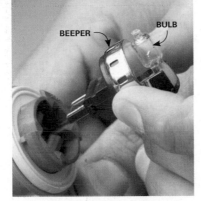

The bulb alarm isn't as loud as a freestanding alarm because the bulb sits inside your light assembly. Choose from two bulb styles: The Hopkins No. 20100VA ($20) replaces a No. 1156 bulb; the No. 20101VA ($20) replaces a No. 3156 bulb (both from amazon.com). If you want a freestanding alarm, try the Wolo BA 52 ($8). Want to sound like a garbage truck? Buy the heavy-duty, extra-loud BA-107 ($24) for 107 dB of beep-beep (both models from amazon.com).

Swap out your backup light with a beeper bulb. Remove the backup light socket and snap in the beeper bulb. Wipe off any fingerprints before you reinstall the socket.

Choosing jumper cables

Cheap jumper cables are a bad investment. They're made with thin 10-gauge wire and cheap clamps. You want a thick (4- or 6-gauge) wire to move the most juice.

High-quality cables (such as the Hopkins BC0860 shown; $41 from amazon.com) have professional-grade clamps that won't pop off. High-quality cables are a once-in-a-lifetime investment. They're priced according to wire gauge, length, clamp quality and the ability of the insulation to flex at minus 30 degrees F.

Phone mounting clip

Do you want to mount your smartphone in the car for easier access to your music, mapping and hands-free calling? You're not alone, but one-size-fits-all mounting systems are often difficult to position properly and can detract from a car's ambience.

ProClip USA takes a different approach. The company sells car mounts customized to a vehicle's make, model and year for a perfect fit. ProClip offers a couple of mounts for my 2010 Mazda 5, and the one I selected installed in a jiffy. It blends right in and holds my iPhone 4 gently but securely. I slide it in and go. These mounts cost $70 to $110. Go to proclipusa.com for more information.

—Julio Ojeda-Zapata

Spiff up your ride with 3M car wrap

If you're just itching to airbrush flames, stripes or logos on your car or truck, put the brakes on the paint and check out "car wrap." 3M vehicle graphics dealers now offer custom design services for 3M's Scotchprint Wrap Films.

The dealers will take your design (or help you create one) and fabricate it out of pressure-sensitive film that applies right over your paint. So you can get the look you want without destroying the paint finish. Change your mind and want to go with a different look down the road? Just peel off the old design.

Go to 3mgraphics.com/1080 to see all the colors and finishes. Then click on "locate an installer" to find a dealer near you.

3M "wraps" a Mustang. 3M "souped up" this Mustang Shelby with carbon fiber–textured Scotchprint wrap film. Was the original color yellow or black? You tell us.

MOTORCYCLE
BUYING TIPS

Don't get taken for a ride when you buy a used mororcycle

by **Rick Muscoplat, Contributing Editor**

The price of used motorcycles has gone through the roof as more people buy them to save on gas. But it's easy to get burned with a lemon needing hundreds in repairs. Ryan Scott, owner of Blue Cat Motors, has been in the motorcycle repair business for 10 years. He shared with us the most commonly overlooked problems a used bike may have.

The good news is that you can spot them yourself and avoid a costly mistake with just a 15-minute look-see. Then, just as you would for any used vehicle, have it inspected by a certified mechanic (motorcycle mechanic, in this case) before you commit to buy.

First, check for engine/transmission leaks. An oil leak can easily cost several hundred dollars to repair and usually requires immediate attention. Valve and side cover leaks are the most common, so start your inspection with those two components. But don't confuse an oil weep with a leak. A weep looks like a darkened grease spot and is usually covered with dust or road grit, and it isn't a deal breaker. An oil leak, on the other hand, looks and feels wet.

If the engine is spotless, it could mean the owner keeps his bike clean. If so, the rest of the bike should be just as spotless. But if it's not, be suspicious. The owner may have degreased the engine to mask an expensive-to-repair oil leak.

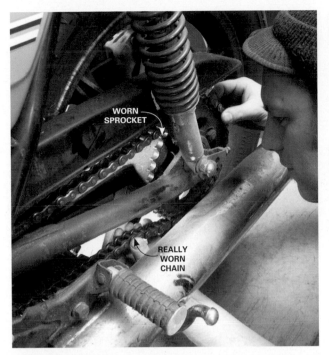

New chain and sprockets: $400 to $500. Press up on the chain to check tension. It shouldn't move more than an inch. Then examine the sprocket teeth. The wear on the leading and trailing edges of each tooth should be the same. If one side is worn more than the other, both sprockets and the chain must be replaced as a set.

New tires: $300 to $500. Compare the tread depth with the height of the wear bar. If the wear bar is close to or even with the tread, the tire is worn out and must be replaced. Also, check for cracks in the rubber. That's a sign of tire aging, requiring immediate replacement.

Fork seal replacement: $300. Pry off the fork seal protective covers. Then run your fingers along the fork to detect any fluid leakage. If your fingers come up wet, the seals and the fluid must be replaced.

Brake job: $125. Shine a flashlight through the spokes to light up the inboard brake pad. If the pad is worn to within 1/8 in. of the steel backing plate, it's time to replace the set.

NEW BRAKE PAD

The test ride

Check out the engine and fuel delivery systems with a "cold-start" test drive. When cold, the engine should start right up and idle smoothly. As it warms up, it should accelerate with power and without hesitation. The same goes for clutch lever operation and gear shifting—smooth, with positive engagement. And you shouldn't hear any knocking or metallic sounds coming from the engine or transmission. After the test drive, let the engine idle. It should be smooth with no coughing, idle speed variation or misfires.

START A **DEAD SMALL ENGINE**

When you're staring at a yard full of grass that desperately needed cutting two weeks ago, the last thing you want is a lawn mower engine that won't fire up.

Before you have a heart attack pulling on the rip cord of your lawn mower (or snow blower), check the fuel and carburetor. They're the root causes of more than 80 percent of all no-starts. I'll walk you through the steps.

You'll need hand tools and a socket set, a can of carburetor cleaner and your air compressor. And you'll probably have to make a trip to the small-engine parts store. But after an hour of effort, you just might have an operational engine, and you'll save a bundle by fixing it yourself. Let's dig in.

Check the plug

I'll assume you've cleaned the air filter, so the next step is to remove the spark plug to see if it's wet. If it is, there's no way the engine will start. So clean the plug with carburetor cleaner and let it dry. Cleaning it with compressed air isn't enough; you need a solvent to remove oil residue. If the plug was wet, move on to Step 2. If it was dry, skip to Step 3.

If the fuel is more than a month old, dispose of it properly and refill the tank with fresh gas. Then reinstall the spark plug and try starting. It may take quite a few pulls to suck the new gas into the carburetor, so be prepared to clean and dry the plug a few more times.

Check the carburetor bowl for gas

The engine can't get gas if the fuel filter is plugged or the carburetor inlet needle is stuck. Check the fuel filter (if equipped) by removing the fuel line at the carburetor. Gas should run out. If it doesn't, remove the fuel line ahead of the fuel filter inlet. If gas flows, the filter is clogged. Replace it. If you still don't get any gas, the fuel line is kinked or plugged. And check inside the tank for any debris that might clog the outlet.

If you're getting gas to the carburetor, check to see if there's any fuel in the bowl. Clamp off the fuel line with a

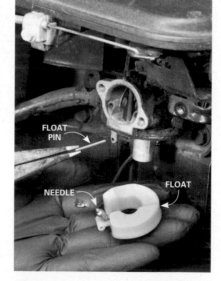

1 Remove the bowl. Set a small cup under the carburetor to catch any spills. Then loosen the bowl nut with a socket. Once the nut is loose, unscrew it by hand and lower the bowl. Gas should drip out.

2 Remove the inlet needle and seat. Pull the float pin straight out. Catch the float, inlet needle and retaining spring with a rag. Remove the rubber seat with a small pick. Reverse the procedure to install the new parts.

3 Check carb condition. Examine the inside of the carburetor. If you see chalky/powdery white corrosion like this, the carb is a goner.

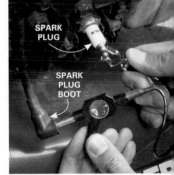

Fuel stabilizer for small engines

Preventing corrosion in small-engine carburetors is so important that Briggs & Stratton developed its own Advanced Formula Fuel Treatment & Stabilizer. The product contains three antioxidant ingredients to protect the fuel system. One chemical forms a protective barrier on metal parts to prevent corrosion. A second acts as a metal "deactivator" to stop the chemical reactions caused by dissolved metal ions in the fuel. The third prevents water separation and gum and varnish buildup.

A 4-oz. bottle ($5.50) treats 10 gallons of fuel, and the treated gasoline is good for three years. You can buy it at a Briggs & Stratton dealer or online at briggsandstratton.com.

C-clamp. Then remove the bowl (**Photo 1**). If the bowl is empty, the problem is a stuck inlet needle and seat. They're easy and cheap to replace (**Photo 2**). But before you buy the parts, check the condition of the rest of the carburetor's interior (**Photo 3**). If you see any corrosion, it's "game over." A corroded carburetor is a dead carburetor. Replace it. One source for parts is Reeds Sales & Service (651-774-9515).

Clean the jet

A clogged main jet is a pretty common problem. You can try cleaning it with spray carburetor cleaner (**Photo 4**). Then try starting. If the engine still isn't getting gas, replace the carburetor.

If it starts but runs rough

If you got the engine to start by cleaning the main jet, but it runs rough or the idle speed surges, you have two choices—rebuild or replace the carburetor. For rebuilding instructions, go to familyhandyman.com and search for "carburetor." Otherwise, disconnect the old carburetor from the linkage, remove the two retaining bolts and slap on a new carburetor.

Check the ignition system on a small engine

Most people think you can check a small engine's ignition system by removing the spark plug and grounding it while cranking the engine and watching for a spark. Nope. That just confirms that the spark plug fires in open air. It doesn't mean the ignition coil is strong enough to fire the plug when under full compression.

Here's a better way to check. Buy an inexpensive spark tester (Briggs & Stratton No. 19368; $24 at tulsaenginewarehouse.com). Then connect the tester between the spark plug boot and the engine. Watch for a spark in the tester window as you pull the starter cord. To test the operation of both the ignition coil and the spark plug, connect the tester between the spark plug boot and the spark plug. Then start the engine and watch the tester window. A spark plug misfire will immediately be evident in the tester window. You can use the tester on any small engine (mower, snow blower, chain saw, string trimmer, etc.).

4 Clean the main jet. Remove the carburetor bowl nut. Insert the carburetor cleaner straw directly into the main jet passage and squeeze the trigger on the can several times until the spray shoots into the venturi of the carburetor. That'll confirm the passage is open.

VEHICLES & GARAGES

SPECIAL SECTION

The Sporting Life

2-1/2" PLATE

2" BALL MOUNT

BALL MOUNT GUARD

Everybody's done it— walked right into the ball mount and gotten a really banged-up shin. Now you can soften the blow by adding a ShinShield protective rubber cushion ($20 from shin-shield.com). The cushion curves downward to prevent contact with the sides of the ball mount and the ball stud. Right now the ShinShield fits only the 2-1/2-in. plate found on most 2-in. ball mounts. If yours is a different size, you'll have to wait for new models to come out. Contact the manufacturer for release dates.

To install the guard, remove the ball. Then slide the guard onto the mount and reinstall the ball, lock washer and nut. Tighten to the specified torque.

—Rick Muscoplat, Contributing Editor

FISHING ROD ORGANIZER

I got sick and tired of my fishing rods getting tangled, so I came up with this easy fishing rod organizer. All you need is a length of 3-in.-diameter PVC pipe and a foam swimming pool noodle.

Drill 1-in. holes spaced every 4 in. in the PVC pipe. Use a utility knife to cut slits in the foam noodle, spacing them 4 in. apart. Line up the pool noodle on the wall so that at least two of the slits sit over studs. Pull those slits apart, slide in a fender washer, and screw the noodle to the wall with 2-in. screws. Then screw the PVC pipe to the wall beneath it at a comfortable height and insert your fishing rods. Look Ma, no more tangles!

Robert Rempel

GreatGoofs®

Tippecanoe and Chia too

I bought a used canoe at a garage sale. The canoe was sea-worthy, but I figured that a fresh coat of marine paint might give the old gal an updated look. I waited for a sunny day and perched the canoe upside down on two sawhorses and painted the entire canoe in short order. After several hours, I returned to admire my handiwork only to find the entire canoe covered in a coat of white fuzz! The wind had come up, causing a nearby cottonwood tree to shed its cotton, turning my canoe into a giant Chia Pet.

—Stacy Gibson

IBALL (2)

NO SPOTTER REQUIRED

I used to hook up to my work trailer at least twice a week. Even with a spotter guiding me into place, the process was always a pain. I recently picked up the iBall trailer hitch camera. This thing is super-cool and really simple. The monitor plugs into my truck's power port (cigarette lighter), and the camera is equipped with a magnet, so it can be stuck to my truck or trailer. I stick it to the top of my tailgate for an overhead view.

The first time I used it, the camera was telling me to adjust to the right while my brain was telling me "left." Then I discovered the button that reversed the image so my brain and the camera could come to terms (!). My only complaint is that I wish I had had this thing for those several hundred times I was forced to rely on a spotter with sketchy depth perception and even worse hand signals. They're under $140 at amazon.com.

—Mark Petersen, Associate Editor

TOUGH LABELS FOR SOFT BAGS

If you carry around soft-sided bags like camping duffels, sports bags and tool cases, you'll want labels that stand up to being squashed, mashed, soaked, yanked, dropped and rolled around. They can be tough to find, but a good solution is nylon webbing (found at camping and fabric stores for $3 a yard) or short lengths of tie-down straps. Just tie the webbing around the handle of your bag and label it using a water-proof marker.

—Casey Norman

SELECTING THE RIGHT BALL MOUNT

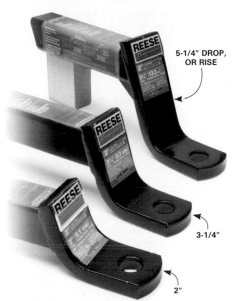

5-1/4" DROP, OR RISE

3-1/4"

2"

Buying the right ball mount for receiver hitches is critical to the safe operation of your trailer. If you install the wrong mount, the weight imbalance may break either the ball mount or the trailer coupling, causing a huge accident that could easily kill people. Follow the measuring instructions below to find the right "drop" or "rise" height.

—Rick Muscoplat, Contributing Editor

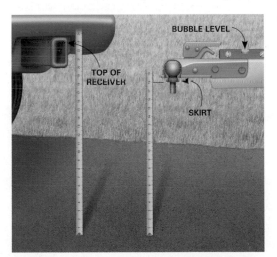

BUBBLE LEVEL

TOP OF RECEIVER

SKIRT

Park the vehicle and the trailer on level ground. Drop the trailer jack and level the tongue with a bubble level. Then lock the proper-size trailer ball into the trailer coupling. Measure from the ground to the skirt of the ball. Then measure from the ground to the top of the vehicle hitch receiver. The difference between the two measurements is the "drop," or "rise." Find the ball mount that's closest.

TheSportingLife

WINTERIZE YOUR BOAT

A little attention at the end of the season ensures a trouble-free spring

by Rick Muscoplat, Contributing Editor

If you've been paying the marina $150 or more to winterize your boat every fall, it's time to do the job yourself and save some dough. We brought in marine mechanic Sam Kelley to guide you through the process and share his expert tips for winterizing an inboard/outboard (I/O) drive boat.

An I/O is full of water. So if you don't drain the water properly, it can freeze and cause major damage. However, if your boat will be in heated storage, you can skip the draining part.

The job isn't hard, but we have to warn you: If you skip a step or miss a drain plug, you could wind up with a repair bill of at least $3,000 for a replacement engine. (And none of that cost will be covered by insurance.) So if you're at all nervous, invest in a factory service manual to locate all the drain ports and cooling units.

Before you start the winterizing procedure, pick up a few gallons of RV antifreeze, a can of fogging oil, motor oil, an oil filter, lower-unit lube and drain plug gaskets, an oil suction pump and a lower-unit lube injection pump. Then gather up your screwdrivers, sockets and combination wrenches.

Start by sucking out the oil and changing the filter (**Photo 1**). (Oil suction pumps can be found at most auto parts stores.) Then run the boat over to the marina and top off the gas tanks with non-oxygenated fuel (if

MEET A PRO

Sam Kelley owns Sam's Marine and Performance in Stillwater, MN. He's been maintaining, repairing and installing performance upgrades for almost 25 years. We asked Sam to help with this story because he winterizes about 150 boats a year and hasn't cracked a block yet.

available). Add a marine fuel stabilizer to the tank and run the boat to a landing. With the boat still in the water, remove the spark arrester from the carburetor and fog the engine (**Photo 2**). Then trailer it and perform the rest of the procedure on land.

Tip the trailer up (so it drains well) and place a bucket under the hull drain plug. Then remove the plug (**Photo 3**).

Hop in the boat and start draining near the top of the engine. Remove the drain plugs (or the hoses) for the exhaust manifolds, power steering cooler (**Photo 4**), oil cooler (if equipped) and block drain plug(s); **Photo 5**. See tip on p. 281.

Leave the block drain plugs out, but reinstall all the other drain plugs and hoses. Then remove the thermostat or the hose attached to the thermostat housing and pour in RV antifreeze until it drains out the block drains (**Photo 6**). Once the antifreeze stops draining, reinstall

1 Change your oil. Yank the dipstick. Then shove the suction hose down the dipstick tube and suck out all the old oil. Change out the oil filter and then refill the engine with fresh oil.

OIL SUCTION PUMP

2 Spray fogging oil down the carb. Hold the carburetor choke open (if closed), start the engine and spray fogging oil directly down the carb until the engine chokes out.

3 Yank the hull plug. Remove the hull plug with an open or box-end wrench. Don't use an adjustable wrench—it will round off the shoulders on the brass plug.

BILL ZUEHLKE (3)

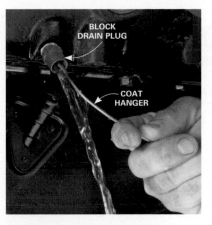

BLOCK
DRAIN PLUG

COAT
HANGER

UPPER
HOSE

4 **Drain the power steering cooler.** Loosen the hose clamp and remove the drain hose from the power steering cooler (if it doesn't have a drain plug).

5 **Drain the block.** Locate and remove the block drain plug(s) at the bottom of the block. Cooling systems always suck in sand, so as soon as you remove a drain plug, shove a bent coat hanger inside the drain port and wiggle it around to loosen any sand or rust dams.

6 **Flush the engine with RV anti-freeze.** Pour RV antifreeze directly into the thermostat opening or into the large hose attached to it. Keep pouring until you see a steady stream of the pink stuff running out of the block drain plug.

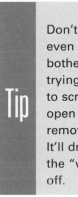

Don't even bother trying to screw open drain petcocks. Just remove the entire valve. It'll drain much better and the "wings" won't break off.

Tip

the block drain plugs and the hull drain plug.

Note: Sam likes to leave the engine block flushed but empty for the winter. However, some marine engine manufacturers recommend filling the entire engine with RV antifreeze. Always follow your engine manufacturer's advice.

Next, unscrew the bottom drain plug on the lower unit. Allow the lube to drain a few minutes before removing the upper vent plug. Once the old lube is out, refill with fresh lube (**Photo 7**). Sam recommends refilling with high-performance lube.

Finally, remove the battery terminals and give it a full charge. Sam has had better luck leaving the fully charged battery in the boat. But you can also bring it inside and attach a battery maintainer.

Cover the boat and dream about spring.

LOWER
UNIT

SCREW IN
FILLER
TUBE

7 **Refill the lower unit.** Screw in the pump nozzle and pump in the new lube until it comes out the top vent. Insert new gaskets in the drain and vent holes and install the plugs.

Specialty tool for drain petcocks

If you're winterizing a boat, there are two ways to deal with drain petcocks. The better one is to remove the entire petcock, as mentioned above. But if you can't get a wrench in place to do that, try using this nifty petcock socket (Thexton No. 485; $11 at amazon.com). The kit contains two sockets, one for brass and one for the plastic style. Just slip it over the petcock "wings" and turn it with a ratchet.

BRASS
PETCOCK
SOCKET

PLASTIC
PETCOCK
SOCKET

GreatGoofs®
Water, water everywhere

Plumber? What plumber?

In the middle of trying to sell our house, my husband accidentally broke the hot water pipe to the washing machine while trying to unscrew the rusted connection from the wall. Hot water started gushing inside the wall, and I ran for buckets and towels as my husband raced to turn off the water main. Two hours later, as the emergency plumber was cutting into the drywall, the doorbell rang. Our real estate agent was standing outside with potential buyers!

As my husband greeted them, I ran around the house and threw the towels, buckets and mops into the garage, pushed the washer back into place, and told the plumber to go wait in his truck, which was prominently sitting in our driveway. The couple toured the house while my husband and I suffered heart palpitations. They ended up buying our house. And luckily they never did ask what the plumber was doing in the driveway...

—Kiersten Jarvis

Totally hosed

When we moved into our new house, we brought along a few things, including our water bed, but most of our stuff was being delivered the next day. We decided to set up the water bed. When it was ready to fill, I realized that we didn't have our garden hoses. Luckily, the previous owner had left one behind, so I ran it out the window and went outside to hook it up to the outdoor faucet.

I turned on the faucet and paused to meet my new neighbor. When I finally got up to the bedroom, I discovered the hose was actually a soaker hose. I had thoroughly watered my new bedroom!

—Joshua Koch

One step at a time

For several months, we'd been having a problem with water pooling in the basement below our front steps. I coated the basement wall with a waterproofing paint, hoping that would solve the problem, but no dice. The water was still there each morning. I figured the water must be coming in through the cracked steps that were pulling away from the wall.

I rented a jackhammer, demolished the front steps and dug along the foundation, assuming I'd find the leak. Nothing! Frustrated, I put a layer of poly down and filled the hole back in, ready to give up and live with a wet basement. A few days later, I went down to the utility room to put salt in the water softener, and I noticed that one of the hoses was loose. Turns out that every time the water softener recharged, it was spraying water all over the floor. Now I have a dry basement, but no front steps!

—Erik Laine

Please don't drink the water

I was moving our washer and dryer to the first floor of our house from the basement. In preparation for tying into the main drain line, I told my wife to please not run any water and that I would be turning off the main in case she forgot. Just after I finished cutting off the drain pipe to add a wye fitting, a rush of water came down the main line and I got drenched! The water was still off, but I failed to remember that toilets will flush one more time, even without water pressure. Let's just say I was highly motivated to finish the job and turn the water back on so I could jump in the shower. Yuck.

—Travis Fisher

Pinpoint accuracy

I was assembling a new drain for the toilet in my master bath remodel, and I accidentally bumped an old 2x4 that was leaning against the wall. The 2x4 had a nail sticking out of its end, and when it fell into the open floor cavity, the nail landed point first on top of a new pressurized copper water line. Instantly I had a 4-ft. geyser shooting out of the pipe, which started to flood the ceiling of the room below. After shutting off the main water supply and vacuuming up all the water, I sat my drenched self down to have a laugh. I'll lay odds that I could try bumping that 2x4 a hundred more times and never get the nail to hit that copper water line again. If only I were that accurate when throwing darts!

—David Nogle

Homeowner 0, Moles 1

Each year the moles arrive and wreck my perfect lawn with their earthworm mining tunnels. I've tried all sorts of traps and solutions over the years, and last year I decided to try a different approach. One evening, I stamped down the mole trails and waited with a pitchfork. As soon as I saw a little quiver in the stamped down trail, I knew a mole was moving and I attacked, plunging the sharp tines into the soil over and over to spear the varmint. I figured I must have speared the critter, but who knows?

The next morning I noticed something odd about my lawn irrigation system. The ground was rising and bulging and occasionally sending up an errant spray of water where no sprinkler head was located. Upon closer investigation, I found that even if I hadn't speared any varmints, I'd done a nice job of perforating the underground water lines.

—Kent Stever

Is it just me, or is it hot in here?

A friend of mine was opening a coffee shop, and I offered to help him out by taping the drywall. Since it was late January in Michigan, with no heat in the building, I brought in a big commercial propane heater to keep things warm enough to tape.

I noticed that it was getting pretty warm up near the ceiling at the front of the store, but I didn't pay it much mind. I went on to mud the back of the store, thinking how nice and toasty the shop was getting. When I finished up the first coat in the back, I went up front to check how well the mud was drying in the heat, and it looked pretty good. But just as I was starting the second coat, I heard a loud SNAP and HISSSSSSSS as the overhead sprinklers came on. That very long day turned into a very long night.

—John Klube

INDEX

*Visit **familyhandyman.com** for hundreds of home improvement articles.*

ACKNOWLEDGMENTS

FOR THE FAMILY HANDYMAN

Editor in Chief — Ken Collier
Senior Editors — Travis Larson
Gary Wentz
Associate Editors — Elisa Bernick
Jeff Gorton
Senior Copy Editor — Donna Bierbach
Art Directors — Vern Johnson
Becky Pfluger
Marcia Roepke
Photographer — Tom Fenenga
Production Artist — Mary Schwender
Office Administrative
Manager — Alice Garrett
Production Manager — Judy Rodriguez

CONTRIBUTING EDITORS

Spike Carlsen   Mark Petersen
Dave Munkittrick   David Radtke
Rick Muscoplat

CONTRIBUTING ART DIRECTORS

Roberta Peters   Becky Pfluger

CONTRIBUTING PHOTOGRAPHER

Bill Zuehlke

ILLUSTRATORS

Steve Björkman   Trevor Johnston
Concept3d   Don Mannes
Mario Ferro   Frank Rohrbach III
Jeff Gorton   Eugene Thompson

OTHER CONSULTANTS

Charles Avoles, plumbing
Al Hildenbrand, electrical
Joe Jensen, Jon Jensen, carpentry
William Nunn, painting
Julio Ojeda-Zapata, high-tech
Dean Sorem, tile
Costas Stavrou, appliance repair
John Williamson, electrical
Les Zell, plumbing

For information about advertising in
The Family Handyman magazine, call (646) 293-6150

To subscribe to *The Family Handyman* magazine:
■ By phone: (800) 285-4961
■ By Internet: FHMservice@rd.com
■ By mail: The Family Handyman
Subscriber Service Dept.
P.O. Box 6099
Harlan, IA 51593-1599

We welcome your ideas and opinions.
Write: The Editor, The Family Handyman
2915 Commers Drive, Suite 700
Eagan, MN 55121
Fax: (651) 994-2250
E-mail: editors@thefamilyhandyman.com

Photocopies of articles are available for $3.00 each. Call (800) 285-4961 from 8 a.m. to 5 p.m. Central, Monday through Friday for availability and ordering, or send an e-mail to FHMservice@rd.com.